THE CIVIL SERVICE

Vol. 3 (2)

Surveys and Investigations

Evidence submitted to the Committee under the Chairmanship of Lord Fulton 1966–1968

LONDON
HER MAJESTY'S STATIONERY OFFICE
1968

SBN 11 630003 5

Members of the Committee

LORD FULTON (Chairman)

SIR NORMAN KIPPING, G.C.M.G., K.B.E., J.P. (Vice-Chairman)

SIR PHILIP ALLEN, K.C.B.

MR. W. C. ANDERSON, C.B.E.

RT. HON. SIR EDWARD BOYLE, Bart., M.P.

SIR WILLIAM COOK, C.B., F.R.S.

SIR JAMES DUNNETT, K.C.B., C.M.G.

DR. NORMAN HUNT

MR. R. R. NEILD

MR. R. SHELDON, M.P.[1]

PROFESSOR LORD SIMEY

SIR JOHN WALL, O.B.E.

[1]Mr. Sheldon succeeded Mrs. Shirley Williams, M.P., on her appointment as Parliamentary Secretary, Ministry of Labour in April, 1966.

Preface

Volume 3 consists of the reports of surveys and investigations submitted to the Committee. It is divided into two parts, published separately; Part 1, to be published later, contains the report by Dr. Halsey and Mr. Crewe on their social survey of the Civil Service; Part 2 contains the rest of the surveys and investigations. Some of the reports published in Part 2 were commissioned by the Committee:

Memorandum No. 2 Profile of a Profession, by Dr. R. A. Chapman

Memorandum No. 3 Civil Service Unsuccessfuls, by Dr. J. F. Pickering

Memorandum No. 4 Administrative Class Follow-up Survey, by Dr. E. Anstey

Memorandum No. 10 Reports on the Civil Service since the Northcote-Trevelyan Report, by Mr. J. B. Bourn

The rest were undertaken under the aegis of the Treasury (including some that arose from the recommendations of the Sixth Report of the Estimates Committee (1964–65) on recruitment to the Civil Service) and were made available to the Committee:

Memorandum No. 5 Executive Class Follow-up Survey

Memorandum No. 6 School backgrounds of members of the Administrative Class

Memorandum No. 7 Survey of Wastage of Executive and Clerical Officers

Memorandum No. 8 Study of Ability, Efficiency and Job Satisfaction among Executive and Clerical Officers

Memorandum No. 9 Recruitment of Graduates: Survey of Student Attitudes

These surveys and investigations were already in hand when the Committee began its work. Nos. 5 to 8 were produced within the Civil Service, No. 9 by the Psychological Research Centre. In one case (No. 5), the Committee was able to take part in planning the scope of the survey in order to suit its needs; in the other cases, this was not possible because they had already reached a more advanced stage.

Contents

MEMORANDUM No. 2

submitted by

RICHARD A. CHAPMAN

(University of Liverpool)

February, 1967

Profile of a Profession: The Administrative Class of the Civil Service

A. Introduction

(*i*) *General*

This paper is based on a detailed study of men and women in the Administrative Class who joined the Civil Service as Assistant Principals in 1956. The object of the study was to gather background information about people in the Administrative Class, and in particular to find out how they see themselves and what they like and dislike about their work.

There were forty entrants in that year (thirty-five men and five women), though not all sat the Civil Service examinations in 1956—some had competed earlier but had their entry delayed because of National Service. Of the forty, thirty-eight were direct entrants by open competition and two were successful candidates from the 1955 Limited Competition (they were both graduates, one of whom was transferred from the Tax Inspectorate and one from the Ministry of Labour Cadet Grade). At the time of the research late in 1966 eight (20%) of the 1956 entry, a fairly typical proportion,[1] had resigned from the service.

In the summer of 1966 a letter was sent to the current official address, or in the case of those who had left the service, the last known address, of each of the 1956 entrants. The letter explained that a research project on the entry for that year was being carried out for the Fulton Committee and outlined the objects of the research. It asked each of the 1956 entrants to co-operate by completing a questionnaire[2], and explained that they would probably also be asked oral questions about themselves and their work. The project had the agreement and co-operation of the Treasury, the First Division Association and the Establishment Officers in each of the Departments where a 1956 entrant was then serving. The questionnaire contained fifty-eight questions and often took up to four hours to complete; the average follow-up interview took an hour and a half.

Thirty out of the thirty-two Civil Servants completed the questionnaire and

[1] The Treasury supplied information about other years so that a comparison could be made.
[2] Printed at the end of this Memorandum.

were interviewed. Of the eight who had left the service three completed the questionnaire and were interviewed, two completed the questionnaire but were not interviewed and three failed to reply. This represents an exceptionally high response and thanks are due to all those who generously gave their time and took such trouble to help with the research.

Most of the questions in the questionnaire were deliberately open-ended, and this factor should be remembered when considering the results. Therefore, the 1956 entrants were asked to provide specific information in answer to fairly general questions, and consequently it is very significant that a number of people have provided similar answers. For example, one question asked the Civil Servants what they dislike about the service, and it seems reasonable to attach more significance to the number of answers that referred to the absence of secretarial assistance than would be attached if the same proportion of persons had been critical when asked a specific question about the adequacy of secretarial assistance.

(*ii*) *The 1956 sample*

There were both advantages and disadvantages in selecting one year, and in particular 1956, as the basis for a research project such as this. Ideally, one would wish to select a sample representative of all levels in the Administrative Class but the size of such a task, and the resources available within the very limited time made this impossible. It was therefore decided that all the entrants for one particular year might be followed up. This means that the significance and limitations of the sample must constantly be borne in mind in interpreting the results.

The advantages of selecting this particular group are as follows. They were a group small enough to be within the scope of one spare-time academic researcher, yet on the other hand large enough to be statistically viable. They are a group of people whose education was not seriously disrupted by the war but who were recruited to the Civil Service before the recent period of university expansion was under way (this is significant as the universities are at present fiercely competing with the Civil Service for highly qualified graduates and a number of the 1956 entry might have become dons had they been a few years younger). They are a group of people who have now been in the Civil Service sufficiently long for them to expect to remain there for the rest of their working lives, and in twenty years some of these people will probably be filling top posts in the service. In addition, after ten years in the service they may be expected to have a pretty good idea of its good and bad features, but at the same time it may be hoped that they have not become too steeped in service mores as to be beyond making valuable, perhaps even radical, suggestions for reform. And apart from this method of research, there is no other effective means of presenting the views of such a group as this.

However, there are also disadvantages in selecting this group. The size of the sample in relation to the service as a whole must not be disregarded. The Administrative Class is roughly one half per cent of the total non-industrial Civil Service. It is composed of both direct entrants (who form roughly only one half the men and women in the Class), and the others have been recruited from within the Civil Service. This means that the 1956 entrants constitute one year's recruits into a group which in total is only about a quarter per cent of the whole Civil Service. But this is a very significant quarter per cent because from it are chosen most of the holders of the senior posts in the Administrative Class and therefore in the service as a whole.

However, 1956 was a difficult year for recruitment to the Administrative Class. In their 1957 Annual Report the Civil Service Commissioners noted that " There was a further diminution this year in the size of the field of candidates for the open competitions of the Administrative Group: the number entering for the Administrative Class itself was the lowest since 1949. Only 33 of the 50 vacancies allotted to this competition were filled . . . In order to fill vacancies which the 1955 Open Competition had not filled we held in the summer of 1956 a Supplementary Competition for the Administrative Class. Candidates had to be up to two years above the normal competition age limits, and to have a first class honours degree. The aim of this competition was to offer an opportunity to people who had stayed on at Universities to do research, or taken up other employment, and who had outstanding intellectual ability to enable them to catch up with those who entered the service two years earlier. There was no written competition; short-listed applicants were given tests at the Civil Service Selection Board before going on to the Final Selection Board. There were 21 candidates, of whom 5 were successful. All 5 had been engaged in research or University teaching since graduation." (Paras. 12, 13).

The results of the Open Competitions in 1956 were as follows:

Results of the 1956 Administrative Class Open Competitions

	No. of vacancies	*No. of applications*		*No. of candidates examined*	
		Men	*Women*	*Men*	*Women*
Method I*	50	217	46	166	38
Method II*		242	48	223	43
Supplementary Comp.	10	19	2	12	0

	No. declared successful			*No. certified for appointment up to 31.5.1957*
	Men	*Women*	*Total*	
Method I*	22	2	24	21
Method II*	18	2	20†	12
Supplementary Comp.	5	0	5	5

* Candidates who competed under both Methods are included in the figures relating to each Method.

† Includes 5 candidates who were also successful for and preferred the Senior Branch of the Foreign Service.

The entrants into the Administrative Class in 1956 who constituted the sample for this research were made up of twenty-four successful candidates by Method I, eleven by Method II, three by the Supplementary Competition and two by Limited Competition.

Two other contemporary developments should be mentioned in order to place the 1956 entrants in relation to the recruitment problems at that time. In 1957 the Civil Service Commissioners stated: " The arrangement first made in 1955 whereby younger members of the Administrative Class act as links between the Civil Service and their own Colleges or Universities appears to fulfil a real need and Your Commissioners have received encouraging comments on the way in which it has worked." In addition, University students were given some knowledge of the work and daily life of the Administrative Class when the first group of sixty undergraduates from nearly all the Universities spent a week visiting government departments in December 1956. (1957 Annual Report, paras. 66, 67).

B. The Civil Servants and Society

(*i*) *Date of birth, national service, school*

Naturally, the age limitations for entering the Civil Service competitions has meant that this group are of similar age—in fact, the average date of birth of the thirty-five who completed the questionnaire was April 1932, which means that they were all about thirty-five years old at the time of the research. But within the group the total age span covers nearly seven years (the youngest was born in December 1934 and the eldest in April 1928).

However, this comparatively large age range was mainly caused by national service; the eldest spent two years in the R.A.F. but the youngest did not do national service. Of the thirty men who completed the questionnaire six were excused for medical reasons, and seventeen of the other twenty-four became commissioned officers.

All thirty-five came from different schools which are difficult to classify beyond saying that twelve are independent (public) schools, ten are direct grant schools and thirteen are local authority (grammar) schools.

These statistics suggest that 1956 may have been a slightly untypical year for recruitment to the Administrative Class, when compared with other years around that time. Evidence presented to the 1965 Select Committee on Estimates shows that the proportion of direct entrant Assistant Principals who attended L.E.A. maintained and aided schools went down from 42% in the period 1948–56 to 30% in the period 1957–63. The 1956 sample is also very different from the sample of eighty higher Civil Servants studied by H. E. Dale in the 1930s. (Of Dale's higher Civil Servants twenty were educated at one or other of the large English boarding schools: Eton produced six, Winchester three, Rugby, Marlborough, and Clifton two each, and no other more than one. Eighteen were educated at one or other of the large English day schools—the main contributions were four from Merchant Taylors', and three each from St. Paul's, Dulwich and King Edward's School, Birmingham. Twelve came from Scottish and Irish schools—George Watson's College at Edinburgh contributing two and no other school more than one. The remaining thirty came from a great variety of schools (one Australian), most of which were day-schools. Two of these thirty were at county schools).

(*ii*) *University education and other occupations before entry*

Of the thirty-five 1956 entrants who completed the questionnaire, fourteen took their first degrees at Cambridge University, nine at Oxford, four at London (two each at the London School of Economics and King's College), two each at Edinburgh and St. Andrews, and one each at Aberdeen, Glasgow, Liverpool and Manchester. Again, this evidence about education suggests that the 1956 entrants were a slightly untypical sample for there was a relatively low proportion from Oxford and Cambridge (66%) compared with the periods 1957–63

(85%) or 1948–56 (78%). It is, however, very similar to H. E. Dale's sample of the higher Civil Service, where the proportion who had attended Oxford or Cambridge was 68%.

The class of honours and the main subject studied in first degrees awarded to the 1956 entrants were as follows:

Class of degree		*Subject of degree*	
1st	20	History	17
2nd (including 2(i))	14	Economics	3
3rd	1	Classics	3
		English	2
		Jurisprudence	2
		Modern Languages	2
		P.P.E. (Oxford)	2
		Government (B.Sc.(Econ.))	2
		Philosophy + Politics	1
		Modern Hist. + Pol. Econ.	1

Nine out of the thirty-five had been awarded further degrees or diplomas by 1966 or had done more than a year's full-time research at a university. These included two Ph.D.s, and one each B.Phil., M.Litt., B.C.L., and a Diploma in Public and Social Administration.

Another five of the thirty-two still in the service at the time of the research had spent a period in industry or business before joining the Civil Service.

(*iii*) *Assessment of educational background*

Nearly all felt their education prior to joining the Civil Service had been a very good background for the sort of work they are now doing. However, twelve out of thirty-two answering the question added that they would have found a study of economics and public and political institutions very useful indeed (these were apart from the five with degrees in Economics or P.P.E.).

(*iv*) *Father's occupation*

Of the sample who answered the questionnaire, twenty-seven out of the thirty-five were first generation university students in their immediate family.

An analysis of the fathers' occupation at the time of their entry into the Civil Service shows that, in terms of the Registrar General's Socio-Economic Classification, 7 were in Class I, 19 in Class II, 6 in Class III, 1 in Class IV and 2 in Class V.

(*v*) *Marital status, children and their schools*

Of the thirty-five, six were unmarried and twenty-nine married at the time of the research. They have a total of fifty-four children, of whom thirty-four are below school age, thirteen attend L.E.A. schools, two attend direct grant schools and two attend independent schools.

(*vi*) *Where they live*

Of the twenty-six 1956 entrants who work in London, four live in Inner London (within about five miles of Whitehall), eleven live in Outer London (elsewhere within the London postal area), five live in Surrey, three in Kent, two in Middlesex and one in Buckinghamshire.

Of the total of thirty in the sample who are still in the service and who completed the questionnaire, twenty-two live in houses which they own or are buying on mortgage and eight live in flats (four owned and four rented). One, with a substantial private income, lives in a flat in London and also has a house in the country. The average annual amount paid in rates by the thirty is £98 (lowest £50, highest £160—though the two above £135 specifically mentioned that they have substantial private incomes).

(vii) Clubs, leisure-time activities, etc.

Only four of these thirty-five belong to a London Club (two belong to the Oxford and Cambridge University, and one each to the Travellers' and United University) but two of the four are in the Scottish Department and therefore resident in Edinburgh. These figures are somewhat different from the impression given by Dale in the 1930s who, writing of higher Civil Servants (though he regarded only Civil Servants *above* the grade of Principal as falling within his scope) said that " nearly all belong to one (rarely to two) of six of the great clubs within easy reach of Whitehall—the Athenaeum, the Travellers', the Reform, the Union, the United University, and the Oxford and Cambridge ". Indeed, some of the 1956 entrants found it almost amusing that they should be seriously asked about membership of London Clubs.

Eighteen are regular church-goers (fifteen C. of E., two non-conformist and one Roman Catholic). Six are members of local Residents Associations. Apart from these memberships they tend to belong to a not surprising cross-section of local history societies, music societies, theatre clubs etc. Two have rather unusual club memberships—one belongs to ten ornithological societies and another belongs to seven climbing and ski clubs.

Several, when asked whether there were any other associations they would like to belong to, said they would like to belong to more clubs and associations (they usually mentioned cultural or benevolent associations) but added that this was impossible because they had not the time, or the demands of their work made it impossible. Only one, in answer to that question, specifically mentioned that he would like to belong to " one or two London Clubs ".

Perhaps it is not surprising that the number of clubs and associations they now belong to is not as large as the number they belonged to when at university. Clearly, this is a reflection of their different style of life, and people tend to join in more activities at University than they are able to keep up when they leave. But the comments of the Civil Servants suggest there is more to this aspect than just that difference.

People who daily spend about nine hours in a government department, doing important work against considerable pressure of time, are likely to be physically and mentally fatigued when they leave the office. But when, in addition, they may have to spend a further two or three hours travelling to and from work, they are more or less completely exhausted, and have little inclination towards leisure activities. A significant proportion of the 1956 entrants specifically said they wanted to do much more with their leisure time, though it should perhaps also be admitted that these were also the people who tended already to be the most active joiners. As one of them put it: " I do not have much leisure time. I normally work late, come home tired, have dinner and that's that. I used to have a wide spread of interests (the list on my form for entry into the C.S. was impressive) and a big circle of friends, but work has eaten into both . . . I feel like a mole nowadays." Another simply explained: " No leisure . . . Go once weekly to theatre or cinema and occasionally entertain."

Apart from membership of clubs and associations, the 1956 group follow a wide and unclassifiable field of other interests and spare-time activities. Some examples will illustrate this: model making; historical research and writing articles for learned journals; music (e.g. membership of a choir or orchestra); university teaching in the evenings; writing books on mountaineering and skiing (author of the Penguin Handbook " Mountaineering "). In addition, most of them mention interests associated with home, garden, motoring, sport, reading etc. If one can legitimately generalise about this information, most of the Principals seem to enjoy a fairly balanced mixture of indoor and outdoor, active and passive, creative and receptive activities.

Perhaps it is appropriate at this stage to mention the demands of work in terms of time, and its intrusion into the private lives of Civil Servants. In terms of hours worked most of the Civil Servants interviewed are usually in the office from about 9.45 a.m. to 7.00 p.m., and in addition take home about five hours work each week, but an average working week of about fifty-five hours in the office is not unusual.

However, all recognise that their work is such that they have to work hours appropriate to its demands, and it is also not unusual to be very hard pressed from time to time. For example, one Civil Servant recalled that during the economic crisis in 1964 he worked regularly from 9.00 a.m. to 7.00 p.m. and took home about twenty hours work each week. Another, concerned with the Rhodesian crisis at the time of the interview, gave details of the hours he had worked in Downing Street during the week of the interview and they amounted to about seventy-five hours. Private secretaries, of whom there were three in the sample may expect to work a regular sixty hour week.

(*viii*) *Motor cars*

Twenty-seven of the sample ran motor cars (one of them had two) and one ran a motor cycle. When bought, ten of the cars were new and eighteen were secondhand. If classified according to the age of the car and engine size the details are:

Engine size		*Age of model*	
Under 1,000 c.c.	3*	1959 or earlier	9
1,000–1,300 c.c.	9	1960–1963	11
1,500–1,800 c.c.	13	1964 or later	8
Over 1,800 c.c.	3		

*None of these is a B.M.C. Mini, one of the three in this category is a van.

The reasons behind this distribution probably include the facts that these Civil Servants tend to have young families and also that, as they tend to live in London surburbs, they are unlikely to use their cars for driving to work.

(*ix*) *Newspapers and journals*

The following tables show the newspapers and periodicals read regularly by the thirty-five people in the sample (" regularly " means for daily newspapers at least three times a week, and for Sunday newspapers and other weeklies it means at least once every two weeks).

Daily newspaper	
The Times	23
The Guardian	15
Financial Times	8
Daily Telegraph	4
Scotsman	3
Glasgow Herald	2
Daily Mirror	2
Daily Mail	1
Daily Express	1
None	2*

Sunday newspaper	
The Observer	23
The Sunday Times	17
Sunday Telegraph	2
Sunday Express	2
None	4

* The two who claimed not to read a daily newspaper were specially questioned about this and confirmed their answers.

Weekly periodicals	
Economist	21
New Society	10
New Statesman	9
Spectator	5
Times Literary Supp.	5
Listener	4
New Scientist	3
Statist	2
Times Educational Supp.	2
Country Life	2
Local Newspaper (various)	3
Church Newspaper (various)	2
None	4

In addition the following are read regularly by one person in the sample:

Aeroplane
Architectural Journal
British Medical Journal
Electrical Times
Engineer
Financial Mail
Motor Cycle
Newsweek
New Yorker
Pulse
Punch
Time
West Africa
Woman's Mirror

(*x*) *Social relationships*

Generally speaking, these Civil Servants like to meet people and go to social gatherings; less than a quarter of them said they preferred not to. But a significant proportion made qualifications which show that they prefer small rather than large gatherings (" it depends very much on the kind of people and social gatherings ") and several specifically said they liked to meet people " anywhere other than at sherry parties and cocktail parties ".

One of the group said she liked to meet people and go to social gatherings but she now has little opportunity to do so; and another, who has now left the Civil Service, said that he was friendly with less people and talked less often to people while he was a Civil Servant than he has since leaving, and this was primarily because of the demands of the service which affected his private life (the same person also said that he had been more regular in church attendance since leaving the service).

They are quite often asked by their friends for advice or comments about social or political matters, this is because friends know they are Civil Servants and it is generally believed that the work they do gives them more insight into social and political matters. One of them added, however, that whilst Civil Servants are more likely to be asked for opinions and advice " people play fair and do not expect more than a certain amount of political comment ".

(*xi*) *Political attitudes*

It was, of course, made perfectly clear to all the 1956 entrants that there was no obligation to answer any of the questions put to them as part of this research, and this was particularly stressed in relation to the questions about politics. However, members of the group were usually very pleased to speak about their attitudes to party politics—indeed many of them welcomed the opportunity to explain how they felt about such matters.

Each was asked how he voted at the last general election (1966). None preferred not to answer, and the results were as follows:

Labour	17
Conservative	6
Liberal	4
Scottish Nationalist	1
Did not vote	2

****

(*xii*) *Social class*

Although the 1956 entrants were all willing to talk about their own political attitudes and political attitudes generally in the Administrative Class, they were much less willing to talk about social class, and some preferred not to talk about it at all. The Civil Servants were asked which social class they would say they belonged to and which social class they would say people in the administrative Civil Service generally belonged to. The answers were:

Which social class would you say you belonged to?

Upper middle or professional middle	12
Middle or middle-middle	16
Lower middle	1
None	5
Prefer not to answer	1

Which social class would you say people in the Administrative Civil Service generally belong to?

Upper middle or professional middle	14
Middle or middle-middle	18
Lower middle	0
None	2
Prefer not to answer	1

* Two paragraphs, which are not printed, followed in Dr. Chapman's confidential report to the Committee.

In discussion, they were also asked what criteria they had borne in mind in reaching their answers. A large number of different criteria were given among which education, income, family background and the subjective assessment of society in general, were the most common. Equally common were answers such as " I don't think in terms of social class ", or " I should try to avoid saying anything, but under pressure I would say . . . ", or " I would say I belong to no social class because I think consciousness of class is the curse of this country ".

Three particularly interesting answers were given to the question about the administrative Civil Service generally. They were: " They are all probably middle *now*, with family backgrounds differing widely ", " If you exclude top civil servants from the upper class, the upper class is drained of any meaning at all; the upper class must include the ' establishment ' and top civil servants are part of the establishment ", " My father once asked me if the people I worked with were gentlemen. I had to admit they weren't, mostly. There is a curious tendency for the women to be of somewhat higher social class than the men ".

One of the most interesting and unexpected aspects of this research was the difficulty of obtaining answers to the questions on social class. In one sense administrative Civil Servants can be regarded as a classless group within society. Some of the Civil Servants who had been perfectly willing to answer all sorts of questions about their private lives and political attitudes became distinctly uncomfortable when talking about social class, and a few simply said they preferred not to discuss it (this was the only aspect of the research on which anyone said he would rather not pursue the subject). Naturally, whilst trying not to cause offence, the researcher tactfully tried to find out why there was this feeling. The most likely conclusion seems to be that a number of these Civil Servants have family backgrounds which they feel are below the social class to which they feel they now belong. On the other hand, at work they often deal with people of a higher social class than themselves. Consequently many of them feel unattached to any particular social class and are quite happy to be in that position, for it means they can easily adjust themselves to various classes and this is both pleasant and sometimes an advantage in their work. Only two seemed really disturbed by this, but about a third of the sample tried to avoid the question or said they just didn't think in terms of class.

C. The Civil Servants and their Work

(i) Career since entry

All of the thirty-two 1956 entrants still in the service are now Principals; a few were promoted in 1960, and a few in 1962, but the majority were promoted in 1961. During the ten years since 1956 they have all had a fairly wide range of experience within their departments, and have had new postings at an average rate of about one a year (though some people in the larger departments tended to have postings every six months during their period as Assistant Principals). Generally speaking, after promotion to Principal their postings average out at about a new posting every eighteen months to two years.

(ii) When they decided to join the Civil Service

The Civil Servants in the sample were asked when they decided that they wanted to join the Civil Service. All thirty-five who completed the questionnaire replied to this question, and the replies fall into the following seven categories:

(*a*) Before entry to University—1.
(" At no particular time . . . I had it in mind as a possible career before I went to Cambridge.")

(*b*) During undergraduate career, but before taking the Civil Service examinations—17.
(" At University—my tutor suggested that I ought to explore the Civil Service as a possible career." " While at University I decided I wanted to join the . . . (Ministry), but no other government department." " As a student . . . I wanted to ' serve the community '; I wanted to avoid any scrambling for position etc. The Civil Service seemed the answer . . . (I also wanted to prove to myself that I could pass those administrative examinations which are spoken of with bated breath).")

(*c*) During, or soon after the Civil Service examination—6.
(" During C.S.S.B. . . . I was impressed by the standard of the selection procedure." " In my last year at Cambridge *after* having sat the Civil Service examination and *after* having been offered a lectureship in classics." " I first took the Method II examination in a light-hearted way, having a first just behind me, with the intention of applying for the Foreign Office and at least partly with the idea of turning it down. They turned me down and I then had to consider the Home Civil Service for which I had been successful. My reasons for joining are coloured by hindsight, and drift played a large part.")

(*d*) While doing research—5.
(" While I was a research student I decided I did not want a University career.")

(*e*) After working for a time in industry—2.
(" Some time after graduating and after working in industrial management for about eighteen months.")

(*f*) After joining the service—2.
(" About eighteen months after I had actually entered it . . . I joined because I had passed the examination." " Probably after I had done so. I was in some doubt when I entered and only did so because I was successful in getting into the . . . (Ministry), which attracted me for quite different reasons.")

(*g*) Other answers—2.
(" At no time did I take a positive decision." " I decided to apply by accident: it was a device for getting home a week or two earlier from West Africa (where I was doing national service).")

They were also asked whether, when they joined, they consciously decided that this was to be a life-long career. Just over 50% (eighteen out of thirty-five) clearly stated that they were not, when they joined, thinking of the Civil Service as a life long-career. Just under 50% (seventeen out of thirty-five) did think in those terms, but about half of this group also added that they were quite prepared to leave if the service was not up to their expectations.

(*iii*) *Why they decided to join*

The answers to " What attracted you to the Civil Service? " were classified by giving a weight of one to each facet mentioned (some replies gave three or four attractions, some gave only one). The following is a list of all the reasons that were quoted more than once:

Interesting, important work; being at the centre of things	20
Belief in the public service; working for the common good	14
Work with congenial colleagues	11
The intellectual quality of the work	9
Attractive pay	6
Lack of enthusiasm for alternative careers	5
Career prospects	3
Difficulty of getting in	3
The attraction of joining an elite group in society	3
Generous leave allowance	2
Opportunity for travel abroad	2
Security	2

Later, during the interview, the Civil Servants were asked specifically whether they felt they had been attracted *to the entry competition* by the fact that it was difficult to pass and that success signified entry into some kind of elite.

Twenty-four out of the thirty-two interviewed said the difficulty of the examination was an important factor. Several mentioned that they took the examination simply for the fun of it, so that they could compete against their contemporaries, but then, when they had been offered a place by the Civil Service Commission, they felt they could not turn it down simply because they had passed the examination against stiff competition. Three specifically said they took the examinations to spite their University careers advisers who had told them they did not stand much chance as they had not been to Oxbridge (these three represented 25% of the Redbrick entry for 1956).

Twenty-four of the thirty-two said they had *not* been attracted by the idea that if they passed the examinations and were offered a place they would be joining some kind of elite (even though several of these twenty-four had taken the examinations for the fun of competing). Of the eight others, one said that this had been an element " but it was an elite of yesterday rather than today ", and three more added that although this element had attracted them, they had since been rather disappointed about this aspect of the Civil Service and did not now feel part of an elite.

In the light of their experience, however, only nineteen out of thirty-five said that the Civil Service had lived up to their expectations (these people gave answers such as " yes ", " on the whole, yes ", " generally, yes ") and five said that the Civil Service had not lived up to their expectations (these were not the same five as had left the service). The other eleven gave heavily qualified answers, often stating that while the Civil Service did not in fact have some of the attractions they had expected before they joined, it had other compensations which meant that they still felt it was a worthwhile career.

(*iv*) *Alternative careers*

Another question was: "If you had not entered the Civil Service, what career would you have followed? " The answers could be classified as follows:

University teaching	17
Industry or management	7
Other public administration	5
Law	4
Miscellaneous	3
Don't know	2

(*v*) *Would you consider leaving the service?*

On the question of whether they would now seriously consider leaving the Civil Service, only eleven out of twenty-eight who answered the question said no. Seventeen out of twenty-eight said they would certainly consider leaving (eight of these had actually been applying for other jobs in the last few years). Many different reasons were given, but only three reasons occurred more than twice, these were: " My job leaves me with less leisure time than I should like ", " I want more pay and better conditions of service " (though it must be pointed out here that of those who had seriously considered other opportunities, the main reason why they had remained in the service was that their pay was better than they could get outside), and " I don't want to work in London for the rest of my working life ".

(*vi*) *Type of work*

Two ways of classifying work done were suggested to the Civil Servants in the sample. One question appeared on the questionnaire as: " Would you describe the work you do as a Civil Servant as primarily (*a*) executive management, (*b*) policy formation, (*c*) regulatory work, (*d*) negotiation, (*e*) other? " The answers were as follows:

Executive management	5
Policy formation	15
Regulatory work	1
Negotiation	3
Other	8

(*Note:* Where two categories were chosen in answer to this question and marked as of equal importance a half-point has been allotted to each in the above table.)

However, it must be stressed that these answers tended to be given only with a great deal of qualification which suggests the form of classification is very imperfect. Two examples will illustrate this: " It depends on the field of work. In my last post (*b*), (*c*), and (*d*) were predominant—but in my present post (*a*) and (*d*). This reflects the very wide division in the work of the service between the traditional policy formation and regulatory work (often closely associated with Ministers and Parliament) and the growing field of executive management of practical tasks (often of great magnitude)." " The work *I* do at the moment is very un-typical Principal work. It is a mixture of (*b*) and (*d*). I have no money or powers to do anything; I work through organizations (some independent, some government financed) and have to try to do policy-planning by discussion, manipulation and purse-string coercion etc." Several of the Civil Servants who said their work was *primarily* (*b*), (*c*), (*d*) or (*e*) above, pointed out that management is a significant part of the work of the Administrative Class, but that as such it is not appreciated.

The second way of classifying work done was based on categories mentioned by H. E. Dale. The question appeared on the questionnaire as: " The following is a list of the types of work you may be doing. Please write 1, 2, 3 etc. against them in the order in which they make demands on your time (so that No. 1 will be the most time consuming for you, No. 2 the next time consuming and so on):

(i) Giving written instructions concerning matters submitted to you by your subordinates and which are to be passed no higher.
(ii) Writing your own minutes, memoranda or letter to indicate your views on matters submitted by your subordinates and which are to be passed to higher authority.
(iii) Writing minutes, memoranda or letters on matters referred to you by your official superiors (whether or not you pass them to subordinates).
(iv) Interviews and telephone conversations with people both inside and outside the Civil Service.
(v) Miscellaneous work not falling under the headings enumerated above."

Unfortunately, the replies here were so qualified and annotated that they are completely unclassifiable.

This does not, however, mean that these two questions were not very valuable. On the contrary, the answers to these questions strongly suggest that a Principal is a grade in a distinct profession, and the work involved cannot be usefully classified according to the simple schemes suggested.[1]

(vii) Demand of work on ability

The nature of the work of Principals is such that most people find its intrinsic quality makes only a moderate demand on their ability, although twelve out of thirty-two said their present work makes a great demand on their ability (ten of the twelve added that this was primarily because of the time factor: " The work is a great demand on physical stamina and quick-wittedness ", " One has to be able to work long and hard under pressure." Four of the thirty-two said that their work was making only a slight demand on their ability, and a few more said they had *recently* been doing work which had been very undemanding.

(viii) Salaries

The sample were asked what they thought the highest salary *should be* at present for Permanent Secretaries, and what they thought the lowest salary *should be* at present for Principals. The answers were:

Highest salary for Permanent Secretaries	
Less than £10,000	1
£10,000	6
£10,001–£12,000	5
£12,001–£15,000	5
£15,001–£20,000	5
More than £20,000	4
No views	4

Lowest salary for Principals	
Between £2,000–£2,500	28
More than £2,500	2

(*Note:* At present the salary scales show £8,600 as the salary for the head of a big Department, and £2,335 as the lowest salary for Principals.)

[1] For two outstanding descriptions of the work of Principals see William Reid, " Civil Service " in *Outlook, A Careers Symposium* (edited by Robin Guthrie), Macdonald, 1963, pp. 163–171, also Camilla Crump, " My Lady Mandarin ", *Outlook Two, A Careers Symposium* (edited by Robin Guthrie and Tony Watts), Macdonald, 1965, pp. 147–154.

The suggestions for the highest salaries tended to come from Civil Servants whose work brought them in contact with industry.

A large majority, in answering these questions, added that what was wrong with the salary scales was that the pay was too low for the people holding the top positions. Increases could be afforded within the same overall budget if there was better management inside the service (for example, some of the work at present being done by Principals could easily be downgraded, and some Principals would be available for more duties if they did not have to waste so much time on low grade secretarial tasks).

(*ix*) *Morale: promotion prospects*

The following question appeared on the questionnaire: " Would you say that a young person of your ability who enters the Civil Service today as an Assistant Principal has an extremely good chance, a fairly good chance, a fairly poor chance or hardly any chance at all of ending up in a top-level post (i.e. *above* Assistant Secretary) ? "

The answer's were:

An extremely good chance	6
A fairly good chance	18
A fairly poor chance	6
Hardly any chance at all	0
No views, or unclassifiable	4

(*x*) *Advice for children*

Although nearly all the sample said they did not intend to influence their children's choice of career, only three said they might advise their children against entering the Civil Service (two because they now feel it is better for a person to have a trade or particular skill or profession as distinct from being a " generalist " in administration, and one because " a Civil Service career can lead to a restricted outlook on social and political problems "). However, one in three added that they would advise against the Civil Service if their children could not get into the Administrative Class. And there appear to be strong views about the Civil Service as a career for women—the general view here seems to be that as a full career the Civil Service is to be recommended, but not as a career for a girl who might get married (mainly because the first few years in the Administrative Class tend to be so much less interesting and less rewarding than later years).

(*xi*) *Present likes and dislikes about the Civil Service*

The answers to " What do you now like about the Civil Service ? " were classified by giving a weight of one to each facet mentioned (some replies gave more facets than others). The following is a list of all aspects of the Civil Service that were mentioned more than once:

Work with congenial colleagues	24
Interesting, important work, being at the centre of things	23
The intellectual quality of the work	10
Being " in the know "; helping to shape policy	7
Working in the public service	6
Pay and/or leave	6

Absence of rat-race, presence of team spirit	6
Enables me to live where I do (London or Edinburgh)	3
Enables me to meet a lot of interesting people	2
Democracy in management (Whitleyism)	2

The answers to " What do you now dislike about the Civil Service? " were similarly classified, and the following is a list of all aspects of the Civil Service that were mentioned more than once:

Bad man-management	19
Lack of clerical assistance	14
Bad office accommodation (e.g. sharing a room when the nature of the work is such that efficiency is seriously reduced)	10
Work interferes with my private life (usually because of long hours)	8
Doing work that I dislike (e.g. that is objectionable on political, social or philosophical grounds or work that comes to nothing because of political pressures)	7
The cult of the amateur	6
Work below my capacity	6
Living in London	5
Anonymity	3
Lack of training	3
The class structure of the service	3

Several of these categories overlap, but this cannot be helped in this type of investigation. For example, " work below my capacity " was quoted for two reasons, either because bad management is causing the Civil Servants to feel that their abilities are not being fully used, or because the supporting staff is so poor (or does not exist) that the Principal has to do minor clerical duties as part of his work. Other people might simply have included these types of experience under the broad heading of " bad management ".

Although a few of the Civil Servants were equipped with them, dictating machines do not yet seem to be generally available to Principals in most departments, and in many cases secretarial assistance does not exist either. It was common to find an ancient typewriter in a Principal's room for his own typing activities. One member of the sample gratefully recalled some typing training he had received during his national service in the R.A.F., another Principal is enrolled as an evening student in a typing class where he is the only man with about thirty women. Many Principals, recalling that there are many unfilled Principal posts at present, pointed out that this need not be so serious if better secretarial assistance was provided, as this would enable more of a Principal's time to be spent on work suited to the grade (and salaries)—typing and addressing envelopes do not need honours degrees or salaries of over £3,000.

Some of the examples of bad management (which one of the Civil Servants defined as " not enough thought being given to how to *use* staff to allow them to earn their salaries ") illustrate such inept staff relations that one is left wondering that there are not more resignations from the service. One Principal learned of his recent posting only by overhearing a telephone conversation in his Assistant Secretary's office, and the posting has never been confirmed by the Establishments Officer. Other criticisms[1] showed serious lack of consideration towards staff as human beings, and some criticisms of staff management were based on incidents that had left individuals feeling very bitter, and not without good cause.

According to several of the Civil Servants interviewed the faults stem basically from the Treasury (management divisions). One or two mentioned that it had been years since they had seen or heard of a visit from a Treasury staff inspector. One or two more, with recent experience of establishments work, gave examples of how unconcerned the Treasury seemed to be about representations or suggestions made to them. Nearly all were highly critical about attitudes to training in the Civil Service (see later), and there were examples in the sample of people with special qualifications or experience who for no apparent good reason are being prevented from using their skills. Several of the Civil Servants interviewed were highly critical of what they called " the cult of the amateur " in relation to postings. As one of them put it: " I have had seven jobs in my department, none lasting longer than two years, none bearing any but the most remote relation to any other; with this kind of career there is not enough scope for getting to know a job thoroughly and for acquiring enough confidence (and time) to produce new ideas and ' make a difference '."

Several in the sample were at the time of the research, or had recently been, filling posts which did not provide a full day's work, but little notice seemed to be taken when they reported this. On the other hand, others were required to work inordinately long hours and were complaining of the intrusion of work into their private lives. As one put it: " In the administrative Civil Service, if one is at all conscientious it is not a job but a way of life. It demands most of one's time and energy and this pressure is kept up so that one can see people becoming paler editions of themselves." Another gave as a dislike " the expectation that civil servants will work inordinate hours without regard to their family life ".

The attraction of working with congenial colleagues tended to mean two things at once. On the one hand, there is the complete absence of class distinction within the service. This applies not only to social class but also to the Civil Service Classes (Executive/Administrative, etc.), for there is a general atmosphere of team spirit in which educational and family backgrounds are totally irrelevant. Graduates from Oxbridge and Redbrick Universities work side by side, even in the same office, with those promoted from within the service, or even those still within the Executive Class itself (in several cases Principals interviewed shared offices with Civil Servants in the Executive Class). What matters is that X or Y is " a decent sort " and " a good person to work with ". On the other hand, working with congenial colleagues often also meant having colleagues who were very intelligent and " civilised " and of a liberal frame of mind.

(*xii*) *Attractiveness of various departments*

Members of the sample were asked to state, with reasons, which three departments in their opinions were the most attractive to work in, and which three departments were the least attractive to work in. A very large majority stated

[1] Based on a number of specific personal experiences which were explained to the author in confidence.

that they felt these were impossible questions to answer because all departments have both attractive and unattractive jobs in them, and the subject matter of civil service work is relatively unimportant in making particular posts or departments attractive. The answers given were almost unclassifiable, but they were interesting for three reasons. First, nearly everyone in the sample included his own department as being attractive—mainly because the work and people were familiar, but also because Civil Servants tend to feel very ignorant of what goes on in other departments. Secondly, two departments emerge, even through the claims of ignorance, with a very attractive image—the Treasury and the Department of Economic Affairs, and two emerge as very unattractive—the Ministries of Defence and Social Security. Thirdly, the main qualities that make a department appear attractive are (*a*) the importance of the work involved, (*b*) interesting subject matter and variety of subject matter, (*c*) people already in the department give the impression of being intellectually stimulating people to work with: the main qualities that make a department unattractive are (*a*) work that seems to be mainly executive in character, and/or (*b*) work that seems to be more concerned with destruction rather than construction.

(*xiii*) *Training*

These Civil Servants have had almost no formal training for the work they are now doing. Twenty-six out of thirty-two (only thirty-two answered this question) spent three weeks on a Treasury course which one of them described as " a child's guide to government and administration "—the other six did not even attend that course (they included one who explained " I was put on the three week A.P. course run by the Treasury but taken off after a day because of urgent departmental work "). The usual story was one of " I spent a day being shown round the department on arrival and three weeks later I was on the three week A.P. course ". Three of the thirty-two have at some stage attended a two week's course on management and communications, two have spent six weeks at the Centre for Administrative Studies (one more was proposed for the C.A.S. course but had to withdraw because of work pressure), two have spent a sabbatical year in the U.S.A. (on Harkness Fellowships) and one has spent three months at the Henley Administrative Staff College. The largest departments in addition arranged for an introduction course in the department (usually lasting about a week) and five of the 1956 entrants attended such courses. But that is the total training during a period of ten years in the service for those thirty-two Civil Servants.

They were also asked to comment on the value of these courses. Those who are serving in large departments said the planned regular postings (" sitting with Nellie ") during their period as an A.P. (sometimes with a regional tour as well) was very profitable, assuming they remained with that department. A couple of the Civil Servants recalled that " the best of my training was serving in the Minister's Private Office for a year and a half " and others commented that " training on the job can be very valuable if you have a good teacher . . . but not everyone is a good teacher ".

Nearly everyone condemned the Treasury course in terms such as " of no value whatever ", " a complete waste of time " or " as satisfactory as a three week introductory course could be ". The only point mentioned in its favour was that it enabled fairly isolated Civil Servants to meet other new entrants of similar age from other departments. The Treasury courses as experienced by the 1956 entrants have since been replaced by the three months course for Assistant Principals at the Centre for Administrative Studies. One Civil Servant, expressing the sentiments of many in the group, said " I would have welcomed the opportunity to attend the present A.P.s course at the C.A.S. . . . many of us need to know about modern techniques of management and administration ". Several in the group bitterly regretted that they have been in the Civil Service not only too long for them to be able to attend the A.P.s course, but also too long for them to take advantage of the new courses at the C.A.S. for Principals (the Treasury recently announced that these would be for entrants from 1957 onwards).

They had many ideas for improving this situation ranging from encouragement for them to get qualifications in administration to short courses at universities or in industry. Indeed, the general consensus was that almost *any* form of training would be welcomed, but particularly the opportunity to get away from the office for a course of guided discussion or seminars where they could exchange ideas.

(*xiv*) *The typical administrative Civil Servant*

When asked to give a description of the typical administrative Civil Servant quite a large proportion found this impossible, often because, as they put it, there are so many exceptions. Others explained that an administrative Civil Servant " cannot be type cast, (sic) what emerges in an attempt to do so is either a caricature or an ideal or platitudes ", and " I know so many administrators so well that it is their differences rather than their similarities that have left their impression . . . you have a general idea about things you don't know well; for example, I have a general idea about stockbrokers ".

On the other hand, those who attempted the description tended to fall between giving a factual description (such as " educated at Oxbridge, with three children, works long hours often taking work home, middle aged, etc.") and only a few described what appeared to them to be general characteristics (" a bit stuffy and short on ideas ", " generally unworldly ", " nearly all have too little money, inclination or time left to be anything but a little dull ", " an idealist with his feet on the ground ", " a little cynical, or at any rate sceptical, not a particularly colourful personality ", " civilised in general approach, but not necessarily cultured because most have no time ").

They tended to find it much easier to say whether they considered themselves to be typical members of the administrative Civil Service. Nineteen out of thirty-two felt they were more or less typical and only ten thought they were definitely not typical.

(*xv*) *Attitudes to recruitment*

In general, most of the sample thought good, suitable people are at present being recruited for the Administrative Class, but several added that the service needs more from Redbrick universities and there needs to be more publicity to tell people what it is really like. Several also added that, " whilst the university material is basically good the best use is not made of that material ". At no time either in answers on the questionnaires or during the interviews was anyone—and this includes the people who have now left the service—really critical of the Civil Service Commission. Indeed, several of the sample went out of their way to comment favourably about the C.S.C.

At the interview they were asked for comments on the Treasury proposal for a common graduate entry where the best performers—on the strength of academic record and performance in the entry competition—should be " starred " and offered the same kind of opportunities for special training(!) and the same course of postings in their early years as A.P.s receive today. In particular they were asked whether they thought it necessary to preserve some form of pre-selection at entry point (i.e. starring) in order to attract the best talent.

Twelve thought starring would be necessary, fifteen were against, and three didn't know. It was not possible, mainly because of the small size of the sample, to usefully correlate these answers with any other information about the Principals who gave them.

The most common comments by people who favoured starring were: " Really good people would be deterred from entering the Civil Service if they were put in a common graduate entry grade ", " Starring would be necessary to preserve the present standard of entry at A.P. grade, especially as more students will now be going to universities ", " I think amalgamation of executive and administrative entry grades would be fatal unless there are also radical management changes in the service ", and " The starring suggestion is only necessary because of present bad man-management ".

Comments of people against the idea of starring included: " We need more graduates of all sorts—there is a great need for people with ordinary degrees as well as for people with honours degrees ", " Big commercial employers don't openly subdivide their graduate entry into categories and they don't appear to do too badly ", " It is better to classify people after they have been in the service a couple of years ", " If you don't star you may lose a few very able people (but these are not necessarily the people you would want anyway) and you might attract a lot of other people who are certainly needed ", " A good honours man wouldn't be put off as long as he was sure his ability would be recognised—but can the service say its man-management is good enough for them to be able to spot him and encourage him? ", " Starring is a gimmick which mature graduates would see through ", " Starring will not help the recruitment problem and nor will a common graduate entry—you need to tell potential entrants what the service is *really* like, and let them see that ability is rewarded ", " Starring will only be of value if you can later ' un-star ' people and that would create bad feeling . . . the service badly needs some means of getting rid of passengers (in the way that the Foreign Service does by using the 1943 Foreign Service Act) ", " Starring won't work—we need to be able to recognise and reward administrative ability—a first class honours degree is not a guarantee that a man will be a good administrator ", " If we are going to have stars they should be awarded after three years in the service, when a person's ability as an *administrator* is known ", " The service needs to concentrate on rewarding merit in the job ", " The Treasury proposals for starring suggests there is some positive correlation between good honours degrees and good administrative ability, is there? ", " Research is needed on what *young people* think about this—you won't necessarily get the most valuable answer by asking a lot of old men; if you want to know what effect the starring proposals might have on recruitment—go and ask some young people! "

The Civil Servants were asked what qualities they thought should be looked for when selecting Administrative Class Civil Servants. The replies tended to be a rather unhelpful catalogue of virtues, and a typical answer: " Analytical ability, judgement, initiative, energy, preparedness for sheer hard work and long hours, courage, integrity, discretion, persuasiveness, intelligence, ability to get on with people, sense of humour, ability to write and speak clearly. (God, move over.) ".

When this subject was introduced at the interviews, however, it was discovered that few people had any clear idea what made a good administrator. Some talked of administrators they admired (several were impressed by reading Harrod's biography of Keynes) but several said the nearest they could get to expressing it was that a person needed a " flair " for administration. One added that bad Civil Servants fail because of lack of judgement, and judgement cannot be taught. Perhaps this also is a subject on which more research could profitably be done.

(*xvi*) *The Government as an employer*

On the question of comparing the service, as an employer, with other employers, the results were:

It is better than other employers	7
It is about the same	21
It is worse	3
Don't know	1

Most of the answers had qualifications added about the good and bad points about the Civil Service. It seems that the main factors on which the Civil Service is better than other employers are sick leave, leave and security. Its bad features are (*a*) its non-contributory pension scheme which results in lack of mobility into and out of the service (" a dictatorial attempt to tie employees for life "), (*b*) bad man-management and in particular career planning, and (*c*) bad working conditions (" offices are frequently shared, dirty, ill-lit and noisy ").

(*xvii*) *The image of the Civil Service*

When asked whether they thought people generally in this country have a true image of what the higher Civil Service is like, the 1956 entrants fell into two distinct groups. On the one hand there were about half who thought that people generally had no idea what administrative Civil Servants did and it doesn't really matter; one of this group added " there would be something wrong with a country with an excessive admiration for its civil service ".

The other half also thought most people had no idea what higher Civil Servants did but thought it did matter, partly because the bad image had a poor effect on morale in the service and partly because it had a disastrous effect on recruiting. One said: " When I told a relative, who is a local businessman and has a pathological hatred of governments and officials, that I was to enter the service, he was genuinely distressed because he thought good material was going to waste. I met this attitude elsewhere among friends, relatives and even other undergraduates who preferred teaching and industry to the Civil Service."

The remedy that a very large majority of the group suggested was less anonymity. " Civil Servants have taken the cult of anonymity too far . . . it would do the image of the Civil Service a lot of good if e.g. Permanent Secretaries appeared on television from time to time (it would also, I suspect, do the Civil Servants a lot of good) ". Many suggested Civil Servants explaining, on television or radio, details of policies that had been decided, taking part in documentaries dealing with particular problems which Civil Servants are trying to solve, more participation in university seminars by senior Civil Servants, and even a television version of the Public Accounts Committee and the Estimates Committee. All these suggestions could do a great deal of good for the service and could be arranged without conflicting with Ministerial responsibility (in any case there would be no obligation for particular Civil Servants to do any of these things, but the argument was that they should be able to do so if they wish).

(*xviii*) *Comments*

Finally, they were asked for comments and given the opportunity to draw attention to anything which had not been covered in questions on the questionnaire.

In this section the replies tended to stress three things.

First, there should be a great deal more career planning and attention given to man-management. One answer summed up this point of view clearly and forcefully:

> " I should like to emphasise the need to improve career planning, based on the fundamental view that Civil Servants ought to be as good as possible throughout their careers (and most will not end up as Permanent Secretaries). To achieve this, the cult of the non-specialist, with postings to unrelated jobs every two or three years, is inadequate and inefficient—even if it is the right way to train Permanent Secretaries, which is doubtful. What is needed is a career pattern related to some specific area of work, theme or subject matter, with a series of jobs lasting, say, four years on average, and all related to this theme (though they could be otherwise widely varied e.g. in different departments). Given the uncertainties of career management (promotions, departmental requirements etc.), this ideal is extremely difficult to realise fully. But it ought to be acknowledged as the aim, and discussed with individual Civil Servants, so that their aptitudes and preferences can be considered. This would make Civil Servants on average more efficient, increase their ' job satisfaction ' and encourage them to study their field in depth to become properly expert. It ought also to mean that individuals with the high innate ability already recruited could be given more responsibility earlier, developing their ability by giving them greater confidence and a chance to ' make their mark '. This could be accommodated within the structure of the Civil Service by securing higher recruitment of less able graduates for Principal/C.E.O. posts (to fill the gap left by quicker promotion of the most able) and by accepting more resignations into industry or academic posts at higher levels (which greater specialisation would itself tend to encourage)."

Secondly, several felt that what is needed is a fundamental change *in attitude* (for the way people think about the Civil Service, and in particular the way Civil Servants think about it themselves, is a major factor in the functioning of the system), and therefore it might be a good idea, though risky, to operate on " the brain " of the Civil Service—that is, the Treasury. The general direction of this argument was that if one sums up all the really important suggestions for reform they amount to questions of management and attitudes (the management questions cover both the need for better career planning and deployment of personnel, and also extensive reclassification of work because a lot of work at present done by Principals could be done by senior executive staff). Of course, it would not necessarily help if you made these changes piecemeal, but if all the changes were made at once they might shock the service, and people outside as well, into a much needed change of attitude.

For example, you could take the Treasury management functions from the Treasury and get a new staff to work on them in a Public Service Commission. One of the troubles with having the Treasury responsible for management is that its staff are selected from other departments because of their ability, and for this reason they tend to be an unrepresentative sample of administrative Civil Servants as a whole. Also, a number of the Treasury management staff have now been in the department (though not necessarily in the same post) so long that they do not appreciate the type of executive management problems that face many Principals in other departments. If many of the suggested reforms were implemented at one time, and in addition there was a " brain operation " on the Treasury, a great deal might be achieved.

Thirdly, there were comments about what was sometimes referred to as " the context of Fulton ". A final quotation from the answers on the completed questionnaires expresses the point forcefully:

> " The really crucial questions—the relationship between Government, Parliament and the Civil Service—are outside your terms of reference, which means that the outcome of ' Fulton ' will be little more than a botching up operation. There will be some ' reforms ': the tripartite class structure will be, if not abandoned, at least modified considerably, to the accompaniment of a great deal of applause: (yet, in practice, the barriers between the three classes only exist on paper even today; and some differential for age, educational standards and aptitude at entry will still have to be maintained). But without tackling questions such as the dogma of Ministerial Responsibility, Parliamentary and Public Accountability, the relationship between the Executive and Legislature, nothing very much is likely to emerge except, I suspect, the ironic conclusion that, given the highly restricting and artificial conventions within which Civil Servants are obliged to work, they manage remarkably well! "

Questionnaire for Administrative Class Civil Servants who were Direct Entrants (by Open Competition) into the Service in 1956

A. Curriculum Vitae

1. Name in full.

2. Date of birth.

3. Home address.

4. Present department, and rank in it.

5. What is the name of the last school you attended? (please also give the type of school, e.g. local authority, direct grant, independent).

6. Which University did you attend? (If Oxford, Cambridge or London please also give college. If a civic university, please give department.)

7. First Degree (please give class, subject(s), and year of graduation).

8. Other qualifications (e.g. second degrees or professional qualifications).

9. Give brief details of your career since entry into the Civil Service (positions held, dates of promotions, changes in departments etc.).

10. Do you feel that your present work makes (*a*) a great demand, (*b*) a moderate demand or (*c*) only slight demand on your ability?

11. (men only) (*a*) Did you do national service?

    (*b*) If so, please give dates, name of service (also regiment or branch), and last rank held.

12. Have you had any other occupation since leaving school? (apart from vacation employment whilst a student), please give dates and nature of the employment.

B. Other Personal Details

13. Marital status (please tick appropriate): (*a*) unmarried
(*b*) married
(*c*) widowed
(*d*) divorced

14. If your status is (*b*), (*c*) or (*d*), please state (*a*) whether you have any children (please give sex and age in each case).
(*b*) the name(s) of the school(s) they now attend, and the type, e.g. local authority, direct grant, independent.

15. Do you live in a house or flat?

16. Do you own or rent your accommodation?

17. (*a*) If you rent your house or flat please give monthly rental.
(*b*) If you own your house or flat please give rateable value.

18. If you have a car please state make, model and year. How long have you had it?

19. What was the occupation of your father when you entered the Civil Service? (Please be as precise as possible; if your father had retired or died please say so and state his last occupation).

20. Were you a first generation university student in your family?

21. While at university, what societies or clubs did you
(*a*) join
(*b*) hold office in.

22. What associations, clubs and other organisations do you belong to?

(*a*) London Clubs (such as Union, United University etc.)

(*b*) Other social clubs.

(*c*) Sporting.

(*d*) Religious (please specify denomination, also if you hold any office such as churchwarden or layreader, please specify).

(*e*) Cultural.

(*f*) Civic.

(*g*) Benevolent.

23. Are you a committee member of any of the organisations you belong to, or do you undertake any special duties for any of them?

24. Are there any other associations which you would like to belong to?

25. What are your other leisure time activities?

26. (*a*) Are there many people with whom you are friendly and talk with fairly often?

(*b*) Please place the following categories of such people in order of frequency of contact (write 1, 2, 3 etc. against them)

(*a*) Relatives outside your own household.

(*b*) Neighbours.

(*c*) Ex-neighbours.

(*d*) People at work.

(*e*) Friends who are not and have not been neighbours.

27. Do you like to meet people, go to social gatherings, and generally get around a lot?

28. Which daily newspaper do you read regularly, that is at least three times a week?

29. Which Sunday newspapers do you read regularly, that is at least once every two weeks?

30. Which other weekly magazines and newspapers do you read regularly, that is at least once every two weeks?

31. Which social class would you say you belonged to?

32. Which social class would you say people in the administrative civil service generally belong to?

33. Have you recently been asked (outside your work) for your views about social or political affairs?

34. Compared with other people belonging to your circle of friends are you more or less likely than most of them to be asked for advice about what one should think about social or political matters?

C. Civil Service Attitudes

35. (*a*) Which three government departments, in your opinion, are the most attractive to work in? (please give reasons why you consider them attractive).

    (*b*) Which three government departments, in your opinion, are the most unattractive to work in? (please give reasons why you consider them unattractive).

36. When did you decide that you wanted to enter the Civil Service?

37. When you joined, did you consciously decide that this was to be your life-long career? (if not, why did you join?)

38. If you had not entered the Civil Service, what career would you have followed?

39. What particularly attracted you to the Civil Service?

40. In the light of your experience, would you say that the Civil Service has lived up to these expectations?

41. Would you advise your son or daughter to enter the Civil Service? (please give reasons).

42. What do you now like about the Civil Service?

43. What do you now dislike about the Civil Service?

44. Would you consider leaving the Civil Service? (If so, give reasons and if possible the career you would like to follow and why you have not in fact left. If you would have liked to leave at any time between entry and now please say when, why, and what deterred you from doing so.)

45. Do you consider yourself to be a typical member of the administrative Civil Service?

46. Would you describe the work you do as a Civil Servant as primarily (*a*) executive management, (*b*) policy formation, (*c*) regulatory work, (*d*) negotiation, (*e*) other?

47. The following is a list of the types of work you may be doing. Please write 1, 2, 3, etc. against them in the order in which they make demands on your time (so that No. 1 will be the most time consuming for you, No. 2. the next time consuming and so on):

    (i) Giving written instructions concerning matters submitted to you by your subordinates and which are to be passed no higher.

    (ii) Writing your own minutes, memoranda or letters to indicate your views on matters submitted by your subordinates and which are to be passed to higher authority.

    (iii) Writing minutes, memoranda or letter on matters referred to you by your official superiors (whether or not you pass them to subordinates).

    (iv) Interviews and telephone conversations with people both inside and outside the Civil Service.

    (v) Miscellaneous work not falling under the headings enumerated above.

48. Do you feel that your education prior to joining the Civil Service was the best background for the sort of job you now hold? (if not please suggest what you feel would have been more suitable.)

49. (*a*) Give details of the training you have received since you joined the service.

    (*b*) Give an assessment of this training, how helpful you feel it has been in equipping you to do (i) your past job(s) (ii) your present job, and (iii) what you expect to do in future (if you are critical please suggest improvements).

50. Do you think that the best (i.e. most suitable) persons are at present being recruited for the administrative Civil Service? (If not, why not?)

51. What main qualities do you think should be looked for when recruiting for the administrative Civil Service?

52. If you were to describe your general idea of what an administrative Civil Servant is like, what sort of person would that be?

53. Would you say that a young person of your ability who enters the Civil Service today as an Assistant Principal has an extremely good chance, a fairly good chance, a fairly poor chance or hardly any chance at all of ending up in a top-level post (i.e. *above* Assistant Secretary)?

54. What do you think the highest salary *should be* at present for Permanent Secretaries?

55. What do you think the lowest salary *should be* at present for Principals?

56. What is your opinion now of the Civil Service as an employer? (State how you think it compares with other employers that you think are comparable—is it better, about the same, or worse? If better or worse please give reasons.)

57. Do you think that people generally in this country have a true image of what the higher Civil Service is like? (If not please suggest why this is so, and what you would suggest to improve the image.)

D. Comments

58. Would you please add any further information or comments that you think may be useful in this investigation.

MEMORANDUM No. 3

submitted by

J. F. PICKERING
(Lecturer in Economics, University of Sussex)

May, 1967

The Civil Service Unsuccessfuls: Fifteen Years Later

Contents

List of Tables

Chapter 1

Introduction

(*a*) *The survey*

At the request of the Committee on the Civil Service, the writer conducted a follow-up survey into the subsequent careers of graduates who had thought of entering the Administrative Class of the Civil Service (and had gone so far as to submit an application) but for one reason or another had not done so. In the majority of cases they had been rejected by the Civil Service Commission following the Open Competitions but a number had withdrawn their applications and a number had been declared successful but decided on other careers. The survey was conducted by means of a mail questionnaire and carried out between November 1966 and February 1967. The report was submitted to the Committee on the Civil Service in May 1967 and minor amendments have subsequently been made prior to publication.

The main object of the inquiry was to throw some light on the career patterns of the people involved and, if possible, to try to assess how far they have achieved success in their chosen careers. In the course of this inquiry information has also been collected on the attitudes of the respondents to their present careers and towards the Civil Service.

It was decided that the survey should be based on the candidates who competed in a particular year. The 1951 applicants were selected for this follow-up. By selecting people who had competed as much as fifteen years before (and had in most cases graduated from University at the same time)[1] it was felt that this would provide a long range picture of career development. The selection of 1951 candidates was also advantageous since it made it possible to draw a more direct comparison with those of their contemporaries who did become Administrative Class Civil Servants, since they are now in the normal course of things becoming due for promotion from Principal to the career grade of Assistant Secretary with a starting salary of £3,585.

The report of the Civil Service Commissioners for the relevant period shows that nearly 1,000 applications were submitted for the 1951 Open Competitions to the Administrative Class but that only just under 600 competitors were

---

[1] Admission to the Administrative Class is either by direct entry through the Open Competitions or promotion from other classes in the Civil Service. The Open Competitions take two forms. Method I consists of written examination papers of honours degree standard and an interview. Method II consists of a series of aptitude and other tests followed by an interview at the Final Selection Board. For a description of the Open Competitions as they apply at the present time see Civil Service Commission, *Civil Service Posts for Graduates*, H.M.S.O., 1966.

In order to qualify for admission by Method II it is necessary to have at least a second class honours degree and since the Method I papers are set at honours degree level it is safe to say that almost all the candidates in the Open Competitions are graduates or about to graduate at the time they compete.

It does not follow from this that all members of the Administrative Class are graduates, since non-graduates may be promoted into the Administrative Class and the recently instituted " over-age " competitions are open to non-graduates also. At the present time some 23 per cent of the members of the Administrative Class are not graduates.

examined and under 100 were declared successful. These figures contain an element of double counting because candidates who competed by both Method I and Method II were included twice.

Table 1.1. Results of Open Competitions to the Administrative Class 1951–1952

	No.	
Applications received	950	
Method I		471
Method II		479
Candidates examined and/or interviewed	583	
Method I		231
Method II		352
Declared Successful	92	
Method I		58
Method II		34

Source: Eighty-fifth Report of Her Majesty's Civil Service Commissioners, 1st April 1949, to 31st March 1952. H.M.S.O. 1953.

It seems that in 1951 the Commissioners were well satisfied with the quality of the candidates offering themselves. " At the beginning of the period 1949–1952 we did not find enough candidates of good quality for the Administrative Class, but subsequently there was no serious difficulty in filling the vacancies."[1] But even by 1952 there seem to be hints of the difficulties which have since become serious in recruiting a sufficient number of good candidates, ". . . our general impression has been that the number of outstanding candidates who wish to join the Home Civil and Foreign Services is smaller than it used to be."[2]

A list was provided by the Civil Service Commission containing the names and addresses of 482 people who had either been unsuccessful in the 1951 Open Competition or withdrew at a late stage or, in the case of ten of the names provided, had been declared successful and subsequently declined appointment in the Civil Service. One of the difficulties in surveying people, most of whom have had no contact with the Civil Service Commission since 1951, is that the majority have moved from the address which the Commission gave, in many cases without trace. In some instances where the 1951 address was the address of parents it was possible to make contact with the graduates but it quickly became apparent that a survey conducted on such an out of date mailing list would prove unsatisfactory. While, therefore, the first mailing of the questionnaire in November 1966 was sent to the addresses provided by the Civil Service Commission, a separate inquiry was sent to the Universities and Colleges attended by these people as students in an attempt to obtain more up-to-date addresses for them. In many instances this proved successful, and second and third mailings of the questionnaires were sent to the addresses provided from this source.

Even so, it has proved impossible to trace over 20 per cent of the candidates. All communications addressed to them have been returned by the G.P.O. as " gone away ". It is perhaps not surprising that fewer graduates from Universities where there is a strong link with former students have proved untraceable

[1] *Op. cit*, para. 13.
[2] *Ibid*

than from those which have less close ties. Whereas only 12 per cent of the candidates from Oxford and Cambridge have proved untraceable, the proportion is between a quarter and one third from London, the Scottish Universities and the English Civic Universities and the University of Wales (to be referred to as the ' Other ' Universities henceforward). Nine of the candidates are known to be deceased. If therefore we exclude these and the untraceables we are left with an effective sample size of 372 of whom 263 (71 per cent have replied). Eleven of these refused to complete the questionnaire leaving an actual response rate of 68 per cent. Six per cent of those replying did not complete questionnaires but sent letters containing information which has been incorporated into the results. In most cases these were housewives who are no longer working and to whom the questionnaire had slightly less relevance than to those who are still in full time employment, but this also includes two or three who have become Civil Servants and whose attitudes have been surveyed in other studies.

Table 1.2. Response to a Survey of Civil Service Unsuccessfuls

	No.
Survey size	482
Untraceable	101
Deceased	9
Effective sample size	372
Refusals	11
Completed questionnaires	237
Other usable information supplied	15
Number of usable replies	252
Response rate	68%

It may be that the actual rate of response is higher than that shown. A number of the graduates who replied following a reminder sent to an address provided by their old College or University remarked that they had not received the first questionnaire sent to the address provided by the Civil Service Commission, though this has not been returned to the sender. It seems reasonable to suppose, therefore, that others from whom we have had no reply also may not have received a questionnaire. The problem of people who prove untraceable does not constitute a major problem in most surveys because the samples can be drawn from up to date address lists and the difficulty experienced here of ensuring that all people are contacted suggests that similar follow up inquiries over a long time period might prove equally difficult.

Some of the respondents came closer to success than others and at certain stages in the discussion of their career development it will be convenient to compare this with their performance in the Open Competitions. Eight different levels of performance will be identified and used in making comparisons. Together with the numbers falling into each category, the different levels of performance are identified in Table 1.5 below. The number of candidatures is greater than the number of candidates because some competed by both Method I and Method II. At certain stages in the discussion it will be convenient to pay particular attention to those who were ' near misses ' in 1951. These we define as people who obtained a mark of 700 or more in the Method I competition, or a mark of more than 200 at the Final Selection Board interview in Method II.

(b) The problem of non-response

In any survey there is a danger that people who do not reply may constitute a significantly different group when compared with those who do reply. This may mean that any general conclusions drawn from the replies obtained may be invalid. In this survey, despite considerable efforts to minimize the extent of non-response, there is the double problem of people who proved impossible to trace and those who have chosen not to reply. Both groups are of almost equal size.

In order to assess whether either of these groups appears to introduce a significant degree of bias into the results as a consequence of their absence we need to compare such information as is available about them with the same data for the respondents. Such comparison can be made in respect of the sex of the candidates, their University background and the level of performance in the Open Competitions to the Administrative Class. This information is presented in Tables 1.3, 1.4 and 1.5.

As has already been pointed out, the proportion of untraceables does vary according to University background but there does not appear to be any significant variation in the incidence of non-response amongst graduates of different University backgrounds. Similarly, we find that almost identical proportions of men and women fall into the three categories of respondents, non-respondents and untraceables. As regards the level of performance in the Open Competitions, we find that a rather higher proportion of those who withdrew their candidature have replied and there is a slight under-representation amongst the respondents of those who scored low marks (less than 600) in the Method I Competition. In all other respects there does not appear to be a significant degree of variation between the respondents, non-respondents and untraceables, and we may tentatively conclude that there does not appear to be any significant degree of non-response bias introduced into the results.

Table 1.3. Response Analysed by Type of University

Type of University	Sample size No.	Untraceable and deceased No.	Effective sample size No.	Usable replies No.	Response rate %
Oxford	129	19	110	77	70
Cambridge	86	8	78	53	68
London	93	28	65	47	72
Scottish	54	15	39	25	64
Other	117	40	77	49	64
None	3	0	3	1	33
Total	482	110	372	252	68

Table 1.4. Sex of Respondents, Non-Respondents and Untraceables

	Respondents		Non-respondents		Untraceable and deceased		Total	
Sex	No.	%	No.	%	No.	%	No.	%
Men	191	52	93	25	85	23	369	100
Women	61	54	27	24	25	22	113	100

Table 1.5. Performance in 1951 Open Competitions by Respondents, Non-Respondents and Untraceables Separately

N=482

Level of Performance	Respondents No.	Non-respondents No.	Untraceables and deceased No.	Total No.
Declared successful	8	1	1	10
Withdrew	69	17	16	102
Method I:				
Less than 600 marks	26	26	28	80
600–699 marks	31	18	11	60
700 marks and over	17	11	7	35
Method II:				
Rejected after qualifying tests	100	38	44	182
Called to Final Selection Board, mark 200 or less	61	26	23	110
Called to Final Selection Board, mark more than 200	17	6	2	25
Total:	329	143	132	604

Note: The totals are greater than the actual number of candidates since those who sat both methods are counted twice.

(*c*) *Some definitions*

The numbers in the survey are quite small and it has therefore proved necessary to group together some categories of respondent in order to provide cells where the numbers are normally sufficiently large to enable conclusions to be drawn with some degree of confidence. The main grouping used is by type of employment. This refers to the main form of business of the employer and does not take account of the fact that within that employment group different people may be exercising different functions e.g. within the University group there will be both teachers and full-time administrators. Where appropriate, an occupational classification has also been adopted. This is based on the nature of the work actually carried out by the respondent.

Employment groupings

In combining employment groups that would normally stand on their own in a larger survey, account has been taken of the nature of the work done and the general employment conditions. In most cases it has been found that the information about each of the parts that go to make up the composite category is very similar. Where there are important variations within a category these are pointed out in the text. Nine separate employment groups are used in the analysis (together with a tenth—those not in full time employment). The groups " school " and " local government " are probably self explanatory except to emphasise that education officers employed by local authorities are classed as local government officers. The other employment groups comprise the following:

Further education includes all teachers employed in polytechnics, colleges of advanced technology, colleges of education, etc.

University includes university teachers, those engaged in university administration and employed in full-time paid research positions in universities.

Finance and law includes all those engaged in accountancy, banking, stockbroking, insurance, legal practice as barristers and solicitors and employees of trade associations.

Civil service includes all grades of the Home Civil Service, the Foreign Service and the Overseas Civil Service. Also included here are members of the British Council and commissioned officers in the armed forces.

Industry includes all those employed in manufacturing industry together with employees of public utilities and nationalised industries.

Research and consultancy includes people employed by organizations specifically concerned with research and consultancy activities, especially in the fields of market research, advertising and management consultancy.

The miscellaneous group mainly comprises people in the fields of journalism, publishing and entertainment but also for the purposes of this study includes an ordained clergyman and two or three employed in agriculture and estate management and in distribution.

Occupational groupings

Classification on an occupational basis is less satisfactory in some areas because of the difficulty of identifying and defining correctly the occupations and of maintaining an adequate number of replies in each occupational group to facilitate meaningful comparison. The line of distinction becomes particularly difficult to draw in the case of people holding managerial positions concerned with a particular function, such as marketing. Wherever possible, the principle adopted has been that such people should be classified according to the specific function rather than as administrators or managers. The occupational classification adopted has the following special features:

Teaching includes one or two who are employed outside the normal fields of education and are engaged in training schemes in industry or are in teaching posts with the British Council.

Financial and legal activities include people working as lawyers, tax and investment advisers in industry and the civil service.

Research and consultancy includes people employed in positions as economists, planners, statisticians together with a few concerned more specifically with information and publicity services whose career details place them more conveniently in this group than elsewhere.

The miscellaneous group is comparable with the "miscellaneous" heading in the employment grouping but also includes women graduates who obtained employment as secretaries.

(d) General comments and acknowledgements

Some general comments about the study may be appropriate. It is hoped that the results of this survey may prove of interest to those who are concerned with the pattern of graduate career development over a fairly long time period. The results of this survey, however, should not be taken as having general applicability since the graduates included were a self-selected group in the sense that it was only because they chose to apply for a position in the Administrative Class of the Civil Service that they were included in the study. We do not have information on the career patterns of their contemporaries who did not compete for a place in the Civil Service so we cannot claim that their career experiences may be taken as typical of all graduates of their age. As a group, there is a strong bias towards graduates in arts and the social sciences. It seems also, that in terms of academic achievement the respondents are above average since three-quarters of them had first or good second class honours degrees and the knowledge that entry standards for the administrative class were high and competition keen was likely to attract only those who had set their sights high.

The survey included both men and women and a high proportion of the women have withdrawn from the labour force since 1951. This means therefore that the tabulations relating to the present work experience and job attitudes etc. have had to exclude married women who are no longer in full-time employment.

In order to keep this report to a manageable length a high proportion of the statistical tables that were computed have had to be omitted. The aim has been to publish the main tables and to draw attention in the text to other interesting and important features of the survey results.

Any survey requires the goodwill and active co-operation of a large number of people, especially where it has to be executed and completed within a short period of time as was the case with this survey. Thanks are especially due to the graduates who completed the questionnaires in great detail and in doing so provided much valuable information. The author wishes to acknowledge the assistance of the Civil Service Commission who provided various items of information required, the registrars and other administrative officers of the Universities and Colleges who provided addresses for the graduates we wished to contact, and the officials of professional bodies for their advice on salary levels in different occupations. Much of the administration of the survey and the coding of the questionnaires was carried out by Mrs. J. R. Pickering, assisted by the members of the Social Research Unit at the University of Sussex. Mr. D. H. Hitchin, also of the University of Sussex, was responsible for the efficient processing of the data. Thanks are also due to Professor Marie Jahoda, University of Sussex and Dr. Richard Chapman, University of Liverpool for helpful comments on an earlier draft of this report. The author remains solely responsible for the opinions expressed and conclusions.

Chapter 2

Characteristics of the Respondents

In this chapter we are concerned with identifying the people who completed the questionnaire, particularly with reference to their educational and social background and their social characteristics at the present time. This information is important on the one hand because it enables us to identify background factors which seem to influence the development of the graduate's career, and on the other hand it allows us to investigate the way in which the career progress seems to influence certain social habits. It should also facilitate comparison with the data provided in Dr. Chapman's study of Administrative Class civil servants.[1] In making such comparisons, however, it should be borne in mind that the graduates in this study are, on average, five years older than those surveyed by Dr. Chapman.

In two respects at least the respondents form a homogeneous group. With one exception, they are all graduates, having obtained their degree in almost every instance in either 1950 or 1951. There is also little difference in their ages. At the time of the survey the average age was thirty-eight and no-one was older than forty-one or younger than thirty-six. The women tend to be about two years younger than the men since most men had already completed National Service before entering the competition.

(*a*) *Educational and social background*

(*i*) *Educational.* The largest number of respondents were Oxford graduates but sizeable numbers had also been to Cambridge, London and the Other Universities. Nearly half had been to L.E.A. schools and, of the remainder, a slightly larger proportion had been to Independent schools than to Direct Grant Schools. Graduates in the arts and social sciences predominate and in terms of academic achievement they represent a high quality group with three quarters of them having either a first or an upper or undivided second class honours degree. Comparing the figures for the " near misses " against those for all respondents, we find that a higher proportion of the " near misses " were educated at independent schools and at Oxford, were graduates in history and classics and had first class honours degrees.

(*ii*) *Social*

One in five of the respondents had fathers who were graduates and one in twelve of the mothers had also been to University. The children of graduate parents were more likely to have been to Oxford, 44 per cent of those with graduate fathers and 42 per cent of those with graduate mothers went to Oxford.

Fifty-eight, or nearly a quarter, of the fathers were either in some form of public service employment in 1951 or had been at the time of their death or

---

[1] R. A. Chapman—*Profile of a Profession: The Administrative Class Civil Servant*, 1967. (Memorandum No. 2.)

Table 2.1. Educational Background

N=237

Type of school attended	All respondents %	"Near misses" only %	Subject read	All respondents %	"Near misses" only %
L.E.A.	49	39	Classics	8	13
Direct Grant	21	20	History	29	45
Independent	27	41	Humanities	26	22
Foreign	3	0	Social Sciences	29	10
Total	100	100	Natural and Applied Sciences	5	10
			Law	3	0
			Total	100	100
University attended			Class of degree		
Oxford	31	43	I	15	32
Cambridge	21	24	II undiv.	29	26
London	19	12	II_I	30	26
Scottish	10	3	II_{II}	14	16
Other	19	18	III	9	0
None	*	0	Other	3	0
Total	100	100	Total	100	100

* Less than 1%

retirement if that was before 1951. Their activities covered a wide range from bus conductor to high level Civil Servant but the majority were either senior Civil Servants or officers in the Armed Forces. Fourteen were members of either the Administrative or the Professional Classes of the Civil Service and a further fourteen were Departmental or Executive Class Civil Servants. Five were clerical officers and three were members of the Overseas Civil Service. In addition there were seven high ranking commissioned officers in the Armed Forces. The remainder were local postmasters, postmen and one or two local government officers, etc.

A broad indication of the social background of the respondents is to be obtained by grouping the occupations of the fathers into the Registrar General's Social Class categories.[1] The largest proportion come from those in Social Class II which contains people holding managerial and executive posts and includes higher Civil Servants, school teachers, shopkeepers etc. When the fairly large proportion of candidates whose fathers were in Social Class I professional occupations are also added in, it will be observed that three quarters of the respondents came from what can probably be described as the upper or middle classes. Whereas three in ten of all the graduates completing the questionnaire had been to Oxford nearly twice as many of those from Social Class I backgrounds were Oxford graduates. There is no evidence that the social background of the "near misses" differed significantly from that of the respondents as a whole since 23 per cent of the "near misses" came from Social Class I and 47 per cent from Social Class II backgrounds.

Table 2.2. Father's Occupation—Percentages

N=237

Social Class category	%	Proportion that had been to Oxford %
I. Professional occupations	21	56
II. Intermediate occupations	54	25
III. Skilled occupations: manual	11	28
Skilled occupations: non-manual	13	7
IV. and V. Partly skilled and unskilled manual	1	0
Total	100	30

Note: In the Registrar-General's classification of occupations members of the Armed Forces are not classified. In the above table the seven high ranking commissioned officers have been included in Social Class I.

(*b*) *Social characteristics now*

(*i*) *Marital status.* By the time that this survey was carried out 88 per cent of those replying had married. A rather smaller proportion of men remained single than women. One in ten of those who are married do not have any children and the average family size amongst all who are married is 2.2 children. It appears that family size depends to some extent upon salary level. Taking only those who are married and have an income from full time employment of their own (i.e. excluding housewives) we find that average family size increases as salary increases.

[1] Using the General Register Office, *Classification of Occupations* (H.M.S.O.) 1966.

Table 2.3 Marital Status—Percentages

N=237

Marital status	Men	Women	Total Men and Women
Single	8	21	12
Married	90	79	87
Separated/Widowed/Divorced	2	0	1
Total	100	100	100

Table 2.4 Family Size in Relation to Salary (married people only)

N207

Salary group	Average family size (number of children)
Less than £2,000	1·9
£2,000–£2,999	2·0
£3,000–£3,999	2·3
£4,000–£4,999	2·5
£5,000 and over	2·5
Overall average	2·2

(*ii*) *Education of children*

Three quarters of the children are now attending school (excluding those under the age of five who may be attending nursery schools etc.), but only 26 per cent of those at school are now in secondary schools. Altogether one third of the children at school are attending a fee paying school, either a preparatory or senior independent school. It may be, of course, that some of those attending a Direct Grant school are also in fee paying places.

Table 2.5. Type of school attended by children—Percentages

N=157

Type of school	(Children at school only) Percentages attending
L.E.A. Primary	44
L.E.A. Grammar/Technical	6
Comprehensive/Secondary Modern	3
Direct Grant	6
Preparatory (under 13s)	28
Independent (over 13s)	5
Foreign	8
	100

While the overriding tendency is for the children to go to the same type of school that their parents attended, a slightly higher proportion of children are now going to fee paying schools than was the case with the respondents themselves. It is not possible to draw hard and fast conclusions at this stage while so many children are either not yet at school or have not gone beyond the primary school level. Some of those at present at an L.E.A. primary school may go on to a fee-paying place in a Direct Grant or an Independent school, and some children at present at preparatory schools may ultimately go to an L.E.A. Secondary or Direct Grant school. What trend there is, is due to a number of graduates who were educated at L.E.A. and Direct Grant schools sending their children to independent schools, though this is partly offset by the fact that some children who are now going to L.E.A. schools have parents who received their education at independent schools. Another trend that seems apparent now but which may in the long run be disproved is the decline in the number of boarders. Whereas 23 per cent of the respondents were boarders at their last schools, only 6 per cent of their children are boarding at present. As these children grow older it would be interesting to see whether the same high proportion do become boarders or whether, despite an apparent increase in the numbers going to independent schools, the proportion boarding remains small.

The likelihood of a child being sent to an independent school seems to depend largely upon the income of the father, and this, as Chapter 4 shows, is determined to a considerable extent by the nature of the father's employment. The highest proportions of children at independent schools, junior or senior, are to be found amongst those whose fathers are employed in research and consultancy organizations (56 per cent), the Civil Service (53 per cent) and manufacturing industry (39 per cent). The high proportion of children of Civil Servants at independent schools is to be explained mainly because these are the children of Overseas Civil Servants who are being educated in this country, and are therefore also boarding. The people in this group of respondents who are now housewives also have a very high proportion of their children at independent schools (57 per cent). At the other end of the scale only four of the fifty-seven children of school teachers, teachers in colleges of further education and local government officers are now at independent schools.

Table 2.6. Type of school attended by first child compared with salary of respondent

N=127

Type of school	Average salary	Median salary
	£	£
L.E.A. (junior and secondary)	2,675	2,680
Direct Grant (secondary only)	3,635	3,250
Independent (junior and secondary)	4,290	4,150

Note: This table is based on replies from men only, since we do not have information on salary levels of the husbands of the women in the sample.

(iii) Membership of Organisations

Just over four-fifths of the respondents belong to some organisations and societies which make calls on their leisure time. On average they spend about eight hours a month on these activities, but if we exclude those who appear to be inactive in this respect the average rises to ten hours. The types of organisations most frequently supported are those connected with the respondents' work e.g. professional associations and groups connected with leisure, especially sports and recreational clubs. All the other groups claim a certain amount of support with religious connections the next most important.

Some check on the validity of these results can be obtained by comparing them with the findings of a survey of local government electors conducted by the Government Social Survey for the Committee on the Management of Local

Government.[1] This survey revealed that 61 per cent of local government electors belonged to one or more organisations and those who were active spent on average 10·6 hours per month on these activities. It was found that a greater proportion of people in the professional and managerial classes belonged to organisations than was the case with those from the lower social classes. Thus, 88 per cent of those in Social Class I and 71 per cent in Social Class II are members of organisations. As all those in our survey of Civil Service Unsuccessfuls who are in full time employment at present are in occupations which would place them in Social Class I or II, these findings suggest that our respondents are neither more nor less active in their leisure time activities than other people of the same social class.

Unfortunately, the Government Social Survey Paper does not give a breakdown of membership of the different types of organisation by social class; but from the information provided about organisation membership for all social classes we find that while a higher proportion of the Civil Service unsuccessfuls belongs to each type of organisation, the rank order of importance is the same in each case, except that organisations connected with education and training (mainly parent-teacher associations) acquire a slightly higher significance in the present survey.

Table 2.7. Organisation Membership

N=237

Type of organisation	Proportion belonging %	Proportion of Local Government Electors belonging* %
Organisations connected with work	57	27
Public bodies and committees	12	1
Organisations connected with politics	16	8
Organisations connected with education or training	18	5
Religious	22	10
Welfare organisations	14	3
Civic or community groups	16	7
Organisations connected with leisure	53	17

* Source: Mary Horton: *op. cit.*

There is little variation between graduates in the different employment groups in the degree of involvement and time spent in organisations. Journalists and those in the arts seem to be the most active and most likely to hold office in the organisations to which they belong. Civil Servants also have an above-average degree of involvement in such ogranisations.

Although salary levels do not appear to influence the level of activity in outside organisations, the extent to which the respondent was an active society member at University does seem to be important. The active University students appear to have remained active in later life and those who held office in student societies are more likely to hold office now.

[1] The results of this survey are summarised in Mary Horton: "*Organisation Membership and the Community*" Government Social Survey G. Paper No. 66. 1966.

Table 2.8. Organisation Membership Now Compared with Society Membership at University—Percentages

N=237

Organisation membership now	Society Membership at University					
	Active and held office	Active, no office	Fairly active, held office	Fairly active, no office	Inactive	Overall proportion
Active and holds office	40	17	22	12	8	21
Active, no office	24	17	11	13	4	14
Fairly active, holds office	14	17	18	13	26	17
Fairly active, no office	16	30	28	42	33	30
Inactive	6	19	21	20	29	18
Total	100	100	100	100	100	100
Average number of hours spent in organisations now.	11	9	8	8	8	8

Note: To be classed as " active", membership of three or more organisations was required. " Fairly active " respondents belong to one or two organisations and those who are termed " inactive " do not belong to any.

(*iv*) *Reading Habits*

Readership of a daily newspaper is heavily concentrated on the three " quality " papers—" The Times ", " The Guardian " and the " Daily Telegraph " with the " Financial Times " a close runner-up. Even amongst this group, " The Times " is easily the most popular and is seen at least once a week by over half those replying.

The questionnaire asked each person to indicate the degree of frequency, from 0 to 6 times, with which they saw each daily newspaper in an average week. If we define regular readership as seeing a paper at least five times a week, and casual readership as anything from once to four times in an average week, we find that there is a considerable amount of casual readership of all newspapers. A particularly high proportion of readers of the " Financial Times ", " Daily Express ", " Daily Mirror ", " The Sun " and the " Daily Sketch " are casual rather than regular readers. On average, each person sees just over two different newspapers a week but this average is clearly raised by those people who in the course of their work find it necessary to read several newspapers.

The highest average number of newspapers seen is therefore to be found amongst people employed in research and consultancy organisations (average 3·1 different papers seen in an average week), the financial and legal professions (2·9), and universities (2·7).

Readership of the " Daily Mail " and " Daily Express " is concentrated mainly upon school teachers and those in manufacturing industry. School teachers tend also to read the " Daily Telegraph ". The " Financial Times " draws its readership mainly from those engaged in financial work, manufacturing industry and research and consultancy. There is also a sizeable readership amongst university teachers. Readers of " The Guardian " are mainly from the financial and legal professions and universities. " The Times " readership is drawn from all employment groups but is more marked amongst university and further education employees, those in the financial and legal professions and those in the miscellaneous group; in all these groups more than 70% see " The Times " at least once a week.

Table 2.9. Readership of Daily Newspapers

N=234

Newspaper	Proportion seeing each paper in an average week			
	At least once 1 %	Three or more times 2 %	Five or more times 3 %	Proportion of " regular " readers col. 3 as a proportion of col. 1. %
The Times	59	48	39	66
The Guardian	43	30	24	56
Daily Telegraph	41	27	24	60
Financial Times	33	23	15	45
Daily Mail	19	11	9	47
Daily Express	15	6	6	40
Daily Mirror	9	2	2	22
Other	9	6	4	44

The pattern of Sunday newspaper readership is even more striking with over three quarters of the total readership in all employment groups concentrated on the " Sunday Times " and " The Observer ". A much higher proportion of Sunday newspaper readers claim to see every issue than is the case with readers of daily newspapers.

Table 2.10. Readership of Sunday Newspapers

N=234

Newspaper	Proportion seeing each paper in an average month		
	At least once 1 %	All four issues 2 %	Proportion of " Regular " readers, col 2 as a proportion of col. 1. %
The Observer	68	56	82
Sunday Times	66	54	81
Sunday Express	23	17	74
Sunday Telegraph	16	7	44
All other papers	9	3	33

In order to investigate the readership of other periodicals the respondents were asked to write-in on the questionnaire details of magazines, journals and other newspapers that they saw regularly. In this case " regular reading " was defined as seeing at least every other issue. Many different journals were listed but the five shown in Table 2.11 occurred most frequently. It is possible that

Table 2.11. Readership of Other Periodicals

Periodical	Number seeing at least every other issue
The Economist	59
New Statesman	37
The Listener	35
The Spectator	32
Times Educational Supplement	28

because the respondents were asked to write-in the names of the periodicals they read rather than tick-off names from a previously prepared list on the questionnaire, the actual extent of the readership of these journals amongst the group surveyed may be understated and so the table is given in terms of absolute numbers rather than in percentage form.

Other periodicals which were mentioned ten or more times are " Which " (18), " New Society " (15), " Time Magazine " (15), " Punch " (10) and the " Times Literary Supplement " (10). A wide variety of other journals were also named covering religion, sport, various leisure pursuits and a substantial number of journals specifically related to the present occupation of the respondent.

Chapter 3

The Career Pattern

(*a*) *Additional qualifications*

Since graduating, just over two-fifths of those replying have obtained an additional academic or professional qualification. Sixteen have obtained a university doctorate, mainly in history, the social sciences or the natural sciences. Half of them had obtained first class honours in their first degree and five had obtained an upper second. Two who graduated with a lower second had also gone on to take a Ph.D. but the figures include only one Oxford graduate with an undivided second. Of these sixteen Ph.Ds we find that in the 1951 Open Competitions to the Administrative Class three had been declared successful and had declined appointment and a further three were " near misses " in that they scored over 700 marks in Method I or over 200 at the Final Selection Board in Method II. In addition six others withdrew from the competition altogether.

Another nineteen have some other higher degree e.g. M.A., M.Sc., B.Phil., which has been obtained by examination either of written papers or dissertation or both. That is, M.A.s which are awarded without further study are omitted. Of these nineteen, one had been declared successful in the Open Competition and six were near misses. In addition another five withdrew from the competition. These figures suggest that the Open Competitions tended to place in the higher orders those who have since achieved further academic recognition but the large proportion who withdrew and the number who did not accept the offer of a position in the Administrative Class suggests that even in 1951 there was a problem of competing with the Universities for the better students.

In addition to those with higher degrees, a further thirty-three, of whom two-thirds are women, obtained a certificate or diploma in education although ten of them did not take a school teaching post as their first employment. A wide range of professional qualifications are also held by other respondents. These include qualifications in law (both Bar Council and Law Society), accountancy, engineering, banking and insurance.

(*b*) *First full time employment*

Two-thirds of the candidates began work in either 1951 (44 per cent) or 1952 (23 per cent). However, a small group of 6 per cent began their working life before 1951 and a larger group of 27 per cent did not enter full time employment until 1953 or later. Of those who had worked before 1951, some had left school at an early age and after serving in the armed forces had gone up to University and from there entered the Open Competition. A few had graduated in 1949 or 1950 and were already working in other occupations (including the Executive Class of the Civil Service) when they entered the Competition.

Many of those who did not begin their first employment until 1953 or later (three quarters of whom were working by the end of 1954) are holders of an additional qualification. Sixty-three per cent of Ph.D.s fall into this group, so too do 50 per cent of those with other higher degrees and so also do 30 per cent of those with a teaching qualification. One or two completed legal or accountancy qualifications before beginning paid employment. There are however, also a number of other people who delayed their employment until 1953 or later, most of these also stayed on at University to do research but have not taken a further degree.

The pattern of first employment taken up by the 247 people for whom we have the necessary information is shown in Table 3.1. The most popular first employment groups were manufacturing industry which accounted for just over a quarter of all the graduates and school teaching which took another 18 per cent including just over half the women respondents. Other important employers were the Civil Service, financial services (accountancy, banking, insurance and stockbroking), the legal profession and the Universities. Almost all who became Civil Servants (seven of whom were women) entered either the Executive or Departmental classes or the Overseas Civil Service.

In the light of this distribution of employment groupings, it is not surprising to find that the most important occupations were teaching and general administration and management. A large proportion of those who went into industry began their careers in general trainee schemes but an equally large proportion were concerned with marketing and advertising activities. Many also found research posts in a wide variety of organisations. The eight shown as holding research positions in Universities held full time paid appointments specifically concerned with research. Post-graduate research studentships are not counted as a first employment.

When the employment pattern is compared with the background of the graduates a number of interesting differences emerge. School teachers came mainly from amongst those who had upper or undivided seconds in an arts subject. Most of them had been educated at an L.E.A. school and a much smaller proportion came from a Social Class I background than is the case with the overall pattern of graduates replying. Local government only attracted graduates who had been educated at L.E.A. schools. University teachers were drawn mainly from the Scottish and Redbrick Universities and a high proportion had been to Direct Grant schools.

Financial and legal activities recruited mainly graduates from Oxford and Cambridge together with a few from London. In most cases these people had been educated at public schools. Civil Service entrants were mostly from Cambridge and the Scottish Universities who had also been to independent schools and came from Social Class I backgrounds. Half the Civil Service entrants were history graduates. Many Oxford graduates went into industry, which was also an important source of employment for social scientists.

Of the eight who were declared successful in the Open Competitions and preferred appointments elsewhere, five took posts in the universities, two in industry and one in school teaching. The Universities also recruited a number of those who withdrew from the competition.

Fourteen per cent of the respondents began their first employment abroad. Most of these were either in Africa (mainly as Overseas Civil Servants) or in North America. Thirty-seven per cent were first employed in the Greater London area[1] and the remainder were fairly evenly distributed throughout the rest of the United Kingdom.

[1] The Greater London area is defined as being within fifteen miles of Charing Cross.

Table 3.1. First Employment

Occupation group	Employment Group										Total
	School	Further Education	Univer-sities	Local Govern-ment	Finance and Law	Civil Service	In-dustry	Research and consult-ancy orgs.	Miscel-laneous	Not in full-time employ-ment	
Teaching	43	5	15	—	—	1	1	—	—	—	65
Administration, Management	—	—	4	10	1	21	2	1	6	—	45
Financial and Legal	—	—	—	1	20	4	1	—	—	—	26
Marketing, Advertising	—	—	—	—	—	—	19	1	2	—	22
Research and Consultancy	—	—	8	1	3	7	7	2	3	—	31
Production, Engineering	—	—	—	—	—	—	4	—	—	—	4
Personnel work	—	—	—	—	—	—	5	—	—	—	5
General Trainee Schemes	—	—	—	—	4	—	21	1	4	—	30
Miscellaneous	—	—	—	—	3	—	3	—	10	—	16
Not in full-time employment	—	—	—	—	—	—	—	—	—	3	3
Total	43	5	27	12	31	33	63	5	25	3	247

(*c*) *Present employment*

Thirty seven of the people who were originally employed are now no longer in full time employment. One of these is again a full-time student and one is not working because of ill health. The rest are all married women and represent nearly two thirds of all the women replying. Rather more than one third of them are now engaged in part time work of one sort or another (in most cases teaching) for which they receive incomes varying between £200 and £800 a year.

Seven per cent of the women who are not in full time employment have never worked. Of the remainder, 31 per cent stopped work before 1955, another 31 per cent between 1956 and 1958, 13 per cent between 1959 and 1962 and the remaining 18 per cent have stopped working since 1962.

The present pattern of employment is shown in Table 3.2 and the changes in employment and occupational groupings between the first and the present employment respectively are identified in Tables 3.3 and 3.4. Eleven of the respondents are self-employed. Six of these are in the finance and law employment group and five in the miscellaneous group.

Altogether, two thirds of the graduates who are still working are now in the same employment group as in their first post. A rather smaller proportion are still in the same occupation group. Higher education and consultancy activities, especially the growth fields of management consultancy and advertising, both show a net increase in the number of respondents employed compared with the first employment group. Offsetting this has been a decline in the number employed in other areas. The decline in the number of school teachers is partly due to a number of married women stopping work and also to a tendency for some teachers to move into higher education, especially colleges of education and technology. The decline in the number of Civil Servants is partly due to married women stopping work and also to a number of Overseas Civil Servants leaving the service. There has also been a substantial reduction in the number of graduates in the group under investigation employed in industry, most of whom have moved into either education or management consultancy.

Looking at the pattern of occupational movement, after allowing for the withdrawal of married women, we find that there has been a net increase in the number engaged in teaching, and a small reduction in numbers employed in marketing. No other occupational groups reveal any significant net change in the numbers employed though there has been a considerable degree of mobility between occupations on the part of individuals. In the Research and Consultancy occupational group it will be observed that although there has been little net change in the numbers employed, only a small proportion of those in this group in their first employment are still there. This is explained by the tendency for people initially employed in pure research activities in Universities and the Civil Service to move into other occupations, especially teaching, and for others with industrial experience to move into this group as management consultants.

Although most people have given detailed descriptions of the nature of the work involved in their present position, the degree of responsibility involved etc., it is not easy to make comparisons of status levels. In some employment groups such as teaching where the descriptions of posts are normally fairly consistent with each other, comparisons can be made with greater ease than in private enterprise occupations. Nearly three quarters of the school-teachers now have some additional measure of responsibility. Three are now heads of schools and a further seven are deputy heads. Two are housemasters at public schools and

Table 3.2. Present Employment

Occupation Group	Employment Group										
	School	Further Education	Univer-sities	Local Govern-ment	Finance and Law	Civil Service	In-dustry	Research and Consult-ancy	Miscel-laneous	Not in full time employ-ment	Total
Teaching	31	11	30	—	—	2	2	—	—	—	76
Administration, Management	3	—	5	6	3	13	8	1	4	—	43
Financial and Legal	—	—	—	—	19	3	4	1	—	—	27
Marketing, Advertising	—	—	—	—	—	—	14	3	—	—	17
Research and Consultancy	—	—	3	4	—	2	10	9	1	—	29
Production, Engineering	—	—	—	—	—	—	5	—	—	—	5
Personnel work	—	—	—	1	—	—	4	—	—	—	5
Miscellaneous	—	—	—	—	1	—	—	—	9	—	10
Not in full time employment	—	—	—	—	—	—	—	—	—	40	40
Total	34	11	38	11	23	20	47	14	14	40	252

Table 3.3. Changes in Employment

First full time employment	Present Full Time Employment										
	School	Further Education	Univer-sities	Local Govern-ment	Finance and Law	Civil Service	Industry	Research and con-sultancy	Miscel-laneous	Not in full-time employ-ment	Total
School	23	5	2	2	—	2	—	—	1	8	43
Further Education	—	2	1	—	—	1	1	—	—	—	5
Universities	2	—	22	—	1	—	—	1	—	1	27
Local Government	—	—	1	6	—	—	1	—	—	4	12
Finance and Law	—	2	1	1	18	—	1	—	3	5	31
Civil Service	2	—	5	1	1	15	2	1	—	6	33
Industry	3	1	5	1	1	—	38	9	1	4	63
Research and consultancy	—	—	1	—	—	—	—	2	—	2	5
Miscellaneous	4	1	—	—	1	—	3	—	9	7	25
Not in full time employment	—	—	—	—	—	—	—	—	—	3	3
Total	34	11	38	11	22	18	46	13	14	40	247

Table 3.4. Changes in Occupation

First occupation	Present Occupation										
	Teaching and Training	Administration and Management	Financial and Legal activities	Marketing and Advertising	Research and Consultancy	General Trainee Schemes	Production/engineering	Personnel	Miscellaneous	No full time employment	Total
Teaching and Training	46	3	2	—	4	—	—	1	—	9	65
Administration and Management	8	16	1	1	4	—	1	—	1	13	45
Financial and Legal activities	2	3	16	1	1	—	—	1	1	1	26
Marketing and Advertising	1	3	2	9	6	—	1	—	—	—	22
Research and Consultancy	11	3	3	2	6	—	1	—	—	5	31
General Trainee Schemes	3	10	2	4	5	—	1	1	1	3	30
Production/Engineering	2	—	—	—	1	—	1	—	—	—	4
Personnel	2	1	—	—	—	—	—	1	—	1	5
Miscellaneous	—	—	1	—	2	—	—	1	7	5	16
No full-time employment	—	—	—	—	—	—	—	—	—	3	3
Total	75	39	27	17	29	—	5	5	10	40	247

a further twelve have head of department status. Two-thirds of the teachers in institutions of further education hold senior positions either as senior lecturers in colleges of education and polytechnics or as heads of department in colleges of further education.

Of the thirty university teachers, seven are professors, three are Readers and five Senior Lecturers. In addition two are Associate Professors in American Universities and three hold Fellowships in an Oxford or Cambridge college, so two thirds have received promotion above the basic level of lecturer. Three hold full-time research appointments, one as director of a large research group. The other five people employed in universities are on administrative staffs as Assistant Registrars etc.

In industry, the line of distinction between strictly managerial functions and a particular activity such as marketing is hard to draw. Is a marketing manager, for example, to be classed as a manager or as a marketing man? In fact this is a problem that arose quite frequently as nearly three fifths of the people now employed in industry have a post which carries the term " manager " in its description. In most cases these are managers controlling a particular section or activity in a company or, in a few cases, a given geographical area. The largest single group (fourteen in number) is concerned with the management of marketing and market research activities. Eight have general managerial responsibilities, five are concerned with corporate planning and financial control, four are personnel managers and three are concerned with the management of production processes. Others are in charge of specialist departments concerned with economic research, statistics, accounting, taxation and purchasing. Five are now directors of their respective companies. Although some respondents did not give the name of the company they are employed by (the questionnaire did not ask for this information) from information provided by those who did name their company it is quite clear that three or four large international commercial organisations each employ several of these graduates.

Amongst employees in the finance and law group of organisations we find a wide spread of status. Two people hold directorships and another seven are either partners in legal or financial organisations or are members of a syndicate in insurance. This group also includes a number in higher and middle management positions, but rather more than half of these are only in secondary positions as assistant or deputy managers. As far as can be judged, probably the highest overall level of responsibility is exercised by people employed in the fields of advertising and management consultancy who include a number of account directors in advertising and senior management consultants among their number.

Of the local government officers, only one is in control of his own section and it is significant that he is only on loan to his particular authority. The majority are either assistant administrative officers or deputy education officers. By virtue of the fact that they failed to enter the Administrative Class those who went into other grades of the Civil Service may be expected to have had less distinguished careers. This may be true of the majority but there are significant exceptions. Five graduates have subsequently entered the Administrative Class despite being turned down in 1951 and one is now an Assistant Secretary. In addition, another three or four have attained equivalent status in other branches of the Civil Service such as the Inland Revenue, the Overseas Civil Service and the professional classes.

The miscellaneous group contains people engaged in a wide range of activities but the largest number of people in this group are engaged in journalism and publishing, three of whom are now employed by leading London daily papers.

Although there have been small reductions in the proportion working abroad and in the Greater London area, the geographical distribution of the place of work of the respondents has not changed substantially. Amongst those working abroad there are now fewer Overseas Civil Servants in Africa but this has been partly offset by an increase in the number of graduates working in Canada and the U.S.A. Despite the small reduction in the number with offices in Greater London there is some evidence of a drift to the south. The number of graduates working in the south of England, excluding the Greater London area, has doubled since 1951 and now accounts for 15 per cent of the sample. The main Areas to lose workers have been the North Midlands and North West England.

Table 3.5. Place of Work in First and Present Employment—Percentages

N=203

Area of first Employment	Area of present employment: Greater London	Rest of U.K.	Abroad	Total
Greater London	22	13	2	37
Rest of U.K.	10	37	2	49
Abroad	3	3	8	14
Total	35	53	12	100

Some types of employment require a much greater degree of concentration of employment in on earea than in another. Teachers, for example, are widely dispersed over the country. On the other hand, 80 per cent of those engaged in the fields of finance and law and 80 per cent of those employed in research and consultancy organisations work in Greater London. The next highest concentration is amongst those employed in industry, 40 per cent of whom work in Greater London.

During the fourteen or fifteen years that most of the graduates had been working up to the time of the survey they have made on average almost two moves each and therefore have had three different employers. This figure seems if anything to be lower than might intuitively be expected for people in the formative years of their careers, though comparing it with the results of a survey of the employment of Cambridge graduates made nine years after they had graduated the results seem to be remarkably similar.[1]

The largest number of moves have been made by those who are now employed by organisations specialising in research and consultancy and by teachers in schools and colleges of further education. At the other end of the scale, Civil Servants and people in the financial and legal professions have moved less frequently. It is to be expected that employment groups where there has been

[1] Christine Craig—"*The Employment of Cambridge Graduates*", Cambridge University Press 1963, pp. 52–55. This information relates only to men and from the data given it seems that they had moved on average 1·01 times. If we assume that over the next seven years they moved with the same frequency (this may or may not be a valid assumption) this would given an average number of moves in sixteen years of 1·8 per person.

Table 3.6. Number of Changes of Employer by Present Employment Group

N=203

Present employment group	Average number of changes of employer	Proportion who have not changed their employer %
School	2·3	18
Further Education	3·1	0
Universities	1·6	16
Local Government	2·0	27
Finance and Law	1·0	36
Civil Service	0·8	64
Industry	1·8	26
Research and Consultancy	2·4	7
Miscellaneous	2·0	23
Overall Average	1·8	24

a high average number of changes of employer would also show a small proportion of graduates who are still with their existing employer and *vice versa*. The right hand column of Table 3.6 indicates the extent to which this is borne out. It will be observed that the expectations are justified in all but two cases. Although university teachers have tended to make rather fewer-than-average moves the proportion who have not moved at all is below average. Amongst local government officers both the average number of moves made and the proportion without a change in employer are slightly above average.

Oxford graduates have had slightly more changes of employer (2·1) and those from Cambridge have moved rather less frequently than the average (1·3 times). There is, however, no evidence that the sex or marital status or the social class background of the graduate have any influence on the propensity to move.

Although they were unable to gain places in the Administrative Class in 1951, 58 of the unsuccessful candidates were offered posts in other grades of the Home Civil Service such as the Professional, Departmental or Executive Classes either in 1951 or subsequently. These offers were made mainly to the people who came closest to success in the Open Competitions and more than one-third of the " near misses " were thereby offered the opportunity of a Civil Service career. According to information supplied by the Civil Service Commission, supplemented with information from the present survey, we find that 25 are still working in the Civil Service, and another is on temporary secondment to a local authority, 11 did not accept a Civil Service appointment at all and 21 entered the service but have since resigned.

Considering only the respondents to the present survey, we find that at some stage or other during their working career (not necessarily their first or present employment) 31 have been employed in the Home Civil Service (not all of whom were shown in the Civil Service Commission's list as having been Civil Servants at one time or another) and another 13 in the Overseas Civil Service. Of these, 15 are still employed in the Home Civil Service. Five are now in the Administrative Class, two in the Diplomatic Service, three in the Inland Revenue and five in the professional classes. Of those who have resigned, one had been promoted into the Administrative Class, five were in the departmental classes (including three inspectors of taxes), six were in the professional classes and two were

Table 3.7. Performance in Open Competitions of Unsuccessful Candidates offered alternative Civil Service Posts

N=482

Level of performance	Unsuccessful candidates offered alternative Civil Service posts No.	All candidates in 1951 Open Competitions No.
Declared successful	—	10
Withdrew	—	102
Method I:		
Less than 600 marks	6	80
600—699 marks	14	60
700 marks and over	12	35
Method II:		
Rejected after qualifying tests	20	182
Called to final selection board, mark 200 or less	6	110
Called to final selection board, mark more than 200	11	25
Total	69	604

Note: Some candidates competed by both Methods and are therefore counted twice in this table.

executive officers. The other person to resign had been employed as a secretary. Five of the resignations were by married women ceasing full-time employment, three others went into university teaching and two into industry.

Only three of the respondents are still employed in the Overseas Civil Service. Of the ten who have resigned from there, four are now University administrators and one is engaged in full-time University research, one resigned for domestic reasons and the remainder are now employed in a variety of different positions including school teaching and local government.

That six people who were initially unsuccessful should have ultimately entered the Administrative Class indicates that lack of success at one time does not necessarily mean the barring of the door for all time though there is evidence that Civil Servants outside the Administrative Class do not rate their prospects of promotion at all highly (see below Chapter 5). It is worth recording also that one other respondent is on temporary secondment to the Civil Service and two others reported that during recent expansion in the Civil Service they had been invited to accept senior positions in the service which they had, for various reasons, not been able to accept.

Chapter 4

Remuneration

(a) Basic Salary

The graduates who were successful in the 1951 Open Competitions and are still Administrative Class Civil Servants will now be senior Principals or will have recently been promoted to the rank of Assistant Secretary. Apparently, the average age for promotion to Assistant Secretary is now 40·2 years and the median age 39. As far as can be ascertained,[1] 26 per cent of the 1951 candidates who were declared successful and are still in the Home Civil Service are still Principals and 74 per cent have already become Assistant Secretaries. The inner London salary scale for Principals is £2,335 to £3,192 and for Assistant Secretaries £3,585 to £4,585. So the 1951 successful candidates who are now Civil Servants will be earning in the region of £3,100 to £3,700.

The average salary for the graduates surveyed is comparable at £3,155 though this hides a wide range of salaries varying from £1,200 to over £8,000. Altogether, 30 per cent of the unsuccessful candidates who are still in full time paid employment and for whom we have salary data are now receiving £3,500 or more and can therefore be considered to have done at least as well as those who entered the Civil Service in terms of the level of the basic salary they are receiving at the present time.

Most graduates started their first employment at a salary of between £450 and £500, though on average women were paid £200 less and Ph.D.s £85 more. Present salary levels seem to be greatly influenced by the employment group of the graduate. People employed in private enterprise activities such as industry, the financial and legal professions and research and consultancy organisations have, on the whole, much higher salaries than those with fixed salary scales such as the teaching profession and public service occupations. The only major exceptions to this broad generalisation seem to be that university teachers receive higher salaries than the rest of those with fixed salary scales and salary levels for those in the miscellaneous group of employments, mainly journalism and the arts, are rather lower than in other private enterprise activities.

The use of the straightforward arithmetic mean as an indicator of salary levels in a particular type of employment is not always satisfactory because it may be unduly affected by extremes at either end of the salary scale. A useful check is available in the calculation of the median salary and upper and lower quartile salaries for each group. The results of these calculations are given in Table 4.1 below together with an indication of the overall pattern of salary levels. Whichever measure of salary we take, the same general conclusions arise. Research and consultancy organisations pay the highest salaries followed by the financial and legal professions. Then comes industry and the universities. After a fairly wide gap the Civil Service and the Miscellaneous group come next, leaving further education, school teaching and local government right at the bottom.

[1] From the *British Imperial Calendar and Civil Service List*, H.M.S.O., 1967.

Table 4.1. Present Salary Analysed by Type of Employment—Percentages and Averages

Basic salary £1 per year	Employment Group									All in full time employment %
	School %	Further Education %	University %	Local Government %	Finance and Law %	Civil Service %	Industry %	Research and Consultancy %	Miscellaneous %	
less than 1,500	7	—	—	27	4	—	—	—	14	4
1,500–1,999	38	37	3	27	10	10	7	7	21	15
2,000–2,499	33	45	12	27	13	14	19	7	14	20
2,500–2,999	19	18	25	—	10	42	19	—	14	19
3,000–3,499	3	—	25	9	20	20	13	7	8	13
3,500–3,999	—	—	9	9	10	14	17	23	8	10
4,000–5,999	—	—	23	—	13	—	15	28	21	12
6,000 and over	—	—	3*	—	20	—	10	28	—	7
Total	100	100	100	99†	100	100	100	100	100	100
Number in group	33	11	35	11	21	21	46	14	14	206
Mean salary	2,125	2,160	3,355	2,070	3,985	2,825	3,545	4,680	2,750	3,155
Median salary	2,080	2,145	3,200	1,925	3,325	2,895	3,200	4,250	2,500	2,800
Lower quartile salary	1,735	1,835	2,700	1,460	2,375	2,375	2,470	3,585	1,710	2,125
Upper quartile salary	2,455	2,420	4,075	2,375	4,875	3,415	3,970	6,625	3,500	3,730

* This respondent is not employed in the United Kingdom!

† Not 100 due to rounding off

The top 30 per cent in terms of salary level are therefore earning at least as much as those who became higher Civil Servant and in some cases considerably more, but the likelihood of any school teachers, teachers in further education or local government officers approaching this salary level seems to be virtually non-existent. On the other hand over three quarters of the people employed in research and consultancy organisations are earning over £3,500 and two fifths of those in industry and finance and the law, and a third of those in universities are receiving salaries above this figure.

The level of the basic salary paid seems also to be related to the place of work. Those working abroad receive £1,200 more than the average for all the respondents and there is a differential of £750 between those working in Greater London and those working elsewhere in the United Kingdom.

Table 4.2. Present Salary Analysed by Place of Work—Averages

N=203

Place of Work	Average Salary
Greater London	£3,300
Rest of U.K.	£2,550
Rest of the World	£4,375

People who have made the fewest changes of employer appear now to have the highest average salary levels. But this does not necessarily mean that the penalty for changing employer rather more frequently than the average is a lower salary. It may be that those who have moved most frequently would have had an even lower salary had they not moved and those who have not moved might be even more highly rewarded had they changed employer.

Table 4.3. Present salary Analysed by Number of Changes of Employer—Averages

N=203

Number of changes of employer	Average salary £
None	3,345
One	3,225
Two	3,035
Three	3,015
Four or more	2,845

Considering these figures from an occupational point of view we find that people employed in general managerial and administrative functions earn less than those who are responsible for a specific activity such as marketing or advertising or the provision of financial or legal services.

The respondents engaged in marketing and advertising activities do, however, show a wide spread of salary levels and there is therefore a major divergence between the arithmetic mean salary and the median salary in this case.

If we consider only those holding managerial positions in industry and analyse their salaries in terms of the occupational basis of the work, we find a wide range of salaries earned both between occupational groups and sometimes within the same group. The numbers are, however, too small to show meaningful upper and lower quartile figures for each group. It will be observed, however, that in

Table 4.4. Present salary Analysed by Type of Occupation—Averages

N=203

Occupation group	Basic salary £ per year: Arithmetic mean £	Median £	Lower quartile £	Upper quartile £
Teaching	2,630	2,435	1,900	3,100
Administration and Management	3,000	2,850	2,175	3,610
Financial and Legal	4,145	3,875	2,450	5,325
Marketing and Advertising	3,905	3,000	2,625	5,375
Research and Consultancy	3,430	3,300	2,800	4,125
Miscellaneous	2,360	2,125	1,565	2,625
Overall average	3,155	2,800	2,125	3,730

industry the holders of general managerial positions have very high average salaries. This is a reflection of the fact that the level of responsibility held is also very high and some of these people are members of the Board of Directors.

The difference between the average and the median salary for marketing managers is a reflection of the wide spread of salaries received by people concerned with this function in industry. Three respondents in this category are

Table 4.5 Present Salaries of Employees in Managerial Positions in Industry Analysed by Type of Occupation

N=40

Occupation	Average salary	Median salary
General Management	4,325	4,350
Marketing	3,820	2,835
Planning, Financial Control	3,770	3,600
Production Management	2,430	2,450
Personnel, Training	2,560	2,150
Management of other specialist functions, e.g. Accounting, Statistics, Taxation, Economics, Market Research	3,580	3,500

earning over £6,000 a year, in one case with a seat on the Board, but on the other hand six are earning less than £3,000. It seems clear that others who are employed as corporate planners, financial controllers, accountants, statisticians, tax advisers, economists and market researchers are also well remunerated but management concerned with production control and personnel work in industry is significantly less well paid.

In order to assess the significance of the data we have collected it is necessary to have information about the salary levels of other graduates who are about the same age as the group under investigation but who did not take the Open Competitions for the Civil Service. Unfortunately, there is, as yet, little available information on which to base judgement. The Civil Service, Local Government and the teaching professions have defined salary scales and the position on these scales depends upon length of service but the extent to which promotion has been obtained determines which salary scale is applicable. It would appear that in most cases these scales are well below comparable salaries in other types of activity.

The best information that we can obtain for purposes of comparison for those in industry and the professions other than teaching is that contained in the *Cornmarket Salary Survey, 1967* prepared by Careers Register Ltd. This organisation exists mainly to help people with a degree or professional qualification and so some measure of comparability is possible. Their data is calculated on an occupational basis and the relevant part is that which deals with people aged 36 to 40 years.

Table 4.6. Comparable Salary Data analysed by Type of Occupation. People aged 36–40—Averages

Type of occupation	Basic salary £ per year		
	Median	Upper quartile	Upper decile
Economists	2,195	2,605	3,660
Sales/Marketing	2,270	3,005	4,060
Accountants	2,270	2,745	3,910
Professions (Architects, Lawyers, Surveyors)	2,110	2,720	3,630
National figures for all categories	2,095	2,550	3,335

Source: *Cornmarket Salary Survey*, 1967

In so far as comparisons can be made between this table and the data for the Civil Service unsuccessfuls given in Tables 4.1 and 4.4, we find that the salaries of the group under investigation appear to be well above average. It would seem that the top half of the Civil Service unsuccessfuls would come in the top 25 per cent of the overall group of graduates and the top 25 per cent of the unsuccessful candidates are now amongst the top 10 per cent in the overall earnings scale. Two other people with considerable knowledge of salary levels in industry whose views were requested on this matter were of the opinion that any graduate in his late thirties who was earning around £3,500 had done well, though it was emphasised that this would depend, amongst other things, on the size of the company employing him.

Some guide as to salaries in other employment groups not covered by the Careers Register report was obtained from the relevant associations representing employees in a particular occupation. They were asked what salary level they would expect a good honours graduate, about 38 years old, to be receiving now. In each case the replies emphasised that the actual salary would depend on the amount of promotion that had been attained and various other factors specific to each occupation e.g. for local government officers on the size of population of the local authority. The figures given below should therefore be treated as merely an indication of a reasonable salary level that would be expected from graduates of this particular age, granted normal promotion.

If these estimates are taken as a guide it would appear that the University teachers in the sample are earning rather more than might be expected, school

Table 4.7. Estimates of Reasonable Salary Levels in Other Employment Groups—Graduates aged 36–40

Employment group	Estimate of a reasonable salary £
School	2,000
Further Education	2,200
University	2,750
Local Government	2,500
Law	3,000–4,000 depending on speciality

teachers, further education teachers and lawyers are about par and local government officers are earning rather less than might be expected.

If we take into account the level of performance in the 1951 Open Competitions, we find that there is some evidence that those who were given the highest marks in 1951 are now earning above average salaries. The group of eight respondents who were declared successful now have the highest average salary and they are closely followed by those who scored more than 700 marks in the Method I competition and those who attended the final selection board for Method II. The much lower salary levels earned by those who scored less than 700 marks in the Method I competition is remarkable and certainly cannot be explained in terms of the present employment group of these people since a number of them are to be found in the employment groups with high average salaries such as industry and research and consultancy.

Table 4.8. Present Salary Analysed by Performance in 1951 Open Competitions—Averages

N=203

Performance in competition	Average salary £
Declared successful	3,750
Withdrew	3,192
Method I—Mark less than 600	2,490
Mark 600–699	2,460
Mark 700 and over	3,380
Method II—Not called to F.S.B.	3,155
Mark less than 200 at F.S.B.	3,375
Mark 200 and over at F.S.B.	3,350

Note: Candidates who competed by both Methods are counted twice.

Although the actual type of employment that the graduate is in seems the most important influence on his salary level a number of social and educational factors also appear to be related.

Women are paid substantially less than men (£2,000 against £3,305) and this is partly explained by the higher proportion of those women who are still working that are to be found in the lower paid occupations especially schoolteaching. It is surprising, however, to find that single men receive on average nearly £1,000 less than their married counterparts. In a survey of this size small numbers are a problem in drawing any very firm conclusions (there are only fifteen single men in the sample) but it does suggest that there are less pressures on single people to maximize their earnings.

As we have seen, the educational and social class factors tend to be interrelated, with candidates from Social Class I backgrounds more likely to have been to independent schools and then on to Oxford and Cambridge. Since all of these factors are associated with above-average salary levels it would be difficult to say which is the most important, if indeed there is a causal relationship at all. Graduates with first and undivided second class degrees are now earning high salaries on average and social scientists are also well remunerated. The numbers of classicists and lawyers contributing to the high average salaries for people in these subject groups are rather too small (15 and 9 respectively) to permit any strong conclusions to be drawn. The classicists with high incomes appear to be employed mainly in industry.

Table 4.9. Present Salary Analysed by Educational and Social Background—Averages

N=203

(a) University background		(b) Class of degree		(c) Subject read	
Type of University	Average salary £	Class of degree	Average salary £	Subject read	Average Salary £
Oxford	3,675	I	3,900	Classics	3,865
Cambridge	3,545	II Undivided	3,410	History	2,855
London	2,500	II_1	2,985	Humanities	2,815
Scottish	3,190	II_{11}	2,410	Social sciences	3,480
Other	2,685	Other	2,800	Science	3,055
				Law	3,915

(d) Social Class grouping		*(e) Type of school*	
Social class	Average Salary £	Type of school	Average Salary £
I Professional	3,520	L.E.A.	2,855
II Intermediate: managerial	3,250	Direct grant	2,855
III Skilled non-manual	2,850	Independent	3,510
III and IV skilled and partly skilled manual	2,775		

(b) *Additional benefits and emoluments*

Most posts nowadays offer some additional benefits and emoluments even if these only consist of contributions by the employer to a pension fund for the employee. The evidence from other studies suggests that those in the more senior positions in industry and some of the professions tend to receive substantial extra benefits in this way which, do, of course, add to the real financial value of the position held.[1] Questions were asked to ascertain the extent and importance

[1] For information on the extent and importance of these "fringe" benefits see: *Survey of Executive Salaries and Fringe Benefits in the United Kingdom*, Associated Industrial Consultants Ltd., 1966. *Motivating Management—Fringe Benefits Findings: Fringe Benefits Survey*, P.A. Management Consultants Ltd., Handout No. 4.

of these additional benefits. In fact these do not appear to have been as widespread as might be supposed. Almost everyone in full-time employment who replied receives some sort of additional benefit but the average number of benefits per person was only about 1·9. If we allow for the fact that just over four fifths of those replying have a pension contribution paid by their employers this means that many have no other form of additional benefit.

Table 4.10. Additional Benefits and Emoluments Received

N=203

Benefit	Proportion Receiving %
Housing, free or subsidised	15
Use of car for business and/or private and business purposes	17
Family allowances	13
Advantageous borrowing arrangements	11
Bonuses and commission	15
Employer contributions to non-contributory pension scheme	18
Employer contributions to contributory pension scheme	65
Miscellaneous	26

The even distribution of the other benefits received is striking. Most of those who are provided with a car are able to use it for private as well as business purposes. The miscellaneous category contained a wide range of additional benefits of which three occurred most frequently—free or subsidised meals including luncheon vouchers, free travel and membership of a private health insurance scheme.

If we distinguish between the 30 per cent earning £3,500 and over and those earning less than this amount we find that those with the higher salaries receive on average more emoluments—2·3 per person, compared with 1·8 in the lower income group. The provision of cars for business and private purposes is more likely in the higher income group and these are the people who are most likely to receive bonuses and commission. One in three in the higher income group belong to a non-contributory pension scheme compared with one in seven of the others.

Apart from one or two teachers in public schools who receive subsidised or free housing and some university teachers who receive family allowances, most people in teaching and local government only have pension contributions as a fringe benefit. Those employed in industry tend to have the largest number of fringe benefits—on average 2·5 each, 45 per cent have a company car and 33 per cent receive a bonus. A quarter are members of a non-contributory pension scheme. Employees concerned with the marketing and advertising aspects of industry have an even higher average number of fringe benefits though in almost every case they belong to a contributory pension scheme.

There is little evidence to suggest that membership of a non-contributory pension scheme reduces significantly the frequency with which a person changes his employer. Those who now belong to a contributory pension scheme have had an average of 1·8 changes of employer though 22 per cent have not moved at all, whereas those in a non-contributory scheme have moved on average 1·6 times and 30 per cent are still with their original employer. It is certainly true that the employment groups where non-contributory pension schemes are most prevalent (the Civil Service and Finance and Law) show the smallest amounts of mobility. But against this must be set the fact that in industry, with a higher degree of mobility, 25 per cent belong to non-contributory schemes. Also, that even though almost all those engaged in marketing and similar activities belong to contributory schemes they have not taken advantage of this (supposedly) greater opportunity to change employer—44 per cent have not moved at all and the average number of moves for this group is only 1·3.

In order to assess the importance of these benefits in relation to the basic salary, each respondent was asked to indicate their approximate total annual value to him. This might have been expected to create some difficulties in obtaining a reliable estimate but does not seem to have been the case and it appears that the majority of the group have a clear appreciation of the value of these additional benefits to them. The arithmetic mean value is about £470 but this figure is inflated on account of the high additional benefits paid to people working abroad and the high value of the benefits received by a fairly small number. The median value is £320.

School teachers, teachers in colleges of further education, local government officers and Civil Servants working in this country receive little in the way of additional financial advantage. Those employed in finance and law, industry and consultancy activities receive larger benefits. People working abroad in the Overseas Civil Service, the armed forces and the British Council receive even more valuable emoluments.

Table 4.11. Value of Additional Benefits Analysed by Employment Group—Averages

N=203

Employment group	Average value £	Median value £	Proportion in group receiving one or more benefits %
School	245	175	84
Further Education	235	175	82
University	415	375	97
Local Government	220	160	90
Finance and Law	825	575	86
Civil Service (home)	230	205	100
Civil Service (abroad)	1,000	810	100
Industry	570	375	96
Research and Consultancy	630	575	86
Miscellaneous	380	325	70
Overall average	470	320	88

The value of the emoluments increases as salary increases. This is partly to be explained by the fact that a large number of benefits are available in the employment groups which offer the highest basic salaries. It is also, in part, a reflection of the fact that contributions to pension funds tend to be related to the size of the basic salary and therefore increase as salary increases.

In fact, for all salary levels above £2,500 the median value of the additional benefits maintains a fairly constant ratio of 12 to 15 per cent of the basic salary.

(*c*) *Income from other work*

Some types of occupation present opportunities to add to income by undertaking additional work. Of the respondents who are now in full time employ-

Table 4.12. Value of Additional Benefits Analysed by Salary Level—Averages

N=203

Salary group £	Average value of benefits £	Median value of benefits £
Less than 2000	255	175
2000–2499	250	210
2500–2999	450	330
3000–3499	495	425
3500–3999	645	560
4000–4499	650	640
4500 and over	810	650
Overall average	470	320

ment just over a third have some extra income but these are largely concentrated in the teaching profession. Three-quarters of those in Universities and two-thirds of further education lecturers have an additional income, mainly from writing, examining and part-time teaching. In addition, some University teachers receive income from broadcasting and a few hold consultancy and advisory posts. One in three of the school teachers have an extra income, mainly from marking examination scripts. Only 20 per cent of the respondents who are working outside the field of education have an additional income. In the majority of these instances this is from writing and translating activities though a few are engaged in part-time teaching and examining.

In the case of University teachers this income represents a substantial addition to their basic income—on average £425 a year to those who receive some income from extra work, and this is equivalent to £310 when averaged over all the University teachers replying.[1] The average addition to the income of the further education employment group is £185 but the average for all other groups is under £100.

[1] The majority of University teachers included in this study are social scientists where the opportunities for outside earnings are greater than in other academic disciplines. This figure should not be taken as representative of the situation for University teachers generally.

Chapter 5

Attitudes to a Career

(*a*) *Job satisfaction*

Although society tends to judge a person's success in his career by the remuneration he receives, since this represents his power to acquire goods and services, to achieve the highest possible level of salary need not necessarily be the main objective of the individual. In an attempt to assess the relative importance of a number of alternative considerations in a career the respondents were asked to rank a group of factors according to the degree of importance which they attached to them.[1] Ten factors were listed on the questionnaire and space was provided for a further three to be written in. A number of additional factors were added by the respondents of which the most important was the quality of the colleagues one worked with. This was mentioned by 10 per cent of those replying. The next important was the opportunity to travel which 4 per cent mentioned. No other additional considerations appear to have strong general support outside those listed on the questionnaire.

Such a procedure involves a considerable element of subjective assessment on the part of each respondent and, as one or two pointed out, the rankings, especially after the first three or four factors, might change each time the factors were considered. However there has been a quite considerable amount of agreement between the respondents over the rank order to be given to each one. The most important was interest in the job, 55 per cent of those replying considered this the most important of all and a further 19 per cent rated it the second most important.

The two next most important factors were level of earnings which was ranked first or second by 25 per cent and independence of action which 26 per cent ranked as one of the top two. Next came a group of four factors—the ability to contribute to the well-being of society, promotion prospects, a sense of vocation in the post and the opportunity to use special skills were all rated as of some importance. The least important factors were geographical location, security and contact with members of the public.

With the exception of vocational considerations which some held important and others gave low ranking to, there was little variation between the rank order given to the factors when analysed in terms of the present employment group of the graduates. School teachers, local government officers and those in the miscellaneous group appeared to be slightly more concerned about the opportunity to contribute to the well being of society and school and university teachers and those in the miscellaneous group gave a lower ranking to earnings considerations. Teachers in further education and employees in research and consultancy organisations were more concerned about their place of work. Civil Servants ranked security higher than other groups of workers.

[1] The factors listed on the questionnaire were: Contact with the public, contribution to well-being of society, earnings, geographical location, independence of action, interest in job, opportunity to use special skills, promotion prospects, security of tenure, sense of vocation.

Table 5.1. Ranking of Factors Contributing to Job Satisfaction Analysed by Employment Group

N = 203

Factor	Employment group									Total
	School	Further Education	Univer-sity	Local Govt.	Finance & Law	Civil Service	Industry	Research & Consult.	Miscel-laneous	
Contact with members of the public	10	10	10	8	10	10	10	10	9	10
Contribution to well-being of society	3	7=	4	2	5	5=	5	6	3	4
Earnings	6	3	6	3	2	2=	2	2	6	2
Geographical location	9	5	9	7	9	9	8	5	8	9
Independence of action	4	2	2	4	4	2=	3	3	4	3
Interest in job	1	1	1	1	1	1	1	1	1	1
Opportunity to use special skills	5	7=	5	5	7	7=	6	7	5	7
Promotion prospects	7	4	7	6	3	4	4	4	7	5=
Security of tenure	8	9	8	10	6	5=	9	9	10	8
Sense of vocation	2	6	3	9	8	7=	7	8	2	5=

On balance, the general impression is that school teachers, university teachers and employees in the miscellaneous group revealed a stronger vocational and social motivation than graduates now in other employment groups. They were more concerned with a sense of vocation, finding the opportunity to use their special skills and to contribute to the well-being of society and less concerned about the level of earnings they might obtain. What we cannot say, however, is whether different types of employment attract people with different values or whether the nature of the employment moulds the attitude of the employee.

By asking the respondents to indicate how well their present position met their requirements, in respect of each of the factors listed we were able to obtain some indication of job satisfaction in respect of each factor. Four alternative answers were offered for the respondents to choose between in respect of each factor listed. These were " Very Well, Well, Fairly Well, Badly ". Few people were prepared to state that their job met their requirements badly in respect of any particular factor but many did not feel able to indicate that their job met their requirements " very well ". By awarding a certain number of points for each answer an index of job satisfaction can be constructed. Thus where a job is held to meet the requirements of a particular factor " very well " a score of four points was given, three for each answer of " well ", two for " fairly well " and one for " badly ". The degree of job satisfaction is then indicated by the proportion of the maximum possible scores actually recorded. Thus if ten people record an opinion about a particular factor the maximum possible score is 40. If four of these say their job meets their requirements " very well ", two say " well ", three " fairly well " and one " badly " the total score is 29 and the index of job satisfaction is 72·5 per cent.

By adopting this procedure for each of the factors listed and analysing the results by employment group we are then able to make a direct comparison of the relative satisfactions of people in different types of jobs in respect of the factors which they seem generally to agree are the most important. Table 5.2 gives the result of these calculations. We find that teachers of all types and local government officers are most satisfied that their career offers them the best opportunities to contribute to the well being of society. Overall there is a fairly low degree of satisfaction with the level of earnings but this is particularly strongly felt by school teachers, local government officers and those concerned with journalism, the arts and the other " miscellaneous " activities. Only those employed in research and consultancy organisations indicated a high level of satisfaction with their earnings. Most positions seem to offer considerable interest and scope for independent action though Local Government is an exception in both cases. University teachers and administrators appear particularly well satisfied with these two aspects, also with the scope which their positions offer to them to use their particular skills. Considerably less satisfaction was shown about promotion prospects and this appears to be a particularly serious problem for Civil Servants, local government officers and school teachers.

The majority of Civil Servants giving information on job satisfaction are not in the Administrative Class and their very low level of satisfaction with regard to promotion prospects highlights one of the serious problems relating to the employment of graduates in the departmental, professional and executive classes of the Civil Service. There is little doubt that the graduates employed in the Civil Service but outside the Administrative Class would welcome any measures which improved their promotion prospects.

Table 5.2. Job Satisfaction with Respect to 10 Ranked Factors—Index = 100

N = 203

Factor	Employment Group									
	School	Further Education	Univer-sity	Local Govt.	Finance & Law	Civil Service	Industry	Research & Consult.	Miscel-laneous	Total
Contact with members of the public	81	68	63	75	67	58	66	69	77	68
Contribution to well-being of society	90	86	82	83	64	75	66	69	73	76
Earnings	56	61	73	58	70	69	72	84	56	68
Geographical location	81	75	76	80	76	73	73	86	75	77
Independence of action	74	75	96	63	70	81	78	86	88	80
Interest in job	91	86	99	73	86	85	89	91	92	90
Opportunity to use special skills	75	82	94	75	72	78	79	83	85	81
Promotion prospects	56	64	69	50	74	50	78	73	62	67
Security of tenure	94	93	91	80	83	81	80	69	75	84
Sense of vocation	89	80	91	60	71	66	61	62	81	74

By aggregating the information so far presented on the factors contributing to job satisfaction and the degree of satisfaction obtained by the respondents in respect of each factor, it is possible to derive an index of job satisfaction for each individual respondent. This is achieved by weighting each factor in proportion to the rank order given to it by each respondent and multiplying by the score for the degree of job satisfaction actually obtained.

Thus the most important factor to each individual carried a weight of ten, the second most important nine and so on down to one for the tenth most important factor listed; where additional factors were written in which were not on the questionnaire (e.g. quality of colleagues) and were ranked in the first ten these were included in the analysis and other listed factors ranked less than tenth omitted. From the questionnaires we know also whether the respondent's present position meets his requirements in respect of each factor " very well ", " well "," fairly well " or " badly ". By scoring from 4 to 1 according to how well satisfied he is with his job in respect of each factor, we now have two numerical values—a weight and a score for each of the factors ranked. The index of job satisfaction is, therefore, the sum of the products of the weighted ranking and the score for each factor treated separately, expressed as a percentage.

This can be expressed in a simple formula:

$$I = \frac{100 \Sigma_1^{10} R.S}{200}$$

where: *R* is the weighted ranking of the order of importance of the factor *S* is the score of job satisfaction in relation to each factor.

This approach to the question of job satisfaction is considerably more complex than most methods used and could probably only be used in surveys of professional groups.[1] It is thought to offer some advantage over other approaches since it makes possible the highlighting of the important constituent parts of job satisfaction, and the identification of aspects where the worker may be particularly well satisfied or on the other hand most dissatisfied. It remains flexible since the index is calculated separately for each respondent and takes account of the individual's own ranking of the factors.

By calculating each individual's job satisfaction index we can observe the extent to which satisfaction does appear to vary between individuals and between employment groups. The arithmetic mean value of the index was 81 and the median value 82. The lower and upper quartile values respectively were 73 and 91 so it will be observed that a fairly high level of satisfaction was expressed and a substantial proportion of respondents had an index of over 90. It was anticipated that the degree of job satisfaction expressed in this way might vary between employment groups and according to salary level.

The highest overall degree of job satisfaction appears to be found amongst University staffs. People in the miscellaneous group of activities, mainly journalism and publishing, also have a high degree of job satisfaction both when seen in terms of the low proportion of people with a low index and the high proportion with a high index and also in terms of the median value of the index.

---

[1] For a discussion of some other approaches to the measurement of job satisfaction see: Robert Blauner " Work Satisfaction and Industrial Trends in Modern Society " in R. Bendix and S. M. Lipset *Class, Status and Power* (Routledge and Kegan Paul) 1967 pp. 473–487.

Table 5.3. Job Satisfaction Analysed by Employment Group

N=188

Employment group	Proportion with job satisfaction index: Less than 75 %	75–89 %	90–100 %	Total	Averages for group index max=100: Mean	Lower Quartile	Median	Upper Quartile
School	30	50	20	100	80	68	83	89
Further Education	40	20	40	100	80	68	79	92
University	7	30	63	100	88	83	90	96
Local Government	56	22	22	100	72	64	74	81
Finance and Law	30	65	5	100	79	72	77	88
Civil Service	57	36	7	100	75	65	75	86
Industry	38	40	22	100	80	71	79	89
Research and Consultancy	14	57	29	100	84	78	87	91
Miscellaneous	10	50	40	100	80	81	82	90
Total	29	43	28	100	81	73	82	91

School teachers and employees in research and consultancy organisations have a high average value for the index but a rather smaller proportion recorded an index of 90 or more. On the other hand, a high proportion of teachers in non-university institutions of further education recorded an index of 90 or more but the overall average for this group was pulled down by the equally large proportion with a low level of job satisfaction. Local government officers and Civil Servants (most of whom are outside the Administrative Class) have a low level of job satisfaction and employees in industry and the financial and legal professions do not have a high level of job satisfaction commensurate with their high average salaries. It does not necessarily seem to follow therefore that job satisfaction is greatest where salaries are highest.

Table 5.4 also indicates that at the level of the individual, a high salary does not necessarily mean high job satisfaction or *vice versa* although there is some correlation between these two variables.

Table 5.4. Job Satisfaction Compared with Salary Level

N=188

Salary level £	Proportion with job satisfaction index: Less than 75 %	75–89 %	90–100 %	Total	Averages for group index max=100: Mean	Lower quartile	Median	Upper quartile
Less than 2,000	45	43	12	100	75	66	79	85
2,000–2,499	28	49	23	100	80	74	80	89
2,500–2,999	33	45	22	100	80	73	82	86
3,000–3,499	20	40	40	100	83	71	79	93
3,500–3,999	26	37	37	100	81	73	88	91
4,000–4,999	14	30	56	100	84	70	79	92
5,000 and over	24	38	38	100	88	85	89	94
Total	29	43	28	100	81	73	82	91

If, however, we analyse the individual's job satisfaction index in terms of employment group and salary together we find there is a marked tendency for job satisfaction within an employment group to increase as salary increases. This seems to suggest that while *absolute* salary levels may not be of overwhelming importance in influencing the level of job satisfaction, *relative* salary levels compared with other graduates in the same type of employment are important. Intuitively, this also seems to be an acceptable proposition since there is a tendency to assess one's own salary against that of one's colleagues and contemporaries who are doing comparable work.

Table 5.5. Job Satisfaction Analysed by Employment Group and Salary Level
Index max = 100 *N = 188*

Employment group	Salary Level £			
	Less than 2,000	2,000–2,999	3,000–3,999	4,000 and over
School teaching	74	84	—	—
Further education	74	85	—	—
University	81	85	90	93
Local Government	68	77	—	—
Finance and Law	—	76	82	82
Civil Service	—	72	82	—
Industry	—	74	80	84
Research and Consultancy	—	—	81	86
Miscellaneous	82	84	—	—
Total	75	80	82	85

Note: — indicates less than 3 entries in the cell.

It is often argued that one of the reasons why some employment groups are able to recruit workers at a lower salary level is that there are non-monetary advantages in those particular careers which will compensate for a lower salary than could be obtained elsewhere. This being so, we would expect an effective index of job satisfaction to reveal areas where this might be the case. It appears from the measure of job satisfaction used in this analysis that such a situation is to be found amongst teachers at all levels but especially school teachers and also amongst employees in the miscellaneous group of activities. In both cases salary levels tend to be below the average for the whole group of respondents but relatively high levels of job satisfaction are recorded. Conversely, where both salary and job satisfaction are below average as in the case of non-Administrative Class Civil Servants and local government officers we would anticipate greater recruitment difficulties and problems over morale and the retention of staff.

The respondents with the highest degree of job satisfaction are those whose academic achievements are greatest. Over fifty per cent of the graduates with a first class honours degree and a similar proportion of holders of higher degrees obtained by academic study had an index of 90 or more. There is some evidence that job satisfaction is higher among graduates from Oxford and the " Other " group of universities. The study also suggests that job satisfaction is greatest amongst graduates from the highest social class backgrounds.

(*b*) *Comparison with a Civil Service Career.*

Assuming that the unsuccessful candidates still have an adequate knowledge of working conditions and prospects in the higher Civil Service, a useful com-

*Table 5.6. Job Satisfaction Compared with Social Class Background of Respondent**

N=186

Social class category	Proportions with job satisfaction index			Group averages Index Max=100			
	Less than 75 %	75–89 %	90–100 %	Mean	Lower Quartile	Median	Upper Quartile
I. Professional occupations	24	43	33	83	75	86	93
II Intermediate occupations	31	43	26	81	73	82	90
III and IV. Skilled and partly skilled manual and non-manual occupations	35	43	22	79	72	79	89
Total	29	43	28	81	73	82	91

* Social class background of respondent as indicated by father's occupation.

parison can be made between their assessment of their present career prospects against a career in the Civil Service. Therefore, the respondents were asked, to compare their career prospects for the next five years with the prospects of people of their own age who are higher Civil Servants. The answers to this question and to other questions relating to the Civil Service lead to the conclusion that the majority of graduates replying are well informed about the Civil Service and so their answers can be treated as having some authority.

Altogether, thirty per cent of the respondents felt that their career prospects were better than those of Administrative Class Civil Servants and 26 per cent felt career prospects were definitely worse. Respondents in employment groups where the highest salary levels are to be found are most satisfied with their career prospects and *vice versa*. Thus the people who think their career prospects are better than those of a Civil Servant are mainly to be found in research and consultancy organisations, industry, the universities and financial and legal organisations. On the other hand, school teachers, local government officers, teachers in colleges of further education and those in the miscellaneous group are almost completely agreed that their career prospects are not better than a Civil Service career would offer and in many cases they think they are definitely worse.

The questionnaire gave a choice of six alternative replies—Very much better, better, about the same, worse, and very much worse. In Table 5.7 the first two and the last two categories have been combined. Only employees in research and consultancy organisations, industry and Universities thought their prospects were very much better. Respondents who thought their prospects were very much worse were school teachers and further education lecturers, local government officers, Overseas Civil Servants and Home Civil Servants in the Executive and Departmental classes.

There is a strong positive association between present salary level and the assessment of career prospects. This suggests that although the graduate may consider other factors to be of considerable importance in contributing to his job satisfaction, very few are prepared to discount the level of salary in making their assessment of career prospects.

Table 5.7. Career Prospects Compared with Civil Service—By employment group—Percentages

N=201

Employment group	Career Prospects are: Very much better and better	About the same	Indefinite	Worse and much worse	Total
School	0	33	20	47	100
Further Education	11	11	33	45	100
Universities	29	44	9	18	100
Local Government	10	10	20	60	100
Finance and Law	38	33	19	10	100
Civil Service	9	25	0	66	100
Industry	57	27	11	5	100
Research and Consultancy	64	21	0	15	100
Miscellaneous	9	33	25	33	100
Overall average	30	30	14	26	100

Table 5.8. Career Prospects Compared with Civil Service—By salary level—Percentages

N=201

Salary level £	Career Prospects are: Very much better and better	About the same	Indefinite	Worse and very much worse	Total
less than 2,000	3	15	33	49	100
2,000–2,499	3	37	14	46	100
2,500–2,999	16	34	16	34	100
3,000–3,499	42	46	4	8	100
3,500–3,999	40	45	5	10	100
4,000–4,999	75	16	9	0	100
5,000–5,999	75	13	12	0	100
6,000 and over	91	0	9	0	100
Overall Average	30	30	14	26	100

Since we have observed that salary levels tend to be related to class of degree and social class background, it is not surprising to find that career prospects follow the same pattern. Thus 34 per cent of graduates with a first class degree think their career prospects are better than those of their contemporaries who are in the Administrative Class, compared with 30 per cent with undivided seconds, 25 per cent with upper seconds and 15 per cent with lower seconds. An exception is to be found in the case of those who obtained third class degrees and below, one third of whom think their prospects are now better than had they become Civil Servants.

Similarly, graduates from the higher social class backgrounds appear to have the best career prospects. Thirty-six per cent from Social Class I backgrounds assess their prospects to be better than those of their contemporaries who are members of the Civil Service compared with 27 per cent from Social Class II and 21 per cent from Classes III and IV.

In relation to the factors that we used in assessing job satisfaction we find that there are only three of the ten factors where it is thought a career in the Civil Service would on balance have proved more satisfactory. These are security of tenure, earnings and promotion prospects. Of these only earnings appear in the rankings of the factors as being of great importance to the graduate and only respondents in the lower paid employments groups mentioned this as an important advantage which a Civil Service career would offer. On the other hand a career in the Civil Service was held to be likely to have proved less satisfactory in respect of a wide range of considerations. The lack of interest in the job and restrictions on the independence of action in the Civil Service are probably the most important since they appear to be considerations which are uppermost in the mind of the graduate in assessing the desirability of a particular job.

Table 5.9. Advantages and Disadvantages of a Civil Service Career—Percentages

N=201

Factor	A career in the Civil Service would have been: Better	The same	Worse	Total	Ranking of factors
Contact with members of the public	21	40	39	100	10
Contribution to the well-being of the society	21	51	28	100	4
Earnings	38	32	30	100	2
Geographical location	9	42	49	100	9
Independence of action	7	20	73	100	3
Interest in job	7	49	44	100	1
Opportunity to use special skills	9	43	48	100	7
Promotion prospects	33	38	29	100	5=
Security of tenure	35	54	11	100	8
Sense of vocation	16	40	44	100	5=

The figures in Table 5.9 should not, however, be taken as implying any overall assessment about the good and bad features of the Civil Service. (This is discussed in the next chapter). This table merely summarises the views of the graduates in comparing their present career with their assessment of how well a career in the Civil Service could have satisfied their requirements in respect of each of these factors compared with the actual satisfaction they have obtained. Thus where a high level of job satisfaction is experienced in the graduate's present career e.g. interest in job, it is not necessarily to be wondered at if few of them consider a Civil Service career would have offered any greater a degree of satisfaction in this respect.

Chapter 6

Attitudes to the Civil Service

Although they were unsuccessful in their attempts to become Administrative Class Civil Servants, many of the graduates we surveyed have had close contact, either business and/or social, with higher Civil Servants. A number are in positions of responsibility in schools and universities where they have the opportunity to advise and influence the attitudes of potential administrative class Civil Servants. Others are in frequent business contact with civil servants and on their co-operation rests, to some extent at least, the ability of the government to make its policies effective. In addition many are now parents of children who might also consider the possibility of a career in the Civil Service in future years. This survey therefore offered the opportunity to investigate the views which these people now hold about the Civil Service. They were questioned on their reasons for applying to join the Civil Service, on the aspects of a Civil Service career that they consider make it attractive or unattractive and on the salary level they would require to join the Civil Service now.

Besides offering a reflection of the general attitude of an informed group of outsiders, we must not lose sight of the fact that these are the views of a group of people most of whom had their applications to enter the Civil Service rejected. There is, therefore, some danger that opinion may be coloured by an element of " sour grapes ", but in reading through the replies the writer has been impressed by an absence of hostility towards the Civil Service in general or the Civil Service Commission in particular. This does not mean, however, that critical comments have not been made, but they are out of a desire to be constructive rather than destructive.

(*a*) *Reasons for applying to the Civil Service*

A few respondents were already working when they entered the 1951 Open Competitions but in most instances the applicant was still at University. It appears that the reasons for competing remain quite clear in the minds of most graduates and there was a wide range of motivational factors behind the decision.

There seems to have been a widespread opinion that the work of higher civil servants was a stimulating experience and presented a challenge to the intellect of the holder and because of this was an occupation in which interest would be maintained. Several referred to the fact that Civil Service posts were held to be jobs for an élite and that this fact, associated in some instances with a competitive examination, encouraged the graduate to apply. Experience of administrative positions in the forces convinced some graduates that administration was the occupation to which they were best suited and on this basis they decided to enter the competition.

The next most important group of considerations concerned the conditions of employment. The security, salary and promotion prospects all had a strong appeal, so too did the feeling that the Civil Service had a higher level of integrity and ethical standards than did the world of business. Several women referred

Table 6.1. Reasons for Applying to the Civil Service

Reason	Number mentioning
Quality of work (stimulation, challenge, interest)	56
Indecision about career	53
Desire to work in a particular branch	47
Public service considerations	44
Use of a particular qualification	36
Family tradition and encouragement	29
Status of Civil Service	28
Desire to travel	26
Encouragement and advice from University	17
Considerations relating to employment conditions:	
Security	44
Remuneration	31
Promotion prospects	29
General integrity and ethics of Civil Service	29
Quality of colleagues	17

particularly to the fact that the Civil Service offered better career prospects to women than industry. The high number of people mentioning security considerations is surprising in a group of people who were then in their early twenties and who do not appear to consider this factor very important now (see above p. 75). This situation is probably explained by the experiences of the depression which were vivid in the minds of the graduates' parents if not of the graduates themselves. By 1951 the economy was still only in the process of recovering from war-time controls and uncertainty still existed about the general ability of a government to sustain the level of economic activity and maintain full employment in peace time conditions.

Parental encouragement, both because the Civil Service offered a secure employment and also to follow in a family tradition of public service, seems to have been rather more important than any influence exerted in the Universities. A few graduates from Oxford, Cambridge and the Scottish Universities referred to advice from their University teachers or Appointments Boards but only two from London and one from the Other Universities referred to any encouragement from this source. The highest proportion of people who mentioned a desire to serve the country were from Oxford and the Scottish Universities. Linguists and social scientists most frequently mentioned the desire to use their particular academic qualifications.

A surprisingly high number stated that they entered the Competition because they wished to work in a particular branch of the Service. The Foreign Office, Commonwealth Relations Office and Diplomatic Service were the main attractions and several claimed that had they been successful but offered an appointment in another department they would not have accepted.

Besides the positive inducements to apply which many felt, a large number admitted that their reasons for applying were negative rather than positive. There seems to have been considerable indecision about careers amongst candidates from all Universities and many drifted into the examination without a strong desire to become Civil Servants—e.g. " because it was the ' done thing ' for an Oxford man ", or because of the example of College acquaintances. A number reported that they were treating the Civil Service as something to fall back upon should they not obtain the position they really wanted (frequently a chance to stay on at University to do research). Others chose the Civil Service because of a reluctance to teach or to enter the world of business.

(*b*) *Attitudes towards the Civil Service now*

(*i*) *Favourable comments.* In the wide range of comments made by the respondents about aspects of the Civil Service that are attractive and unattractive a number of conflicting opinions are to be found. For every person who thinks it an advantage to work in London there are two who consider this a positive disadvantage. For every three people who think the work of Administrative Class Civil Servants to be highly interesting there are two who hold it to be boring and routine.

Table 6.2. Attractive Aspects of the Civil Service

Factor	Number mentioning
Nature of work (interest, stimulation, responsibility etc.)	72
Share in political decision making and organisation of society	67
Public service considerations	48
Opportunity to wield power and influence	36
Status of the Civil Service (social, professional and/or academic)	30
Considerations relating to employment conditions:	
General working conditions (holidays, leisure, quality of colleagues)	48
Security and pension	72
Remuneration	55
Promotion prospects	31

To a considerable extent the attractive aspects which the Civil Service is thought to offer now coincide with the main positive reasons given for making the initial application to enter the Civil Service in 1951. Salary considerations seem to be more important now, so too does the opportunity to share in decision making in society and to wield power and influence. On the other hand no favourable comments were made about the general integrity and ethics of the Civil Service at the present time.

When these opinions are related to the employment group and salary level of the respondents a number of interesting differences become apparent. The levels of remuneration in the Civil Service are most attractive to school teachers but understandably, not to graduates who are now earning over £3,500. Although employees in industry are not attracted by the remuneration offered by the Civil Service, they do find the security of employment and pension arrangements favourable. It is the higher income groups that find the public service aspects of a career in the Civil Service and the variety and interest of the work involved to be particularly attractive.

(*ii*) *Unfavourable comments.* The strongest criticism was centred on factors concerning the method of working—excessive red tape and the stultification of individual initiative, bureaucracy, excessive reliance on traditional procedures—committees, memoranda etc. Inefficient organisation was also mentioned frequently, so too was the view that at least a large part of the higher Civil Servant's work was routine and uninteresting. The rigid hierarchial structure of the service was mentioned by a large number as a disadvantage. Several respondents also mentioned that they felt there was excessive political pressure in the working of various government departments.

Fewer people criticised the conditions of employment than found them attractive, though there was some feeling that the highest talent was less well rewarded in the Civil Service than in industry. The tendency to relate promotion prospects to age and seniority was criticised as this ruled out the possibility of accelerated promotion for the top people. The most frequently mentioned criticism in relation to the conditions of employment was the need to work in London. One graduate who had been declared successful in 1951 stated that it was the necessity of living in or near London and the high costs associated with this that caused him to decline the appointment.

Among other criticisms made were references to poor office conditions and overcrowding, the liability to transfer with excessive frequency, the isolation of Civil Servants from reality in their daily work and the nature of interdepartmental rivalries, and personal rivalries between candidates for promotion. Several suggested that the rules relating to Civil Servants were excessively rigid (though few specifically referred to political restrictions) and that anonymity was taken further than necessary.

Table 6.3. Unattractive Aspects of the Civil Service

Factor	Number mentioning
Red tape, discouragement of individual initiative	71
Bureaucracy	54
Boring, routine work	42
Bad internal organisation, inefficiency	37
Traditionalism in method of working	35
Rigid stratification of Civil Service	33
Subjection to political pressures	18
Isolation from reality	13
Considerations relating to employment conditions:	
Having to work in London	26
Poor general working conditions	16
Poor promotion prospects	15
Liability to transfer with excessive frequency	14
Low earnings	13

The lack of freedom of action was particularly remarked upon by employees in universities, industry and research and consultancy organisations. Workers in industry referred also to the poor earnings and promotion prospects, inefficiency and bad organisation and the excessive stratification in the Civil Service.

(*c*) *Salary required to join the Civil Service now*

Respondents were asked the question " Supposing you were to consider entering the Civil Service now, about what level of salary would you require? " It seems that this was not entirely a hypothetical question, from other comments on the questionnaire it appears that a number of respondents would (and have) seriously consider joining the Civil Service now if the opportunity presented itself.

The level of salary that would be required to attract these people to the Civil Service depends on the degree of satisfaction with present career prospects, employment grouping and existing salary level but the average and median salaries that would be required—£3,845 and £3,425 respectively are closely similar to the level that is being paid to their contemporaries who became Administrative Class Civil Servants in 1951.

Table 6.4. Salary Required to Enter the Civil Service Compared with the Assessment of Present Career Prospects—Percentages

N=201

Salary required to enter the Civil Service £	Comparison of present career prospects with a Civil Service career Present career prospects are:						
	Very much better	Better	About the same	Indefinite	Worse	Very much worse	Proportion in group
less than 2,000	—	—	—	14	—	16	5
2,000–2,499	—	—	12	20	16	24	12
2,500–2,999	—	—	16	26	42	40	20
3,000–3,499	—	17	20	20	21	4	16
3,500–3,999	6	17	16	7	21	12	14
4,000–4,999	19	31	24	3	—	4	15
5,000 and over	75	35	12	10	—	—	18
Total	100	100	100	100	100	100	100
Average salary required	£5,600	4,665	3,695	3,055	2,955	2,645	3,845
Median salary required	£5,800	4,400	3,545	2,825	2,900	2,650	3,425

Higher salaries would be required to attract people in the more highly paid employment groups—research and consultancy, finance and the law and the Universities, while local government officers and school teachers, because of their much lower current salaries, would be attracted by a lower figure.

Table 6.5. Salary Required to Enter the Civil Service Analysed by Employment Group—Averages

N=201

Employment group	Salary required	
	Average salary £	Median salary £
School	2,855	2,800
Further Education	3,565	3,300
University	4,270	4,000
Local Government	2,295	2,250
Finance and Law	4,220	4,500
Civil Service	3,525	3,670
Industry	3,840	3,920
Research and Consultancy	5,185	5,100
Miscellaneous	3,000	3,000

The majority of people would ask for an increase on their present salary of between £300 and £1,000, the average increase required is just over £700. The level of salary that would be required is closely related to present salary levels and it would seem that the *absolute* size of the increase required is fairly constant over all levels of salary. This would therefore mean that a smaller *proportionate* increase in salary would be necessary to attract the more highly paid than would be necessary to attract those receiving lower salaries.

Table 6.6. Salary Required to Enter Civil Service Analysed by Present Salary Level—Averages N=201

Present salary level £	Salary Required to enter Civil Service: Average salary £	Median salary £
Less than 2,000	2,485	2,600
2,000–2,999	3,240	3,200
3,000–3,999	4,370	4,250
4,000–4,999	5,400	5,600
5,000 and over	6,540	6,500

(*d*) *Further comments*

At the end of the questionnaire the respondents were given the opportunity to add any further comments they felt might be of interest. Several remarked that they were pleased not to have been selected as they now felt they were not best suited to a career in the Civil Service. Others indicated that they would still like to become Civil Servants.

The majority of comments, however, were critical and concerned mainly with three problems—the selection procedure, working conditions in the Civil Service as seen by those who at some time or other have been Civil Servants and the quality of the Civil Servants and their outlook as seen by people outside the service who come into contact with them. It is not possible to give a numerical weighting to these comments and it should be borne in mind that remarks on the selection procedure may not be relevant to the present day Open Competitions. Comments about the working conditions and quality of Civil Servants while, no doubt authentic, should not necessarily be seen as reflecting a comment about the Civil Service as a whole but about the particular parts of it with which the respondents have come into contact.

Despite one or two favourable comments on the fairness of the selection procedures, it was this aspect that attracted most critical attention. Several commented on the timing of the Method I written papers suggesting that because they followed hard upon University finals many people were reluctant to take them. One writer suggested that University examination results should be used instead to overcome the need to sit two gruelling examinations within a short time of each other. One London graduate in history suggested that the group of history papers were slanted more in favour of the " Oxbridge " historian than the " Redbrick " candidate. He referred to the existence of questions on the history of art, music, literature to the exclusion of social and economic history questions which the Redbrick candidate was more likely to be able to answer.

The interviews in both Method I and Method II came in for more criticism. One graduate reported that he found the people conducting the interviews and tests less impressive than those involved in a similar " country house " selection procedure used in industry. One candidate who came very close to success and has since had a highly successful career considered the close questioning on his political views, which he described as being of the " fellow traveller type ", very distasteful. Another, writing of the interviews, commented:

" The interviews that I had made it clear to me that my type was undesirable . . . This was one of the most horrible experiences of my life."

It is worth adding that the writer of that comment has since been asked to participate in the selection of Administrative Class Civil Servants and has declined the invitation.

Several graduates suggested that the selection procedure tended to favour candidates who were excessively conformist and might be considered " safe ". It was argued that the emphasis on academic and social ability was at the expense of a closer investigation of the aptitude of the candidate to do the job required. One, with close practical knowledge of the problem, argued that selection to the Diplomatic Service placed undue emphasis on the ability of a candidate to stand up to the social round and paid insufficient attention to his ability to cope with the administrative and technical aspects of the position. Some felt that there was a tendency to deprecate specialised skills, especially in the social sciences. This is reflected in a comment by an unsuccessful economist:

> " My request to be considered for the Treasury was greeted as in a Bateman cartoon. In any sane Civil Service the question should have been why as an economist you do not want to go into the Treasury, Board of Trade etc., not the reverse."

The question of appointments was raised by three respondents. One successful candidate applied to have his appointment held over for a year so that he could continue his studies. This was turned down and so he did not accept the appointment. Another candidate who was declared successful had already accepted another position before the results were announced. A graduate who was offered a Civil Service appointment outside the Administrative Class turned down the offer because of what he described as a disregard for personal preference regarding department.

Four graduates were still sufficiently interested in a career in the Civil Service that in 1966 they considered applying again in the competition for Principals aged 36–52. Two withdrew because they had obtained other posts before the selection procedure was completed. The other two did not submit completed application forms because they were unhappy about certain aspects of the selection procedure. One felt that the Civil Service Selection Board tests were inappropriate for older people. The other was unwilling to arrange the necessary references at the beginning of the candidature since this meant that his professional and social contacts would know that the application was being made and also whether or not it was subsequently successful. Another prospective candidate for the 1966 competition criticised the questions asked on the application forms:

> " The Civil Service Commission would get more applications if they stopped asking for details of education, societies you belonged to at University, etc. The selection should be done by practical tests of administrative ability such as have been in recent years. If the candidate is successful at these tests there is no need for anyone to know whether he acquired that ability at Tulse Hill or Tonbridge, whether he was a member of ' Pop ' or a ' Half-Blue '."

Two graduates who have served in the special departmental classes commented upon their experiences. One remarked that in his first position he felt very isolated from his colleagues. The other complained that the short notice given before being posted to a different part of the country created hardship and the possibility of financial loss in selling property. (This is presumably more of a problem in the departmental classes than the Administrative Class.) Both these graduates have now left the Civil Service.

Two graduates criticised salary and promotion prospects in the professional classes which they found to be much worse than in the Administrative Class. One, who has now left the Civil Service, also commented on the lack of intellectual challenge:

> " I doubt if any other organisation allows its *professional* staff to ' go to seed ' as does the Civil Service. Professional people are still not accepted."

This graduate claimed that during nearly ten years in the Civil Service he did not once have the opportunity to attend a training or refresher course and suggested this is true also of his former colleagues in the same class.

Some businessmen compared the Civil Service unfavourably with industry in certain respects. They held that the organisation of the Civil Service is inefficient and that higher Civil Servants are excessively amateurish in their approach to problems when dealing with industry.

One graduate commented:

> " I have frequent dealings with senior Civil Servants and respect them in many ways, but their position tends to make them defensive and dominated by a desire for a quiet life. A more open attitude to and examination of, their work might be a good thing ".

But the comments were not all on the debit side. One successful businessman at least was aware of a difference in emphasis between the Civil Service and industry:

> " My contemporaries in the Administrative Class don't seem to talk the same language in terms of profitability and accountability in the short term, but they think streets ahead of me on the long range planning of expected resources."

A number of businessmen suggested ways in which these criticisms of the Civil Service might be resolved. The need to recruit more people with a training which fitted them to exercise a specialist function was emphasised and it was also suggested that more might be done to equip top Civil Servants with a better knowledge of the problems they are dealing with especially where this involves close contact with industry. An interchange of staff between industry, the Civil Service and the Universities was frequently suggested as a way of achieving this end.

Chapter 7

The Assessment of Career Success

It was hoped that a follow-up survey of the unsuccessful candidates in the Open Competitions such as that described in this paper might offer the opportunity to assess the extent to which the people rejected by the Civil Service Commission had gone on to successful careers elsewhere. There is evidence that the rankings given to successful candidates are a fairly good predictor of the degree of success which the candidate is likely to experience in the Civil Service,[1] but until the present survey there has been no attempt to follow-up those who did not become Civil Servants. Have the Open Competition rankings any relevance to non-Civil Service careers? Is there any evidence that the Civil Service Commission have overlooked potential top class Civil Servants? At the present time when the problem is to attract a sufficient number into the Service rather than to select the best from a high-class field as seems to have been the case in 1951, a more relevant question is what would be the effect on the general quality of the entrants if standards were lowered slightly in order to fill the existing vacancies without the need for supplementary competitions?[2]

While these questions are important and of considerable interest, it is difficult to provide entirely satisfactory answers on the basis of the results from this survey. In the first place, merely because a person has had a successful career as a businessman or as an academic does not necessarily mean that he would have been equally successful in the Civil Service where there is perhaps less scope for the individualist. Certainly, the fact that a number of those surveyed now report that they would not have been happy as Civil Servants lends support to this view.

There is also the problem of defining "success". Success in the eyes of society is not necessarily success to the individual. We have already seen (Chapter 5) that the most important considerations to the individual in a particular position are interest in the job, earnings and independence of action. But other factors such as the ability to contribute to the well being of society and a sense of vocation are also important. Of these, only earnings are measurable objectively and the evidence of our job satisfaction index is that job satisfaction, which can probably be seen as a reflection of success in the eyes of the individual, is not necessarily high in absolute terms when earnings are high.

Even to measure success from the point of view of society presents problems because of the difficulty of finding an objective test. The criterion of salary alone seems to be unworkable because of the wide variations between the different employment groups. It would be wrong to suggest that a school teacher had

---

[1] E. Anstey, *The Civil Service Administrative Class and the Diplomatic Service: A Follow-up*, Occupational Psychology, 1966, vol. 40 pp. 139–151.

[2] Assuming that it is held to be preferable that all direct entry recruitment to the Administrative Class should be at the age of 21 or 22. It may be that the over-age competitions should have a permanent part in supplying the Civil Service with some of its administrators. Certainly, many businessmen would appear to favour this.

necessarily been any less successful than a management consultant or stock-broker just because there was a difference of £2,500 or more in their annual salaries. To take into account the status of the position held is helpful, but in the case of people in administrative and managerial positions it is not always possible when using a mail questionnaire to differentiate effectively between different levels of responsibility. This could only be done by means of interviews with the employers of the people we wish to follow-up. This method of approach was initially considered for the survey but was rejected because of the difficulties that would have been involved in achieving the co-operation of the employers necessary to obtain confidential information on the assessment of their employees.

In an attempt to derive some sort of assessment of those who appear to have had a successful career, while recognising the limitations inevitably imposed on any conclusions that might be drawn, each completed questionnaire was sorted through by hand using the joint criteria of relative salary level and status. Two groups of graduates were picked out: one group of 40 who seem to have been highly successful "the successfuls" and a second group of 40 who appear also to have had above average success and whom we therefore classify as fairly successful. Excluding those who are no longer working and so cannot be considered this represents 38 per cent of those replying. We would not, however, suggest that this group is exclusive and others have undoubtedly been successful in the light of the criteria they set themselves and others may have had a degree of career success that is not apparent from the questionnaire. Indeed, from the general information on salary levels for graduates in their late thirties that we have been able to collect it seems that, as a group, the graduates we have surveyed have had above average success.

In some types of employment it is fairly easy to distinguish between different status levels. This is certainly true in the teaching profession and the Civil Service where salary is related to the status of the post. When we move away from the groups with a clearly defined hierarchy it becomes even more difficult to employ criteria for success. Here it is necessary to take into account the description given in the completed questionnaire of the status of the post and the nature of the work involved together with the salary received assessed, where possible, against information on average salary levels for graduates in that occupation.

In looking for evidences of success, the emphasis has been on the graduates whose careers so far seems to have progressed further than those of most of their contemporaries in the same employment group. Thus we would class someone who had already reached Professorial status in a University as "successful", also headmasters and headmistresses. In industry, positions carrying high degrees of responsibility have been taken as indicators of success. In some cases status and salary have been high, in others either status or salary has been high while the other has seemed low in comparison.

The people identified as successful or fairly successful cover all the employment groups to a greater or lesser degree. They include head teachers and deputy heads, professors, readers and senior lecturers, some fellows of Oxford and Cambridge colleges, directors of industrial concerns, partners in legal or financial organisations and holders of senior managerial positions in industry. Also included are journalists and publishers, management consultants, company secretaries and planners, University administrators and teachers in colleges of further education. There are also four Civil Servants who, despite being unsuccessful in the 1951 Open Competitions, have still had successful careers in the Civil Service. One is now an Assistant Secretary, one a senior official in the Inland Revenue. The other two are high ranking members of the Overseas Civil Service.

The proportion of successful and fairly successful graduates is higher in research and consultancy organisations than in other employment groups while fewer local government officers, school teachers and further education lecturers seem to have had outstanding success.

Table 7.1. Career Success Analysed by Employment Group—Percentages

N=207

Employment group	Proportion in group assessed to have been successful or fairly successful %
School	29
Further Education	18
Local Government	10
Universities	44
Finance and Law	50
Civil Service	38
Industry	52
Research and Consultancy	64
Miscellaneous	23
Overall percentage	38

It is almost inevitable that successful graduates will be receiving higher average salaries than those who appear to have been less successful. Even by 1958 the people we are now classifying as successful were receiving higher salaries than the rest, and it is significant that the rate of growth of salaries since 1958 has been faster for those classed as successful than for the others.

Table 7.2. Salary Level Analysed by Career Success—Averages

N=206

Assessment of career success	Average Salary 1966 £	Average Salary 1958 £	Median Salary 1966 £	Median Salary 1958 £
Successful	5,130	1,715	4,500	1,460
Fairly successful	3,390	1,300	3,375	1,280
Not successful	2,420	1,205	2,330	985
Overall average	3,145	1,331	2,830	1,135

A much higher proportion of people who have been successful in their careers come from Oxford than is the case with the graduates as a whole. Another important educational factor is the class of degree obtained. The successful graduates are mainly those with either a first class degree (55 per cent of whom are classified as successful or fairly successful) or an undivided second (44 per cent). On the other hand, only 28 per cent of upper seconds and 23 per cent of those with lower classes of degree appear to have had successful or fairly successful careers. While it appears therefore that class of degree obtained at University is a useful predicter of subsequent career success, it should be observed that nearly a quarter of those with lower seconds or below seem to have achieved considerable success in their careers so far. It does not follow therefore that a high class of degree is a *sine qua non* for later career success.

Table 7.3. Relation between University Background and Career Success—Percentages

N=207

University attended	Assessment of career success			
	Successful	Fairly successful	Not successful	Total
Oxford	34	22	44	100
Cambridge	17	16	67	100
London	10	10	80	100
Scottish	9	9	82	100
Other	2	21	77	100
Overall average	19	19	62	100

A slightly higher than average proportion of those who have had successful careers went to independent schools and/or came from Social Class I backgrounds.

There is no evidence that the number of times a graduate has changed his employer is a reflection of either success or lack of success so far. Those we have classed as not successful have made an average of 1·8 moves and the successfuls and fairly successfuls have moved 1·7 times. The possession of additional qualifications does not seem to have had much influence either. One fifth of those without an additional qualification have had some measure of career success compared with one in seven of those with a qualification. There are, however, two types of qualification which do seem to be beneficial—legal and accountancy qualifications—70 per cent of the small number who are professionally qualified in these fields have been successful, and a Ph.D.—44 per cent of the holders of which have been classed as either successful or fairly successful.

While a few of the graduates who scored poor marks in the Open Competition have since had successful careers it seems that the closer the candidates came to gaining admission to the Administrative Class the more likely they are to have had successful careers so far. Those who were declared successful but preferred a career outside the Civil Service have almost without exception had successful careers. Graduates who came close to success in both the Method I and Method II competitions have also been quite successful in their careers and the number of graduates who withdrew from the Open Competition and have since been successful suggests that many good quality candidates were lost by these withdrawals. It will be observed that candidates who competed by Method II have been rather more successful in their careers than the Method I candidates overall.

It seems that the people we have identified as having had successful or fairly successful careers so far are also those who are most satisfied in their own minds with their present positions and career prospects. Very few of the people we have classed as not successful have a high index of job satisfaction while the reverse is true for those identified as successful and fairly successful. The average values of the job satisfaction index for the different classes of respondent also confirm the situation.

Table 7.4. Career Success Compared with Performance in the Open Competitions—Percentages

N=*207*

Performance in competition	Assessment of career success			
	Successful	Fairly successful	Not successful	Total
Declared successful	25	62	13	100
Withdrew	22	13	65	100
Method I:				
Mark less than 600	7	11	82	100
Mark 600–699	7	17	76	100
Mark 700 or more	32	12	56	100
Method II:				
Not invited to final selection board	12	17	71	100
Mark 200 or less at final board	23	16	61	100
Mark more than 200 at final board	43	19	38	100

Note: Candidates who competed by both Methods are included twice in this table.

Table 7.5. Career Success Compared with Job Satisfaction

N=*188*

Proportion with job satisfaction index	Assessment of career success			
	Successful %	Fairly successful %	Not successful %	Overall average %
Less than 75	20	20	35	29
75–89	31	45	47	43
90–100	49	35	18	28
Total	100	100	100	100
Average values of job satisfaction index max=100				
Mean	86	84	78	81
Lower quartile	80	75	72	73
Median	89	85	80	82
Upper quartile	94	94	88	91

Table 7.6. Assessment of Career Prospects Analysed by Career Success—Percentages

N=*203*

Assessment of career success	Compared with a career in the Civil Service, career prospects are:				
	Very much better and better	About the same	Indefinite	Worse and very much worse	Total
Successful	66	23	8	3	100
Fairly successful	42	32	8	18	100
Not successful	13	30	21	36	100
Overall average	30	30	14	26	100

Similarly, very few of the " not successfuls " claim that their prospects are better than they would have been in the Civil Service, whereas two thirds of the " successfuls " rate their career prospects in their present job more highly.

In order to attract those who are having successful careers outside the Civil Service in to the Service a higher salary would have to be paid than to those who have been less successful. But this is merely a reflection of the fact that present career success is already rewarded with above-average salaries. In fact the average increase on his present salary that the successful graduate would require to enter the Civil Service now is lower than that required by those who seem to have had less career success.

Table 7.7. Salary Required to Enter the Civil Service Analysed by Career Success—Averages

N=203

Assessment of career success	Salary required		Increase on present average salary
	Average £	Median £	%
Successful	5,735	5,150	12
Fairly successful	4,255	4,175	26
Not successful	3,175	2,900	31
Overall average	3,765	3,400	20

Attitudes towards the Civil Service also vary according to the extent of career success experienced. Those with less career success emphasise the pay and promotion prospects as attractive features of the Civil Service, especially promotion on merit. They also favour the Civil Service because they consider it offers the opportunity to use their abilities to the full and encourages them to shoulder responsibility. On the other hand, the graduates who have been successful and fairly successful in their careers consider the Civil Service to be attractive now because it offers the opportunity to serve in a capacity that is beneficial to society. The successful graduates are also the people who are most prone to criticise the lack of contact that Civil Servants have with the world of industry and commerce. They condemn the excessive traditionalism in the method of operation of the Civil Service and the limitations on the exercise of individual initiative. Whereas a fairly large number of graduates find the need to work in London an unattractive aspect of the Civil Service it is significant that none of the graduates who have had successful careers considered this a drawback.

Conclusions

A number of general conclusions can be drawn from this survey of people who did not enter the Administrative Class in 1951.

As far as can be ascertained, on balance their careers appear to have been as successful as they would have been had they entered the higher Civil Service. Many are now in positions of considerable responsibility in industry and the professions and some are drawing considerably higher salaries than Assistant Secretaries in the Civil Service.

The choice of career seems to have played a major part in influencing the salary now being received. As a general rule, we can say that most people in public service occupations tend to receive lower basic salaries and fewer fringe benefits than those in private enterprise occupations. Although salary level seems to influence the assessment of career prospects it appears that the degree of job satisfaction experienced does not depend solely upon earnings.

In the light of this survey it is not possible to say whether the Civil Service Commission selected the right people in 1951. The evidence suggests that the overall quality of the candidates was very high. It would appear that in terms of subsequent career achievement many of the graduates who offered themselves as potential Civil Servants have since had a significant degree of success. In general, it can also be claimed that the rankings in the 1951 Open Competition have proved an accurate predictor of the degree of success subsequently experienced by each candidate, though a high proportion of those classed as career successes were lost to the Civil Service either because they declined appointment or because they withdrew from the Competition.

Many of the people surveyed remain in close contact with higher Civil Servants and represent an informed body of opinion about the Civil Service. To some at least, the Civil Service would still prove an attractive field of employment. For these reasons, their comments and criticisms of the higher Civil Service which have been discussed in this paper are all the more important and valuable.

COPY OF QUESTIONNAIRE USED IN FOLLOW-UP STUDY OF ADMINISTRATIVE CLASS "UNSUCCESSFULS"

Please answer all questions in the space provided, either by giving the information requested or by placing a ring around the number or numbers shown against the answer you consider most appropriate

Please leave this column blank

1. How do you think your career prospects for the next five years compare with people of about your age who are Administrative Class Civil Servants?

My career prospects are:

Very much better	1	Indefinite	4
Better	2	A little worse	5
About the same	3	Much worse	6

2. Approximately how many people who are members of the higher Civil Service (i.e. administrative, professional, scientific officer classes etc.) do you come into contact with in an average year?

(*a*) In connection with your work ....

(*b*) Socially ....

3. What considerations made you apply for admission to the Civil Service?

4. (a) Here is a list of factors which some people consider make for a satisfying occupation. How well does your present position meet each of the requirements listed?

Please indicate by placing ticks in the appropriate columns.

(b) If there are any other factors which you think should be included in this list please add them.

(c) Please rank these factors (including your own suggestions) in what you consider to be their order of importance in the last column. (Thus the most important is marked 1, the next most important 2, and so on).

Code	*Factors*	*Extent to which present position meets these requirements*				*Ranking of factors*
		Very well	Well	Fairly well	Badly	
A	Contact with members of the public					
B	Contribution to well-being of society					
C	Earnings					
D	Geographical location					
E	Independence of action					
F	Interest in job					
G	Opportunity to use special skills					
H	Promotion prospects					
I	Security of tenure					
J	Sense of vocation					
	Other factors					
K	....					
L	....					
M	....					

5. Taking the factors listed in Question 4 (including your own suggestions) do you think a career in the Civil Service would have been more satisfactory or less satisfactory than your actual career so far in the light of each of these factors separately? (Please enter the code for each factor in the appropriate box).

A career in the Civil Service would have been;		
	More satisfactory	
	Equally satisfactory	
	Less satisfactory	

6. (a) What particular aspects of the Administrative Class of the Civil Service do you consider make it attractive as an occupation?

(b) What particular aspects of the Administrative Class of the Civil Service do you consider make it unattractive as an occupation?

(c) Supposing you were to consider entering the Civil Service now, about what level of salary would you require?

£.......................p.a.

We are anxious to build up a picture of the development of the careers of people who did not enter the Civil Service. Would you therefore please answer the following questions in as much detail as possible.

7. Please give details of your present and previous employments by filling in the following table. (Temporary and vacation jobs and national service should not be included.) ***This table is reproduced on page 101.***

8. (a) In a number of occupations many people receive benefits and emoluments in addition to their basic salaries. Would you please indicate which, if any, of the following you are receiving now?

Free or subsidised housing	1
Use of car for business only	2
Use of car for business and private purposes	3
Family allowances	4
Interest free or reduced interest loans	5
Bonuses and commissions	6
Payment in kind	7
Contributions by employer to non-contributory superannuation scheme	8
Contributions by employer to contributory superannuation scheme	9
Other (please specify)	

....

Table referred to in Question 7

The Development of A Career

	Industry or Profession	*Position held and nature of work*	*In what town/ city do you work*	*Are you self-employed*	*Year entered*		*Approximate gross salary p.a.*	
							On entering	*Now*
Present employment						/		

If you are at present not in paid employment would you please briefly state the reason (e.g. housewife, ill-health) ....

	Industry or Profession	*Position held and nature of work*	*In what town/ city did you work*	*Were you self-employed*	*Year entered*	*Year left*	*Approximate gross salary p.a*	
							On entering	*On leaving.*
Your first employment								
Second employment								
Subsequent employment								
,,								
,,								
,,								

Please continue on a separate sheet if necessary.

(b) Could you indicate the approximate total annual value to you of these additional emoluments? (i.e. How much extra salary would you require to compensate you if they were not available?)

£..................

9. Have you any income from other work (e.g. fees, including directors' fees, royalties)?

Yes 1
No 2

If yes

(a) What kind of work is this

(b) How much did you receive from this source last year? £.........

In order that the results of this investigation can be compared with the findings of other similar studies would you please provide the following information about yourself.

10. What is your age? ....**years**

11. (a) What type of school did you last attend?

L.E.A. Grammar School 1
Direct Grant School 2
Independent School 3
Foreign School 4
Other (please specify) ....

....

(If you are uncertain about the type of school, please give the name of school and town) ....

....

(b) Were you:

a day pupil 1
a boarder 2

12. Please give details of your undergraduate University career. (If your degree consisted of two or more parts, each of which were classified, please indicate the subject read and the class awarded in each part.)

University/college	*Year*		*Subject read*	*Class of degree awarded*
	Entered	*Left*		

Was your degree:

Internal 1
External 2

13. What other qualifications have you obtained? (e.g. second degree, professional qualifications)

Qualification	***Awarded by (name of University Association etc.)***	***Year obtained***

14. (a) Did you do national service?

Yes 1
No 2

(b) *If yes* please give dates, name of service and last rank held.

15. (a) Are you:

Single 1
Married 2
Separated/widowed/divorced 3

(b) How many children have you?

16. For each of your children who are still at school, will you please indicate the type of school they are now attending.

Type of school	*1st child*	*2nd child*	*3rd child*	*4th child*	*5th child*
L.E.A. Primary	1	1	1	1	1
Preparatory (under 13s)	2	2	2	2	2
L.E.A. Grammar/ Technical	3	3	3	3	3
Secondary modern	4	4	4	4	4
Comprehensive	5	5	5	5	5
Direct Grant	6	6	6	6	6
Independent (over 13s)	7	7	7	7	7
Other (describe)	8	8	8	8	8
Are they:					
Day pupils	9	9	9	9	9
Boarders	10	10	10	10	10

17. What was the occupation of your father when you left University? (Please be as precise as possible, giving industry or profession, occupation and grade of post held. If your father had retired or died please say so and state his last occupation.)

18. Did either of your parents go to University as full-time students?

Father Yes 1 No 2
Mother Yes 1 No 2

19. Can you remember which clubs and societies you belonged to at University? Please indicate whether you held office in any.

Club/Society	*Office held*

20. (a) Please list the associations, clubs and other organisations that you belong to now. Do you hold office in any of them?

Organisation Membership	*Office held*
(i) *Organisations connected with your work*	
(ii) *Public bodies or committees* e.g. boards of govenors	
(iii) *Organisations connected with national or local politics*	
(iv) *Organisations connected with education or training* (e.g. W.E.A., youth organisations)	
(v) *Church or religious organisations*	
(vi) *Organisations connected with welfare* (e.g. charitable organisations)	
(vii) *Civic or community groups* (e.g. ratepayers or consumer associations)	
(viii) Groups connected with leisure (e.g. sporting, cultural)	
(ix) *Any other* (please specify)	

(b) How much time do you spend on all these organisations in an average month? ....hours.

21. Would you please indicate the degree of frequency with which you read the following newspapers.

(a) *Daily Newspapers*

Paper	*Number of issues seen in an average week*						
	None	*One*	*Two*	*Three*	*Four*	*Five*	*Six*
Daily Express	0	1	2	3	4	5	6
Daily Mail	0	1	2	3	4	5	6
Daily Mirror	0	1	2	3	4	5	6
Daily Sketch	0	1	2	3	4	5	6
Daily Telegraph	0	1	2	3	4	5	6
Financial Times	0	1	2	3	4	5	6
The Guardian	0	1	2	3	4	5	6
The Sun	0	1	2	3	4	5	6
The Times							
Other (please specify)	0	1	2	3	4	5	6
....	0	1	2	3	4	5	6
....	0	1	2	3	4	5	6

(b) *Sunday Newspapers*

Papers	*Number of issues seen in an average month*				
	None	*One*	*Two*	*Three*	*Four*
News of the World	0	1	2	3	4
Sunday Express	0	1	2	3	4
Sunday Mirror	0	1	2	3	4
Sunday Telegraph	0	1	2	3	4
Sunday Times	0	1	2	3	4
The Observer	0	1	2	3	4
The People	0	1	2	3	4
Other (please specify)					
....	0	1	2	3	4
....	0	1	2	3	4

22. Which other magazines, newspapers and journals, if any, do you read regularly—that is at least every other issue?

23. If you have any further comments you would like to make that may be of interest in this investigation, please add them here.

Name ....

(If you have changed your name since 1951 (e.g. because of marriage) would you please indicate also your name in 1951..............................**)**

Present address ....

....

....

Thank you for your co-operation in this survey. When you have completed the questionnaire please return it as soon as possible to;

Dr. J. F. Pickering,
School of Social Studies,
University of Sussex,
Falmer,
Brighton

MEMORANDUM No. 4

submitted by

THE CIVIL SERVICE COMMISSION

June, 1967

Administrative Class Follow-up 1966

Introduction

1. At the request of the Fulton Committee, a follow-up survey of present members of the Administrative Class has been carried out with the following aims:

(i) To compare the relative progress and performance of different types of entrant to the Administrative Class (i.e. those who entered as Assistant Principals by the Method I or Method II Open Competitions or by Limited Competitions—both Methods—those who entered direct as Principals by Competition, and those who joined the class as Principals by departmental promotion, mainly from the Executive Class).

(ii) For Competition entrants only, to check the validity of the selection procedure.

2. The survey was carried out by Dr. E. Anstey, Senior Principal Psychologist and head of the Commission's Research Unit. His report covering the major aspects of the review is attached; its coverage has been largely determined by the need to bring the main conclusions to the attention of the Committee at the earliest possible date. The Committee has also asked for information about the correlation of progress and performance with educational background—school, university, degree subject, degree class. Work is continuing on this and a supplementary report will be made as soon as possible, though it may be said now that

(*a*) the current relevance of some of the conclusions will be affected by the marked changes that have occurred since 1963 in the pattern of recruitment by open competition, and

(*b*) many of the sub-groups in the further analysis will be too small for statistically significant conclusions to be drawn.

The survey material

3. Departments were asked by the Treasury to furnish reports as at 1st September 1966, using a special follow-up form, on all entrants to the Administrative Class between 1948 (when " Normal " Competitions were resumed) and 1963. It was clear that rank attained, while an important index of success, needed to be supplemented by subjective assessments of efficiency and potential. The follow-up form therefore asked for the following information:

(A) Ratings on a five-point scale, each fully defined, in respect of:

1. Short-term contacts
2. Relations with colleagues (long-term)
3. Paper work
4. Figure work
5. Meetings (effectiveness at)
6. Drive
7. Stability

(B) Gradings for Present Performance, on the following five-point scale:

Very good indeed	5
Distinctly above average	4
Well up to standard	3
Not quite so good as most officers of his rank	2
Among the less able	1

(C) Gradings for Future Promise, on a three-point scale, worded as follows:
" Please tick below the highest rank which you think he is or will be capable of filling successfully "

The rank of Under Secretary or above	3
The rank of Assistant Secretary	2
A rank not beyond Principal	1

4. The numbers covered were:

Entrants as Assistant Principal by:		
Open competition:	Method I	297
,, ,,	Method II	219
Limited Competition		80
		596

Entrants as Principal:	Direct entry	76
,, ,, ,,	Departmental promotion from other classes	387
,, ,, ,,	Limited Competition	5
		468

5. The first step, as soon as all follow-up reports had been received, was to check whether the standard of reporting in different Government departments was sufficiently uniform to justify pooling the reports, and the batches of departmental reports were closely scrutinised from this aspect. As was to be expected, there were considerable variations between departments in mean rank; but it was found that mean scores (para. 7) bore a reasonable relationship to mean rank, even comparing the departments in which promotion had been particularly rapid

with those where promotion had been slow. The conclusion reached was that there was a satisfactory degree of uniformity of reporting standards.

Interpretation of the material

6. One major difficulty in interpreting the material was the wide variation during the sixteen years under review in the proportions of the different types of entrant to the Administrative Class. For example, of the 165 Assistant Principal entrants in the years 1948–51, 94 were Method I entrants, 40 were Method II entrants and 31 were Limited Competition entrants. Over the years however the proportion of entrants from Method I and the Limited Competition decreased, and the proportion of entrants from Method II increased. Thus the 158 Assistant Principal entrants in 1960–63 consisted of 82 from Method II, but only 59 from Method I and only 17 from the Limited Competition. The fact that more of the earlier entrants will have been promoted than of the later ones has to be borne in mind in any comparison based solely on rank attained. In the case of one important comparison—that between open competition entrants as a whole and departmental promotees—the difficulty has been avoided by comparing samples of people exactly matched according to length of service. In many instances however matched samples of sufficient size were not available, and some other way round the difficulty had to be sought.

7. It was decided that the fairest comparisons would be obtained by the use of a single index of progress and success derived from the three criteria of Rank, Present Performance and Future Promise, with appropriate weightings as described in the report. The index is referred to throughout as the " Combined Criterion Score "; it is thought to be the fairest that could be devised, and there is no reason to think that it is weighted in favour of any one kind of entrant.

Scope of the report

8. The main matters covered in the report are:

(i) a comparison between Method I entrants and Method II entrants, in terms of their progress in the Administrative Class;

(ii) an examination of the validities of the Method I and Method II selection procedures;

(iii) a comparison of all types of entrant (including not only Method I and Method II entrants, but also Limited Competition entrants, Departmental Promotees and Direct entry Principals);

(iv) a more detailed comparison between two equal and matched samples, one of Open Competition entrants, the other of Departmental Promotees, to show specific ways in which their performances differ.

Comparison between Method I and Method II entrants

9. In the sixteen years under review (1948–63) there were 297 Method I entrants and 219 Method II entrants. In terms of rank attained there is not much difference between the two types of entrant: 25% of Method II entrants are Assistant Secretaries as against 23% of Method I entrants. On the other hand a higher proportion of Method I entrants are Principals (67% compared with 57%). But a comparison based on rank attained is misleading since it reflects the pattern of recuitment in the earlier years covered by the survey when Method I provided the majority of entrants. Under the criteria of Present Performance and Future Promise, Method II entrants have a very marked superiority. Over half the

Method II entrants (56%) are graded above average for present performance, compared with only a third (34%) of the Method I entrants. Moreover fewer of the Method II entrants were given the two lowest gradings (7% against 15% of the Method I entrants). Similarly two-thirds of the Method II entrants are thought capable of filling the rank of Under-Secretary or above, compared with half the Method I entrants. On the fairest overall basis of comparison, the "Combined Criterion", the Method II entrants had significantly higher scores than the Method I entrants.

10. A separate study of 167 Assistant Principals who attended long courses at the Centre for Administrative Studies between October 1963 and July 1966, nearly all later entrants to the A.C. than those included in the main follow-up, points to similar conclusions. The 115 entrants by Method II obtained significantly better reports than the 52 entrants by Method I.

11. In any comparision between Method I and Method II one important factor must be kept in mind. The main Method II competition takes place earlier in the year than that by Method I and attracts many candidates who might otherwise had competed by that Method. Many do in fact apply by both Methods but after success by Method II have then no need to continue their Method I candidatures. Thus, though it is factually correct to say that on the criteria of present performance and future promise Method II entrants show a marked superiority, this may be a reflection of the quality of the Method II candidate field: in short, Method II by its very timing recruits a higher proportion of the abler candidates.

Validity of the Method I and Method II selection procedures

12. In order to check the validity of the Method I and Method II selection procedures, correlations were made between marks in the competitions and Combined Criterion Scores. The validity of the Method I procedure as a whole is rather low, precisely how low it is impossible to estimate with accuracy. It is clear however that the marks for the Written Examination part of Method I have no relation to subsequent progress in the Service. Detailed analysis of the fairly large sample of 284 entrants for whom full particulars were available showed no relationship between examination marks and Combined Criterion score. For example, the 13 Method I entrants with the highest Written Examination marks did neither better nor worse than the 13 with the lowest Written Examination marks. This is not to say that the Method I selection procedure has been inefficient in terms of the quality of recruits it has produced; on the basis of the assessments of Present Performance and Future Promise the present review confirms the conclusions of earlier ones, that very few Method I entrants are rated below standard by their Departments. 85% were rated well up to standard or better, and only 2% as poor, while 93% were judged capable of attaining at least Assistant Secretary rank (Method II did even better in these respects—para. 9 above).

13. Evidence about the validity of the Method II procedure is more clear-cut. Comparison of final Method II marks and Combined Criterion scores gives a correlation co-efficient of 0·424, a result not greatly different from those obtained in earlier studies of the validity of the Method II procedure. For reasons explained in the report, correlation co-efficients of the order of 0·4 to 0·5 are probably as high as have been obtained in the field of high-grade selection.

Comparison of all types of entrant

14. To compare all types of entrant, including Departmental Promotees to Principal and Direct-entry Principals, a further analysis was made of all those who became Principals in the years 1948–63. Of the total of 883, 217 were Method I entrants, 132 Method II entrants, 71 Limited Competition entrants, 76 Direct-entry Principals and 387 Departmental Promotees. The fairest basis of comparison seemed to be the Combined Criterion score, adjusted to compensate for the effects of varying lengths of service. Method II entrants obtained significantly higher scores than any other type of entrant. Limited Competition and Method I entrants came next. It seems that Limited Competition entrants fare better than Method I entrants in the early years, because, being on average about five years older, they tend to obtain more rapid promotion from Assistant Principal to Principal, but their advantage disappears with increasing service. Departmental Promotees as a whole obtained significantly lower scores than all other entrants combined, but fared as well as Direct-entry Principals.

15. More detailed analysis showed a connection between the scores of both Departmental Promotion and Direct-entry Principals and the age at which they became Principals, though some of the categories were too small for firm conclusions to be drawn. Officers promoted to Principal when over 40 were given relatively low ratings. Similarly among the Direct-entry Principals scores tended to decline the higher the age of entry.

Detailed comparison between Open Competition entrants and Departmental Promotion

16. It would have been interesting to have made detailed comparisons between different types of entrant, taking account not only of Combined Criterion score, Rank, Present Performance and Future Promise but also of the ratings given under the seven headings in Part 2 of the form (Relations with colleagues, Paper work, etc.). To give meaningful results however the samples needed to be matched exactly according to length of service and also large enough to be significant.

17. The only groups which satisfied those conditions were Open Competition entrants (by Method I or II) and Departmental Promotees. Comparisons were made between two groups, each of 312, matched exactly according to length of service. In terms of rank the Promotees do not fare much worse than the Open Competition entrants (68 Promotees have become Assistant Secretaries as against 100 in the Open Competition sample). The superiority of the Open Competition sample was however more marked in gradings for Present Performance (150 had the two highest gradings as against 51 in the Promotees sample), and most marked for Future Promise (185 of the Open Competition sample are thought capable of promotion above Assistant Secretary as against 32 of the Promotees sample).

18. Comparison between the two samples was also extended to the ratings given under the seven separate headings in Part 2 of the follow-up form. The superiority of the Open Competition sample was most marked for " Paper Work ", marked for " Drive ", " Stability", " Performance at Meetings " and " Figure Work ", and least marked for the two " Personal Contacts "

items. With regard to those two " Personal Contacts " items, the Open Competition sample provided more people rated Very Good (more than half from Method II) but also more people rated Poor (nearly all from Method I).

Summary of Conclusions

19. The main conclusions of the report are as follows:

(i) Method II entrants have made better progress in the Administrative Class than Method I entrants, although it must be borne in mind that the Method II competitions are held earlier in the year, that candidates can compete by both Methods and that the best of these " dual " candidates succeed by Method II and then drop out of Method I.

(ii) The validity of the Method I procedure as a whole is rather low; the Method I written examination marks bear no relation to subsequent progress in the Service.

(iii) Method II has a higher validity, as high as could be expected for selection from a field of candidates of this kind.

(iv) Comparison of all types of entrant to the Administrative Class shows that Method II entrants fare best; that Limited Competition and Method I entrants are the next best; and that Direct-entry Principals Departmental Promotees do least well, especially those who were 35 or more when they became Principals.

(vi) More detailed comparisons show that Open Competition entrants are superior to Departmental Promotees not only in terms of rank attained, but even more markedly in terms of present performance and future promise, and are graded higher under all seven of the separate headings in Part 2 of the Follow-up Report.

20. The Treasury have seen a copy of this note and the accompanying report. They accept the broad conclusions.

Report on the Administrative Class Follow-up (1966)

Aims of the Follow-Up

1. The aims of this Administrative Class follow-up were:

(1) To compare the relative progress and performance of different types of entrant to the Administrative Class (i.e. those who entered as Assistant Principals by the Method I or Method II Open Competitions or by Limited Competitions, those who entered direct as Principals, and those who joined the Class as Principals by departmental promotion mainly from the Executive Class).

(2) For Competition entrants only, to check the validity of the selection procedure.

The field

2. Through the good offices of the Treasury, Departments were asked to furnish reports as at 1st September 1966, using a special follow-up form, on all entrants to the Administrative Class between 1948 (when " Normal " Competitions were resumed) and 1963. Comparisons were complicated by variations

in (*a*) length of service and (*b*) rank on entry to the Administrative Class. Though the same form of report was used for all entrants, those with longer service would have had a greater chance of earning promotion and of obtaining better reports than recent entrants. For statistical purposes, to facilitate comparison of like with like, entrants were divided into four groups, each covering four years of entry. The numbers who originally entered Departments as Assistant Principals are given in Table 1.

Table 1. Classification of Entrants as Assistant Principals (A.P.)

Period	Entry as A.P. years	Method I	Method II	Limited Competition	Total
a	1948–51	94	40	31	165
b	1952–55	81	49	21	151
c	1956–59	63	48	11	122
d	1960–63	59	82	17	158
Total	1948–63	297	219	80	596

It will be seen that during this 16 year period the proportion of entrants from Method I and Limited Competitions decreased and the proportion of entrants from Method II increased (this trend has continued and intensified since).

3. For comparison with the Departmental Promotees to Principal (who were never Assistant Principals) and with Direct-entry Principals, the other entrants must be reclassified with reference to their date of promotion to Principal. Of the people in Table 1, 74 (30 entrants by Method I, 40 by Method II and 4 Limited Competition entrants) were still Assistant Principals on the operative date of 1st September 1966. The remainder are included with the entrants as Principals (including 5 other Limited Competition candidates promoted direct to Principal) in Table 2.

Table 2. Classification of entrants as Principals

Group	Entry as Principal years	Method I	Method II	Limited Competition	Direct Entry	Promotees	Total
A	1948–51	5	3	10	27	66	111
B	1952–55	45	27	27	—	57	156
C	1956–59	100	48	20	9	136	313
D	1960–63	67	54	14	40	128	303
Total	1948–63	217	132	71	76	387	883
E	1964–66	50	47	10	—	—	107
Grand Total	1948–66	267	179	81	76	387	990

4. To make comparison with Competition entrants fairer, Departmental Promotees were themselves classified (see paras. 41 to 47) according to:

(*a*) age on promotion to the Administrative Class,

(*b*) rank immediately before entry to the Administrative Class, and

(*c*) rank on first entering the Civil Service.

Criteria of progress and success

5. Rank attained is obviously an important index of success, but it is not by itself sufficient. It may be affected by variations in promotion prospects among Departments and by other chance factors; it is inevitably affected also by length of service, at least to the extent that no officer can expect promotion until he has served a certain number of years in his present grade. In addition, rank is a crude index, having for most post-war entrants only the three steps of Assistant Principal, Principal and Assistant Secretary. It is thus difficult to adjust for length of service so as to permit the possibility, for example, of giving roughly equal assessments of merit to a " Very Good " Principal on the verge of promotion and a newly promoted Assistant Secretary who has not yet made good in that grade. For these reasons, the basic criterion of Rank attained needed to be supplemented by subjective assessments of efficiency and potentiality. To obtain these assessments on as uniform a basis as possible, a special follow-up form was used, a copy of which is attached as Annex 1 to this report.

6. Part 1 of the follow-up form convered personal particulars and details of the entrant's record and promotions. Part 2 asked for ratings on a five-point scale, each fully defined, under the seven headings of:

1. Short-term contacts
2. Relations with colleagues (long-term)
3. Paper work
4. Figure work
5. Meetings (effectiveness at)
6. Drive
7. Stability

The main purpose of Part 2 was to stimulate the reporting officer to consider the person thoroughly from these seven aspects before making his gradings in Part 3. Some results obtained with the seven separate ratings are given in paragraphs 36 to 40. This part of the analysis provided strong evidence that reporting officers had tackled their job conscientiously and effectively.

7. Part 3 contained the two important gradings. Overall Grading for efficiency at present duties, Present Performance for short, and Future Promise. The grading for Present Performance was on the five-point scale:

Very good indeed	5
Distinctly above average	4
Well up to standard	3
Not quite so good as most officers of his rank	2
Among the less able	1

The grading for Future Promise was on a three-point scale, worded as follows:

" Please tick below the highest rank which you think he is or will be capable of filling successfully."

The rank of Under Secretary or above	3
The rank of Assistant Secretary	2
A rank not beyond Principal	1

8. These assessments of Present Performance and Future Promise had their limitations also, mainly because, however carefully the follow-up reports were

made (and evidence will be quoted that they were made with considerable care and discrimination) they were of course subjective, especially those of Future Promise. Assessments of Present Performance are based on considerable evidence, but the majority are related to performance in grades below the main career grade of Assistant Secretary.

9. One of the difficulties in this follow-up stems from the wide variations during the sixteen years under review in the proportions of people entering the Administrative Class by different methods of entry. If a high proportion of entrants by one method came in during the early years, they would have had greater chances of promotion by 1966 than would entrants by another method who came in, mainly, during the later years. Where it has been possible (as in paras. 34 to 40 of the report) to compare samples of people exactly matched according to length of service, this has been done. In such circumstances, any of the criteria can yield fair comparisons. In many instances, however, matched samples of sufficient size were not available, and some other way round this difficulty had to be sought.

10. For the fairest comparisons, and in order to obtain the clearest evidence of whether differences were statistically significant, it was necessary to use some single index of progress and success, derived from the three criteria of Rank attained, Present Performance, and Future Promise. In order to allow for the greater variation in Present Performance scores (on a five-point scale), compared with Future Promise (three-point scale) or Rank (Assistant Principals marked 0, Principals 1, Assistant Secretaries 2), it was decided to adopt as this index a " Combined Criterion Score " (C.C. score) defined as follows:

$$\text{C.C. score} = 3 \times \text{Rank} + \text{Present Performance} + 2 \times \text{Future Promise}.$$

This definition was an arbitrary one but can be justified by the following considerations. Making allowance for the different scales, Present Performance and Future Promise carry about equal weight in the determination of C.C. scores. The weighting of 3 given to Rank is such as to allow some overlap in C.C. score between ranks, but not too much. Applying the above formula, it will be seen that the limits of variation in C.C. score according to rank attained were:

Assistant Principals	3–11
Principals	6–14
Assistant Secretaries	11–17

Thus, A " Distinctly above average " Principal (if expected to rise to Under-Secretary) and a moderate Assistant Secretary (not expected to rise above Assistant Secretary) would each receive a C.C. score of 13. The much wider variation in C.C. scores derived from combining the three criteria created a more flexible index of assessment. This made it possible both to review departmental standards of reporting (see para. 16) and to consider schemes of adjustment for length of service (see paras. 24 and 32).

11. Finally it should be remarked that, though this particular index may be criticised on other grounds (some people have argued, for instance, that more weight should be attached to Rank, and others that less weight should be attached to it), it is not open to the criticism of being weighted so as to favour one kind of entrant, since it was determined in a plan of analysis settled and circulated before any follow-up forms were received.

12. It was regarded as impracticable to request reports on Under-Secretaries (eight of the entrants had been promoted to this rank), and they were automatically awarded a C.C. score of 18.

13. The actual distributions of C.C. scores are given in Table 3.

Table 3. Distributions of C.C. scores obtained by each Rank

C.C. score	Assistant Principals	Principals	Assistant Secretaries
17			28
16			64
15			69
14		42	9
13		114	109
12		45	20
11	6	45	1
10	14	257	
9	9	31	
8	6	52	
7	28	78	
6	7	18	
5	0		
4	3		
3	1		
Mean	8·0	10·3	14·4
No. of people	74	682	300

Within each rank there was, as expected, a peak corresponding to the "normal" entrant graded 3 for Present Performance (Well up to standard) and 2 for Future Promise (Potentiality up to Assistant Secretary)—the corresponding C.C. scores are 7 for Assistant Principals, 10 for Principals, and 13 for Assistant Secretaries. There was also a peak corresponding to the " fliers " graded 4 for Present Performance (Distinctly above average) and 3 for Future Promise (Potentiality above Assistant Secretary)—the corresponding C.C. scores are 10 for Assistant Principals, 13 for Principals, and 16 for Assistant Secretaries. With Assistant Secretaries, the second peak was somewhat flatter, being shared with people obtaining C.C. scores of 15, most of whom were graded 3 for Present Performance and 3 for Future Promise. Among Principals, there was a third, lower peak at C.C. score of 7, obtained mainly by older Principals graded 2 for Present Performance (Not quite so good as most officers of the rank) and 1 for Future Promise (Potentiality not beyond Principal).

14. The variation of mean C.C. scores with length of service in rank is shown in Table 4.

15. Since this follow-up related to entrants to the Administrative Class between 1948 and 1963, there are no entries in the Assistant Principal columns for 1964–66. For the same reason, entries in the Principal columns for 1964–66 relate only to Competition entrants as Assistant Principals promoted to Principal during those years, and not to Departmental Promotees. To this extent, the high mean C.C. scores for those years are misleading. The only safe conclusion from Table 4 is that, within each rank, mean C.C. score is much the same for officers

Table 4. Variations of mean C.C. score with year of entry into Rank

Year of entry into rank	Assistant Principals		Principals		Assistant Secretaries	
	No.	Mean C.C. score	No.	Mean C.C. score	No.	Mean C.C. score
1966	—		[32	11·0]	58	14·6
1965	—		[41	11·4]	73	14·2
1964	—		[38	11·3]	57	14·8
1963	43	7·8	74	10·7	28	14·7
1962	13	8·6	73	10·7	24	14·6
1961	15	7·8	70	10·6	16	14·2
1960	3	7·7	81	10·1	8	14·6
1959	0		79	10·2	7	14·9
1958	0		53	10·6	4	15·0
1957	0		40	9·8	9	13·6
1956	0		35	9·0	4	13·5
1954–5	0		29	9·0	7	13·4
1952–3	0		14	9·8	1	12·0
1950–1	0		11	7·6	0	—
1948–9	0		12	8·3	4	12·2
Total	74	8·0	682	10·3	300	14·4

with different lengths of service up to about nine years after which it begins to fall off. A likely explanation for this comparative stability of C.C. score is that the tendency for reports on individual officers to improve gradually with increasing experience is roughly balanced by the tendency for more efficient officers to be promoted out of the rank in question. Any more detailed conclusion from Table 4 would be unjustified because of the variation during the period 1948–63 in the proportions from different modes of entry.

Review of departmental standards of reporting

16. The first step, as soon as all follow-up reports had been received, was to compare the C.C. scores recorded for officers according to Department, in order to check whether the standard of reporting in different Government Departments was sufficiently uniform to justify pooling the reports. Had one or more Departments seemed markedly out of step with the others, it would have been necessary to exclude the reports from that Department. Attached as Annex 2 is a list of the 30 Departments which contributed follow-up reports, 10 " major " Departments each supplying 40 or more reports, and 20 " minor " Departments. 1,064 reports were furnished in all, with a mean rank of 1·23 (counting Assistant Principals as 0, Principals as 1, Assistant Secretaries as 2, and Under-Secretaries as 3) and a mean C.C. score of 11·4. As expected, there were considerable variations between Departments in mean rank. In the Ministry of Technology, for instance, it was as high as 1·6 (No Assistant Principals, 7 Principals, and 10 Assistant Secretaries), so that it was not surprising that this Department should also have recorded the highest mean C.C. score, namely 12·8. In the four Scottish Departments, on the other hand, the mean rank was 1·1, and the mean C.C. score 10·9. Despite these variations, it was reassuring to note that for each Department the mean C.C. score bore a reasonable relationship to the mean rank, particularly when regard was paid to the make-up of the Administrative Class within that Department. In the Post Office, for instance, an unusually high proportion of Administrative Class

officers (58 out of 77) were Departmental Promotees who entered the Administrative Class as Principals. It was not surprising therefore that the mean rank of 1·3 was slightly higher than average, though the mean C.C. score of 11·2 was slightly lower than average. After close scrutiny of each batch of reports, it was decided that there were no grounds for supposing that any Department was seriously out of step as regards standard of reporting in parts 2 and 3 of the follow-up form. It was therefore concluded that reports from all Departments could be combined for statistical analysis.

Entrants at Assistant Principal level

17. Entrants at Assistant Principal level were classified according to method of entry (Method I, Method II or Limited Competition), and according to period

Table 5. Progress made by Method I, Method II, and Limited Competition entrants (percentages shown in brackets)

	Period a 1948–51		Period b 1952–55		Period c 1956–59		Period d 1960–63		Total 1948–63		
	I	II	I	II	I	II	I	II	I	II	L.C.
Rank attained											
Assistant Secretary	57 (61)	37 (92)	11 (14)	15 (31)	—	3 (6)			68 (23)	55 (25)	39 (49)
Principal	37 (39)	3 (8)	70 (86)	34 (69)	63 (100)	45 (94)	29 (49)	42 (51)	199 (67)	124 (57)	37 (46)
Assistant Principal							30 (51)	40 (49)	30 (10)	40 (18)	4 (5)
Total	94 (100)	40 (100)	81 (100)	49 (100)	63 (100)	48 (100)	59 (100)	82 (100)	297 (100)	219 (100)	80 (100)
Present Performance											
Very good indeed	12 (13)	13 (33)	7 (9)	8 (16)	6 (10)	12 (25)	1 (2)	10 (12)	26 (9)	43 (20)	4 (5)
Distinctly above average	22 (23)	9 (22)	23 (29)	26 (53)	17 (27)	19 (40)	13 (22)	26 (31)	75 (25)	80 (36)	22 (27)
Well up to standard	44 (47)	17 (43)	40 (49)	13 (27)	30 (47)	14 (29)	38 (64)	38 (47)	152 (51)	82 (37)	50 (63)
Not quite so good as most others	14 (15)	1 (2)	9 (11)	2 (4)	8 (13)	3 (6)	7 (12)	7 (9)	38 (13)	13 (6)	4 (5)
Less able	2 (2)		2 (2)		2 (3)			1 (1)	6 (2)	1 (1)	
Total	94 (100)	40 (100)	81 (100)	49 (100)	63 (100)	48 (100)	59 (100)	82 (100)	297 (100)	219 (100)	80 (100)
Future Promise											
Under-Secretary or above	51 (54)	32 (80)	40 (50)	39 (80)	28 (45)	33 (69)	29 (49)	42 (51)	148 (50)	146 (67)	32 (40)
Assistant Secretary	35 (37)	8 (20)	35 (43)	10 (20)	30 (47)	15 (31)	27 (46)	38 (47)	127 (43)	71 (32)	45 (56)
Principal	8 (9)		6 (7)		5 (8)		3 (5)	2 (2)	22 (7)	2 (1)	3 (4)
Total	94 (100)	40 (100)	81 (100)	49 (100)	63 (100)	48 (100)	59 (100)	82 (100)	297 (100)	219 (100)	80 (100

of entry into the Administrative Class, as described in para. 2 and Table 1. Table 5 compares the progress made by the three kinds of entrant, using the criteria of Rank attained, Present Performance, and Future Promise. Because of the smallness of their numbers, figures for Limited Competition entrants are shown for the total period only, in the right hand column of the table. The percentages corresponding to each row of figures are given immediately below that row.

18. Table 5 illustrates some of the advantages but also some of the pitfalls of simple comparisons. First comparing Method I with Method II entrants, within each period the Method II entrants fare generally better as regards Rank attained, Present Performance and Future Promise. The better performance of Method II entrants in respect of both gradings was reflected also in the figures for the total period. In respect of Rank attained, however, over the total period only a slightly higher proportion of Method II entrants (25% against 23%) had been promoted to Assistant Secretary and a higher proportion (18% against 10%) had remained Assistant Principals. This was entirely because a much higher proportion of Method II entrants had come into the Administrative Class during the latest period 1960–63 and had thus had less chance of promotion.

19. Comparing the figures for Limited Competition entrants in the right-hand column of Table 5 with the corresponding figures for Open Competition entrants, it will be seen that a much higher proportion (49%) had been promoted to Assistant Secretary. But this finding could be accounted for by the fact that a high proportion (31 out of 80) of Limited Competition entrants had come into the Administrative Class during the earlier period (a) from 1948–51 and had thus had greater chance of promotion. Moreover Limited Competition entrants were on average some five years older than Open Competition entrants (average ages about 28 and 23 respectively) and could thus expect more rapid promotion from the cadet grade of Assistant Principal to Principal. For Present Performance, Limited Competition entrants obtained a high proportion (63%) of gradings of 3, " Well up to Standard ", with lower proportions graded either " Very Good Indeed " or " Below average ". For Future Promise, Limited Competition entrants obtained less favourable assessments, 40% being graded as having the potentiality to make successful Under-Secretaries, compared with 50% of Method I entrants and 67% of Method II entrants. The evidence is thus somewhat mixed, and overall comparison between Limited and Open Competition entrants is difficult without calculating Combined Criteria scores.

20. The mean C.C. score for each group of entrant to the Administrative Class at Assistant Principal level is shown in Table 6 immediately under the entry for number of people in the group. It is immediately apparent from Table 6 that C.C. score is appreciably affected by period of the entry, earlier entrants by each method having higher mean scores than later entrants. As the proportion of entrants by different methods during the total period varied considerably (falling for Method I and Limited Competition and rising for Method II), this complicates the position and prevents any significance being attached to differences between the crude overall mean C.C. scores. Any such figure would be inflated if a high proportion of officers entered the Administrative Class early and would be depressed if a high proportion entered late.

Table 6. Mean C.C. scores of entrants as Assistant Principals

Period	Entry as A.P. years	Method I	Method II	Limited Competition	Total
a	1948–51 Mean C.C. score	94 13·07	40 15·22	31 13·71	165 13·72
b	1952–55 Mean C.C. score	81 11·56	49 13·33	21 13·14	151 12·35
c	1956–59 Mean C.C. score	63 10·97	48 12·40	11 11·55	122 11·58
d	1960–63 Mean C.C. score	59 9·51	82 10·00	17 9·47	158 9·76
Total	1948–63 Crude Overall mean	297 11·50	219 12·23	80 12·36	596 11·88
Mean *adjusted* C.C. score (as defined in paragraph 24)		10·99	12·39	11·75	11·61

21. The relationship between C.C. score and the classification by rows and columns in Table 6 was investigated by Analysis of Variance. The difference between rows was found to be significant, the probability that this result was due to chance being less than 1%. This confirms the obvious fact that C.C. score is appreciably affected by period of entry, and that C.C. scores from different periods should not be combined without making an appropriate adjustment to allow for length of service.

22. The difference between columns was also found to be significant, showing that C.C. score depends significantly upon method of entry. Method I entrants clearly fared worst, but it was not obvious at first sight whether there was a significant difference between entrants by Method II and Limited Competition. The mean C.C. score was higher for Method II entrants than for Limited Competition entrants in each row of Table 5, but the crude overall mean was slightly higher (12·36 as against 12·23) for Limited Competition than for Method II. This was because the Limited Competition column contained a high proportion of entrants from the early periods (tending to inflate the overall mean), whereas the Method II column contained a high proportion of entrants from the later periods (tending to depress the overall mean).

23. The next step was to devise a method of compensating for the effect of length of service on C.C. score. Table 7 shows, for each method of entry, the increase in mean C.C. score between successive periods. Because of the smallness of some of the groups, some of the fluctuations in this table may be attributed to chance, but the average figures in the final row indicate a clear trend.

24. The average increase in C.C. score was about $\frac{4{\cdot}34}{3} = 1{\cdot}45$ points every four years, or about 0·36 points per annum. The increase was greater, about 2 points, between periods d and c, i.e. after about 5–7 years of service. This was to

Table 7 Average increase in C.C. scores between successive periods (Assistant Principals)

Method of entry	Between d and c	Between c and b	Between b and a	Between d and a
Method I	1·46	0·59	1·51	3·56
Method II	2·40	0·93	1·89	5·22
Limited Competition	2·08	1·59	0·57	4·24
Total	5·94	3·11	3·97	13·02
Average	1·98	1·04	1·32	4·34

be expected, since a high proportion of Assistant Principals become promoted to Principal after that length of service. Promotion automatically increases their C.C. score by 3, but their grading for Present Performance may fall for a time by 1 point (A Distinctly above Average A Assistant Principal newly promoted to Principal is unlikely to be graded higher than Well up to Standard), thus resulting in a net gain of 2 points. Between periods c and b, and between b and a, the average increase was rather more than 1 point. The slightly higher increase between periods b and a, i.e. after about 13–15 years of service (particularly for Method I and Method II entrants) may be attributed to the fact that after this length of service some of the " fliers " are beginning to be promoted to Assistant Secretary. From this evidence it was concluded that the effects of varying lengths of service could be compensated for by adjusting the raw C.C. score to an " Adjusted C.C. score " as follows:

Adjustment of C.C. scores for entrants as Assistant Principals

Entrants from group a (1948–51)	Subtract 2
Entrants from group b (1952–55)	Subtract 1
Entrants from group c (1956–59)	No change
Entrants from group d (1960–63)	Add 2

25. Mean adjusted C.C. scores were calculated for each method of entry, and these figures were added to Table 5, for comparison with the unadjusted means. The adjusted means were:

Method II	219 entrants	12·39
Limited Competition	80 entrants	11·75
Method I	297 entrants	10·99

Limited Competition entrants obtained significantly higher mean C.C. scores than Method I entrants. The difference of 0·76 points is entirely attributable to the fact that, being on average about five years older, they tend to obtain more rapid promotion in the early years, and is equivalent to about two years of service.

26. Method II entrants obtained rather higher mean C.C. scores than Limited Competition entrants and significantly higher mean C.C. scores than Method I entrants. The margin of their average superiority over Method I entrants was about 1·4 points. This could be expressed in different ways according to the criteria used: thus, it is approximately equivalent to half the entrants being graded

a point higher both for Present Performance and for Future Promise. As in all previous reports commenting on follow-up results for entrants by Methods I and II, one important reservation must be stressed. Since Method II competitions are held earlier in the year than Method I competitions, they tend to attract candidates eligible to compete by either Method who, if successful by Method II, have then no need to compete by Method I. Thus, though it is factually correct to state that Method II entrants have made better progress in the Administrative Class than Method I entrants, their superiority may (on this evidence alone) be wholly or partly due to the superior quality of the Method II candidate field. Evidence as to the validity of the two methods of selection will be given later in this report, in paras. 48 to 53.

Entrants at Principal level

27. Entrants at Principal level were classified according to the process by which they became Principals and the year of appointment to that grade, as described in para. 3 and Table 2. Departmental Promotees were divided into three groups, P(H) who had been Higher Executive Officers immediately before promotion to Principal; P(S) who had been Senior Executive Officers; and P(O) who had held a variety of other ranks immediately before promotion. The mean C.C. scores (unadjusted) for each group are shown in Table 8 immediately under the entry for number of officers in the group.

Table 8. Mean C.C. scores: Classifications according to year of appointment as Principal

Period	Method I	Method II	Limited Competition	Direct Entry	P(H)	P(S)	P(O)	Total
A 1948–51	5 14·60	3 15·67	10 14·00	27 12·07	10 13·30	16 13·13	40 12·40	111 12·84
B 1952–55	45 13·20	27 15·41	27 14·30	0 —	7 11·86	28 10·93	22 12·23	156 13·27
C 1956–59	100 12·10	48 13·94	20 11·35	9 10·11	47 9·79	53 9·62	36 11·19	313 11·41
D 1960–63	67 11·00	54 12·33	14 11·21	40 10·15	36 9·75	57 9·82	35 9·97	303 10·65
E 1964–66	50 11·14	47 11·70	10 10·20	—	—	—	—	107 11·30
Total	267 11·94	179 13·11	81 12.49	76 10·83	100 10·27	154 10·30	133 11·41	990 11·62
Adjusted Mean A-D only (see para. 33)	217 12·17	132 13·78	71 12·35	76 10·64	100 10·36	154 10·28	133 10·90	883 11·57

28. With Principals as with Assistant Principals, C.C. score is appreciably affected by period of entry, the earlier entrants by each method having higher mean scores than later entrants. The seeming reversals in trend between the

overall means for period A and B, and between D and E, are explained by the fact that the officers promoted in period A were mainly Departmental Promotees, whereas the officers promoted in period E were all Competition entrants. These officers were included in Table 8 since they had all entered the Administrative Class between 1948 and 1963.

29. The relationship between C.C. score and the classification by rows and columns in Table 8 was investigated by Analysis of Variance. The difference between rows was found to be significant, the probability that this result was due to chance being less than 1%. This confirms that C.C. score is appreciably affected by period of entry, and that C.C. scores from different periods should not be combined without making an appropriate adjustment to allow for length of service.

30. The difference between columns was also found to be significant, the probability that this result was due to chance being less than 1%. Method II entrants clearly fared best, followed by Limited Competition entrants. A separate comparison, contrasting all Competition entrants combined with all Departmental Promotees combined, showed that the Competition entrants obtained significantly higher C.C. scores than the Departmental Promotees, the probability that this result was due to chance being less than 1%. Comparing the mean scores in Table 8 obtained by P(H), P(S) and P(O) entrants—people who immediately prior to promotion had been Higher Executive Officers, Senior Executive Officers, and in a variety of other ranks—there was little difference between P(H) and P(S), but P(O) entrants tended to fare better than either.

31. The next step was to estimate the effect of length of service on C.C. score. Table 9 gives, for each method of entry, the increase in mean C.C. score between successive periods. Figures shown in brackets were based on comparatively few cases and were given half weight when calculating the average figures shown in the final row of the table.

Table 9. Average increase in C.C. scores between successive periods (Principals)

Method of Entry	Between D and C	Between C and B	Between B and A	Weighted total between D and A
Method I	1·10	1·46	(1·04)	3·08/2½
Method II	1·61	1·47	(0·26)	3·21/2½
Limited Competition	(0·14)	(2·95)	(−0·30)	1·40/1½
Direct-Entry Principals	(−0·04)	(0·98)	(0·98)	0·96/1½
Departmental Promotees	0·26	1·44	1·17	2·87/3
Weighted Total	3·02/4	6·34/4	2·16/3	11·52/11
Average	0·76	1.58	0·72	1·05

32. The average increase in C.C. score was about 1·05 points every four years, or about 0·26 points per annum. The increase was somewhat greater, about 1·58 points, between periods C and B, i.e. after about 9–11 years of service. This was to be expected, since a fair proportion of Principals promoted to Assistant Secretary after that length of service, with a consequent likely net gain of 2 points in their C.C. score (plus 3 points for promotion with a probable loss of

1 point in grading for Present Performance). The differences did not seem sufficiently great, however, to warrant departing from the most simple scheme of adjustment. It was concluded that the effects of varying lengths of service could be roughly compensated for by adjusting the raw C.C. score to an "Adjusted C.C. score" as follows:

Adjustment of C.C. scores for entrants as Principals

Entrants from group A (1948–51)	Subtract 2
Entrants from group B (1952–55)	Subtract 1
Entrants from group C (1956–59)	No change
Entrants from group D (1960–63)	Add 1

33. Mean adjusted C.C. scores were calculated for each method of entry, and these figures were added to Table 8, for comparison with the unadjusted means. At this stage, no account was taken of entrants from group E, Competition entrants promoted Principal in 1964–66, since there were no Departmental Promotees with whom to compare them. The adjusted means were:

Method II	132 entrants	13·78
Limited Competition	71 entrants	12·35
Method I	217 entrants	12·17
Promoted from a rank other than Higher or Senior Executive Officer	133 entrants	10·90
Direct-Entry Principals	76 entrants	10·64
ex-Higher Executive Officers	100 entrants	10·36
ex-Senior Executive Officers	154 entrants	10·28
Total	883 entrants	11·57

Method II entrants obtained significantly higher mean C.C. scores than any other type of entrant. Limited Competition and Method I entrants came next; the initial superiority of Limited Competition over Method I entrants as Assistant Principals was due to more rapid promotions in the early years (see paragraph 25) and would seem to disappear with increasing service. Departmental Promotees as a class obtained significantly lower C.C. scores than all other entrants combined, but fared as well as Direct-Entry Principals. P(O) entrants obtained significantly higher mean C.C. scores than P(H) or P(S) entrants and slightly higher scores than Direct-Entry Principals (this difference was not significant). The margin of superiority of other entrants by all methods combined (mean C.C. score 12·39) over Departmental Promotees (mean C.C. score 10·51) was about 1·9 points. This would be equivalent to all the Competition entrants being graded a point higher for Present Performance and nearly half of them a grade higher also for Future Promise.

Comparison between Open Competition entrants and Departmental Promotees

34. One would have liked to have made more detailed and extensive comparisons between different types of entrant, taking account not only of total C.C. score but of its three components (Rank, Present Performance and Future Promise) and also of the ratings given under the seven separate headings on Part 2 of the form. To give meaningful results, however, the samples would have to be matched exactly according to length of service and also large enough to make it possible for observed differences to achieve statistical differences.

The only groups that seemed to satisfy these conditions were Open Competition Entrants (by Methods I or II) and Departmental Promotees. Because so few Open Competition entrants were to be found in group A of Table 8 (only 8 in all), this group was omitted. The numbers of follow-up forms available within the other groups and the numbers included in the sample are given in Table 10.

Table 10. Composition of Matched Samples

Period	Numbers available in		Included in sample from each group
	Open Competition group	Promotees group	
B 1952–55	72	56	56
C 1956–59	148	135	135
D 1960–63	121	128	121
Total	341	319	312

35. The 29 forms omitted from the Open Competition group (16 from period B and 13 from period C) were selected in representative proportions from Methods I and II and from the various C.C. scores. The 7 forms omitted from the Departmental Promotees group (all period D) similarly were representative of the C.C. scores obtained by Promotees in period D. Thus the two samples were matched exactly according to years of entry as Principal and were representative of the two modes of entry into the Administrative Class.

36. Table 11 compares, for each sample, the numbers who had been promoted to Assistant Secretary and the distributions according to gradings for Present Performance, Future Promise, and C.C. score (unadjusted).

Table 11. Comparison between Matched Samples, various criteria

Criterion		Score	Competition sample	Promotees sample
Rank attained	Assistant Secretary	1	100	68
	Principal	0	212	244
	Mean score		0·321	0·218
Present Performance	Very good indeed	5	47	4
	Distinctly above average	4	103	47
	Well up to standard	3	129	198
	Not quite so good as most	2	29	55
	Among the less able	1	4	8
	Mean score		3·513	2·949
Future Promise (Potentiality)	Under Secretary	3	185	32
	Assistant Secretary	2	111	188
	Principal	1	16	92
	Mean score		2·542	1·808
C.C. score (unadjusted)		16–17	46	9
		14–15	60	14
		12–13	101	59
		10–11	74	133
		8– 9	16	42
		6– 7	15	55
Mean combined criterion score			12·349	10·211

37. With all four criteria, the Open Competition sample obtained significantly higher mean scores than the sample of Departmental Promotees, the probability that this result was due to chance being less than 1% in each case. To assess the relative superiority of the Competition sample under the four headings, it was necessary to convert the differences in mean scores into " Standardised mean differences " by dividing them by the standard deviation of the scores in question. Standardised mean differences have the advantage of being on the same scale and therefore directly comparable. These additional data are given in Table 12.

Table 12. Comparison between Matched Samples, Standardised Mean Differences

Criterion	Mean scores			Standard deviation of scores	Standardised mean difference
	Competition entrants	Departmental promotees	Difference		
Rank attained	0·321	0·218	0·103	0·443	0·231
Present performance	3·513	2·949	0·564	0·752	0·750
Future promise	2·542	1·808	0·734	0·700	1·049
C.C. score (unadjusted)	12·349	10·211	2·138	2·794	0·765

The superiority of the Open Competition sample was least marked for Rank attained, most marked for Future Promise. The superiority in C.C. score was about the same as for Present Performance and intermediate in value between the figures for Rank attained and Future Promise. The fact that Departmental Promotees are nearly always older than Competition entrants when they become Principals and have had longer experience may explain why they do not fare much worse in obtaining promotion to Assistant Secretary (68 against 100); but they are judged to have far less potentiality for promotion above Assistant Secretary (32 against 185).

38. Comparison between the two samples was now extended to the ratings given under the seven separate headings on Part 2 of the form. This comparison served the obvious purpose of indicating the particular respects in which the superiority of Competition entrants was thought to be most and least marked. It served another important purpose in showing to what extent reporting officers in general had managed to discriminate effectively between the different items in Part 2. If broadly similar results were obtained for all items, this would cast grave doubt on the discrimination of reporting officers and would suggest that they had succumbed to " halo effect " (tending to rate people up or down in all respects depending on their general impression of the people concerned). Conversely, if very different patterns of results emerged, this would strengthen confidence in the ability of reporting officers to make accurate and fair appraisals. Actual results for the two samples are given in Table 13.

39. The patterns of results obtained for different items varied very considerably, pointing to the care and discrimination with which the follow-up forms had been filled in. It was noticeable, for example, that, whereas for items 3–7 the Competition sample obtained both more high ratings and fewer low ratings than the Promotees sample, with items 1 and 2 this was not so. For both these " Personal

Table 13. Comparison between Matched Samples, different Items in Part 2

	Score	Comp.	Prom.
Item 1 Short term contracts	5 4 3 2 1	33 156 99 22 2	13 163 119 14 3
Mean score		3·628	3·543
Item 2 Relations with colleagues (long term)	5 4 3 2 1	56 161 73 21 1	26 173 99 13 1
Mean score		3·801	3·673
Item 3 Paper work	5 4 3 2 1	16 178 100 17 1	1 103 172 34 2
Mean score		3·612	3·215
Item 4 Figure work	5 4 3 2 1	15 126 116 4 0	10 108 147 5 2
Mean score		3·582	3·437
Item 5 Meetings (effectiveness at)	5 4 3 2 1	42 159 103 8 0	15 148 138 10 1
Mean score		3·752	3·532
Item 6 Drive	5 4 3 2 1	57 132 102 18 3	21 119 135 30 7
Mean score		3·711	3·375
Item 7 Stability	5 4 3 2 1	104 128 63 15 2	50 139 97 23 3
Mean score		4·016	3·673

With Item 4 (figure work) the entries do not add up to 312, since on a number of forms no rating was made (insufficient evidence).

Contacts " items, the Competition sample obtained more ratings of 5 (33 against, 13, and 56 against 26), but also more ratings of 1 or 2 (24 against 17, and 22 against 14). This interesting result followed from the fact that the Competition sample was a mixture of 197 entrants by Method I and 115 entrants by Method II. Taking items 1 and 2 together, of the 89 high ratings (of 5) in the Competition sample, 43 were awarded to Method I entrants and 46 to Method II entrants. Of the 46 low ratings (1 or 2) in the Competition sample, 37 were awarded to Method I entrants and only 9 to Method II entrants.

40. Here again, in order to assess the relative superiority of the Competition sample under the seven headings, it was necessary to convert the differences in mean scores into " Standardised mean differences ", which are directly comparable. These additional data are given in Table 14.

Table 14. Comparison between Matched Samples, Standardised Mean Differences

Item	Mean scores			Standard deviation of scores	Standardised mean difference
	Competition entrants	Departmental promotees	Difference		
1. Short-term contacts	3·628	3·543	0·085	0·774	0·110
2. Relations with colleagues	3·801	3·673	0·128	0·765	0·168
3. Paper work	3·612	3·215	0·397	0·701	0·567
4. Figure work	3·582	3·437	0·145	0·633	0·229
5. Meetings	3·752	3·532	0·220	0·693	0·318
6. Drive	3·711	3·375	0·336	0·865	0·389
7. Stability	4·016	3·673	0·343	0·892	0·385

The superiority of the Open Competition sample was:

Most marked for	Paper work
Marked for assessments of	Drive, Stability, Performance at Meetings, and Figure work
Least marked for	The two Personal Contacts items (Short-term contacts and Relations with Colleagues)

These findings make sense. The Open Competition entrants, by virtue of their superior academic training, ought to be very much better at Paper Work; but there is no obvious reason why the Departmental Promotees should be inferior at making short-term contacts or at achieving satisfactory relationships with colleagues.

Effects of age of appointment as Principal

41. In the preceding comparisons with Competition entrants, it was suspected that Departmental Promotees might be at a disadvantage since they nearly always became Principals at a later age, and this fact tended to restrict their prospects of obtaining promotion beyond Assistant Secretary. The possibility was therefore investigated that there might be a significant connection between age on promotion to Principal and subsequent progress and success in the Administrative Class. In this event, even though Departmental Promotees as a whole fared significantly worse than Competition entrants as a whole, it might be the case that some kinds of Departmental Promotee, if promoted while young, might do as well as certain kinds of Competition entrant.

42. Departmental Promotees were classified into four groups, W, X, Y and Z according to their age on becoming Principals, and the distributions of their (unadjusted) C.C. scores are shown in Table 15.

43. It is clear from Table 15 that age on promotion to Principal does have a significant connection with C.C. score for Departmental Promotees. All 883

Table 15. C.C. scores of Promotees classified according to age on becoming Principals

Unadjusted C.C. score	W under 35	X 35–39 years	Y 40–44 years	Z 45–54 years	Total
16–18	9	13	3	1	26
14–15	10	5	5	2	22
12–13	30	40	12	3	85
10–11	14	73	46	10	143
8– 9	2	16	20	10	48
6– 7	5	24	25	9	63
Total	70	171	111	35	387
Mean score	12·50	10·78	9·77	9·37	10·67

entrants as Principal during 1948–63 (i.e. excluding only those Competition entrants as Assistant Principals during 1948–63 who were promoted to Principal in 1964–66) were therefore reclassified into the four groups W, X, Y and Z. P(O) entrants, those who immediately prior to promotion had been serving in some grade other than Higher Executive Officer or Senior Executive Officer, had already been shown to do better than other Promotees (see paragraph 30). These P(O) entrants were therefore further subdivided into four groups depending on whether their rank immediately before promotion had been Executive Officer, Chief Executive Officer, some G.P.O. grade, or any other grade (M for Miscellaneous). This increased the chance of identifying any sub-groups which had achieved unusually good reports. Comparison was first made between Departmental Promotees as a class and the various kinds of Competition entrant, with the results shown in Table 16.

Table 16. Mean adjusted C.C. scores. Classifications according to age of appointment as Principal

Age on Promotion	Method I	Method II	Limited Competition	Direct Entry	Departmental Promotees	Total
W Under 35	222 12·25	124 13·72	66 12·56	12 12·08	70 11·83	494 12·60
X 35–39	—	1 15·00	4 9·25	23 10·87	171 10·56	199 10·59
Y 40–44	—	1 13·00	1 11·00	28 10·36	111 9·83	141 9·96
Z 45–54	—	1 13·00	—	13 9·54	35 9·41	49 9·52
Total	222 12·25	127 13·72	71 12·35	76 10·64	387 10·51	883 11·56

The group W promotees, those promoted when under 35, obtained much higher C.C. scores than those promoted when older. Even so, their mean C.C. score of 11·83 was slightly below that of Direct-Entry Principals, 12·08 (this difference was not significant) and considerably below the mean C.C. scores for Method II, Limited Competition, and Method I entrants (these differences were significant).

44. Comparison was now made between the different kinds of Departmental Promotee, with the results shown in Table 17.

Table 17. Mean adjusted C.C. scores of different kinds of Departmental Promotee

Age on promotion	Rank immediately before promotion						Total
	E.O.	H.E.O.	S.E.O.	C.E.O.	G.P.O. grade	Miscel-laneous	
W under 35	4 7·25	21 12·48	17 11·88	3 12·0	1 9·0	24 12·08	70 11·83
X 35–39	1 11·0	51 10·22	71 10·51	8 10·88	11 10·36	29 11·28	171 10·56
Y 40–44	—	20 9·55	53 9·58	13 10·69	13 10·38	12 9·83	111 9·83
Z 45–54	1 6·0	8 8·11	13 9·77	5 10·20	1 13.0	7 10·0	35 9·41
Total	6 7·67	100 10·36	154 10·28	29 10·79	26 10·42	72 11·21	387 10·51

The numbers in most cells of Table 17 were too small for significant differences to emerge, but the following conclusions could be drawm:

(*a*) Among people promoted to Principal when under 35, those promoted from Higher Executive Officer were the most successful. They did about as well as Limited Competition entrants and rather better than Method I entrants or Direct-Entry Principals, though much less well than Method II entrants. Higher Executive Officers promoted when over 35 were much less successful.

(*b*) Apart from the under 35 Higher Executive Officers, the most successful Departmental Promotees were those promoted from miscellaneous grades when under 40 years of age. A high proportion of these officers had been specialists with University degrees, such as Scientific Officers, Statisticians, Economists, and Inspectors of various kinds.

(*c*) People promoted to Principal when over 40 years of age had comparatively little chance of further success, whatever their previous service and experience.

45. This stage of the analysis was rounded off by tabulating the mean (adjusted) C.C. scores of all the groups of entrants as Principal hitherto considered. The results are shown in Table 18.

46. Finally, Departmental Promotees were reclassified according to original rank when they first entered the Civil Service. For this purpose, they were divided into the following five groups:

A Entered as Clerical Assistants, or an equivalent rank
C Clerical Officers
E Executive Officers

Table 18. Mean adjusted C.C. scores of different kinds of Principal

Kind of entrant	No. of people	Mean C.C. score
Method II (all)	132	13·78
Limited Competion entrants (all)	17	12·35
Method I (all)	217	12·17
Direct-Entry Principals (all)	76	10·64
of whom, W (aged under 35 on entry)	12	12·08
X (aged 35–39 on entry)	23	10·87
Y (aged 40–44 on entry)	28	10·36
Z (aged 45–54 on entry)	13	9·54
Departmental Promotees (all)	387	10·51
of whom, W (aged under 35 on entry)	70	11·83
X (aged 35–39 on entry)	171	10·56
Y (aged 40–44 on entry)	111	9·83
Z (aged 45–54 on entry)	35	9·41
Total Entrants, 1948–63	883	11·56

M Minor and Manipulative grades, Boy Messenger, Postman, Typist, Telephonist, etc.

O Other (mainly specialist) grades

Their mean (adjusted) C.C. scores are given in Table 19.

Table 19. Mean adjusted C.C. scores of Promotees classified according to rank on first entering the Civil Service

	A	C	E	M	O	Total
W under 35	10 12·20	15 11·93	19 11·84	3 7·67	23 12·13	70 11·83
X 35–39	27 10·22	74 10·86	21 9·71	1 11·00	48 10·65	171 10·56
Y 40–44	18 9·50	45 10·23	14 9·36	7 9·14	27 9·78	111 9·83
Z 45–54	7 8·00	3 9·33	6 9·67	5 7·40	14 10·85	34 9·41
Total	62 10·08	137 10·74	60 10·30	16 8·44	112 10·77	386 10·51

47. The numbers in most cells of Table 19 were too small for differences in means to attain statistical significance, but one interesting fact emerged. A surprisingly small proportion of Promotees, namely 60 out of 387 or 15·5%, had started their careers in the Executive Class [It must be remembered that a number of the best young Executive Officers or Higher Executive Officers, 71 officers with a mean C.C. score of 12·35, had been successful in Limited Competitions]. 55% started their careers in clerical or minor grades; the mean C.C. score of the 35% who entered as Clerical Officers was slightly higher than that of Executive entrants, though this difference was not significant.

Validity of the selection procedures

48. For Competition entrants only, the validity of the selection procedures was checked by correlating marks in the entrance examinations with C.C. score.

For Departmental Promotees, no such check up could be made, since no selection data were available.

49. With Method I candidates, the final order of merit was determined by adding marks in the Written Examination (out of a total in the years 1948–62 of 1,000, in the year 1963 of 900) and in the Board Interview (out of a total of 300). Full selection data were available for 284 out of the 297 entrants by Method I. Product-moment correlation coefficients were calculated between (adjusted) C.C. score, Written Examination mark, Board Interview mark and Total mark, based on the sample of 284, and were then corrected for selectivity i.e. estimates were made of the correlation coefficients that would have been obtained if follow-up reports had been available on all candidates, not only on those who actually entered the Service. The relevant data are given in Table 20.

Table 20. Validity of selection variables, 284 entrants by Method I

Selection variable	Raw correlation with C.C. score	Standard deviation of variable		Corrected coefficient
		Among successes	Candidate field	
Written examination	−0·0042	47·40	—	—
Interview Board	0·1232	15·05	55·70	About 0·4
Total mark	0·0620	46·32	135·65	About 0·18

50. The raw correlation of 0·062 between Total Mark and C.C. score was not statistically significant. The estimate of the validity of the whole selection procedure, corrected for selectivity, namely about 0·18, must therefore be treated with considerable reserve.

51. What is certain is that the Written Examination had no validity. For all papers (compulsory general subjects and optional specialist subjects) combined, the raw correlation coefficient was −0·0042; the corresponding coefficient for the optional papers only was +0·046, not significantly different from zero. Detailed inspection of the full scatter for this fairly large sample of 284 people showed no relationship between Written Examination marks and C.C. score. To illustrate this point in terms of individual people, full particulars are given in Annex 3 of the 13 Method I entrants obtaining the highest Written Examination marks, 701 or more (Group A), and of the 13 Method I entrants obtaining the lowest Written Examination marks, 551 or less (Group B). In terms of all the criteria, Rank obtained, Present Performance, Future Promise, and C.C. score, Group B fared just as well as Group A. Both groups contained 8 people who were making relatively good progress (as defined in Annex 3) and 5 people who were making relatively poor progress. On the other hand, the raw correlation of 0·1232 between Interview Mark and C.C. score, though low, is statistically significant at the 5% level. When corrected for selectivity, it attains the fairly high figure of about 0·4. To illustrate this point, the mean C.C. score of the 15 Method I " fliers " at interview (with Board marks of more than 260) was 11·60, whereas the mean C.C. score of the 9 candidates with lowest interview marks (160 or less) was 8·78. [The 30 recent entrants by Method I still serving as Assistant Principals were included in this analysis, so that these mean scores are not comparable with those quoted in Table 18.] In the middle of the range of

interview marks, the relationship with C.C. score, though less dramatic, was still positive.

52. With Method II candidates, the final order of merit was determined by the Final Selection Board (F.S.B.), though they had studied, and been strongly influenced by, reports from the Civil Service Selection Board (C.S.S.B.). Product-moment correlation coefficients were calculated between (adjusted) C.C. score, C.S.S.B. mark and F.S.B. mark, based on the sample of 219 entrants, and were then corrected for selectivity. The relevant data are given in Table 21.

Table 21. Validity of selection variables, 219 entrants by Method II

Selection variable	Raw correlation with C.C. score	Standard deviation of variable		Corrected coefficient
		Among successes	Among candidates reaching CSSB/FSB	
C.S.S.B.	0·1054	13·73	41·06	0·302
F.S.B.	0·1485	13·50	42·06	0·424

53. The raw correlation of 0·1054 between C.S.S.B. mark and C.C. score is of borderline significance (the probability that this was a chance result being about 1/7), and the corrected validity of 0·302 must therefore be taken as only a rough estimate. The raw correlation of 0·1485 between F.S.B. mark and C.C. score is statistically significant at the 5% level.

54. It is interesting to compare these figures with the corresponding validity coefficients obtained in the 1965 Foreign Service follow-up and in Professor P. E. Vernon's (end of probation) 1950 follow-up of Reconstruction entrants to the Administrative Class.

*Table 22. Comparative validity of C.S.S.B. and F.S.B., three follow-ups**

	A.C. 1966	F.S. 1965	Vernon 1950
C.S.S.B.	0·302	0·387	0·505
F.S.B.	0·424	0·463	0·563

* These correlation coefficients of the order of 0·4 to 0·5 may not sound impressive, but they are probably as high as have ever been obtained in the field of high-grade selection. One limiting factor is the reliability of the criterion itself which, for the reasons discussed in the report, is hardly likely to exceed 0·7. The reliability of the criterion imposes an upper limit on all validity coefficients. Some writers go so far as to make a further correction for attenuation, i.e. compensating for the estimated unreliability of the criterion, but this procedure has not been resorted to in this follow-up.

In each case, F.S.B. succeeded in increasing the validity of C.S.S.B. predictions. For the rather higher validities obtained by Professor Vernon there are two likely explanations:

(*a*) Reconstruction candidates (aged up to 30 or 31) were older than Normal Competition candidates (aged mainly 22–25), so that more factual information was available about them.

(*b*) During the Reconstruction period, C.S.S.B. was operated by a small team of regular assessors, which made it much easier for the same standards to be maintained. During the 16 year period 1948–63 there was inevitably some variation in standards both at C.S.S.B. and at F.S.B., despite the care taken to maintain standards. For example, though 240 remained the official F.S.B. pass mark throughout this period, a proportion of candidates awarded 230–235 marks during the years 1948–51, though not immediately declared successful, were in fact later offered appointments. This variation in standard inevitably depressed all the correlation coefficients.

55. Turning now to Direct-Entry Principals, the 49 entrants since 1959 had passed through C.S.S.B., but the 27 entrants before 1959 had not. (These earlier candidates were given a personal interview followed by the Board Interview). For the 49 entrants who passed through C.S.S.B., the correlation coefficient between C.S.S.B. mark and adjusted C.C. score was very low and did not differ significantly from zero. The product-moment correlation between F.S.B. mark and adjusted C.C. score, based on all 76 entrants, was 0·097, a figure which is not significant for so few cases. If corrected for selectivity (competition for these posts had been extremely severe) this validity coefficient would be about 0·4.

56. Finally validity coefficients were calculated for the 80 Limited Competition entrants, who had passed through C.S.S.B. and F.S.B. The product-moment correlation coefficient between C.S.S.B. mark and adjusted C.C. score was 0·141. For such a small number of cases, this correlation was not significant —the probability that this was a chance result being about 1/4. If corrected for selectivity, the validity coefficient would be about 0·37. The raw correlation coefficient between F.S.B. mark and adjusted C.C. score was −0·058, a figure which of course did not differ significantly from zero. This was the one instance where F.S.B. did not seem to improve on C.S.S.B.'s predictions, but in view of the smallness of the sample and the lack of statistical significance little, if any, weight can be attached to the Limited Competition correlations.

Reports from the Centre for Administrative Studies

57. Since 1963 new Assistant Principals have been attending long (20 week) courses at the Centre for Administrative Studies. Though the function of these courses is to train Assistant Principals, mainly in administration and economics, rather than to assess their operational efficiency, the Director of the Centre has very kindly furnished to the Civil Service Commission the best reports that could be made on the information available, for reference as an independent interim assessment of the Assistant Principal's progress. The criterion used, as in the main follow-up, was a combination of assessments of Present Efficiency and Future Promise. Reports have been studied for 167 Assistant Principals who attended courses between October 1963 and July 1966. As these were nearly all later entrants to the Administrative Class than those included in the main follow-up, the two studies could not be fused directly together.

58. The 52 Assistant Principals who had entered by Method I obtained a mean criterion score of 5·827. The 115 Method II entrants obtained a mean criterion score of 6·348. This difference was significant, the probability that this result was due to chance being less than 5%.

59. For the 115 Method II entrants, the correlation coefficients obtained with criterion score were:

C.S.S.B. mark 0·240, significant at 1% level
F.S.B. mark 0·222, significant at 2% level

If corrected for selectivity, either of these correlations would exceed 0·5, but for this size of sample there would be little point in attempting a more detailed estimate.

60. It is of interest to compare the gradings of these 115 Method II entrants by F.S.B. as " fliers " (260 marks or more) and other entrants (240–255 marks) with the corresponding division at the Centre for Administrative Studies. For this purpose, students at the Centre could be regarded as " fliers " if graded " Very Good indeed " or " Distinctly above average " for present duties, and with potentiality above Assistant Secretary. The comparative grouping is shown in Table 23.

Table 23. Comparison between F.S.B. marks and reports by Centre for Administrative Studies

	Report by Centre for Administrative Studies		
F.S.B. mark	Normal	" fliers "	Total
260 or more	14 (56%)	11 (44%)	25
240–255	73 (81%)	17 (19%)	90
Total	87	28	115

The tetrachoric correlation coefficient is 0·45 with F.S.B. mark (and 0·52 with C.S.S.B. mark), which is highly significant. The probability that this result was due to chance is less than 1%. If corrected for selectivity, this correlation would be even higher, exceeding 0·7. Though the number of cases was small, there is thus some evidence that, with reports from the Centre for Administrative Studies as an interim criterion, C.S.S.B. and F.S.B. were quite successful in picking out people regarded as potential fliers.

Staff—In Confidence

Annex 1

This report will be used for research purposes only, and no note of its contents will be made on an officer's personal file.

Civil Service Commission

FOLLOW UP REPORT

(for all entrants to the Administrative Class between 1948 and 1963 inclusive, either by Open or Limited Competitions (but *excluding* Reconstruction Competitions or by internal promotion.)

PART 1

Surname and Christian names..

Male or Female..

Surname on entry to A.C. if different from above..

Date of birth..19.........

Department..

Date of assignment to Department..19.........

Present rank..

Date of appointment to present rank..19.........

Method of entry into Administrative Class:

(1) By Open Competition (give date against whichever Method applies)

(*a*) Method I..19.........

(*b*) Method II..19.........

(*c*) Direct Entrant Principal..19.........

(2) By Limited Competition (give rank on first entering Civil Service and date of entry into Administrative Class)

Rank.. Date..19.........

(3) By Internal Promotion (give rank on first entering Civil Service and date of entry into Administrative Class)

Rank.. Date.......................................19.........

For entrants by (2) or (3), give rank immediately before entry into Administrative Class ....

Record of previous promotions within the Administrative Class

	Date		Rank
(1) On	....19.........	promoted to	....
(2) On	....19.........	promoted to	....
(3) On	....19.........	promoted to	....

Parts 2 and 3 need not be completed for any officer who has already reached the rank of Under Secretary

PART 2

Report on aspects of performance. Please tick the appropriate box.

1. *Short-term Contacts*

Very impressive in manner and address	1	☐
Usually makes a good impression	2	☐
Handles people quite well	3	☐
His manner tends to be unfortunate	4	☐
Poor at making intitial contacts	5	☐

2. *Relations with Colleagues* (long-term)

Wins and retains their highest regard	1	☐
Is generally liked and respected	2	☐
Gets on well with everyone	3	☐
Not very easy in his relationships	4	☐
A difficult colleague	5	☐

3. *Paper Work*

Brilliant on paper	1	☐
Written work always clear, cogent and well set out	2	☐
Generally expresses himself clearly and concisely	3	☐
Written work just good enough to get by	4	☐
Paper work is a weakness	5	☐

4. *Figurework*

Exceptionally good at all kinds of figure work 1 ☐
Handles and interprets figures very well 2 ☐
Competent at figurework 3 ☐
Handling of figures leaves something to be desired 4 ☐
Not good with numerical data 5 ☐

5. *Meetings*

Extremely effective 1 ☐
Puts his points across convincingly 2 ☐
Expresses himself adequately 3 ☐
Barely competent 4 ☐
Ineffective 5 ☐

6. *Drive*

Exceptional vitality, well directed to the job 1 ☐
More effective than most in getting things done 2 ☐
Usually gets a move on 3 ☐
Rather inclined to take things easy 4 ☐
Needs constant chasing 5 ☐

7. *Stability*

Highly dependable; adapts well to new situations 1 ☐
Takes most difficulties in his stride 2 ☐
Reacts quite well to normal stress 3 ☐
Occasionally flustered or put out 4 ☐
Easily thrown off balance 5 ☐

PART 3

Present Performance

Comparing him with other established officers of the same grade in the Civil Service as a whole, I consider him to be on his present duties:

(*Please tick the appropriate box*)

Very good indeed	Distinctly above average	Well up to standard	Not quite so good as most officers of his rank	Among the less able

Future Promise

Please tick below the highest rank which you think he is or will be capable of filling successfully.

The rank of Under Secretary or above	
The rank of Assistant Secretary	
A rank not beyond Principal	

COMMENTS

Please add free comments on any officer who has been graded as not quite up to standard or is unlikely to be successful in a rank beyond Principal, and on any other officer whose performance does not seem to have been covered adequately by the ratings in Parts 2 and 3.

Signature of Reporting Officer..

Date..

Annex 2
to Report on Administrative Class Follow-up

Comparison between Departments, Entrants to A.C. during 1948–63

Department	No.	Mean Rank	Mean C.C. Score
1. M.A.F.F.	63	1·1	11·7
2. Aviation	65	1·3	12·2
3. Education and Science	44	1·1	10·4
4. Health	50	1·2	10·8
5. Home Office	56	1·1	10·5
6. Housing and Local Government	57	1·2	10·4
7. Post Office	77	1·3	11·2
8. Trade	81	1·1	11·5
9. Transport	47	1·4	11·8
10. Treasury	62	1·2	11·8
11. C.R.O.	17	1·35	12·2
12. Customs and Excise	38	1·3	10·6
13. Defence (Central)	25	1·2	12·4
14. Defence (Air)	29	1·3	11·6
15. Defence (Army)	39	1·2	11·2
16. Defence (Navy)	23	1·5	12·4
17. Economic Affairs	15	1·2	10·9
18. Exports Credit Guarantee	11	1·4	11·8
19. Revenue	21	1·4	12·8
20. Labour	29	1·4	12·8
21. Overseas Development	21	1·4	12·8
22. Power	24	1·3	12·2
23. Public Building and Works	25	1·4	11·6
24. Social Security	34	1·1	11·5
25. Technology	17	1·6	12·8
26. Scottish Ag. and Fish.	19	1·0	10·3
27. Scottish Develop.	19	1·1	10·8
28. Scottish Education	20	1·3	11·7
29. Scottish Home	29	1·1	10·8
30. Welsh	7	1·1	9·1
Ten "Major" Departments	602	1·20	11·3
Twenty other Departments	462	1·26	11·5
Grand Total	1064	1·23	11·4

Mean rank was obtained counting A.P. as 0, Principal 1, Assistant Secretary 2, and Under-Secretary 3.
C.C. Score = 3 Rank + Present Performance + 2 × Future Promise.

Annex 3
to Report on Administrative Class Follow-up

Method I Entrants to A.C.
Relationship between W.E. Marks and Follow-Up Reports

Statistical findings in paragraph 51 of the report could be illustrated in terms of individuals by comparing the progress made in the Civil Service by the people with the highest and lowest Written Examination marks. From the 284 Method I entrants between 1948 and 1963 we therefore identified two groups, each of 13 people:

Group A, the entrants obtaining the highest W.E. marks, 701 or more.
Group B, the entrants obtaining the lowest W.E. marks, 551 or less.

For each entrant is listed Year of entry, Rank attained by 1st September, 1966; grading for Present Performance on a scale from 5 (Very Good indeed) to 1 (Among the less able); and grading for Present Performance on a scale from 3 (Potentiality above Assistant Secretary) to 1 (Potentiality not above Principal). Finally the entrants' overall progress was judged to be

Good if he had been promoted to Assistant Secretary and was giving satisfaction (graded 3 or better),

or if still a Principal or A.P. was graded above average (4 or better) or as having Potentiality above Assistant Secretary.

(relatively)
Poor if not qualifying for Good as defined above.

Group A. Entrants with Highest W.E. Marks

Number	Year of entry	Rank attained	Present performance	Future promise	Overall progress
1	1948	Assistant Secretary	4	3	Good
2	1949	Principal	1	1	Poor
3	1949	Assistant Secretary	4	3	Good
4	1950	Principal	3	2	Poor
5	1952	Principal	4	3	Good
6	1953	Principal	3	3	Good
7	1953	Principal	3	2	Poor
8	1954	Principal	2	2	Poor
9	1954	Principal	4	3	Good
10	1954	Principal	3	2	Poor
11	1956	Principal	3	3	Good
12	1956	Principal	5	3	Good
13	1957	Principal	4	3	Good
Average	1952·7	2 A.S. 11 Principals	3·3	2·5	8 Good 5 Poor

Group B. Entrants with lowest W.E. marks

Number	Year of entry	Rank attained	Present performance	Future promise	Overall progress
1	1948	A.S.	3	3	Good
2	1949	A.S.	3	2	Good
3	1949	A.S.	2	2	Poor
4	1950	A.S.	4	3	Good
5	1951	Principal	3	2	Poor
6	1951	A.S.	2	2	Poor
7	1951	A.S.	5	3	Good
8	1956	Principal	4	3	Good
9	1957	Principal	4	3	Good
10	1957	Principal	2	2	Poor
11	1959	Principal	3	2	Poor
12	1961	Principal	4	3	Good
13	1961	Assistant Principal	3	3	Good
Average	1953·9	6 A.S. 6 Principals 1 Assistant Principal	3·2	2·5	8 Good 5 Poor

Comparing the two groups, Group B, although averaging one year service less than Group A, has the better promotion record with 6 promotions to Assistant Secretary as against 2 such promotions. In other respects the average performance is practically identical. Each Group contains 8 people making good progress and 5 people making (relatively) Poor progress.

This comparison is in accord with the statistical conclusion that the Written Examination has zero validity. Those obtaining very high marks in it have on average fared no better than those obtaining low marks in it.

FURTHER NOTE

submitted by

THE CIVIL SERVICE COMMISSION

August, 1967

Administrative Class Follow-up 1966

1. Paragraph 2 of a Note by the Civil Service Commission on the Administrative Class Follow-up 1966, submitted to the Fulton Committee in June, said that the Committee had asked additionally for information about the correlation of progress and performance with educational background—school, university, degree subject, and degree class—and that work was being done on this. A supplementary report covering these matters is attached. The opportunity has been taken to include figures relating the progress of Method II entrants with their performance in three parts of the selection procedure: the intelligence tests, the Qualifying Examination, and the interview by the Final Selection Board.

Educational factors

2. Since the aim of the selection procedure is to test intellectual and personal qualities and to apply a uniform standard of assessment regardless of educational background, the expectation was that the differences in follow-up performance between the sub-categories of entrants classified according to educational factors would be small. This is borne out by the conclusions of the report. The differences in performance between entrants from different types of school, either by Method I or by Method II, were extremely small and definitely not significant. With regard to entrants from different Universities and different degree subjects, the differences in performance were small and in no case attained clear statistical significance though, as pointed out in the earlier main paper, many of the sub-groups are too small for firm statistical conclusions to be drawn. With regard to Degree Class, again the differences were small and not quite statistically significant, but, both for Method I and Method II entrants, they are consistent with the expectation that entrants with Firsts would include a slightly higher proportion of people of the higest quality than those with Seconds.

Intelligence test ratings

3. With Method II candidates, the relationship between Intelligence Test ratings and follow-up performance was investigated and showed that C.S.S.B. and F.S.B. had attached just about the right amount of weight to Intelligence Test rating as one piece of evidence among the many to be taken into account in the overall assessment.

Qualifying Examination marks

4. With Method II candidates, the relationship between Qualifying Examination mark and follow-up performance was investigated. It was found that,

among the highly selected group of entrants followed-up, those with very high Qualifying Examination marks had received on average rather better reports than those who had only just reached the qualifying standard—full particulars are given in Annex 1. However, from the very limited data available it is not possible to make any reliable estimate of the validity of the Qualifying Examination when corrected for selectivity.

Final Selection Board marks

5. With Method II candidates, more detailed studies have confirmed the positive relationship between F.S.B. mark and follow-up reports already demonstrated in the main report (para. 53 and Table 21). Full particulars are given in Annex 2, Part A.

6. During the years 1964–1966 there has been a marked increase in the proportion of Method II entrants from universities other than Oxford and Cambridge. Though it is too early for any follow-up information for these years, the 1948–1963 figures of Method II candidates awarded the highest F.S.B. marks have been continued for 1964–1966 in Part B of Annex 2 and classified to show how the educational background of this top group compares with that of the other successful candidates.

Supplementary Report on the Administrative Class Follow-Up (1966)

Purpose of this Additional Investigation

1. The main report issued in June compared the relative progress and performance of different types of entrant to the Administrative Class and, for Competition entrants only, checked the validity of the different selection procedures. The main purpose of this additional work is to see how assessments of progress and performance were related to educational background—school, university, degree subject and degree class. With Method II entrants, the opportunity was taken to investigate also the relationship between progress and intelligence test ratings and Qualifying Examination and Final Board marks.

2. It should be made clear at the outset that in all this work the hypothesis tested was a null hypothesis. In other words, if the Civil Service Commission had done its job of selection well, the expectation was that no marked differences would emerge between the overall progress made by different sub-categories of entrant when classified according to such factors as school, university, degree subject, degree class and (for Method II candidates) intelligence test rating and Qualifying Examination mark. Doubtless there would have been differences in the quality of the candidate field when classified into the different sub-categories, but, if a uniform standard of assessment had been applied to all candidates, the hypothesis was that any differences in the quality of sub-categories would properly be reflected in varying selection (success) ratios. If within a particular sub-category an unusually high proportion of candidates was of an acceptable standard, the proportion of successes would be unusually high; the overall progress of entrants within this sub-category would not be expected to be any better or any worse than that of entrants as a whole (unless within the unusually high proportion of candidates up to acceptable standard there was also an unusually high proportion of candidates of exceptionally high quality, in which case the overall progress made by entrants from this sub-category would be

expected to be slightly above the general average). Taking Method I candidates, for example, the selection ratio among candidates studying P.P.E. at Oxford has been about 3:1 (3 candidates per place gained) compared with an overall selection ratio among all candidates during the period 1948–63 of about 5½. This difference in selection ratios could reflect the high quality of P.P.E. students as a whole, or the fact that the choice of the Administrative Class as a career had a special appeal to able people in this group, or a combination of both factors. In any event, if this favourable selection ratio resulted from applying a uniform standard of assessment to all candidates, one would expect the overall progress made by ex-P.P.E. entrants to be only slightly better than that of other categories of entrant —the difference (if any) being attributable to the higher proportion of candidates of exceptionally high quality or the special relevance of the P.P.E. course to the work of an Administrative Class civil servant.

3. Method II candidates take a series of tests at C.S.S.B., including 2 or 3 intelligence tests. The combined intelligence test rating is one of the many pieces of evidence about a candidate taken into account by C.S.S.B. and F.S.B. assessors. The selection ratio among candidates with very high intelligence test ratings has been about 4:1 (4 such candidates at C.S.S.B. per place gained) compared with a selection ratio among candidates with comparatively low intelligence test ratings of about 8. The intelligence test rating is only one ingredient in assessing intellectual ability, let along general suitability. A candidate with a modest intelligence test rating may be judged to make good use of his native ability, and a candidate with superior native ability may be judged not to make effective use of it. Nevertheless, a low[1] intelligence test rating does give pause for thought. Candidates known to have low intelligence test ratings would need strong compensating personal qualities, and in this category only a small proportion, judged to have the best personalities, were successful. One might expect these people to have fared about as well in the follow-up as the much larger proportion of extremely intelligent entrants, some of whom might have been less well qualified in other ways. In short, if due weight (not too little, not too much) had been attached to intelligence test rating in the selection process, the result should be that no significant differences in performance could be found among different sub-categories of entrant. If any significant differences did emerge—contrary to the general null hypothesis —this would suggest that more (or less) importance should have been attached by the selectors to the intelligence test rating.

4. Similar expectations would apply to the written Qualifying Examination (Q.E.) for Method II candidates. This was used first as a sieve, eliminating the weaker candidates outright. The Q.E. marks of those candidates reaching C.S.S.B. and F.S.B. were also taken into account by the assessors as one relevant piece of evidence. Here again therefore it could be expected that differential selection ratios would be found, and that there would be no appreciable difference between the average progress made by entrants with high and low Q.E. marks, except that possibly among entrants with the highest Q.E. marks there might be a slightly higher proportion of " flyers ".

---

[1] Throughout this section of the report, the term " low " is used relative to the general level of C.S.S.B. candidates, which is extremely high. A candidate with a " low " intelligence test rating, by C.S.S.B. standards, may still be well above the average of the general population.

5. In all this work the follow-up criterion used was " Combined Criterion Score ", as defined in paragraph 10 of the main report. This was a combination of Rank and gradings for Present Performance and Future Promise, each carrying about equal effective weight. C.C. score was adjusted to allow for varying lengths of service, as explained in paragraph 24 of the main report.

Method I Entrants, Schools and Universities

6. Results for entrants classified according to type of school are given in Table 1.

Table 1. Method I entrants 1948–63, Schools

Type of School	Number of entrants	Mean C.C. score	Selection ratio
Public, boarding	57	11·05	About 4·0*
Public, day	28	11·11	
Independent and Direct Grant	61	10·90	5·6
Local Education Authority	151	11·00	6·2
Total	297	10·99	5·5

* This is the selection ratio for "All Boarding Schools" (most of which are Public Schools).

The differences in mean C.C. scores are extremely small and clearly not significant.

7. Results for entrants classified according to university are given in Table 2.

Table 2. Method I entrants, Universities

University	Number of entrants	Mean C.C. score	Selection ratio
Oxford	124	11·02	3·8
Cambridge	85	10·85	3·4
London	40	10·65	10·9
Scottish	30	11·30	5·4
Others	18	11·78	16·6
Total	297	10·99	5·5

The differences in mean C.C. score are small; none approaches statistical significance.

8. Results for entrants classified according to degree subject are given in Table 3. Most of the differences in C.C. score are small and none is significant. It is of some interest, however, that P.P.E. candidates had the highest proportion of successes (1 in 3) and obtained the highest mean C.C. scores. Modern Languages candidates had the lowest proportion of successes (1 in 8·6) and obtained the lowest mean C.C. scores.

Table 3. Method I entrants, Degree Subjects

Degree Subject	Number of entrants	Mean C.C. score	Selection ratio
Greats	45	11·31	3·5 (Greats and Classics)
Classics	27	11·74	
History	106	10·74	4·7
P.P.E.	18	11·78	3·0
Modern Languages	38	10·34	8·6
Maths and Science	14	11·57	6·3
Economics	25	11·20	6·5
Other subjects	24	10·54	8·6
Total	297	10·99	5·5

9. Results for entrants classified according to degree class are given in Table 4.

Table 4. Method I entrants, Degree Class

Degree Class	Number of entrants	Mean C.C. score	Selection ratio
Firsts	93	11·43	1·8
All Seconds,	200	10·81	6·3
Upper	73	10·64	5·1
Undivided	116	10·83	4·8
Lower	11	11·64	36·2
Thirds (or Passes)	4	10·50	34·7
Total	297	10·99	5·5

The difference between mean C.C. scores for entrants with Firsts (11·43) and with Seconds (10·81) was found to be not quite statistically significant, the odds against this being a chance result being rather less than 20:1. This finding was consistent with the expectation that, not only would candidates with Firsts have a much more favourable selection ratio than other candidates, but also entrants with Firsts would include a slightly higher proportion of people of the highest quality than those with Seconds.

Method II Entrants, Schools and Universities

10. Results for entrants classified according to type of school are given in Table 5.

Table 5. Method II entrants 1948–63, Schools

Type of School	Number of entrants	Mean C.C. score	Selection ratio
Public, boarding	71	12·46	About 7.6* (Public, boarding and Public, day)
Public, day	29	12·41	
Independent and Direct Grant	36	12·50	10·9
Local Education Authority	83	12·29	15·3
Total	219	12·39	10·7

* This was the selection ratio for "All Boarding Schools" (most of which are Public Schools).

The differences in mean C.C. score are extremely small and clearly not significant.

11. Results for entrants classified according to university are given in Table 6.

Table 6. Method II entrants, Universities

University	Number of entrants	Mean C.C. score	Selection ratio
Oxford	102	12·18	7·7
Cambridge	73	12·82	7·5
London	18	12·33	23·3
Scottish	15	12·73	20·5
Others	11	11·27	61·5
Total	219	12·39	10·7

The differences in mean C.C. score are small. Setting aside " Others ", the largest difference, between Cambridge entrants (12·82) and Oxford entrants (12·18), was found to be of borderline statistical significance, the odds against this being a chance result being just over 20:1.

12. If this apparent superiority of Cambridge entrants by Method II was not due to chance, possible explanations would be either that Cambridge candidates were slightly under-rated by C.S.S.B. and the F.S.B. or that they included an unusually high proportion of people of the highest quality. In any case, in the following analysis by degree subjects, it was considered advisable for Oxford and Cambridge entrants to be distinguished from the others. This would make it possible to judge to what extent any apparent differences between the mean C.C. scores of entrants with different degree subjects might be attributed to their being drawn largely from Oxford or Cambridge.

Table 7. Method II entrants, Degree Subjects

Degree Subject	Number of entrants				Mean C.C. score				Selection ratio
	Oxf.	Camb.	Other	All	Oxf.	Camb.	Other	All	
Greats	43	—	—	43	12·21	—	—	12·21	5·4 (Greats and Classics)
Classics	—	11	5	16	—	12·64	11·60	12·29	
History	27	19	7	53	12·00	13·05	11·57	12·32	10·0
P.P.E.	14	—	—	14	12·71	—	—	12·71	8·5
Modern Languages	13	17	3	33	12·31	12·12	14·33	12·39	19·4
Maths and Science	1	6	1	8	8	12·67	9	11·63	9·8
Economics	—	12	16	28	—	13·25	12·38	12·75	12·2
Others	4	8	10	22	11·75	13·50	11·89	12·48	12·3
None	—	—	2	2	—	—	13	13·00	28·3
Total	102	73	44	219	12·18	12·82	12·10	12·39	10·7

The differences in mean C.C. score are small and, for these small sub-groups, none approaches statistical significance. For example, students of History, Economics and " Other subjects " from Cambridge would appear to have made rather better progress than other entrants, but these apparent differences may well be due to chance.

13. Results for entrants classified according to degree class are given in Table 8.

Table 8. Method II entrants, Degree Class

Degree Class	Number of entrants	Mean C.C. score	Selection ratio
Firsts	74	12·62	3·4
All Seconds,	143	12·25	12·4
Upper	57	12·40	10·9
Undivided	76	12·16	9·7
Lower	10	12·10	36·8
None	2	13·00	59·0
Total	219	12·39	10·7

The slight positive relationship (not statistically significant) between Degree Class and C.C. score was consistent with the hypothesis that a uniform standard of assessment had been applied, but that entrants with Firsts included a slightly higher proportion of the highest quality.

Method II entrants, Intelligence Test Ratings and Qualifying Examination Marks

14. Method II candidates have taken two or more intelligence tests at C.S.S.B., the scores of which are combined into a single intelligence test or " g " rating, on a scale from 7 (top 2% of C.S.S.B. candidates) to 1 (bottom 2% of C.S.S.B. candidates). Due account is taken on the " g " rating as one piece of relevant evidence when overall assessments are made by C.S.S.B. or F.S.B. Results for entrants classified according to intelligence test rating are given in Table 9.

Table 9. Method II entrants, Intelligence Test Rating

Intelligence Test Rating	Number of entrants	Mean C.C. score	Selection* ratio
High, 6 or 7	49	12·57	3·7
Medium, 3, 4 or 5	162	12·39	5·6
Low, 1 or 2	8	11·87	8·1
Total	219	12·39	5·4

* These selection ratios relate to the candidates who reached C.S.S.B. and took the C.S.S.B. intelligence tests.

Though entrants with high intelligence test ratings obtained a slightly higher mean C.C. score (12·57) than those with low intelligence test ratings (11·87), the difference is not statistically significant.

15. Method II candidates had also taken a written, Qualifying Examination, comprising an Essay, English and General Papers and, between 1948 and 1958 only, an Intelligence Test. Because of four changes during 1948–63 in the detailed composition of the Qualifying Examination, it has not been possible to extend this investigation to the follow-up of individual papers.

Rather more than half the candidates, 2,925 out of 5,369, failed the Qualifying Examination. For the remaining 2,445 candidates who reached C.S.S.B. (apart from 43 who had been exempt from the Qualifying Examination), their Qualifying Examination mark was one piece of relevant evidence taken into account when overall assessments were made by C.S.S.B. or F.S.B. Results for entrants classified according to Qualifying Examination mark are given in Table 10. Sixteen candidates had for various reasons been exempt from the Qualifying Examination.

Table 10. Method II entrants, Qualifying Examination Marks

Qualifying Examination Mark	Number of entrants	Mean C.C. score	Selection ratio
Extremely high, more than 65%	21	13·00	2·9
High, 52–65%	164	12·53	10·6
Medium, 44–51%*	18	11·33	21·3
Exempt from Q.E.	16	11·25	—
Total	219	12·39	10·7

* No candidate scoring less than 44% reached C.S.S.B. Candidates with low Q.E. marks, between 18 and 43%, are not therefore represented in Table 10.

16. The 21 entrants with extremely high Qualifying Examination (Q.E.) marks obtained a relatively high mean C.C. score (13·00), and the 18 entrants with medium Q.E. marks obtained a relatively low mean C.C. score (11·33). Full particulars of these individuals are given in Annex 1 to this report. Of the first group with extremely high Q.E. marks, 20 have made good progress (in the sense defined in the Annex), and one relatively poor progress. Of the second group with medium Q.E. marks, eleven have made good progress, and seven relatively poor progress. This comparison, for what it is worth, is in accord with the expectation that among entrants with the higher Q.E. marks there might possibly be found a slightly higher proportion of " flyers ". Too much importance should not be attached to this indication, however, since the numbers are too small for the differences in mean C.C. scores quoted above to attain statistical significance.

17. Over the rest of the Q.E. mark range, i.e. for entrants who had obtained Q.E. marks between 256 and 329, there was no positive relationship between Q.E. mark and C.C. score. For the total group of 203 entrants who had taken the Q.E. the " raw " correlation coefficient between Q.E. mark and C.C. score was 0·039. In view of the sharply contrasting selection ratios shown in the right hand column of Table 10, a low figure was expected and little meaning could be attached to that obtained without making an appropriate correction for selectivity.

18. Unfortunately from the very limited data available it is not possible to make any reliable estimate of the " corrected " validity of the Qualifying Examination. Out of the total of 5,369 candidates, C.C. scores are available only for the small number of 203, namely those entrants who had passed successfully through the Q.E., C.S.S.B. and the F.S.B., had taken up appointment and who were still serving in November 1966. Within this small number, such relationship as exists between Q.E. mark and C.C. score is accounted for almost entirely by the relatively poor performance of the 18 entrants with Q.E. marks between 44% and 51%. On this slender evidence it is not possible to estimate how successful the Q.E. was in its primary task of eliminating candidates who would

have had little chance of passing C.S.S.B. and the F.S.B. and being successful in the Administrative Class.

Annex 1
to Supplementary Report on Administrative Class Follow-Up

Method II Entrants to A.C. Relationship between Qualifying Examination Marks and Follow-Up Reports

Statistical findings in paragraph 16 of the report could be illustrated in terms of individuals by comparing the progress made in the Civil Service by the people with the highest and lowest Qualifying Examination (Q.E.) marks. From the 203 Method II entrants between 1948 and 1963 we therefore indentified two groups:

Group A, the 21 entrants obtaining the highest Q.E. marks, more than 65%.

Group B, the 18 entrants obtaining the lowest Q.E. marks, less than 52%.

For each entrant are listed Year of entry; Rank attained by 1st September, 1966; grading for Present Performance on a scale from 5 (Very Good indeed) to 1 (Among the less able); and grading for Future Promise on a scale from 3 (Potentiality above Assistant Secretary) to 1 (Potentiality not above Principal). Finally the entrant's overall progress was judged to be:

Good if he had been promoted to Assistant Secretary and was giving satisfaction (graded 3 or better),

or if still a Principal or A.P. was graded above average (4 or better) or as having Potentiality above Assistant Secretary.

(Relatively)

Poor if not qualifying for Good as defined above.

These definitions were the same as used in Annex 3 to the main Report.

Group A. Entrants with Highest Q.E. Marks (more than 65%)

Number	Year of entry	Rank attained	Present performance	Future promise	Overall progress
1	1948	Assistant Secretary	4	3	Good
2	1950	Assistant Secretary	5	3	Good
3	1950	Assistant Secretary	5	3	Good
4	1951	Assistant Secretary	5	3	Good
5	1951	Assistant Secretary	3	3	Good
6	1953	Principal	5	3	Good
7	1954	Principal	4	3	Good
8	1954	Principal	4	2	Good
9	1955	Principal	4	3	Good
10	1955	Principal	5	3	Good
11	1956	Principal	5	3	Good
12	1958	Principal	5	3	Good
13	1959	Principal	5	3	Good
14	1960	Principal	4	3	Good
15	1960	Principal	4	3	Good
16	1961	Principal	5	3	Good
17	1961	Principal	3	2	Poor
18	1962	Assistant Principal	4	2	Good
19	1963	Assistant Principal	5	3	Good
20	1963	Assistant Principal	4	2	Good
21	1963	Assistant Principal	4	2	Good
Average	1956·5	5 Assistant Sec. 12 Principals 4 Assistant Principals	4·4	2·8	20 Good 1 Poor

Group B. Entrants with Lowest Q.E. Marks (less than 52%)

Number	Year of entry	Rank attained	Present performance	Future promise	Overall progress
1	1948	Assistant Secretary	2	2	Poor
2	1951	Assistant Secretary	3	3	Good
3	1952	Principal	4	3	Good
4	1952	Principal	2	2	Poor
5	1954	Principal	4	3	Good
6	1954	Principal	4	2	Good
7	1955	Principal	4	2	Good
8	1958	Principal	4	3	Good
9	1958	Principal	3	2	Poor
10	1959	Principal	4	3	Good
11	1960	Principal	5	3	Good
12	1960	Principal	5	3	Good
13	1961	Principal	2	2	Poor
14	1961	Assistant Principal	3	2	Poor
15	1962	Assistant Principal	3	2	Poor
16	1962	Assistant Principal	4	3	Good
17	1963	Assistant Principal	3	3	Good
18	1963	Assistant Principal	3	2	Poor
Average	1957·4	2 Assistant Secretaries 11 Principals 5 Assistant Principals	3·4	2·5	11 Good 7 Poor

Comparing the two groups, Group A had on average slightly (nearly a year) longer service, and this may have accounted for their somewhat better promotion record. Group A's average grading for Present Performance was a point higher than Group B's (4·4 as against 3·4) and their assessments of Future Promise were also slightly more favourable. Consequently Group A appeared to have made better progress overall (20 Good and 1 Poor) than Group B (11 Good and 7 Poor).

It will be noticed incidentally that, though the performance of the Method II Group B seemed poor relative to that of the Method II Group A, it had done about as well overall as either of the Method I groups listed in Annex 3 to the main report.

Annex 2

to Supplementary Report on Administrative Class Follow-Up

PART A

The following table compares the progress made in the Civil Service by Method II entrants awarded Very High marks (270–300) by the Final Selection Board, High marks (260–265), and other Method II entrants. As in Annex 1, an entrant's overall progress was judged to be:

Good if he had been promoted to Assistant Secretary and was giving satisfaction (graded 3 or better),

or if still a Principal or A.P. was graded above average (4 or better) or as having Potentiality above Assistant Secretary.

(Relatively)

Poor if not qualifying for Good as defined above.

	1948–1963			
	Entrants with F.S.B. mark of			
	270–300	260–265	less than 260	Total
Number of entrants	24	38	157	219
Average service in years	10·2	9·6	10·1	10·0
Ranks Attained				
Assistant Secretary	4	7	44	55
Principal	17	27	80	124
Assistant Principal	3	4	33	40
Present Performance (Score)				
Very good indeed (5)	9	7	27	43
Distinctly above average (4)	9	17	54	80
Well up to standard (3)	6	12	64	82
Not quite so good as most (2)	0	2	11	13
Among the less able (1)	0	0	1	1
Mean score	4·1	3·8	3·6	3·69
Future Promise (Potentiality)				
Under Secretary (3)	21	26	99	146
Assistant Secretary (2)	3	12	56	71
Principal (1)	0	0	2	2
Mean score	2·9	2·7	2·6	2·66
Overall Progress				
(As defined above) Good	22	30	114	166
Poor	2	8	43	53
Percentage " Good " progress	92%	79%	73%	76%

There is little difference between the ranks so far attained by the three groups of entrants. With regard to gradings both for Present Performance and for Potentiality, however, entrants with Very High marks (270–300) have obtained better reports than entrants with High marks (260–265), and they in turn have obtained better reports than other entrants. Consequently, though the proportion making " Good " progress is high for all Method II entrants (76%), it is particularly high (92%) for entrants awarded 270–300 marks by the Final Selection Board.

PART B. Successful Method II candidates with high marks in 1964–1966

The further tables below cover the three years subsequent to the follow-up period, during which there has been a marked increase in the proportion of entrants from universities other than Oxford and Cambridge. As in Part A they show the number of Method II candidates awarded High and Very High marks by the Final Selection Board. No follow-up information is of course yet available for more recent entrants, but it is of some interest to compare the educational background of the best of the candidates recruited under the changed pattern with that of the remaining successful candidates (degree subjects have been omitted because within a fairly small total the sub-categories would not be meaningful). The figures in the final column give a general comparison with Method II entrants over the whole follow-up period 1948–1963.

Table (a) shows a rather larger proportion of candidates from the public schools in the high-mark group than in the rest; there is little difference in the proportions from L.E.A. schools in the two groups. A recent survey by Dr. J. F. Pickering[1] for 1960–1964 showed that the proportion of high-mark candidates from " independent " schools (i.e. public and other independent, but not

[1] " Recruitment to the Administrative Class 1960–1964: Part 2, Table VI, in the Summer 1967 issue of the Journal of the Royal Institute of Public Administration.

direct grant) was 64 per cent. The corresponding proportion for 1964–1966, excluding direct grant schools, was 51%.

Table (b) shows that about four-fifths of candidates awarded high marks were from Oxford and Cambridge (93% in 1960–1964), against about two-thirds of the other candidates.

Table (c) shows that one-third of the high mark group had Firsts (42% in 1960–1964); the proportion amongst the rest was about one-fifth.

Administrative Class: successful Method II candidates 1964–1966

	1964–1966						1948–1963 percentages for comparison (*all* entrants)
	F.S.B. mark 260–265	F.S.B. mark 270–300	F.S.B. mark 260–300		Other successful candidates		
	No.	No.	No.	%	No.	%	
(a) *Schools*							
Public	24	11	35	(51)	77	(42)	(36)
Indept. and Dir. Grant	11 (all D.G.)	3 (all D.G.)	14	(21)	50	(27)	(19)
L.E.A.	16	2	18	(27)	54	(29)	(45) (L.E.A. and Other)
Other	—	1	1	(1)	3	(2)	
	51	17	68	(100)	184	(100)	(100)
(*b*) *Universities*							
Oxford	17	5	22	(32)	61	(33)	(47)
Cambridge	24	8	32	(47)	63	(34)	(33)
	41	13	54	(79)	124	(67)	(80)
London	2	—	2	(3)	17	(9)	(8)
Scottish	4	1	5	(8)	13	(7)	(7)
Other	4	3	7	(10)	30	(17)	(5)
	51	17	68	(100)	184	(100)	(100)
(c) *Degree Classes*							
First	17	6	23	(34)	39	(21)	(34)
Second:							
Upper	16	6	22	(32)	62	(34)	(26)
Undivided	16	4	20	(29)	55	(30)	(35)
Lower	2	1	3	(5)	21	(11)	(5) (Lower and Other)
Other	—	—	—		7	(4)	
	51	17	68	(100)	184	(100)	(100)

MEMORANDUM No. 5

submitted by

THE CIVIL SERVICE COMMISSION

September, 1967

Executive Class Follow-up

I. Introduction

1. The Sixth Report of the Estimates Committee (August 1965) recommended that " the Treasury and the Civil Service Commission undertake a follow-up survey of Executive Officers, if necessary on a sampling basis, to determine the efficacy of selection methods and to isolate particular reasons for wastage in the early years of service ". Two separate enquiries were initiated accordingly, and the present report is concerned with the former, i.e. with selection methods. The Committee on the Civil Service asked for the report of the survey to be submitted to them and were consulted during the planning of the survey. The present report deals with part only of the results and it is being submitted now, in advance of the remainder of the material, at the request of the Committee.

II. Summary and Conclusions

2. The report covers officers still serving who entered the General Executive Class by competition during the post-war period to the end of 1963, excluding entrants through reconstruction competitions during the immediate post-war years. It also includes a one in five sample of entrants to the Class by promotion during the same period. It examines the quality of entrants by 9 methods of entry (see below) as indicated by rank attained and by departmental assessments of overall grading and fitness for promotion.

Methods of Entry

(1) School leavers: written examination/interview
(2) School leavers: G.C.E./interview
(3) School leavers and others up to 23 years of age: G.C.E./interview
(4) Ex-National Service: written examination/interview
(5) Ex-Regular Service: written examination/interview
(6) Ex-H.M. Overseas Civil Service: written examination/interview
(7) Graduates: written examination/interview (linked with recruitment to the Administrative Class via the traditional written examination)
(8) Serving Civil Servants: written examination/interview (Limited Competition)
(9) Serving Civil Servants: internal departmental promotion by interview

The various methods of entry are described more fully in Annex. 1. The methods were not all in operation throughout the period covered by the follow-up but, in terms of annual intakes, methods 1, 2, 3, 8 and 9 were substantially more important than the rest; the actual figures are given in Table 1, following para. 24.

3. After careful checking it is clear that the follow-up returns have covered approximately 90% of the expected population. There does appear to be a falling short of expectation in some categories within the total field, chiefly in the case of G.C.E. entrants. This particular shortfall may be largely accounted for by wastage rate, since this is greater for women than for men and the G.C.E. methods have relatively larger proportions of women entrants. Because the shortfall is comparatively severe in the case of G.C.E. entrants it will be necessary to establish, at a later date, just how representative the officers covered by the follow-up are of the original intakes, when compared in terms of individual selection variables (i.e. number and quality of G.C.E. qualifications, interview mark etc.)

4. The report indicates (paras. 30 and 35 and Tables 3 and 5) that the most successful methods of entry, overall (i.e. successful in terms of quality of the officers, not in terms of the efficiency of selection), have been 1, 4, 7 and 8 with no very marked differences amongst them. In terms of numbers much the most important of these methods of entry, as indicated above, are 1 and 8. National Service entry has now ceased, and so has separate graduate recruitment, though graduates can and do enter by the continuing method 3.

5. Men show up consistently better than women. At initial selection there is very little difference in performance, and it may be that the much heavier wastage of women officers, especially in their twenties, is a factor in the later difference. However, the data from the follow-up provide little opportunity to test relevant hypotheses, since the follow-up form was not designed to cover these, quite unforeseen, findings and in order to account adequately for the difference it would be necessary to mount another investigation.

6. The results are re-assuring so far as the general standard of ability is concerned. Over 90 per cent of both men and women are rated "well up to standard" or better, with limited competition entrants showing up best.

7. It is satisfactory that methods 1 and 8 make a good showing. A less satisfactory feature is the comparatively low scores for the G.C.E. methods of recruitment of school leavers (method 2 and most of method 3), which were introduced alongside method 1 in 1956–63 and have wholly replaced it since 1963. The G.C.E. method, though quicker and much preferred by school leavers and the schools, is a less exacting process of selection than the full written examination/interview method which it has superseded. But during the period 1956–1963 there was a good supply of G.C.E. candidates and selection was usually from amongst candidates who had more to offer than the minimum qualifications laid down. Wastage after entry could be a factor, since it has been particularly heavy from the G.C.E. intakes; but the available evidence, such as it is, does not suggest that those who remained would be inferior in quality to those who left, rather the reverse (Treasury Interim Report on Survey of Wastage, June 1967, para. 4.6). Further study of the reasons for the differences between the ratings of school leaver entrants by method 1 and method 2/3 respectively is necessary and will be

undertaken. Meanwhile it may be noted that for all three methods the reports shown an encouragingly high level of Overall gradings over the whole period covered by the survey:

	Method 1	2	3
Better than " well up to standard "	43%	36%	29%
Below that standard	7%	7%	9%

8. Comparison of the school leaver entrants by methods 1, 2 and 3 in Group D (see para. 14) with method 8 is of some interest, since many of the method 8 entrants would originally have come into the Service as school leavers also but at clerical level. The small table below sets out the mean values for rank, overall grading, and fitness for promotion (see Tables G-L in Annex 3), which derive from officers of all ranks.

	Men (Tables G–I)				*Women* (Tables J–L)			
Method	1.	2.	3.	8.	1.	2.	3.	8.
Rank	0·12	0·05	0·04	0·14	0·02	0·04	0·03	0·18
Overall Grading	3·28	3·29	3·25	3·36	3·27	3·28	3·08	3·46
Fitness for Promotion	2·24	2·23	2·24	2·44	2·10	2·07	2·00	2·50

The ratings are generally close together for methods 1, 2 and 3, except for women entrants by method 3; but all are inferior to those by method 8.

9. Method 3 is rightly treated in the previous paragraph as primarily a school leaver form of entrant. It does however include a small graduate element amounting, in terms of original intakes, to about one-tenth of the method 3 total. At the present stage it has not been possible to separate out this type of entrant and analyse the relevant follow-up information. It is known that, for graduates, their academic level, generally speaking, is mediocre; but a further study of the performance of this type of entrant will be made.

10. Of the remaining methods of entry not so far discussed methods 6 and 7 hardly call for comment because the numbers are so minute. Method 5 (ex-Regular Service) is rated lowest of all methods in the overall placings in Table 3. Mostly these are older men, capable of good work at the level at which they are recruited but with no great promotion potential; thus, of the earlier entrants in Groups A and B about 10 per cent of method 5 entrants had progressed beyond H.E.O., against an overall proportion for other methods of 22 per cent.

11. There remains method 9, entry by promotion. The ratings of the promotees compare on the whole rather unfavourably with those of competition entrants, a not unexpected result seeing that most of the promotees were recruited originally from a lower education stratum than, for example, the school leaver categories. It is of interest to compare method 9 with method 8, the Limited Competition, since entrants by these methods come from the same, clerical, field within the Service. The Limited Competition shows a marked superiority, and this is to be expected. First, the selection process is more rigorous, with a written examination and interview plus a departmental report, as against departmental interview plus reports. Secondly, the promotees are recruited from a field out of which the Limited Competition has already drawn off the best of the under 28s,

since the Limited Competition has been the main avenue of promotion from the Clerical Class up to age 28. Thirdly, one is not comparing similar age groups, since many promotees achieve promotion much later than their twenties; the average age of promotion to Executive Officer has been 40 or 41 for at least the last six years.

12. Finally, it must be noted that the findings of this report concern only differences in merit between officers who entered by the various methods. Later stages of the analyses will consider in detail individual components (test scores, interview mark, etc.) of each method of selection, and age and experience (which may be of significance in contrasting methods 1 and 2, primarily designed for school leavers, against methods 4, 5, 6, 7, 8 where candidates are more mature) as factors contributing to the differences. The later analyses will, further, evaluate any differences in merit between officers with different types of school background. Also, a subsidiary analysis, incorporating data for the Reconstruction Competition entrants and linking with an earlier follow-up, will be made of the predictive value of end-of-probation reports and the relative weighting of various components underlying the subjective criteria used in the follow-up.

III. Description of the Survey

13. It was agreed that the follow-up should cover:

(*a*) competition entrants to the General Executive Class from 1st July 1945 to the end of 1963 who were still serving in the Class at the time their Departments completed the reports on them, about the end of last year; and

(*b*) entrants to the General Executive Class by promotion in the same period, on the basis of a random sample of 1 in 5.

Included in the survey were some officers who had originally entered the Executive Class but had subsequently moved into the Administrative Class (see para. 21). The returns also included officers who entered the Service through the Reconstruction Competitions, but all such officers have been excluded from the present report and will be the subject of a separate review (see para. 12).

14. Competition entrants were divided into four Groups as follows:

Group A: entrants from 1945 to 1950
B: „ „ 1951 to 1955[1]
C: „ „ 1956 to 1958
D: „ „ 1959 to 1963

15. They were also classified according to the type of competition by which they had entered. The various methods have been outlined in para. 2 and are described more fully in Annex 1, but they are set out briefly below for immediate reference.

Method	*Duration*
(1) School leavers: written examination/interview	1946–1963
(2) School leavers: G.C.E./interview	1956–1963
(3) School leavers and others up to 23 years of age: G.C.E./interview	1959–1963

[1] Chosen as the year for separating Groups B and C because the G.C.E. method of entry was introduced in 1956.

	Method	*Duration*
(4)	Ex-National Service: written examination/interview	from 1948[1]
(5)	Ex-Regular Service: written examination/interview	from 1948[1]
(6)	Ex-H.M. Overseas Civil Service: written examination/interview	from 1958[1]
(7)	Graduates: written examination/interview (linked with recruitment to the Administrative Class via the traditional written examination)	1949–1962
(8)	Serving civil servants: written examination/interview (Limited Competition)	1948–1963
(9)	Serving civil servants: internal departmental promotion by interview	1945–1963

Serving civil servants within the appropriate age bands could also apply by the other methods if they wished, provided that in the case of methods 2 and 3 they possessed the relevant academic qualifications and in the case of methods 4,5 and 6 the appropriate experience. Those who have done this are included in the figures for the relevant methods, rather than in those for methods 8 and 9, but their numbers are small, and their service in the lower grades of the Service is in all cases short.

Procedure

16. A follow-up form (Annex 2 attached) was constructed by the Research Unit of the Civil Service Commission in collaboration with the Treasury and, after consultation with Establishment Officers and the Society of Civil Servants it was issued to Departments. The Departments reported on rank, performance and promotability (see para. 17) and returned the forms to the Commission where they were scrutinised to ensure that the ratings showed reasonable variation within a given Department, e.g. that there was not an excessively high proportion of officers given one particular Overall Grading. Selection data were added and the completed forms were then passed to H.M. Stationery Office with detailed instructions for machine analysis in the Central Computer Bureau. Finally, the data from the machine analysis were passed back to the Commission for further calculations and analyses to be made.

Criteria of performance and promise

17. The follow-up form provided three kinds of assessment to be utilised in this investigation. First, the *Rank* held by the officer at the time of the study, which could be taken as a reasonably objective measure of the Officer's merit. It would, of course, be partially dependent on the variation between Departments in promotion prospects, but it seemed acceptable to assume that these would be randomly related to methods of entry and would not lead to any consistent bias in the results. The ranks distinguished in the exercise were given the following numerical values for the purposes of calculation:

Executive Officer	=0
Higher Executive Officer	=1
Senior Executive Officer	=2
Chief Executive Officer and above	=3

The second assessment available was the " Overall Grading for performance of

[1] Methods 4 and 5 were combined from 1955 and methods 4, 5 and 6 from 1959.

present duties " and the third was the officer's " Fitness for Promotion ", both being expressed on a 5-point scale. Unlike the objective criterion of rank both the latter assessments were subjective and to that extent less reliable indexes of an officer's merit. These three aspects were dealt with in sections A, B and C respectively of the follow-up form.

18. To permit clear-cut comparisons, and to provide a measure which would best allow an evaluation of the statistical significance of any differences between methods of entry, a single index of the merit of the officer was constructed. This, the *Combined Criterion* score, combined in suitable proportions the separate assessments of rank, present performance and promotability, the components being weighted in the composite index in the following manner:

C.C. score = 4 × Rank plus 2 × Overall Grading plus Fitness for Promotion.
Officers could thus obtain C.C. scores within the following ranges:

Executive Officer	3–15
Higher Executive Officer	7–19
Senior Executive Officer	11–23
Chief Executive Officer or above	15–27

The weights applied here differ from those used in devising the C.C. score for the Administrative Class follow-up. There are two reasons for this. First, in the Administrative follow-up the scales for Present Performance and Future Promise differed in length and the weightings used approximately equated the contributions of these assessments to the C.C. score. In the Executive Class follow-up the two scales were of the same length, which eliminated this particular need for differential weighting. However, while the Administrative Class study provided the, rather more important, assessment of the officer's ultimate ceiling (Future Promise), the comparable measure (Fitness for Promotion) in the Executive Class study, which was based on the standard Annual Report form for administrative convenience, gave only a short-term estimate of the officer's future development i.e. his promotability to the next higher grade. For this reason it was thought preferable, in the Executive Class study, to give a relatively smaller weighting to this assessment of future development. Second, bearing in mind the difference between the two studies in the number of levels of rank involved, the weighting of 4 used in the Executive Class follow-up meant that, on average, Rank and Overall Grading (Present Performance) contributed about equally to the C.C. score, as was the case in the Administrative Class study.

19. The primary value of the C.C. score is that it permits finer discrimination between individuals than does Rank alone, and that it presents a composite overall evaluation. Thus, the C.C. score differentiates between officers of the same Rank and can also allow more credit to be given to, say, an outstanding E.O. than to a poor H.E.O.

20. The follow-up covered a total span of 18½ years and this made it necessary to consider the effect of length of service on the Rank attained. To make some allowance for this, and for the different times at which the various methods of entry came into being, officers were divided into the four Groups, described in para. 14 above, according to the period in which they entered the Executive Class, these Groups being distinguished in the course of the subsequent analyses.

21. Included within the investigation were officers who originally entered the Executive Class during the follow-up period but later became members of the Administrative Class, and who were still serving when departments reported. These officers (100 in number) were given the Rank value of 3 (C.E.O. and above) but since assessments of Overall Grading and Fitness for Promotion were not obtained for them the Combined Criterion as defined above could not be applied. They were instead allotted the following C.C. scores:

Entry in Group (A) or (B): C.C. score 27
" " (C): " 23
" " (D): " 19

These scores, though somewhat arbitrary, made allowance for length of service. They provide an officer with a score at least as high as any other in his Group, but not excessively high. (Since only partial information was available for these officers the tables in Annex 3 show slightly smaller total numbers for Overall Grading and Fitness for Promotion, than for Rank and C.C. score).

22. A number of officers had been promoted to their stated Rank only a short time before the follow-up investigation and assessments of Overall Grading and Fitness for Promotion were not available. These officers, who totalled approximately 8 per cent of the follow-up population, were allotted necessarily arbitrary ratings of 3 (" well up to standard ") for Overall Grading, and of 2 (" likely to qualify in time ") for Fitness for Promotion. This consistent form of treatment, together with the likelihood that the cases would have occurred at random over the various methods of entry, makes it improbable that any significant bias was introduced into the data. A similar consideration, of course, applies to the Administrative Class cases referred to in the previous paragraph; a slight bias may be present but the number of cases is too small for the effect to be significant.

IV. Statistical Analysis and Tables

23. The tables which follow compare the nine categories of entrant to the Executive Class, eight by competition and the ninth by promotion, in respect of (*a*) Rank attained, Overall Grading, Fitness for Promotion and (*b*) Combined Criterion score. Within each type of entry the comparison is made separately for each of the four Groups (A)–(D), and separate comparisons again are made for men and for women.

Methods of entry

24. Table 1 below gives the number of entrants, men and women separately, by each method of entry for the four successive periods covered by the survey, with totals for the whole period. The entries by methods 4, 5 and 6 are combined in this table but they are dealt with separately in later analyses, partly in order to allow for differences in age and experience between the three kinds of entrant concerned.

Comparisons of rank, overall grading and fitness for promotion

25. In Annex 3, Tables A, B and C show, for men only, the numbers of cases at each level of Rank, Overall Grading and Fitness for Promotion, within each method and period of entry. Tables D, E and F provide the same data for women. This information is summarised in Tables G to L which show, again for each

Table 1. Methods of Entry and Numbers

Method	Group A (1945–50)		B (1951–55)		C (1956–58)		D (1959–63)		Total (1945–63)	
	M	W	M	W	M	W	M	W	M	W
1	532	80	475	38	220	38	255	107	1482	263
2	—	—	—	—	86	22	465	258	551	280
3	—	—	—	—	—	—	675	264	675	264
4–6 combined	138	—	245	—	150	1	296	3	829	4
7	7	8	23	9	8	3	20	7	58	27
8	409	27	521	38	300	17	553	28	1783	110
9	773	251	640	161	544	114	1393	265	3350	791
Totals	1859	366	1904	246	1308	195	3657	932	8728	1739

method and period, the mean levels for each of the three evaluations. Since methods 4 and 6 showed nil returns they have been omitted from all the tables for women.

26. The tables show consistent differences in favour of men in the Rank attained after equivalent lengths of service and after selection by the same procedures. Thus, with promotion to H.E.O. counted as 1, to S.E.O. as 2, and to C.E.O. as 3, the mean figures for Rank attained in the four successvie periods are:

Men (Table G): 1·25, 0·85, 0·49, 0·09
Women (Table J): 0·74, 0·52, 0·28, 0·05

Because of the differences men and women are considered separately in the following statistical analyses, in which the more comprehensive Combined Criterion score is used; here again men show up better for each of the Groups A to D (see Tables 2 and 4).

Analyses using the C.C. score

27. Table 2 shows the mean C.C. score for men, for each method of entry and each Group.

Table 2. Mean C.C.: Men

Method	Group A No.	A Mean C.C.	B No.	B Mean C.C.	C No.	C Mean C.C.	D No.	D Mean C.C.
1	532	15·26	475	13·53	220	11·18	255	9·29
2	—	—	—	—	86	10·15	465	9·03
3	—	—	—	—	—	—	675	8·89
4	68	14·48	100	14·67	66	11·65	91	9·81
5	70	12·63	145	12·24	84	9·81	196	8·63
6	—	—	—	—	—	—	9	8·55
7	7	15·14	23	13·30	8	12·12	20	9·40
8	409	15·03	521	13·11	300	11·93	553	9·71
9	773	13·76	640	11·51	544	10·83	1393	9·01
Mean C.C.		14·46		12·70		11·08		9·12
F ratio d.freedom probability		12·29 5/1853 Less than 1%		31·56 5/1898 Less than 1%		12·38 6/1301 Less than 1%		10·13 8/3648 Less than 1%

Analysis of variance demonstrates that within each Group the differences between the various methods are statistically significant at less than 1% level, i.e. the probability that the observed differences are not real but simply random variations among groups which are really the same, is less than 1 in 100.

28. The pattern of variation within the data is more clearly shown in Table 3. Here, within each Group, the means of the individual methods are expressed as percentages of the overall mean for the Group, showing the methods which are relatively above and below average in the Group.

Table 3. Individual means as % of Overall Group mean: Men

Method	Group				Average all groups
	A	B	C	D	
1	105·5	106·6	100·9	101·9	103·7
2	—	—	91·6	99·0	95·3
3	—	—	—	97·5	97·5
4	100·19	115·5	105·1	107·6	107·1
5	87·34	96·4	88·5	94·7	91·7
6	—	—	—	93·8	93·8
7	104·73	104·8	109·4	103·1	105·5
8	103·93	103·3	107·7	106·5	105·3
9	95·21	90·7	97·7	98·8	95·6

29. Apart from showing an order of merit Tables 2 and 3 reveal also a tendency for methods to cluster into groups. Since a standard analytical technique was not available a special procedure was used to examine this clustering more precisely. From the overall averages in Table 3, which give weight to all four periods, methods grouped:

Above average = methods 1, 4, 7, 8
Below average = methods 2, 3, 5, 6, 9

Group D however is the only one in which all methods are represented and the following treatment is restricted to this Group.

(*a*) Considering only Above average methods, Analysis of Variance shows the following:

(i) Differences between methods (1, 4, 7, 8) are not significant at the 5% level.[1]

(ii) On addition, to the cluster, of the most successful of the Below average methods (method 2), differences between methods are significant at the 1% level.

(*b*) Considering only Below average methods, analysis shows the same outcome.

(i) Differences between methods (2, 3, 5, 6, 9) are not significant at the 5% level.

[1] In paragraph 16 it was said that significance at (less than) the 1% level indicates that the probability of the observed differences being simply random variations is (less than) 1 in 100. This, as a decision-aiding device, allows the inference that the differences are real and meaningful. Here, the probability that the differences are simply random variations is much greater, i.e. even greater than 1 in 20, and the inference is that the differences may more realistically be regarded as chance variations among groups which are really the same.

(ii) On addition, to the cluster, of the least successful of the Above average methods (method 1), differences are significant at the 1% level.

(*c*) Finally, comparison between the two clusters by Analysis of Variance shows the difference to be significant at the 1% level.

30. In summary then, analysis indicates that, for men, methods of entry fall into two strata:

I. More successful: methods 1, 4, 7, 8
II. Less successful: methods 2, 3, 5, 6, 9

It should be added that method 6 is really somewhat indeterminate since it is represented by only 9 cases. Its exclusion from the analysis would not have altered the outcome.

This classification, of course, applies specifically to Group D. As a general pattern, however, it is supported by the consistency with which methods are ordered in the other groups.

(The data suggest that alternative analyses incorporating other information might reveal some further differentiation into clusters. The dichotomy presented here, however, offers the simplest firmly based categorisation.)

31. The analysis above dealt with the overall index of an officer's merit, the C.C. score. That the difference between the two strata identified in the analysis relates to each of the components of the C.C. score is illustrated in the following figures, derived from Group D:

Differences between strata: individual criteria (Group D): Men

	Percentage of all officers in	
	Stratum I (N=919)	Stratum II (N=2738)
Rank attained		
Officers above level of E.O.	13·2	6·7
Overall Grading		
Below average (ratings 1, 2)	7·0	9·6
Average (rating 3)	52·9	58·3
Above average (ratings 4, 5)	40·1	32·1
Fitness for Promotion		
(*a*) Ready for promotion (ratings 3–5)	30·2	25·6
(*b*) Unlikely to qualify for promotion (rating 1)	2·2	10·4

The figures show consistently the differences between the two strata. These are only broad comparisons, for illustrative purposes, but they are thought to be fair despite some variation in the composition of the strata in respect of rank. For officers recruited within the period (1959–1963), the proportion gaining promotion (almost entirely to H.E.O., of course) is nearly twice as great for Stratum I methods as for Stratum II methods. In the performance of duties Stratum I, though not differing greatly from Stratum II in the proportion of satisfactory officers (i.e. those rated as " Well up to standard " and above), shows a noticeably greater incidence of more able officers. Stratum I, again, shows a higher percentage of officers who were suitable for promotion at the time of the follow-up, and a markedly smaller proportion of officers of such poor quality as to be unlikely to achieve promotion.

32. Table 16 shows the mean C.C. score for women, for each method of entry and each Group. Methods 4 and 6 show nil returns and are omitted.

Table 4. Mean C.C.: Women

Method	Group A		Group B		Group C		Group D	
	No.	Mean C.C.	No.	Mean C.C.	No.	Mean C.C.	No.	Mean C.C.
1	80	13·42	38	13·34	38	10·89	107	8·72
2	—	—	—	—	22	9·68	258	8·77
3	—	—	—	—	—	—	264	8·26
5	—	—	—	—	1	12·00	3	9·67
7	8	13·00	9	14·44	3	9·33	7	9·71
8	27	12·07	38	11·82	17	10·82	28	10·14
9	251	10·88	161	9·78	114	9·52	265	8·84
Mean C.C.		11·57		10·82		9·92		8·69
F ratio	9·79		20·46		1·90		6·46	
d. freedom	3/362		3/242		5/189		6/925	
probability	Less than 1%		Less than 1%		Greater than 5%		Less than 1%	

In Group C, differences between methods are not great enough to reach statistical significance (at the 5% level): for the other three Groups, however, statistical significance is achieved at less than the 1% level and it may reasonably be accepted that the differences, overall, among methods are real.

33. The pattern of variation is shown again in Table 5 which gives, within each Group, the means of the individual methods expressed as percentages of the overall Group mean.

Table 5. Individual means as % of Overall Group Mean: Women

Method	Group A	Group B	Group C	Group D	Average all groups
1	116·0	123·3	109·8	100·3	112·4
2	—	—	97·6	100·9	99·2
3	—	—	—	95·0	94·0
5	—	—	—	111·2	111·2
7	112·4	133·5	94·1	111·8	112·9
8	104·4	109·2	109·1	116·7	109·8
9	94·0	90·4	96·0	101·7	95·5

34. Tables 4 and 5 again show a tendency for methods to cluster together and the procedure adopted for the previous analysis is used again here. From the overall averages in Table 5, which are representative of all periods, methods are grouped:

Above average = methods 1, 5, 7, 8
Below average = methods 2, 3, 9

It is, again, only in Group D that all methods are represented and the following analysis is applied to this Group alone.

(*a*) Considering only Above average methods, but discarding method 5 which is represented by only 3 cases, Analysis of Variance shows the following:

(i) Differences between methods 1, 7 and 8 are significant at the 1% level.
(ii) After eliminating the least successful (method 1), the difference between methods 7 and 8 is not significant at the 5% level. Methods 7 and 8 thus constitute a homogeneous set, with higher C.C. scores than method 1.

(*b*) Considering only Below average methods, analysis shows:
(i) Differences between methods 2, 3 and 9 are significant at the 1% level.
(ii) After eliminating the least successful (method 3) the difference between methods 2 and 9 is not significant at the 5% level. Method 3 constitutes a single unit, with lower C.C. scores than methods 2 and 9.

(*c*) Finally, when the least successful of the Above average methods (method (1) is amalgamated with the most successful of the Below average methods (methods 2 and 9), the differences between methods is not significant at the 5% level.

35. In summary, the analysis indicates that, for women, the methods of entry fall into three strata:

I. Most successful: methods 7, 8
II. Intermediate: methods 1, 2, 9
III. Least successful: method 3

Method 7 may be regarded as of indeterminate status since it is represented by only 7 cases.

This statistical treatment has been confined to Group D, as in the previous analysis for men. However, while the ordering of methods within Groups shows rather less consistency for women than for men, the general patterning does provide support for the specific findings.

36. The three-part stratification has arisen from analysis of the comprehensive C.C. score. However, as with the previous analysis (para. 31), the differences are manifest in each of the three components of the overall index, as is illustrated below for Group D:

Differences between strata: individual criteria (Group D): Women

	Percentage of all officers in		
	Stratum I (N=38)	Stratum II (N=630)	Stratum III (N=264)
Rank attained			
Officers above level of E.O.	13·2	5·1	2·6
Overall Grading			
Below average (ratings 1, 2)	5·3	7·0	14·0
Average (rating 3)	44·7	61·6	64·8
Above average (ratings 4, 5)	50·0	31·4	21·2
Fitness for Promotion			
(*a*) Ready for promotion (ratings 3–5)	37·0	16·0	10·6
(*b*) Unlikely to qualify for promotion (rating 1) (Method 5 is included in Stratum I)	2·6	11·6	11·7

The trend across the three strata appears fairly consistently throughout. Again, these are only broad illustrative comparisons, but they are thought to be fair despite some variation in the composition of the strata in respect of rank. The superiority of Stratum I methods shows in all criteria, most obviously perhaps in the Overall Grading where half the officers were rated above average for the performance of duties, and again in the criterion of promotability where more than one third were rated as capable of performing the duties of the next higher grade. (It must be remembered, of course, that in a total of 38 cases percentages are not very reliable indexes). Strata II and III differ in most respects, though showing some similarities. Thus, both show much the same proportion of officers rated as average (" Well up to standard ") for performance of duties, though appropriately Stratum III has a higher percentage of officers rated below average, and both show the same proportion of officers unlikely to gain promotion.

Conclusion (from paras. 27–36)

37. The separate analyses, for men and women, have given rise to two classifications of methods of entry; a two part grouping for men and a three part grouping for women. These groupings derive from the most recent entrants to the Service (Group D), but the general pattern among previous entrants provides support to the classifications.

The difference in the numbers of clusters of methods makes an overall evaluation difficult (and in a sense such an overall evaluation would be meaningless). However, one simplification, which would not do gross injustice to the data, would be to divide the intermediate category for women appropriately between the two categories for men. This would lead to the simple dichotomy, already obtained for men of

More successful = methods 1, 4, 7, 8
Less successful = methods 2, 3, 5, 6, 9

Annex 1

Description of Methods of Entry[1]

Method 1

Two competitions were held each year (in April and October) from 1946 until 1957, and one competition a year (in April) from 1958 to 1963. This scheme was intended for school leavers who had followed a Sixth Form course for the Higher School Certificate and later the Advanced level of the G.C.E. (or a course for an equivalent Scottish or Northern Ireland qualification) and was open to boys and girls who were at least 17½ and under 18½ (until 1951), under 19 (from 1952), or 19½ (from 1959).

The competitions consisted of a written examination and interview. All candidates took papers in English and Arithmetic and a General paper, together with three from a list of optional academic subjects set and marked at the standard of the Higher School Certificate (and later the Advanced level of the G.C.E.).

Until 1952 all candidates who obtained a certain minimum mark in the written examination were interviewed, and the results were determined by the aggregate

1 All the methods of entry except those numbered 1, 4 and 7 are still in use (1967).

of written examination and interview marks. In order to speed recruitment, from 1953 onwards candidates who scored high marks in the written examination were declared successful without interview.

With the introduction in the autumn of 1956 of recruitment by interview from among candidates with certain educational qualifications (see method 2 below) the number of candidates taking the October written examination declined. This examination was discontinued after 1957, and the success of methods 2 and 3 led to the abandonment of the April written examination competition after 1963. The protracted method of recruitment by means of academic written examination and interview has many disadvantages, and the wide variety of advanced level subjects and courses had made it impossible for the Commission's examination to reflect fairly and adequately the many syllabuses that candidates were following in the Sixth Form.

Method 2

Recruitment by interview from among candidates between 17½ and 19 years of age (19½ from 1959) with prescribed academic qualifications was introduced in the autumn of 1956. The minimum qualification was five G.C.E. passes, one being in English Language and two being academic subjects at Advanced level (obtained in the same examination), or an equivalent Scottish or Northern Ireland qualification. During the latter part of the period 1956 to 1963 entry was competitive, and only those candidates who had rather more to offer than the minimum qualifications were invited to interview.

Method 3

This method was introduced in 1959. It was the same as method 2 except that the upper age limit was 24 so that older candidates with the qualifications specified for method 2 could be considered for Executive Class posts.

During the period 1961–1963 about 250 graduates entered the Executive Class through this method.

Method 4

A competition was held in August 1948 and then twice annually until 1954 for men who had completed a period of compulsory national service. The scheme consisted of papers in English and Arithmetic, General papers to test knowledge of matters of interest and importance at the time (social, economic, political, cultural, and scientific topics), and an intelligence test. Candidates who reached a certain standard in the examination were invited to interview, and the final order of merit was determined by combining the marks obtained in the written examination and for interview.

Method 5

A scheme of recruitment similar to method 4 was held each year in the period 1948 to 1954 for men and women who had served on regular engagements in H.M. Forces, but the examination was qualifying only, and the result was determined by the interview mark alone.

In 1955, methods 4 and 5 were replaced by an annual competition with quotas of vacancies for national servicemen and for those who had served on regular engagements, success for each group being determined in the manner used before the schemes were combined.

Method 6

In 1958 a competition on the same lines as method 5 (and using the same question papers) was introduced for candidates with service in H.M. Overseas Civil Service.

From 1959, methods 4, 5 and 6 were combined, but with separate quotas of vacancies for the different groups of candidates.

Method 7

This method, open only to university graduates, (or those about to graduate) was introduced in July 1949 and held annually until and including 1962. It consisted of a full academic examination, the question papers being the same as those taken by candidates taking the traditional academic examination for the Administrative Class, and an interview. The result was determined by the aggregate of marks for written examination and interview.

By 1962 the number of final-year university students coming forward for the Executive Class through method 3 led to the abandonment of this more elaborate and protracted method of selection.

Method 8

A limited competition among established clerical officers for appointment in the Executive Class was introduced in 1948 and held annually thereafter. Candidates had to be between 21 and 28 years of age, and the written examination consisted of papers in English and Arithmetic, a General paper, and an intelligence test. Success was determined by the aggregate of marks obtained for written examination and interview.

Method 9

This was promotion by departmental selection (i.e. it is not a competition conducted by the Civil Service Commission) among established members of the Clerical Class aged 28 and over who were therefore no longer eligible to take the limited competition.

In methods 1–8 the Interview Board usually consisted of three or more interviewers, including serving Civil Servants, who questioned each candidate mainly on subjects connected with his own experience and interests. The Board's object was to bring out the candidate's personal qualities, and to take account of his experience, the use he had made of his opportunities, the range or depth of his interests, and the quality of his thought and expression; candidates were expected to have some knowledge of current affairs. The Board took into account each candidate's previous record as well as his performance at interview, and in those schemes in which the written examination mark was not added to the interview mark (methods 5 and 6), also gave full weight to the candidate's results in the written examination. No candidate was given a mark denoting suitability for appointment unless the board considered that he had the potential to become at least a Higher Executive Officer.

Annex 2

Form 1 *STAFF IN CONFIDENCE* Serial no.........................
FOLLOW-UP REPORT (for C.S.C. use)

This report is to be completed for those established officers who entered the General Executive Class as Executive Officers between July 1st 1945 and the end of 1963 and are currently serving in the Department in the General Executive or Administrative Classes and who:

(i) were competition entrants to the General Executive Class or

(ii) have been selected on the sample of promotees (one fifth—see note on procedure paragraph 3)

The only *boxes* in which you have to make entries are Nos. 40–44 on page 2 of this form. Please enter surname and Christian names in BLOCK CAPITALS.

Surname ....

Surname on entry to Executive Class, if different

....

Christian names ....

Date of birth............................Sex (M or F)..

Department ....

7	8	9

Date of commencement in

(i) Civil Service (a) Temporary..

(b) Permanent..

(ii) Department ....

(iii) Executive Class..

10

Method of entry into Executive Class

(i) If by " Reconstruction Competition ", give
month.......................... year..........................

(ii) If by " Normal " Limited Competition (for serving civil servants), give
month.......................... year..........................

(iii) If by " Normal " Open Competition give
month.......................... year..........................
Type of Competition (see notes on procedure, paragraph 10) ....
....

(iv) If by internal promotion, write I.P...........................

11

OVER

For C.S.C. use only

Type of school.. | 12 |
|---|
| |

University education, yes/no.........................

Class of University degree, if any.................

13

Degree subject (Arts/Science).........................

14

G.C.E./S.C.E. entrants

Interview mark ....

15	16	17

Total number of subjects.................................

18	19	20

Range of subjects...

21	22	23

No. of Advanced (or Higher) passes of quality

A	B	C	D	E	F

24	25	26

Where relevant

A. *Date of last promotion*

(i) Within the Executive Class

On.................................. promoted to..................................

(ii) From the Executive Class

On.................................. promoted to..................................

[39]

If an entry is made in (ii) it is not necessary to complete the remaining sections of this form. For other officers Sections B to F should be completed on the basis of the last Annual Report available. In each case, please enter the appropriate number in the box provided in the right hand margin.

B. *Overall grading for qualities and performance of duties in present grade*

Outstanding	5	
A very able and effective officer	4	
Well up to standard	3	[40]
Rather below standard	2	
Unsatisfactory	1	

C. *Fitness for promotion*

This officer is now capable of performing the duties of the next higher grade	Exceptionally well	5	
	Very well	4	
	Satisfactorily	3	[41]
This officer is not now capable of performing the duties of the next higher grade. He is	Likely to quality in time	2	
	Unlikely to qualify	1	

General gradings for various aspects of the officer's performance

	Out-standing	Very Good	Good	Fair	Unsatis-factory	
D. Intellectual ability	5	4	3	2	1	[42]
E. Personal relations	5	4	3	2	1	[43]
F. Drive	5	4	3	2	1	[44]

Date.................................Signature..Rank ....

For C.S.C. use only

			15	16	17
Non-G.C.E./S.C.E. entrants	Interview mark				
			18	19	20
	Paper 1				
			21	22	23
	Paper 2				
			24	25	26
	Paper 3				
			27	28	29
	Paper 4				
			30	31	32
	Paper 5				
			33	34	35
	Total W.E.				
			36	37	38
	Interview & W.E.				

Annex 3

Tables A to F show the numbers of cases at each level of Rank, Overall Grading and Fitness for Promotion, within each method and period of entry. This information is summarised in Tables G to L which show, again for each method and period of entry, the mean levels for each of the three criteria.

Table A. Numbers at each level of Rank: Men
B. Numbers at each level of Overall Grading: Men
C. Numbers at each level of Fitness for Promotion: Men
D. Numbers at each level of Rank: Women
E. Numbers at each level of Overall Grading: Women
F. Numbers at each level of Fitness for Promotion: Women
G. Mean Rank attained: Men
H. Mean Overall Grading: Men
I. Mean Fitness for Promotion: Men
J. Mean Rank attained: Women
K. Mean Overall Grading: Women
L. Mean Fitness for Promotion: Women

The description attached to each of the ratings for Overall Grading, and Fitness for Promotion are to be found in the follow-up form at Annex 2. They are however given here for convenience of reference to the following tables.

Overall Grading for qualities and performance of duties in present grade

Outstanding	5
A very able and effective officer	4
Well up to standard	3
Rather below standard	2
Unsatisfactory	1

Fitness for Promotion

This officer is now capable of performing the duties of the next higher grade	Exceptionally well	5
	Very well	4
	Satisfactorily	3
This officer is not now capable of performing the duties of the next higher grade. He is	Likely to qualify in time	2
	Unlikely to qualify	1

*Table A. Number at each level of Rank: Men. (For percentages * indicates trace only)*

Method		Group A					Group B					Group C					Group D i				
		EO	HEO	SEO	CEO+	Tot.	EO	HEO	SEO	CEO+	Tot.	EO	HEO	SEO	CEO+	Tot.	EO	HEO	SEO	CEO+	Tot.
1	No.	44	290	160	38	532	80	340	36	19	475	114	99	0	7	220	230	22	1	2	255
	%	8	55	30	7	100	17	71	8	4	100	52	45		3	100	90	9	*	1	100
2	No.	—	—	—	—	—	—	—	—	—	—	67	19	0	0	86	441	23	1	0	465
	%											78	22			100	95	5	*		100
3	No.	—	—	—	—	—	—	—	—	—	—	—	—	—	—	—	649	25	1	0	675
	%																96	4	*		100
4	No.	3	44	20	1	68	14	64	17	5	100	24	40	1	1	66	75	16	0	0	91
	%	4	65	29	2	100	14	64	17	5	100	36	60	2	2	100	83	17			100
5	No.	21	37	10	2	70	41	95	9	—	145	56	28	0	0	84	185	11			196
	%	30	53	14	3		28	66	6		100	67	33			100	94	6			100
6	No.	—	—	—	—	—	—	—	—	—	—	—	—	—	—	—	7	2	0	0	9
	%																78	22			100
7	No.	1	4	1	1	7	4	16	2	1	23	4	3	0	1	8	17	3	0	0	20
	%	14	58	14	14	100	17	71	8	4	100	50	37		13	100	85	15			100
8	No.	27	262	95	25	409	92	377	50	2	521	117	177	4	2	300	475	77	1	0	553
	%	7	64	23	6	100	18	72	10	*	100	39	59	1	1	100	86	14	*		100
9	No.	181	336	183	73	773	259	349	28	4	640	313	229	1	1	544	1271	121	1	0	1393
	%	23	44	24	9	100	40	55	4	1	100	58	42	*	*	100	91	9	*		100

*Table B. Numbers at each level of Overall Grading: Men (For percentages * indicates trace only)*

Method		Group A 1	2	3	4	5	Tot.	Group B 1	2	3	4	5	Tot.	Group C 1	2	3	4	5	Tot.	Group D 1	2	3	4	5	Tot.
1	No.	1	29	230	228	15	503	0	33	220	193	12	458	0	15	115	80	3	213	1	15	149	87	1	253
	%	*	6	46	45	3	100		7	48	42	3	100		7	54	37	1	100	*	6	59	34	*	100
2	No.	—	—	—	—	—	—	—	—	—	—	—	—	1	4	44	34	3	86	0	39	255	166	5	465
	%													1	5	51	40	3	100		8	55	36	1	100
3	No.	—	—	—	—	—	—	—	—	—	—	—	—	—	—	—	—	—	—	0	51	409	212	3	675
	%																				8	61	31	*	100
4	No.	0	3	36	28	0	67	0	3	38	52	3	96	0	6	34	25	0	65	1	5	47	38	0	91
	%		4	54	42		100		3	40	54	3	100		9	52	39		100	1	5	52	42		100
5	No.	0	7	33	28	0	68	0	12	74	55	4	145	0	9	49	26	0	84	0	25	117	54	0	196
	%		10	49	41		100		8	51	38	3	100		11	58	31		100		13	60	27		100
6	No.	—	—	—	—	—	—	—	—	—	—	—	—	—	—	—	—	—	—	0	2	6	1	0	9
	%																				22	67	11		100
7	No.	0	0	4	2	0	6	0	3	11	7	1	22	0	1	3	3	0	7	0	2	11	7	0	20
	%			67	33		100		14	50	32	4	100		14	43	43		100		10	55	35		100
8	No.	0	14	172	201	9	396	0	31	257	220	11	520	0	13	153	126	6	298	1	39	278	230	5	553
	%		4	43	51	2	100	*	6	49	43	2	100		4	52	42	2	100	*	7	50	42	1	100
9	No.	0	84	391	282	6	763	0	66	333	233	6	638	0	42	288	212	2	544	3	143	811	432	4	1393
	%		11	51	37	1	100		10	52	37	1	100		8	53	39	*	100	*	10	58	32	*	100

*Table C. Numbers at each level of Fitness for Promotion: Men (For percentages * indicates trace only)*

Method		Group A 1	2	3	4	5	Tot.	Group B 1	2	3	4	5	Tot.	Group C 1	2	3	4	5	Tot.	Group D 1	2	3	4	5	Tot.
1	No.	21	262	120	93	7	503	8	254	120	65	11	458	2	145	45	21	0	213	5	197	38	12	1	253
	%	4	52	24	19	1	100	2	56	26	14	2	100	1	68	21	10		100	2	78	15	5	*	100
2	No.	—	—	—	—	—	—	—	—	—	—	—	—	2	54	18	11	1	86	7	372	61	24	1	465
	%													2	63	21	13	1	100	2	80	13	5	*	100
3	No.	—	—	—	—	—	—	—	—	—	—	—	—	—	—	—	—	—	—	10	532	99	32	2	675
	%																			1	79	15	5	*	100
4	No.	3	36	17	11	0	67	0	47	23	24	2	96	2	46	12	5	0	65	2	62	16	11	0	91
	%	5	54	25	16		100		49	24	25	2	100	3	71	18	8		100	2	68	18	12		100
5	No.	21	21	15	11	0	68	31	59	26	21	8	145	29	31	14	9	1	84	46	96	40	14	0	196
	%	31	31	22	16		100	27	41	18	14	6	100	35	37	17	10	1	100	24	49	20	7		100
6	No.	—	—	—	—	—	—	—	—	—	—	—	—	—	—	—	—	—	—	3	4	2	0	0	9
	%																			33	45	22			100
7	No.	0	3	3	0	0	6	2	9	9	2	0	22	0	6	0	1	0	7	1	13	5	1	0	20
	%		50	50			100	9	41	41	9		100		86		14		100	5	65	20	5		100
8	No.	15	183	109	80	9	396	29	261	133	84	13	520	9	174	66	44	5	298	12	348	133	58	2	553
	%	4	46	28	20	2	100	6	50	26	16	2	100	3	58	22	15	2	100	2	63	24	11	*	100
9	No.	178	240	236	97	12	763	145	243	156	85	9	638	79	235	125	103	2	544	218	750	319	96	10	1393
	%	23	31	31	13	2	100	23	39	24	13	1	100	15	43	23	19	*	100	16	54	23	7	*	100

*Table D. Numbers at each level of Rank: Women (For percentages * indicates trace only)*

Method		Group A					Group B					Group C					Group D				
		EO	HEO	SEO	CEO+	Tot.	EO	HEO	SEO	CEO+	Tot.	EO	HEO	SEO	CEO+	Tot.	EO	HEO	SEO	CEO+	Tot.
1	No.	16	46	16	2	80	3	35	0	0	38	26	10	0	2	38	105	2	0	0	107
	%	20	58	20	2	100	8	92			100	69	26		5	100	98	2			100
2	No.	—	—	—	—	—	—	—	—	—	—	19	3	0	0	22	250	7	0	1	258
	%											86	14			100	97	3		*	100
3	No.	—	—	—	—	—	—	—	—	—	—	—	—	—	—	—	257	7	0	0	264
	%																97	3			100
5	No.	—	—	—	—	—	—	—	—	—	—	0	1	0	0	1	3	0	0	0	3
	%												100			100	100				100
7	No.	1	5	2	0	8	1	7	1	0	9	2	1	0	0	3	7	0	0	0	7
	%	12	63	25		100	11	72	11		100	67	33			100	100				100
8	No.	7	17	3	0	27	13	23	2	0	38	12	5	0	0	17	23	5	0	0	28
	%	26	63	11		100	34	61	5		100	71	29			100	82	18			100
9	No.	122	107	17	5	251	108	50	3	0	161	86	27	1	0	114	243	22	0	0	265
	%	49	42	7	2	100	67	31	2		100	75	24	1		100	92	8			100

Methods 4 and 6 show nil returns and have been omitted.

*Table E. Numbers at each level of Overall Grading: Women (For percentages * indicates trace only)*

Method		Group A 1	A 2	A 3	A 4	A 5	A Tot.	Group B 1	B 2	B 3	B 4	B 5	B Tot.	Group C 1	C 2	C 3	C 4	C 5	C Tot.	Group D 1	D 2	D 3	D 4	D 5	D Tot.
1	No.	0	6	38	34	0	78	0	0	19	17	2	38	0	3	17	16	0	36	0	5	68	34	0	107
	%		8	49	43		100			50	45	5	100		8	47	45		100		5	63	32		100
2	No.	—	—	—	—	—	—	—	—	—	—	—	—	0	2	11	8	1	22	0	16	157	81	3	257
	%														9	50	36	5	100		6	61	32	1	100
3	No.	—	—	—	—	—	—	—	—	—	—	—	—	—	—	—	—	—	—	1	36	171	54	2	264
	%																			*	14	65	20	1	100
5	No.	—	—	—	—	—	—	—	—	—	—	—	—	0	0	1	0	0	1	0	0	2	0	1	3
	%															100			100			67		33	100
7	No.	0	0	6	2	0	8	0	0	2	7	0	9	0	0	3	0	0	3	0	0	4	2	1	7
	%			75	25		100			22	78		100			100			100			57	29	14	100
8	No.	0	1	17	9	0	27	0	2	23	13	0	38	0	0	11	5	1	17	0	2	11	15	0	28
	%		4	63	33		100		5	66	34		100			65	29	6	100		7	39	54		100
9	No.	0	28	148	71	2	250	1	28	85	46	1	161	0	14	67	32	1	114	0	23	163	78	1	265
	%	*	11	59	29	1	100	*	17	53	28	*	100		12	59	28	1	100		9	62	29	*	100

Methods 4 and 6 show nil returns and have been omitted.

*Table F. Numbers at each level of Fitness for Promotion: Women (For percentages * indicates trace only)*

Method		Group A 1	A 2	A 3	A 4	A 5	A Tot.	B 1	B 2	B 3	B 4	B 5	B Tot.	C 1	C 2	C 3	C 4	C 5	C Tot.	D 1	D 2	D 3	D 4	D 5	D Tot.
1	No.	7	44	19	8	0	78	1	21	10	6	0	38	2	22	8	4	0	36	1	94	12	0	0	107
	%	9	57	24	10		100	3	55	26	16		100	6	61	22	11		100	1	88	11			100
2	No.	—	—	—	—	—	—	—	—	—	—	—	—	1	14	4	3	0	22	12	222	18	4	1	257
	%													5	63	18	14		100	5	86	7	2	*	100
3	No.	—	—	—	—	—	—	—	—	—	—	—	—	—	—	—	—	—	—	31	205	25	3	0	264
	%																			12	78	9	1		100
5	No.	—	—	—	—	—	—	—	—	—	—	—	—	0	1	0	0	0	1	0	2	0	1	0	3
	%														100				100		67		33		100
7	No.	1	6	1	0	0	8	0	3	4	2	0	9	0	3	0	0	0	3	0	5	0	2	0	7
	%	12½	75	12½			100		33	45	22		100		100				100		71		29		100
8	No.	5	15	7	0	0	27	4	19	11	4	0	38	0	7	7	2	1	17	1	16	7	4	0	28
	%	18	56	26			100	5½	50	29	5½		100		41	41	12	6	100	4	57	25	14		100
9	No.	102	63	70	12	3	250	59	39	43	17	3	161	31	45	29	7	2	114	60	139	51	15	0	265
	%	41	25	28	5	1	100	36	24	27	11	2	100	27	40	25	6	2	100	23	52	19	6		100

Methods 4 and 6 show nil returns and have been omitted.

Table G. Mean Rank attained: Men

Method	Group A No.	Group A Mean R	Group B No.	Group B Mean R	Group C No.	Group C Mean R	Group D No.	Group D Mean R
1	532	1·36	475	0·98	220	0·52	255	0·12
2	—	—	—	—	86	0·22	465	0·05
3	—	—	—	—	—	—	675	0·04
4	68	1·28	100	1·13	66	0·68	91	0·17
5	70	0·90	145	0·78	84	0·33	196	0·06
6	—	—	—	—	—	—	9	0·22
7	7	1·28	23	1·00	8	0·75	20	0·15
8	409	1·28	521	0·93	300	0·64	553	0·14
9	773	1·19	640	0·65	544	0·43	1393	0·09
Total No.	1859		1904		1308		3657	
Mean R		1·25		0·85		0·49		0·09

E.O. = 0 H.E.O. = 1 S.E.O. = 2 C.E.O. + = 3

Table H. Mean Overall Grading: Men

Method	Group A No.	Group A Mean OG	Group B No.	Group B Mean OG	Group C No.	Group C Mean OG	Group D No.	Group D Mean OG
1	503	3·45	458	3·40	213	3·33	253	3·28
2	—	—	—	—	86	3·40	465	3·29
3	—	—	—	—	—	—	675	3·25
4	67	3·37	96	3·57	65	3·29	91	3·34
5	68	3·31	145	3·35	84	3·20	196	3·15
6	—	—	—	—	—	—	9	2·89
7	6	3·33	22	3·27	7	3·29	20	3·25
8	396	3·52	520	3·40	298	3·42	553	3·36
9	763	3·28	638	3·28	544	3·32	1393	3·21
Total No.	1803		1879		1297		3655	
Mean OG		3·38		3·36		3·34		3·26

Table I. Mean Fitness for Promotion: Men

Method	Group A No.	Group A Mean FP	Group B No.	Group B Mean FP	Group C No.	Group C Mean FP	Group D No.	Group D Mean FP
1	503	2·61	458	2·60	213	2·40	253	2·24
2	—	—	—	—	86	2·48	465	2·23
3	—	—	—	—	—	—	675	2·24
4	67	2·54	96	2·80	65	2·31	91	2·40
5	68	2·24	145	2·42	84	2·12	196	2·11
6	—	—	—	—	—	—	9	1·89
7	6	2·50	22	2·50	7	2·29	20	2·30
8	396	2·71	520	2·60	298	2·54	553	2·44
9	763	2·38	638	2·33	544	2·47	1393	2·23
Total No.	1803		1879		1297		3655	
Mean FP		2·52		2·50		2·44		2·26

(The totals in Tables G and H differ from those in Table I because of the Administrative Class officers referred to in para. 21)

Table J. Mean Rank attained: Women

	Group							
	A		B		C		D	
Method	No.	Mean R	No.	Mean R	No.	Mean R	No.	Mean R
1	80	1·05	38	0·92	38	0·42	107	0·02
2	—	—	—	—	22	0·14	258	0·04
3	—	—	—	—	—	—	264	0·03
5	—	—	—	—	1	1·00	3	0·00
7	8	1·12	9	1·00	3	0·33	7	0·00
8	27	0·85	38	0·71	17	0·29	28	0·18
9	251	0·62	161	0·35	114	0·25	265	0·08
Total No.	366		246		195		932	
Mean R		0·74		0·52		0·28		0·05

E.O.=0 H.E.O.=1 S.E.O.=2 C.E.O.+=3

Table K. Mean Overall Grading: Women

	Group							
	A		B		C		D	
Method	No.	Mean OG	No.	Mean OG	No.	Mean OG	No.	Mean OG
1	78	3·36	38	3·55	36	3·36	107	3·27
2	—	—	—	—	22	3·36	257	3·28
3	—	—	—	—	—	—	264	3·08
5	—	—	—	—	1	3·00	3	3·67
7	8	3·25	9	3·78	3	3·00	7	3·57
8	27	3·30	38	3·29	17	3·41	28	3·46
9	250	3·18	161	3·11	114	3·18	265	3·22
Total No.	363		246		193		931	
Mean OG		3·23		3·23		3·25		3·21

Table L. Mean Fitness for Promotion: Women

	Group							
	A		B		C		D	
Method	No.	Mean FP	No.	Mean FP	No.	Mean FP	No.	Mean FP
1	78	2·36	38	2·55	36	2·39	107	2·10
2	—	—	—	—	22	2·41	257	2·07
3	—	—	—	—	—	—	264	2·00
5	—	—	—	—	1	2·00	3	2·33
7	8	2·00	9	2·89	3	2·00	7	2·57
8	27	2·07	38	2·39	17	2·82	28	2·50
9	250	2·00	161	2·17	114	2·16	265	2·08
Total No.	363		246		193		931	
Mean FP		2·08		2·29		2·29		2·07

(The totals in Tables J and K differ from those in Table L because of the Administrative Class officers referred to in para. 21)

MEMORANDUM No. 6

submitted by

HER MAJESTY'S TREASURY

(First submitted to the Royal Commission on the Public Schools)
February, 1967

School Background of Members of the Administrative Class

1. The Public Schools Commission asked for a comparison, by school background, of members of the Administrative Class, with direct and indirect entrants shown separately, by categories of those who have done markedly well, those whose performance has been average and those whose careers have fallen below expectation. The Commission also asked for whatever relevant information was available about members of the Executive, Scientific, Professional and Technical Classes. We were asked to distinguish between former public school pupils who were day boys and those who were boarders.

2. Information was sought in two different ways; in both cases however only those serving in late 1966 were covered. A follow-up survey of those who entered the Administrative Class between 1948 and 1963, excluding those who entered by the reconstruction competitions, was already being prepared for the Fulton Committee. The aim of the follow-up is to compare the progress made by entrants from different methods of entry and, in the case of competition entrants, to correlate follow-up reports with factors in selection and background. Follow-up reports have now been completed by Departments. These reports include individual gradings for overall performance and future promise. The Civil Service Commission are analysing this information and correlating it with a number of factors including type of school attended. The analyses will not be available until the Spring and will then be the subject of a further note to the Public Schools Commission.

3. For the rest, the members of the general service classes of the Home Civil Service are the employees of their individual departments, unlike their nearest counterparts in the Diplomatic Service who have a single employer. While considerable information is held centrally in the Treasury about members of the Administrative Class, it would not justify a comprehensive classification of staff into groups with the precision for which the Commission has asked and which the Diplomatic Service have been able to undertake. A further approach to departments to produce and co-ordinate such information could not, unfortunately, be attempted at this time. An analysis has therefore been made, by

rank achieved and type of school attended, from information available centrally about current members of the Administrative Class who entered before 1948. In fact rank achieved for those who have already served for a substantial period is a useful criterion.

4. Because the analysis is made according to rank achieved those who entered before the war have been included in separate tables; there are also separate tables for entry by different methods. There are thus five tables for the immediate post-war period, since not only were there direct entrants to Assistant Principal and promotions mainly to Principal, but there was also a limited competition which officers in the Civil Service could take to become Assistant Principals. In addition a number of officers entered as Principals through reconstruction competitions, including ex-Forces, ex-Indian Civil Servants and some temporary Civil Servants. A further group which consisted mainly of officers who came in to the Service during the war were later established by nomination. A minority were established at more senior ranks, but to facilitate comparisons the table has been restricted to those established as Principals. The Annex therefore contains the following tables:

1. Pre-war direct entrants to Assistant Principal Grade
2. Pre-war promotees to Administrative Class
3. Open Competition to Assistant Principal 1945–47
4. Promotees to the Administrative Class 1945–47
5. Limited Competition Assistant Principals 1945–47
6. Competition Entrants to Principal 1945–49
7. Nominations to Principal 1945–49

5. Without making enquiries of each individual it was not possible to say who was a boarder and who was a day boy, but on the basis of a list supplied by the Public Schools Commission the public schools have been placed in the following categories:

Boarding
Mainly Boarding
Mainly Day
Day

Other schools have been categorised into direct grant and other.

6. Table 8 summarises the information for all pre-war entrants (i.e. Tables 1 and 2 combined) and Table 9 is a summary of Tables 3 to 7 covering post-war entrants.

7. Tables 1 to 9 include both men and women; the latter only form a small proportion of the Administrative Class. A further series of tables give separate analyses for women. It should be noted that these contain numbers only and no percentages. The numbers of the relevant main tables are given in brackets:

10. Pre-war entrants to the Administrative Class (1 to 2)
11. Open Competition entrant Assistant Principals 1945–47 (3)
12. Promotees to Administrative Class 1945–47 (4 and 5)
13. Entrants to Principal 1945–49 (6 and 7)

8. Table 14 contains an analysis of rank achieved of those who entered as Assistant Statisticians from 1947–55.

9. Information about the schools attended by members of other classes is not available centrally. The Civil Service Commission is carrying out a follow-up of post-war entrants to the Executive Class on similar lines to that being conducted for the Administrative Class. From sample analyses made by the Commission of recent entrants to the Class the proportion of former public school pupils in the Executive Class of the Home Civil Service is too small to warrant making any analysis based on school attended of the large number of officers covered by this enquiry.

10. Tables 15 and 16 contain analyses on the same basis for direct entrants to the grades of Scientific Officer and Legal Assistant, respectively, in the period 1946–52. The period was selected as one which would be likely to give a satisfactory number of entrants still in the Service who had now had time to make their way to the middle range of posts in their respective classes, but not normally to the very top. In these classes one might expect a sufficient proportion of former public school pupils to enable useful comparisons to be made. As there are only six women included in the table for Scientific Officers and four in the table for Legal Assistants, separate analyses are not given.

ANNEX

Table 1. Pre-war Direct Entrants to Assistant Principal Grade

	Total	Public Schools					Other Schools		
		Boarding	Mainly Boarding	Mainly Day	Day	All	Direct Grant	Remainder	All
Number still in class	237	46	30	15	1	92	48	97	145
	%	%	%	%	%	%	%	%	%
Proportion of above who have reached:									
Permanent or Deputy Secretary	25·3	32·6	20·0	33·3	—	28·3	35·4	17·5	23·4
Under Secretary	41·8	37·0	56·7	46·7	—	44·6	33·3	43·3	40·0
Assistant Secretary	29·1	26·1	23·3	13·3	—	22·8	29·2	35·1	33·1
Principal	3·8*	4·3	—	6·7	100·0	4·3	2·1	4·1*	3·5*

* Includes one Assistant Principal.

Table 2. Pre-war Promotees to Administrative Class

	Total	Public Schools					Other Schools		
		Boarding	Mainly Boarding	Mainly Day	Day	All	Direct Grant	Remainder	All
Number still in class	41	3	4	—	—	7	2	32	34
	%	%	%	%	%	%	%	%	%
Proportion of above who have reached:									
Permanent or Deputy Secretary	19·5	66·7	25·0	—	—	42·9	—	15·6	14·7
Under Secretary	26·8	—	25·0	—	—	14·3	100·0	43·8	47·1
Assistant Secretary	41·5	33·3	50·0	—	—	42·9	—	25·0	23·5
Principal	12·2	—	—	—	—	—	—	15·6	14·7

Table 3. Open Competition to Assistant Principal 1945–47

		Public Schools					Other Schools		
	Total	Boarding	Mainly Boarding	Mainly Day	Day	All	Direct Grant	Remainder	All
Number still in class	287	34	27	28	10	99	44	144	188
	%	%	%	%	%	%	%	%	%
Proportion of above who have reached:									
Permanent or Deputy Secretary	1·4	5·9	—	3·6	—	3·0	—	0·7	0·5
Under Secretary	15·3	32·4	18·5	17·9	—	21·2	20·5	9·7	12·2
Assistant Secretary	70·7	58·8	66·7	67·9	80·0	65·7	65·9	75·7	73·4
Principal	12·5	2·9	14·8	10·7	20·0	10·1	13·6	13·9	13·8

Table 4. Promotees to the Administrative Class 1945–47

		Public Schools					Other Schools		
	Total	Boarding	Mainly Boarding	Mainly Day	Day	All	Direct Grant	Remainder	All
Number still in class	93	6	5	7	3	21	8	64	72
	%	%	%	%	%	%	%	%	%
Proportion of above who have reached:									
Permanent or Deputy Secretary	2·2	—	—	—	—	—	—	3·1	2·8
Under Secretary	23·7	33·3	40·0	28·6	—	28·6	12·5	23·4	22·2
Assistant Secretary	49·5	33·3	60·0	57·1	66·7	52·4	37·5	50·0	48·6
Principal	24·7	33·3	—	14·3	33·3	19·0	50·0	23·4	26·4

Table 5. Limited Competition Assistant Principals 1945–47

	Total	Public Schools					Other Schools		
		Boarding	Mainly Boarding	Mainly Day	Day	All	Direct Grant	Remainder	All
Number still in class	38	—	—	1	—	1	7	30	37
	%	%	%	%	%	%	%	%	%
Proportion of above who have reached:									
Permanent or Deputy Secretary	—	—	—	—	—	—	—	—	—
Under Secretary	13·2	—	—	—	—	—	14·3	13·3	13·5
Assistant Secretary	65·8	—	—	—	—	—	57·1	70·0	67·6
Principal	21·1	—	—	100·0	—	100·0	28·6	16·7	18·9

Table 6. Competition Entrants to Principal 1945–49

	Total	Public Schools					Other Schools		
		Boarding	Mainly Boarding	Mainly Day	Day	All	Direct Grant	Remainder	All
Number still in class	50	6	6	4	1	17	9	24	33
	%	%	%	%	%	%	%	%	%
Proportion of above who have reached:									
Permanent or Deputy Secretary	6·0	16·7	—	—	—	5·9	11·1	4·2	6·1
Under Secretary	24·0	16·7	33·3	25·0	—	23·5	11·1	29·1	24·3
Assistant Secretary	52·0	66·7	33·3	50·0	100·0	52·9	55·6	50·0	51·5
Principal	18·0	—	33·3	25·0	—	17·6	22·2	16·7	18·2

Table 7. Nominations to Principal 1945–49

		Public Schools					Other Schools		
	Total	Boarding	Mainly Boarding	Mainly Day	Day	All	Grant	Remainder	All
Number still in class	62	9	8	4	2	23	13	26	39
	%	%	%	%	%	%	%	%	%
Proportion of above who have reached:									
Permanent or Deputy Secretary	9·7	11·1	25·0	—	—	13·0	7·7	7·7	7·7
Under Secretary	24·2	—	25·0	—	50·0	13·0	46·2	23·1	30·8
Assistant Secretary	35·5	55·6	50·0	25·0	—	43·5	7·7	42·3	30·8
Principal	30·6	33·3	—	75·0	50·0	30·4	38·5	26·9	30·8

Table 8. Pre-war Entrants to Administrative Class

		Public Schools					Other Schools		
	Total	Boarding	Mainly Boarding	Mainly Day	Day	All	Direct Grant	Remainder	All
Number still in class	278	49	34	15	1	99	50	129	179
	%	%	%	%	%	%	%	%	%
Proportion of above who have reached:									
Permanent or Deputy Secretary	24·5	34·7	20·6	33·3	—	29·3	34·0	17·1	21·8
Under Secretary	41·7	34·7	52·9	46·7	—	42·4	36·0	43·4	41·3
Assistant Secretary	28·8	26·5	26·5	13·3	—	24·2	28·0	32·6	31·3
Principal	5·0	4·1	—	6·7	100·0	4·0	2·0	7·0	5·6

Table 9. Post-war Entrants to the Administrative Class 1945–47. (But also including some Competition Entrant or Nominated Principals 1948–49)

	Total	Public Schools					Other Schools		
		Boarding	Mainly Boarding	Mainly Day	Day	All	Direct Grant	Remainder	All
Number still in class	530	55	46	44	16	161	81	288	369
	%	%	%	%	%	%	%	%	%
Proportion of above who have reached:									
Permanent or Deputy Secretary	2·8	7·3	4·3	2·3	—	4·3	2·5	2·1	2·2
Under Secretary	18·5	25·5	23·9	18·2	6·2	21·1	22·2	16·0	17·3
Assistant Secretary	60·8	56·4	58·7	59·1	68·8	59·0	51·9	64·2	61·5
Principal	17·9	10·9	13·0	20·5	25·0	15·5	23·5	17·7	19·0

Table 10. Pre-war Entrants to the Administrative Class (including one promotee) (Women only)

	Total	Public Schools			Other Schools		
		Boarding	Mainly Boarding	All	Direct Grant	Remainder	All
Present Grade:							
Permanent or Deputy Secretary	2	—	1	1	—	1	1
Under Secretary	3	—	—	—	1	2	3
Assistant Secretary	5	1	—	1	1	3	4
Total	10	1	1	2	2	6	8

Table 11. Open Competition Entrant Assistant Principal 1945–47 (Women only)

	Total	Public Schools				Other Schools		
		Boarding	Mainly Boarding	Day	All	Direct Grant	Remainder	All
Present Grade:								
Under Secretary	2	—	—	—	—	1	1	2
Assistant Secretary	16	—	2	—	2	5	9	14
Principal	12	1	2	2	5	2	5	7
Total	30	1	4	2	7	8	15	23

Table 12. Promotees to Administrative Class 1945–47 (includes two limited competition Assistant Principals) (Women only)

	Total	Public Schools		Other Schools		
		Boarding	All	Direct Grant	Remainder	All
Present Grade:						
Assistant Secretary	3	—	—	—	3	3
Principal	6	1	1	1	4	5
Total	9	1	1	1	7	8

Table 13. Entrants to Principal Grade 1945–49 (Open Competition or Nomination) (Women only)

	Total	Public Schools			Other Schools		
		Mainly Boarding	Day	All	Direct Grant	Remainder	All
Present Grade:							
Under Secretary	2	—	—	—	1	1	2
Assistant Secretary	3	—	—	—	1	2	3
Principal	5	1	1	2	1	2	3
Total	10	1	1	2	3	5	8

Table 14. Direct Entrants to Assistant Statistician 1947–1955

	Total	Public Schools					Other Schools		
		Boarding	Mainly Boarding	Mainly Day	Day	All	Direct Grant	Remainder	All
Number still in class	22	4	1	—	—	5	1	16	17
Proportion of above who have reached:									
Chief Statistician	54·5	75·0	—	—	—	60·0	100·0	50·0	52·9
Statistician	45·5	25·0	100·0	—	—	40·0	—	50·0	47·1

Table 15. Direct Entrant Scientific Officers 1946–52

		Public Schools					Other Schools		
	Total	Boarding	Mainly Boarding	Mainly Day	Day	All	Direct Grant	Remainder	All
Number still in class	310	11	5	6	2	24	27	259	286
	%	%	%	%	%	%	%	%	%
Proportion of above who have reached:									
Deputy Chief Scientific Officer	0·3	—	—	—	—	—	—	0·4	0·3
Senior Principal Scientific Officer	12·9	18·2	20·0	—	—	12·5	7·4	13·5	12·9
Principal Scientific Officer	68·1	81·8	80·0	66·7	50·0	75·0	63·0	68·0	67·5
Senior Scientific Officer	18·7	—	—	33·3	50·0	12·5	29·6	18·1	19·2

Table 16. Direct Entrants to Legal Class 1946–52

		Public Schools					Other Schools		
	Total	Boarding	Mainly Boarding	Mainly Day	Day	All	Direct Grant	Remainder	All
Number still in class	209	36	35	16	3	90	21	98	119
	%	%	%	%	%	%	%	%	%
Proportion of above who have reached:									
Higher Grades	1·4	—	—	6·2	—	1·1	—	2·0	1·7
Principal Assistant Solicitor	2·9	2·8	5·7	—	33·3	4·4	—	2·0	1·7
Assistant Solicitor	25·8	25·0	22·9	37·5	—	25·6	28·6	25·5	26·1
Senior Legal Assistant	64·1	72·2	71·4	50·0	66·7	67·8	66·7	60·2	61·3
Legal Assistant	5·3	—	—	6·2	—	1·1	4·8	9·2	8·4
Other Grades	0·5	—	—	—	—	—	—	1·0	0·8

MEMORANDUM No. 7

submitted by

HER MAJESTY'S TREASURY

June, 1967

Interim Report on a Survey of Wastage of Executive and Clerical Officers

Contents

List of Tables

Interim Report on Survey of Wastage of Executive and Clerical Officers

Section 1—Introduction and Summary

A. Introduction

1.1. The Estimates Committee in their report on recruitment to the Civil Service (Sixth report, 1964–65) recommended that the Treasury and the Civil Service Commission should undertake a follow-up survey of Executive Officers, to determine the efficiency of selection methods and to isolate particular reasons for wastage in the early years of service. In pursuance of this recommendation it was decided to mount two separate enquiries. This report deals with wastage. The Civil Service Commission is preparing a separate report on the follow-up survey of entrants to the Executive Class.

1.2. Although the recommendation of the Estimates Committee was only concerned with the Executive Class, it was decided that the enquiry into wastage should cover both Executive and Clerical Officers, as similar factors seemed to be affecting both grades.

1.3. The Treasury, in conjunction with the Civil Service Commission and Departments, is therefore carrying out an enquiry to ascertain the reasons why Executive and Clerical Officers voluntarily left the Civil Service in the period from 1st September, 1966 to 31st August, 1967. All such Executive Officers and a sample of Clerical Officers are being asked to complete a questionnaire indicating their reasons for leaving and their Departments are completing a complementary questionnaire giving details of the officers concerned. The present document is an interim report based on the responses of those who left in the period 1st September, 1966 to 31st December, 1966.

1.4. The enquiry was organised by the Treasury in conjunction with the Civil Service Commission and Establishment Officers were consulted. The two staff associations concerned were also informally consulted and their views were taken into account.

1.5. Recent trends in wastage in the Executive and Clerical Officer grades, which form the background to the wastage survey, are analysed in Sections 2 and 3 respectively. The results of the first four months of the enquiry are to be found in Sections 4 (Executive Officers) and 5 (Clerical Officers) and the Tables E.1 to E.11 and C.1 to C.11. Particulars of the way in which the Survey is being carried out are to be found in Appendix 1. Appendix 2 consists of copies of the two questionnaires.

B. Summary

Background to the survey

1.6. Between 1958 and 1966 the number of voluntary losses and the overall wastage rates increased markedly for both Executive and Clerical Officers. Much of this was accounted for by the growing proportion of the younger people, who are more likely to leave (2·5 and 2·6 and 3·4 and 3·5; Tables E.2 and C.2).

1.7. Nevertheless in the case of Executive Officers there was a rise in the wastage rate for men aged 25–34. For women the rise was more evenly spread throughout the age groups. In the case of Clerical Officers wastage rates were generally higher than for Executive Officers and have themselves risen since the early 1960s, particularly for men and women in their twenties (2·6 and 2·7 and 3·5–3·7; Tables E.2 and C.2).

The survey findings—Executive officers

1.8. The men's wastage rate was twice as high in London than it was elsewhere, but there was little difference for women. The average length of service of those living in London was less than elsewhere (4·3 and 4·4; Tables E.3 and E.4).

1.9. Half those leaving had served for less than two years and only 3 per cent had served for more than ten years (4·4; Table E.4).

1.10. Three-fifths of those leaving were regarded as being well up to standard with the rest evenly divided above and below this grading. The evidence is not conclusive, but a comparison with the findings of the Ability, Efficiency and Job Satisfaction Survey suggests that the grading of those leaving was somewhat lower than the generality of staff in the grade (4·5 and 6).

1.11. Men Executive Officers were evenly divided between those generally satisfied with the Civil Service and those generally dissatisfied. Twice as many women were satisfied with the Civil Service as were dissatisfied, but, if those leaving for family or domestic circumstances are omitted, the remainder of the women were divided equally into the two categories (4.8; Table E.6).

1.12. Half the women (but only a twelfth of the men) left for family or domestic reasons. Half of such women were leaving because of marriage or pregnancy while two-thirds of such men were leaving to work nearer home (4.12; Table E.8).

1.13. If those leaving for family or domestic reasons are excluded, Executive Officers were evenly split between those going to full-time education and those taking an outside job. This may however be affected by seasonal factors (4.9).

1.14. Most Executive Officers going to a job found more than one feature which appealed to them. The most popular reason was that the job would provide more scope or more interesting work, or would broaden their experience. The reason mentioned least was that they would have better conditions of service (4.14; Table E.9).

1.15. About a third of those leaving were going to full-time education; of these, 40 per cent were going to a university or college of advanced technology and another third to a college of education. Of those stating an eventual job, half aimed to be teachers (4.15; Table E.10).

1.16. There was particular lack of satisfaction with Departmental postings, with the extent to which the work was thought to use a person's ability and with the amount of responsibility. There was satisfaction with colleagues and superiors and with conditions of employment. The dissatisfied thought poorly of career prospects, the amount of interest in the work, training courses provided by the Department, and interest taken in personal progress and development, while on the whole those expressing satisfaction did not comment adversely on these items (4·17–4·19).

Clerical officers

1.17. The men's wastage rate was higher in London than elsewhere, though there was little difference for women. For jobs in London and elsewhere the rates for men were much higher than the Executive Officer Grades, though the women's rates were similar. The average length of service in London was shorter (5·3 and 5·4; Tables C.3 and C.4).

1.18. Seven in ten were graded as being well up to standard and the remainder were equally divided above and below this level. Again there is a suggestion that those leaving are of slightly lower standard than the generality of staff in the grade (5·5 and 5·6; Table C.5).

1.19. Men Clerical Officers were evenly divided between those generally satisfied with the Civil Service and those generally dissatisfied, but among the women leaving there were four who were satisfied with the Civil Service for every one dissatisfied. (If women leaving for family or domestic reasons are omitted the ratio of satisfied to dissatisfied falls to 2:1.) (5·7; Table C.6).

1.20. Nearly half the women Clerical Officers (but only 5 per cent of the men) left for family or domestic reasons. Half of the women in this category gave marriage or pregnancy as a reason and 40 per cent mentioned travelling difficulties. For men the most important reason was returning to work nearer home (5·7–5·11; Tables C.6 and C.8).

1.21. Apart from those going for family or domestic reasons, two-thirds of the remaining Clerical Officers were going to a new job and one-third to full-time education. Seasonal factors may affect this (5·8; Table C.6).

1.22. Three quarters of the men going to another job mentioned higher pay, better prospects and the expectation that they would have more scope or more interesting work or broaden their experience as reasons for leaving (5·12; Table C.9).

1.23. Three in five of those going to full-time education were going to a College of Education (5.13; Table C.10).

1.24. There was general satisfaction with people with whom the officers worked, their superiors and conditions of service. There was general dissatisfaction with the amount of use made of a person's ability, with the interest in the work and with the Departmental posting arrangements. Men were generally dissatisfied with pay while women were on the whole satisfied. Those dissatisfied with the Service tended to criticise career prospects, departmental training, interest taken in personal progress, and accommodation, while those satisfied do not generally comment on these items adversely (5·14–5·18).

Section 2—Wastage of Executive Officers 1958–1966

2.1. In order to set the results of the Wastage Survey in their correct perspective a number of special analyses were made of losses of permanent staff in the 1958–66 period. These not only permit the position in 1966 to be compared with earlier years but also relate voluntary losses (i.e. wastage) to all losses.

Relationship between wastage and other losses

2.2. Table E.1 shows that during the 1958–1966 period the total losses of men changed relatively little, but there was a shift in the balance between voluntary losses (wastage) and other losses. The proportion of total losses accounted for by wastage rose from 14 per cent in 1958 to 38 per cent in 1966. For women total losses increased by two-thirds between 1958 and 1966, but there was also an increase in the proportion of wastage particularly if those leaving on marriage are left out of account. But changes of this kind in the balance between wastage and other losses do not necessarily mean an absolute rise in wastage, as retirements at and above the normal age are by far the largest element in " other losses ". Such retirements vary from year to year largely as a result of an irregular age structure and substantial changes took place in the period under review.

2.3. Among men Executive Officers the proportion of all voluntary losses accounted for by resignations grew from just over half in 1958 to nearly nine out of every ten in 1966. The proportions in the other causes varied somewhat but there was little discernible trend. Among the women the share attributable to resignation also increased throughout the period and there was also some increase in the number of voluntary retirements[1] from around 20 a year in the early part of the period to over 30 a year at present. For women there has been little trend in the numbers leaving on marriage.

Wastage rates of Executive Officers, 1958–66

2.4. Wastage rates i.e. voluntary losses as a percentage of the mean number of staff in post for Executive Officers for the 1958–66 period are shown in Table E.2. These are based on voluntary losses only, and differ from the losses as a percentage of staff in post which have appeared in " Civil Service Manpower " which are based on all losses and include all grades in the Executive Class.

2.5. We have already noted that the total losses are influenced by the varying number of retirements. Similarly the number of staff leaving voluntarily cannot be taken as a guide to the intensity of wastage because an increase in numbers leaving may merely reflect an increase in the number of staff at risk of leaving. Table E.1 shows that whereas in 1958 voluntary losses amounted to 85 men and 141 women, but in 1966 to 246 men and 395 women (and as Table E.2 shows the overall wastage rate rose from 0·5 per cent (men) and 2·5 per cent (women) to 1·1 per cent and 5·5 per cent respectively in 1966 (provisional rates)). It does not necessarily follow that wastage has risen in the same proportions for each age group or even at all, if the age composition of the grade has changed over the period. This in fact has happened. In 1958, of those under 60 years of age 4 per cent of the men and 6 per cent of women were under 25. In 1966 the corresponding percentages were 10 and 22 respectively. Wastage rates are highest for the

[1]See note to Table E.1, p. 211.

youngest age groups for men and for women are highest for those in their 20s as can be seen from the wastage rates classified by age which relate those leaving from voluntary reasons to the number of staff in post which are given in Table E.2 for the 1958–66 period. Women leaving on marriage have been included in Table E.2 and accounted for nearly a third of all voluntary losses of women during the 1958–66 period.

2.6. Table E.2 suggests that the increase in wastage to a large extent reflects increasing numbers of staff in post in the age groups at which the likelihood of wastage is greatest. For men wastage rates in most years tended to fall with increasing age from around 5 per cent under the age of 25 to around 1 per cent at ages 30–34 and to well under 1 per cent for those over 35. There was little change between 1958 and 1965 in the level of wastage rates for men aged 35 or for those under 25. There was however a slow rise in the wastage rate for men aged 25–34 which was particularly clear for those aged 25–29 whose wastage rate increased from 1·1 per cent in 1958 to 3·3 per cent in 1965 and to 2·5 per cent in 1966.

2.7. During the 1958–65 period there has been some increase in wastage rates for women but not to the extent suggested by the number of women leaving shown in Table E.1. There has been some increase for most of the age groups identified in Table E.2, though the greater year to year fluctuations make the discernment of trends more difficult than for men. Apart from those aged under 20, wastage rates for women Executive Officers were higher throughout the period than those of men in the same age group. The wastage rate for women aged 25–29 (20 per cent in 1965) was four times as high as the corresponding rate for men and at ages 50–59 the wastage rate for women was some six times as great as the rate for men in 1965. It is also noticeable that wastage rates for women have a different pattern from those of men. This was to be expected on account of the women who leave because of marriage or pregnancy. Wastage rates of men tended to decrease consistently with age but wastage rates for women rose with age to reach a peak for the 25–29 age group and only thereafter do they start to fall with age.

Seniority on wastage

2.8. No comprehensive analysis of the seniority in their grade of those leaving voluntarily has been attempted because tabulations of the staff in post according to age and seniority are not available for the period under consideration. Figures for those leaving show that in 1958 60 per cent of those leaving voluntarily had five or more years service in the grade while in 1966 this proportion had fallen to 24 per cent for men and 35 per cent for women. This change is likely to be linked with the changes in the age distribution of the grade already noted.

Section 3—Wastage of Clerical Officers 1958–66

Relationship between wastage and other losses

3.1. Table C.1 gives losses of Clerical Officers during 1958–1966 similar to those for Executive Officers in Table E.1. The numbers retiring at the normal age who form the bulk of those appearing as " other losses ", depend on the age distribution of the grade. No clear trend is visible for men. For women, on the other hand, there was a relatively steady upward trend from 1958 to 1966.

3.2. For men " total losses " tended to increase during the period, an increasing number of " voluntary losses " (wastage) being added to an irregular number of losses from other causes. The proportion of total losses which were voluntary has practically doubled since 1958. For women, the numbers of voluntary losses and other losses both increased during the period so that the proportion accounted for by voluntary losses changed relatively little. However, the proportion of " resignations " to total losses increased markedly during the period from 29 per cent in 1958 to 56 per cent in 1966.

3.3. For men " resignations " accounted for some 80 per cent of all voluntary losses in 1958 but since 1960 this proportion has been about 90 per cent. For women, if those leaving on marriage are omitted a broadly similar picture is seen. " Resignations " comprised 85 to 90 per cent of all voluntary losses.

Wastage rates of Clerical Officers 1958–1966

3.4. Table C.2 shows voluntary losses as a percentage of the mean number of staff in post (i.e. " wastage rates "). Women resigning on marriage who accounted for about one in three of women leaving voluntarily have again been included in these rates. Wastage rates are generally higher for Clerical Officers than for Executive Officers shown in Table E.2.

3.5. The wastage rate for men under 60 was around one per cent a year up to 1961 and rose thereafter to 1·7 per cent in 1962 and 1963, 2·9 per cent in 1964, 3·4 per cent in 1965 and 4·1 per cent in 1966 (provisional rate). This is partly due to changes in the age structure, but the wastage rates for specific age groups have increased in the last few years with the possible exception of rates for men aged 20–24. Otherwise the rise started in the early 1960's and the increase has been most marked for those aged 25–29 for whom the rate more than trebled between 1961 and 1966.

3.6. The rate for women under 60 has been increasing since 1961; 4·4 per cent in that year, the rate reached 9·3 in 1966 (provisional). Changes in the age distribution account for much less of this rise than in case of Executive Officers and men Clerical Officers. For those over 35 there has been no clear change in wastage rates since 1958 and relatively little change for women aged 30–34. For younger women there has been a clear increase which started either in 1963 (for those aged 25–29) or in 1964 (for those under 25). The picture is slightly confused because wastage rates for women Clerical Officers show rather more year to year variation than is evident for men.

3.7. Wastage rates for women Clerical Officers are generally higher than for men of the same ages, with the exception of those under 20 for whom they were similar. At other ages the wastage rates for women are generally two or three times higher than for men. As was noticed with Executive Officers the pattern of wastage rates differs between men and women. For men the rates tend to decline regularly with age but for women wastage rates rise to a peak between 20 and 29 and only thereafter start to decline with increasing age.

Seniority on wastage

3.8. Because of the lack of the necessary tabulations of staff in post according to seniority for the period under consideration no full analysis of the losses of Clerical Officers according to their seniority in the grade has been possible. The numbers leaving show that in 1958, 56 per cent of the men and 46 per cent of the women who left had less than five years' service as Clerical Officers. By 1966 these proportions had risen to 81 per cent and 70 per cent respectively. These changes are likely to be linked with the changes in the age distribution of Clerical Officers during the period.

Section 4—The Interim Results of the Wastage Survey—Executive Officers

4.1. Particularly because this Interim Report relates only to the first 4 months of the year that the full Survey will run, the numbers included in the tables in this report are not large and caution is needed in drawing conclusions from these figures. These small numbers have limited the scope of the classifications used considerably since multiple cross-classification would have produced extremely small numbers in the cells of the resulting tables.

Age

4.2. Table E.3 gives the age of those included in the survey. Their ages are generally similar to those of all Executive Officers leaving voluntarily during 1966. The only significant difference is the higher proportion of women under the age of 20 in the survey. For both men and women the total number leaving is slightly in excess of the one third of the annual total which might be expected to occur during a 4-month period. The right hand section of Table E.3 relates to those who did not complete the personal questionnaire (Form 1) and who have therefore had to be omitted from most of the tabulations from the wastage survey. The numbers are not sufficient to show any significant difference between the age distributions of those replying and those not replying to the questionnaire. There is no significant difference between the ages of those leaving offices in London and those leaving offices elsewhere.

4.3. However, comparison of Table E.3 with the relevant total numbers of staff suggests that total wastage rates for men in London are about twice as high as those for staff elsewhere but that there is little difference for women. Dividing those under 40 in Table E.3 by the strength under 40 at 1st January, 1966 gives the rates shown below.

	Men	Women
London	0·017	0·060
Elsewhere	0·008	0·057
All areas	0·012	0·059

Seniority

4.4. Table E.4 classifies those people who replied to the questionnaire by their seniority as Executive Officers. Of those leaving 32 per cent had served for less than a year as Executive Officers, 52 per cent for less than 2 years and only 3 per cent had served for more than 10 years. The average seniority of men (3·38 years) and women (3·52 years) were virtually identical. Although the numbers were too small for the differences to be statistically significant, there is some suggestion in Table E.4 that the proportion of men who leave with less than a year's service is higher than for women while conversely the proportion of women leaving with more than 1 but less than 5 years' service is greater than for men. One significant difference is between the 3·0 years average length of service of those leaving in London and the 4·2 years' elsewhere, for men and women combined.

Grading

4.5. Table E.5 gives the overall grading for qualities and performance of duties in their present grade of those replying to the questionnaire. These gradings were made by the employing departments and were taken from the normal report form. Out of the total of 225 no grading was given for 49 (22 per cent) most of whom had less than a year's service. Among all Executive Officers included, three fifths were regarded as being " well up to standard " with the rest evenly divided above and below this grading. The gradings of men and women were generally similar but with a tendency for more women than men to be graded as " well up to standard ", and fewer women below this level.

4.6. Fully comparable data is not available for the generality of Executive Officers. However, the following proportions extracted from a survey on ability, efficiency and job satisfaction carried out by MS(G) Division of the Treasury (which the Committee have seen) are of some help:

Percentage who are:

	Above standard	Standard	Below standard
Men Under 25	30	68	2
25–39	36	59	5
40–49	27	70	3
50 or over	25	67	8
Single Women Under 25	35	62	3
25–39	26	68	6
40–49	30	66	4
50 or over	27	64	9

These figures suggest that the grading of those leaving was somewhat lower than the generality of staff in the grade; the proportion who are below the " well up to standard " grading is significantly higher among the leavers than the whole grade. However, the general sample covered only nine departments which may not be completely representative. Further the above three-point gradings represent a summary from longer scales which varied between departments. Some caution is therefore needed in making a comparison between the two sets of figures.

Reasons for decisions to leave

4.7. Sections A and B of Form 1 in Appendix 2 provided for the listing of items which had been of major importance in the decision to leave the department in which the person was serving. One or more items could be marked in Section A as well as Sections B.9 (new job) or B.10 (full-time education) but if items in both Section B.9 and Section B.10 were marked, one marking was eliminated on the basis that only the immediate destination should be retained. This was usually full-time education. Section C gave the opportunity for the person to state whether they were generally satisfied or dissatisfied with the Civil Service. 22 people failed to complete Section C which is not enough to seriously weaken the general applicability of any difference between the satisfied and the dissatisfied.

4.8. From Table E.6 it can be seen that the men were evenly divided between satisfied and dissatisfied whereas twice as many women stated they were generally satisfied as were dissatisfied. However, if people indicated an item only in

Section A (family or domestic circumstances) are omitted both men and women are evenly divided into generally satisfied and generally dissatisfied. There were no marked age differences between the satisfied and the dissatisfied but all the women who left over 30 did so for family or domestic reasons.

4.9. Nearly half the women Executive Officers in the sample indicated that family or domestic circumstances had been of major importance in their decision to leave. These come predominantly from those generally satisfied with the Civil Service. Leaving this group aside, the remaining men and women were evenly divided between those who stated they were taking a job outside the Civil Service and those who stated they would be undertaking full time education or other training. As far as can be judged from this sample, this even split holds for both the satisfied and the dissatisfied.

4.10. Because the Survey relates to the period September to December and places of education start their year in the early autumn, those going to full time education are likely to be over-represented in the sample. For the sample period 30 per cent went to full time education but over half those so doing left in September. If it is assumed that the remaining months in the year are similar to October–December this proportion would fall to 24 per cent for the year as a whole.

4.11. In Table E.7 those leaving are classified not only by the items which were of major importance in their decision to leave and whether they were satisfied but also by their grading for qualities and performance of duties in their present grade (from Section G on Form 2 of Appendix 2). Table E.7 shows no evidence that the people who were dissatisfied with the Civil Service were better or worse civil servants than those satisfied with the Civil Service. There was no significant grading difference between those taking a job outside the Civil Service and those undertaking full-time education or other training.

Those leaving for family or domestic reasons

4.12. The next three tables give some further details about the different items listed in reply to Sections A and B of Form 1. Tables E.8 and E.9 are basically in terms of items listed so that for example a person answering both " I am returning to work near home " and " I am leaving because of travelling difficulties " will appear against each of these items in Table E.8. Some indication of the extent of entry of multiple items is given by the figures of the total number of people at the foot of each table. Also anyone who gave an answer in Section A and one in Section B will appear in Table E.8 as well as in Table E.9 or E.10.

4.13. Table E.8 deals with the items listed in Section A which are broadly family or domestic items " Cost of Accommodation " was not specifically listed on the form but was written into item A.8 with much greater frequency than any other individual item. For men, of the 42 items listed, 20 were " returning to work near home " and a further 9 (8 in London) were " travelling difficulties ", these two accounting for seven out of ten of the total. Two thirds of the men mentioned that they were returning to work near home. For women, 120 reasons were mentioned of which 32 were " marriage " and 24 " pregnancy ", nearly half the total was accounted for by these two. After these women made most frequent reference to " returning to work near home " (17), " husband leaving the district " (15) and " travelling difficulties " (9).

Those taking a job outside the Civil Service

4.14. Table E.9 deals with those who said they were taking a job outside the Civil Service and gives the frequency that particular aspects of this job were stated to have been the reason for the person taking it. The figures for " total people answering " includes some taking a job who did not indicate any of the possible features listed on the Form 1. The high number of items compared with the number of people indicates that Executive Officers usually found a number of attractive features about the job outside. For both men and women the answer " I shall have more scope, or more interesting work, or will be broadening my experience " was clearly the most popular and " I shall have better conditions of employment " was least mentioned. This held whether people were leaving from London or elsewhere. The other three features, " higher pay ", " better prospects " or " I shall be better suited to it " were in an intermediate position and cannot be ranked further except that women seem less attracted by better prospects. These features are repeated for staff leaving from London but for staff employed outside London the numbers in this sample only allow one to conclude that " better conditions " were mentioned less frequently than any other features except " better prospects ".

Those going to full-time education

4.15. Table E.10 gives some further details about those going to some form of full-time education or training. Sixty-seven out of the total of 225 in the sample were going to some such education or training. Of this total 29 were going to a university or college of advanced technology, 22 to a college of education and 16 elsewhere. As regards the subjects to be studied, arts subjects headed the list followed by teaching and then social sciences. Out of the 51 stating an eventual job, 28 aimed to be teachers, 7 were going into local government work and 4 into commerce.

Attitudes to aspects of the Civil Service

4.16. Section D of Form 1 of the Wastage Survey asked for the respondent's attitude to certain aspects of his work. For Executive Officers the results appear in Table E.11. Separate distributions are given for men and women and for those satisfied and dissatisfied with the Civil Service. In order to facilitate comparison between these distributions, the attached summary table has been produced. This is based on an index of satisfaction in which a reply of " very good " counted $+1$, " good " counted as $+\frac{1}{2}$, " adequate " as 0, " poor " as $-\frac{1}{2}$ and " very poor " as -1. Equivalent values were assigned to analogous replies on other aspects of the work. The resulting figures have then been adjusted proportionately so that the value of the index ranges between $+100$ and -100. Some figures for a general sample of Executive Officers in nine departments have been included for comparative purposes for some aspects. These come from the survey on ability, efficiency and job satisfication carried out by the MS (G) Division of the Treasury, already referred to in para. 4.7. The figures for men are restricted to those under 40 years of age and for women to those under 25 years of age.

4.17. There was clear satisfaction with the colleagues with whom people work. This holds for all groups and for the general sample as well as those included in the Wastage Survey. All the groups in the Wastage Survey show satisfaction with their superiors (less marked for the dissatisfied) and also with their conditions of

Satisfaction Index—Executive Officers

Aspects of work	Men				Women			
	General sample from nine departments	Wastage survey			General sample from nine departments	Wastage survey		
		All	Generally satisfied	Generally dissatisfied		All	Generally satisfied	Generally dissatisfied
Pay		− 2	+10	−20		+27	+30	+20
Conditions of employment (hours, leave etc.)		+42	+49	+36		+41	+43	+41
Career prospects	+ 8	− 1	+12	−20	+ 2	− 2	+ 6	−22
Interest of work	+20	+ 4	+30	−26	+19	+ 3	+21	−29
Use made of ability (" to the full " to " not at all ")	−15	−36	−17	−55	−22	−21	− 2	−54
Departmental training courses	−15	− 8	+12	−36	− 2	− 4	+ 6	−17
" On the job " training	−16	−11	+ 0	−22	− 4	−14	− 3	−30
Departmental posting for experience and development	−26	−30	−17	−43	−37	−29	−22	−43
Interest taken in personal progress etc.		−12	+ 7	−34		−10	+ 8	−44
Superiors " good " or " difficult " to work for		+33	+48	+14		+28	+44	− 6
Whether others are " good " or " difficult " colleagues	+60	+60	+67	+56	+64	+62	+67	+55
Office accommodation	−13	+ 5	+17	−17	−40	−12	− 2	−27
Amount of responsibility (" far too much " (+1) to " far too little " (−1))	−25	−29	−19	−42	−17	−18	−14	−28
Amount of work (" far too much " (+1) to " far too little " (−1))	+14	− 6	+ 1	−12	+28	− 2	+ 1	−18

employment. There was also a general feeling among those included in the Wastage Survey that the amount of work is right, although the dissatisfied have a tendency to think they have too little work. There is an interesting contrast here with the general sample where the general feeling was that there is too much work.

4.18. On the other hand there was marked lack of satisfaction with departmental posting to give the experience required for the full use and development of an officer's abilities, about the extent to which the work was thought to use a person's ability—i.e. not enough, particularly for the dissatisfied—and about the amount of responsibility expected to be taken which was generally thought to be too little. All these adverse aspects among leavers were found to hold in the general sample. With the few exceptions mentioned these features of satisfaction or lack of satisfaction held equally for the satisfied and the dissatisfied, and for men and women. On the whole men and women took a similar attitude to most aspects of the work. The main exceptions were pay which women generally thought was good and about which men were generally neutral with the dissatisfied tending to think it was poor. Women were slightly less satisfied with office accommodation than were men.

4.19. Apart from the features already mentioned, career prospects, the amount of interest taken in personal progress and development appear to discriminate relatively well between the satisfied and the dissatisfied although for the last two the satisfied were not on the whole enthusiastic.

Section 5—The Interim Results of the Wastage Survey—Clerical Officers

5.1. Although the number of Clerical Officers leaving in the four month period and included in the sample was larger than the number of Executive Officers (453 compared with 251) it is still relatively small and precludes detailed cross-classification of replies and also limits the conclusions which can be drawn from the data.

Age

5.2. Table C.3 shows the age distributions of those included in the Wastage Survey and identifies separately those who replied to Form 1. This table provides no evidence that the ages of those failing to complete Form 1 were different from those who did so on which the later tables are based. Comparison with the ages of all Clerical Officers leaving voluntarily during 1966 which are shown in Table C.2 suggests that the Wastage Survey was unbiased from this point of view. After allowance has been made for the relevant sampling fractions the numbers included in the Wastage Survey do not differ from the one third of the annual total which might be expected.

5.3. The ages of those leaving from London offices were not significantly different from those leaving from elsewhere. If the figures from Table C.3 for those under 40 are grossed-up and related to the number of Clerical Officers in post at 1st January, 1966 the following set of wastage rates is produced.

	Men	Women
London	0·049	0·065
Elsewhere	0.038	0.068
All areas	0·042	0·067

The above figures for Clerical Officers show that wastage rates are higher for women than for men. For men the rate is higher in London than elsewhere but there is no real difference for women.

Seniority

5.4. Table C.4 classifies those Clerical Officers who completed Form 1 according to their length of service as Clerical Officers. Seventeen per cent left after less than one year's service and 38 per cent after less than two years' (which indicates little reduction of wastage with increasing duration up to that point) while only 6 per cent left with ten or more years' seniority. The average seniority was 3·8 years for men and 4·6 years for women. This comparison is distorted because a relatively smaller proportion of women in the sample left in London. The average seniorities of men and women leaving from London do not differ significantly. Nor is there a significant difference between the seniorities of men and women leaving from elsewhere. On the other hand there was a significant difference between London and elsewhere; for London staff the average length of service was 3·3 years compared with 4·6 years elsewhere.

Grading

5.5. Table C.5 gives the overall grading for qualities and performance of duties in their present grade of those leaving and completing Form 1. These gradings have been taken from the normal departmental report forms. No grading was given for 60 out of a total of 399 Clerical Officers (15 per cent) of whom the great majority had less than two years' service. Seven in ten were graded as being " well up to standard " and the remainder were equally divided above and below this level. There was no real difference between men and women.

5.6. Completely comparable data are not available for all Clerical Officers, as opposed to those who are leaving. The following proportions come from the Survey on ability, efficiency and job satisfaction carried out by MS(G) Division of the Treasury.

		Percentage who are:		
		Above standard	Standard	Below standard
Men	Under 25	15	77	8
	25–39	19	75	6
	40–49	31	57	12
	50 or over	20	66	14
Women	Under 25	20	75	5
	25–39	31	59	10
	40–49	19	62	19
	50 or over	11	75	14

As already indicated leavers among Clerical Officers are concentrated in the younger age groups and for such groups the above figure suggests that those leaving are of slightly lower standard than the generality of Clerical Officers; as for Executive Officers the proportion who are below the " well up to standard " grading is higher among the leavers than among the grade in general. However, since the two sets of data come from different sources caution is needed in making such a comparison (see para. 4.7).

Reasons for decision to leave

5.7. Table C.6 indicates the reasons which were of major importance in decisions by Clerical Officers to leave. Separate figures are given according to age and whether or not they were generally satisfied with the Civil Service. As for Executive Officers the men were roughly equally divided between the generally satisfied and the generally dissatisfied. On the other hand for every woman who was dissatisfied four were satisfied. If those women for whom family or domestic circumstances were of major importance are omitted the ratio becomes one dissatisfied for every two satisfied. There was no marked difference between the ages of the generally satisfied and the generally dissatisfied.

5.8. As among Executive Officers, nearly half the women who left gave family or domestic reasons as being of major importance in their decision to leave, and some 80 per cent of these were generally satisfied with the Civil Service. If this group is omitted then about twice as many men and women gave a new job as a reason for leaving as stated that they were taking up some form of full-time education. Full-time education was less popular for Clerical Officers than for Executive Officers but it was still by no means negligible. As mentioned earlier the period of the year to which this part of the Wastage Survey relates is one that might well be expected to contain an unduly large proportion of people going on to full-time education; two thirds of the Clerical Officers going on to full-time education left in September. Without figures for the whole year no precise estimate of the relative over-statement of the numbers going on to full-time education is possible but for a complete year the proportion could well be nearer a fifth than the third suggested by the figures under discussion here.

5.9. Table C.7 classifies Clerical Officers not only by the items which were of major importance in their decision to leave but also their grading. There is no evidence from this table that those dissatisfied with the Civil Service were of lower grading than the generally satisfied. Similarly there was no significant difference in grading between those taking a job outside the Civil Service and those leaving to undertake full-time education or other training.

5.10. The next three tables C.8–C.10, analyse further the factors stated to be of major importance in the decision to leave. The entries in the main parts of Tables C.8 and C.9 are of items listed; a person marking more than one item will be represented more than once. The total number of persons shown at the foot of these Tables indicates the extent to which people marked more than one item.

Those leaving for family or domestic reasons

5.11. In Table C.8 the items " cost of accommodation " and " emigration " did not appear originally on Form 1 but were written-in most frequently as other reasons. Of the reasons given by men, " I am returning to work near home " accounted for half and " travelling difficulties " for a further fifth. There is some suggestion that the frequency of returning to work near home was even greater for men in London but the sample was not large enough for such a difference to be statistically significant. No significant difference was apparent between satisfied and dissatisfied. Among women rather over half the reasons given were accounted for " Pregnancy " or " Marriage ". If these are left out of account nearly two fifths of the remainder were accounted for by " Travelling difficulties ". The features noted for all women appear to be repeated for those generally satisfied with the Civil Service while the number of those generally dissatisfied is too small for any useful conclusions to be drawn. Again no significant difference is apparent between those leaving from London and those leaving from elsewhere, apart from a suggestion that the proportion accounted for by " Pregnancy " was lower in London than elsewhere.

Those taking a job outside the Civil Service

5.12. Table C.9 summarises the frequency that particular aspects of a new job were stated to have been the reason for the person taking it. For both men and women the total number of features far exceeded the total number of people which indicates that most people found a number of attractive features in the job they were to take. For men three in every four mentioned higher pay, better prospects, or that they would have more scope, about a half thought they would be better suited to the new job and one in five thought they would have better conditions of employment. This general pattern seems to hold for the sub-groups identified except that the proportion expecting better conditions was lower (about one in eight) outside London than within London (one in three). The section of Table C.9 relating to women is based on smaller numbers and fewer conclusions can be drawn; markedly fewer expected to have better conditions of employment than expected to have more scope etc., in their job. The numbers are too small to show any differences between the groups identified.

Those going to full-time education

5.13. Table C.10 gives further information about those Clerical Officers going on to some form of full-time education. 81 Clerical Officers (63 of them men) indicated they were going to full-time education, that is one in five of the total leaving. Colleges of education were the most popular place of full-time education accounting for 49 of the total (35 men and 14 women). Among the subjects indicated there was no similar concentration on teaching which indicates that some of those intending to take up teaching had given the subject they were expecting to teach. School teaching was the job most frequently mentioned, though one in four did not state their anticipated job.

Attitudes to aspects of the Civil Service

5.14. The attitude distributions obtained from Section D of Form 1 are given in Table C.11. To permit ready comparison between different groups the distributions have been summarised in the attached table by a " satisfaction index " whose calculation was described in para. 4.17. As mentioned there some comparison figures are given for certain aspects from the Survey on ability, efficiency and job satisfaction taken in nine departments.

5.15. Among Clerical Officers there was general satisfaction with other people with whom the officers worked, their superiors and their conditions of service. This general satisfaction, which was also found for Executive Officers, was general for men and women and for satisfied and dissatisfied leavers. The favourable attitude towards colleagues was also found in the general sample but those in the general sample tended to think that the amount of work was too much as did those in the general sample of Executive Officers.

5.16. There was overall dissatisfaction with the amount of use made of a person's ability, with the interest in the work and with the departmental posting arrangements. These included in the general sample were also dissatisfied with these

Satisfaction Index—Clerical Officers

Aspects of work	Men				Women			
	General sample from nine departments	Wastage survey			General sample from nine departments	Wastage survey		
		All	Generally satisfied	Generally dissatisfied		All	Generally satisfied	Generally dissatisfied
Pay		−33	−16	−46		+26	+32	+11
Conditions of employment (hours, leave, etc.)		+39	+52	+32		+40	+43	+35
Career prospects	+ 1	−11	+ 7	−24	−16	+ 9	+20	−27
Interest of work	− 7	−31	− 9	−46	+ 0	− 8	− 0	−39
Use made of ability (" to the full " to " not at all ")	−30	−40	−33	−45	−24	−13	− 6	−39
Departmental training courses	−11	− 8	+11	−16	+ 4	+ 3	+ 9	−23
" On the job " training	− 1	− 2	+13	−12	+10	− 8	− 3	+ 8
Departmental posting for experience and development	−34	−21	+ 2	−37	−31	−16	−13	−27
Interest taken in personal progress		−18	+ 7	−37		− 2	+ 6	−42
Superiors " good " or " difficult " to work for		+31	+58	+10		+33	+36	+19
Whether others are " good " or " difficult " colleagues	+55	+61	+68	+54	+51	+58	+59	+60
Office accommodation	−13	+ 3	+23	−13	−22	− 2	+ 5	−26
Amount of responsibility (" far too much " (+1) to " far too little " (−1))	−31	−23	−16	−30	−24	− 7	− 4	−22
Amount of work (" far too much " (+1) to " far too little " (−1))	+20	+ 6	− 4	+13	+21	+ 9	+ 9	+ 8

aspects. There was some contrast with Executive Officers who were generally satisfied with the interest of the work and the extent to which the work used their ability. On the other hand Executive Officers were also dissatisfied with departmental posting arrangements. Clerical Officers and Executive Officers also thought that the amount of responsibility they were expected to take was too low.

5.17. Pay revealed a difference between men and women; men were generally dissatisfied with pay while the women were on the whole satisfied. These features were also apparent for Executive Officers but the contrast was greater for Clerical Officers, particularly the dissatisfaction of the men.

5.18. There were a number of aspects which were effective indicators of satisfaction in the sense that those generally satisfied with the Civil Service tended to be content with these aspects and the reverse was true for those who were generally dissatisfied with the Civil Service. Examples were career prospects (though the general sample does not follow suit here), departmental training, interest taken in personal progress (where the generally dissatisfied were markedly discontented) and accommodation (for which the general sample showed a general adverse reaction).

Notes to Tables E.1 and C.1

1. These tables show the total losses of Executive Officers and Clerical Officers during the years 1958–1966. Separate figures are shown for men and women.

2. The classification of reasons for leaving in these tables derives from the Central Staff Record and is based on superannuation categories. It does not permit any classification of those leaving voluntarily according to the factors which influenced their decision to leave. The main groups identified are " Voluntary Losses " and " Other Losses ". " Voluntary Losses " are sub-divided into the groups shown in the table of these groups.

Resignations includes all those who leave the service voluntarily before normal retiring age except those included under the four other specific headings in the voluntary losses section of the table.

Voluntary retirement represents people leaving after 50 but before normal retiring ages, who have acquired pension rights and put them into " cold storage ", other than by going to approved employment.

Marriage. Women resigning on marriage have been included. Some, however, are not lost, immediately at least, to the Civil Service, as they resign their position as established civil servants and obtain the marriage gratuity for which they qualify after 6 years' service, but are re-engaged in a temporary capacity. Because the Central Staff Record is confined to established staff they are included in the figures with other resignations on marriage in these tables.

Those classified as Voluntary Losses in these tables would have been asked to complete a Wastage Survey Questionnaire if they had left during the relevant period, apart from women resigning on marriage but re-engaged in a temporary capacity.

3. " Other Losses " contains the remainder of which normal retirement (age 60 or over) provides much the largest component.

Table E.1. Losses of Executive Officers—1958–1966*

Year	Voluntary losses						Other losses	Total losses	Percentage of voluntary losses	Percentage of voluntary losses (excluding "Marriage")
	Resignation	Voluntary retirement	Transfer to Public Authority	To approved employment	On marriage	All voluntary losses				
Men										
1958	45	10	—	30		85	514	599	14·2	
1959	52	7	—	31		90	558	648	13·8	
1960	49	5	—	23		77	485	562	13·7	
1961	59	5	10	19		93	382	475	19·6	
1962	110	11	5	11		137	422	559	24·5	
1963	115	7	6	7		135	458	593	22·8	
1964	134	7	17	14		172	449	621	27·7	
1965	160	11	21	46		238	413	651	36·6	
1966	215	9	8	14		246	393	639	38·5	
1958–1966	939	72	67	195		1273	4074	5347	23·8	
Women										
1958	43	17	—	7	74	141	147	288	49·0	23·3
1959	62	15	—	16	103	196	156	352	55·7	26·4
1960	68	27	1	11	52	159	143	302	52·6	35·4
1961	82	24	3	4	45	158	146	304	52·0	37·2
1962	120	32	4	6	79	241	152	393	61·3	41·2
1963	154	25	4	8	80	271	141	412	65·8	46·4
1964	186	32	11	1	79	309	127	436	70·9	52.8
1965	211	30	9	20	63	333	137	470	70·9	57·4
1966	278	34	9	6	68	395	132	527	75·0	62·0
1958–1966	1204	236	41	79	643	2203	1281	3484	63·2	44·8

*See note on page 210.

Table E.2. Wastage Rates of Executive Officers by Age—1958–1966
(Voluntary Losses expressed as percentage of mean number of staff in post)

Age Group	1958	1959	1960	1961	1962	1963	1964	1965	1966*
MEN									
50–59	0·3	0·2	0·2	0·2	0·3	0·2	0·2	0·3	0·2
40–49	0·2	0·1	0·2	0·1	0·2	0·1	0·2	0·4	0·2
35–39	0·3	0·1	0·3	0·3	0·2	0·3	0·3	0·5	0·2
30–34	0·6	0·5	0·3	0·4	0·7	0·3	0·8	1·0	1·2
25–29	1·1	1·5	0·9	1·3	2·5	2·3	2·8	3·3	2·5
20–24	4·7	6·1	4·3	4·0	5·1	5·0	4·9	5·2	6·9
Under 20	4·1	7·6	2·4	5·0	2·4	2·6	4·5	5·6	4·1
Under 60	0·5	0·5	0·4	0·5	0·7	0·7	0·8	1·1	1·1
WOMEN									
50–59	1·2	1·2	1·7	1·5	2·1	1·6	1·9	1·8	1·4
40–49	0·8	1·1	1·0	0·6	1·3	1·3	1·1	1·1	0·6
35–39	2·1	3·3	2·0	1·2	3·3	2·6	3·2	4·8	2·7
30–34	2·1	7·5	5·1	5·9	3·9	5·5	11·0	5·5	5·6
25–29	15·3	21·8	9·8	20·5	20·8	22·5	20·8	19·5	23·3
20–24	11·7	14·1	13·5	10·1	14·5	14·3	14·1	14·6	16·4
Under 20	3·7	9·0	3·0	4·5	3·6	9·0	10·4	5·4	8·9
Under 60	2·5	3·5	2·8	2·7	4·0	4·4	4·9	5·0	5·5

*Provisional. Subject to correction.

Table E.3. Wastage Survey: All Executive Officers (including those not replying to questionnaire) by age

	Those replying to Questionnaire				Those not replying			
	London		Elsewhere		London		Elsewhere	
Age	Men	Women	Men	Women	Men	Women	Men	Women
50–59	2	2	—	2	—	2	1	1
40–49	4	1	1	2	—	—	—	1
35–39	—	1	—	3	—	—	—	—
30–34	4	2	6	1	—	—	1	2
25–29	11	6	6	13	—	2	—	2
22–24	21	28	7	20	1	4	1	1
20–21	11	21	4	9	2	3	1	—
18–19	8	16	5	8	—	—	—	1
Total	61	77	29	58	3	11	4	8

Table E.4. Wastage Survey: Executive Officers: Seniority in grade of those replying to questionnaire

Seniority	London		Elsewhere	
	Men	Women	Men	Women
15 years or over	—	2	—	1
10–years	2	1	—	—
7–years	6	4	6	10
5–years	7	6	5	10
4–years	1	6	—	8
2–years	10	11	4	8
1–years	11	19	4	10
6–months	12	23	6	4
Under 6 months	12	5	4	7
Total	61	77	29	58

Table E.5. Wastage Survey: Executive Officers: Overall grading for qualities and performance of duties in present grade of those officers replying to questionnaire

Grading	Men	Women
Outstanding	1	—
Very able and effective Officer	15	21
Well up to standard	31	75
Rather below standard	15	13
Unsatisfactory	2	2
None given	26*	23†
Total	90	134

*Twelve have less than six months' seniority, 10 less than 1 year and 1 less than 2 years.
†Seven have less than six months, 8 less than 1 year and 6 less than 2 years.

Table E.6. Wastage Survey: Executive Officers: Reasons Given as Being of Major Importance in Decision to Leave the Civil Service

	REASONS						
MEN	Family or domestic circumstances	Job outside	Both job outside and family or domestic circumstances	Full time education	Both full-time education and family or domestic circumstances	Others	Total
Generally satisfied with Civil Service							
Aged 30 years and over		4	2	2	1		9
20–29 years	6	9	2	10	1		28
Under 20 years	1	1		3		1	6
All	7	14	4	15	2	1	43
Generally dissatisfied with Civil Service							
Aged 30 years and over		4			2		6
20–29 years		9	7	6	2	1	25
Under 20 years			2	2	3		7
All		13	9	8	7	1	38
Expressing no views							
All		2	1	4		2	9
Total	7	29	14	27	9	4	90
WOMEN							
Generally satisfied with Civil Service							
Aged 30 years and over	11						11
20–29 years	35	5	13	3	4	1	61
Under 20 years	4			5			9
All	50	5	13	8	4	1	81
Generally dissatisfied with Civil Service							
Aged 30 years and over							
20–29 years	3	8	4	7	4	1	27
Under 20 years	1	5	2	3	3		14
All	4	13	6	10	7	1	41
Expressing no views							
All	6	1	3	2		1	13
Total	60	19	22	20	11	3	135

Table E.7. Wastage Survey: Executive Officers: Reasons given by Grading

MEN Grading	Reasons						
	Family or domestic circumstances	Job outside	Both job outside and family or domestic circumstances	Full time education	Both full-time education and family or domestic circumstances	Others	Total
Generally satisfied with Civil Service							
Outstanding		1					1
Very able and effective		4		1			5
Well up to standard	3	4	1	7	2	1	18
Rather below standard		3	2	4			9
Unsatisfactory							
None given	4	2	1	3			10
Total	7	14	4	15	2	1	43
Generally dissatisfied							
Outstanding							
Very able and effective		4	1	2	1		8
Well up to standard		4	3	2		1	10
Rather below standard		3		2	1		6
Unsatisfactory		1			1		2
None given		1	5	2	4		12
Total		13	9	8	7	1	38
All (including those expressing no views)							
Outstanding		1					1
Very able and effective		9	1	4	1		15
Well up to standard	3	8	4	11	2	3	31
Rather below standard		6	2	6	1		15
Unsatisfactory		1			1		2
None given	4	4	7	6	4	1	26
Total	7	29	14	27	9	4	90

Table E. 7—continued

Women

Grading	Reasons: Family or domestic circumstances	Job outside	Both job outside and family or domestic circumstances	Full time education	Both full-time education and family or domestic circumstances	Others	Total
Generally satisfied with Civil Service							
Outstanding							
Very able and effective	13	1	2		1		17
Well up to standard	29	1	9	5	1		45
Rather below standard	2	2	1	1		1	7
Unsatisfactory	1						1
None given	5	1	1	2	2		11
Total	50	5	13	8	4	1	81
Generally dissatisfied							
Outstanding							
Very able and effective		1	1	1	1		4
Well up to standard	3	7	4	5	2		21
Rather below standard		1		1	2		4
Unsatisfactory			1				1
None given	1	4		3	2	1	11
Total	4	13	6	10	7	1	41
All (including those expressing no views)							
Outstanding							
Very able and effective	13	2	3	1	2		21
Well up to standard	37	8	15	11	3	1	75
Rather below standard	2	4	1	3	2	1	13
Unsatisfactory	1		1				2
None given	7	5	2	5	4	1	24
Total	60	19	22	20	11	3	135

Table E.8. Wastage Survey: Executive Officers: Those Leaving for Family or Domestic Circumstances

Items listed	London			Elsewhere		
	Generally satisfied	Generally dissatisfied	All	Generally satisfied	Generally dissatisfied	All
Men						
Family leaving district	—	—	—	—	—	—
Returning to work near home	6	8	15	2	3	5
Moving for health or personal reasons	2	2	4	—	—	—
Travelling difficulties	2	6	8	1	—	1
Cost of Accommodation	1	—	1	2	—	2
Others	3	1	4	2	—	2
All Items	14	17	32	7	3	10
Total men answering	9	13	23	4	3	7
Women						
Family leaving district	—	1	1	—	—	—
Returning to work near home	7	5	12	—	4	5
Moving for health or personal reasons	5	1	6	1	—	2
Marriage	16	1	19	10	1	13
Pregnancy	7	1	10	11	2	14
Husband leaving district	8	1	10	5	—	5
Travelling difficulties	4	1	5	2	2	4
Cost of accommodation	5	—	6	—	—	—
Others	—	—	—	6	1	8
All Items	52	11	69	35	10	51
Total women answering	36	8	48	31	9	45

Table E.9. Wastage Survey: Executive Officers Taking Job Outside

Attractions of outside job	London			Elsewhere		
	Generally satisfied	Generally dissatisfied	All	Generally satisfied	Generally dissatisfied	All
Men						
Higher pay	4	9	13	7	3	11
Better prospects	4	9	14	3	4	8
More scope, more interesting or to broaden experience	7	11	20	7	4	12
Better suited	5	5	10	2	4	7
Better conditions of employment	1	3	4	1	—	2
All attractions	21	37	61	20	15	40
Total men answering	10	16	28	8	6	15
Women						
Higher pay	3	2	5	2	3	6
Better prospects	2	3	5	—	2	3
More scope, more interesting or to broaden experience	6	10	16	4	7	12
Better suited	3	6	11	3	5	9
Better conditions of employment	1	3	4	2	2	4
All attractions	15	24	41	11	19	34
Total women answering	11	12	25	7	7	16

Table E.10. Wastage Survey: Executive Officers Going to Full-time Education

	Generally satisfied with Civil Service	Generally dissatisfied with Civil Service	All (incl. those expressing no views)
1. *By sex*			
Men	17	15	36
Women	12	17	31
	—	—	—
Total	29	32	67
2. *By place of education*			
University	12	13	29
College of Education (no. of women in brackets)	11 (5)	9 (7)	22 (13)
Other Place	6	10	16
3. *By subject studied*			
Arts subjects	8	7	17
Social sciences	4	2	8
Pure or applied science	1	—	1
Nursing	—	2	2
Professional training	3	2	5
Teaching	6	8	15
Librarianship	—	1	1
Other subjects	3	4	7
Undecided	—	1	1
Not known	4	5	10
4. *By anticipated job*			
School teacher	9	14	28
Commerce	1	2	4
Manufacturing	2	—	2
Local Government—Social Welfare Work	3	2	5
Local Government—Other	1	1	2
Other	5	5	10
Undecided	4	2	6
Not stated	4	6	10

Table E. 11. Wastage Survey: Executive Officers: Attitude towards various aspects of the work

Men

	43 generally satisfied with Civil Service						38 generally dissatisfied with Civil Service						All (90)					
Aspects	Very good	Good	Ade-quate	Poor	Very poor	Not stated	Very good	Good	Ade-quate	Poor	Very poor	Not stated	Very good	Good	Ade-quate	Poor	Very poor	Not stated
Pay	—	16	20	7	—	—	—	4	19	11	4	—	—	23	44	19	4	—
Conditions of employment (hours, leave, etc.)	12	19	11	1	—	—	4	21	11	2	—	—	16	46	25	3	—	—
Career prospects	3	10	24	6	—	—	—	5	17	12	4		3	20	43	20	4	—
Interest of work	8	15	14	5	—	1	1	2	15	17	3	—	9	18	34	24	3	2
Use made of abilities ("To the full" to "not at all")	3	4	15	17	4	—	1	1	—	27	9	—	4	5	16	51	13	1
Departmental training courses	7	11	11	9	3	2	1	4	12	12	7	2	8	16	25	24	11	6
"On the job" training	2	12	12	12	2	3	1	3	14	14	4	2	3	18	27	28	8	6
Departmental posting for experience and development	—	4	20	7	6	6	—	—	10	17	8	3	—	5	33	24	17	11
Interest taken in personal progress, etc.	4	12	13	10	2	2	2	4	6	16	9	1	7	17	22	27	13	4
Superiors "good" or "difficult" to work for	10	23	7	—	1	2	4	15	8	6	3	2	16	42	16	7	4	5
Whether others are "good" or "difficult" colleagues	19	20	3	—	—	1	11	21	5	—	—	1	34	43	10	—	—	3
Office accommodation	3	18	14	7	1	—	—	9	18	4	7	—	4	30	34	13	8	1
	Far too much	Too much	About right	Too little	Far too little	Not stated	Far too much	Too much	About right	Too little	Far too little	Not stated	Far too much	Too much	About right	Too little	Far too little	Not stated
Responsibility	—	—	29	10	3	1	—	2	8	22	6	—	—	2	41	36	9	2
Work	2	8	23	9	1	—	3	4	15	13	3	—	5	12	43	24	4	2

Table E. 11—continued

Women

Aspects	81 generally satisfied with Civil Service						41 generally dissatisfied with Civil Service						All (135)					
	Very good	Good	Ade-quate	Poor	Very poor	Not stated	Very good	Good	Ade-quate	Poor	Very poor	Not stated	Very good	Good	Ade-quate	Poor	Very poor	Not stated
Pay	8	42	21	8	1	1	3	16	18	2	2	—	13	64	42	10	4	2
Conditions of employment	14	46	16	3	1	1	8	21	9	3	—	—	23	73	29	7	1	2
Career prospects	1	23	44	9	3	1	—	8	14	12	7	—	1	36	63	23	10	2
Interest of work	5	29	41	5	—	1	1	2	15	16	6	1	6	33	62	24	6	4
Use made of abilities	5	19	26	28	2	1	—	2	3	26	10	—	5	21	32	61	13	3
Departmental training courses	6	19	30	16	3	7	—	6	15	10	5	5	6	26	47	30	10	16
On the job training	3	18	35	19	5	1	—	3	14	16	6	2	3	22	52	40	13	
Departmental posting for experience and development	—	8	30	37	3	3	—	1	11	14	11	4	—	10	44	54	17	10
Interest taken in personal progress, etc.	12	17	29	16	6	1	1	2	7	16	12	3	13	21	39	35	20	7
Superiors "good" or "difficult" to work for	16	42	19	2	—	2	2	9	15	6	6	3	21	55	38	9	6	6
Whether others "good" or "difficult" colleagues	32	44	4	—	—	1	11	25	3	2	—	—	48	73	9	2	—	3
Office accommodation	5	22	24	21	7	2	1	3	16	13	7	1	6	27	42	41	15	4
	Far too much	Too much	About right	Too little	Far too little	Not stated	Far too much	Too much	About right	Too little	Far too little	Not stated	Far too much	Too much	About right	Too little	Far too little	Not stated
Responsibility	—	1	58	19	2	1	—	3	17	14	6	1	1	5	80	36	10	3
Work	3	16	45	13	2	2	3	5	16	8	9	—	7	26	64	23	11	4

Table C1. Losses of Clerical Officers 1958–66*

Year	Voluntary Losses						Other losses	Total losses	Percentage of voluntary losses	Percentage of voluntary losses excluding "Marriage"
	Resignation	Voluntary retirement	Transfer to Public Authority	To approved employment	Marriage	All voluntary losses				
Men										
1958	447	20	—	70		537	1786	2323	23·1	
1959	323	19	—	52		394	1767	2161	18·2	
1960	490	17	—	49		556	1704	2260	24·6	
1961	406	13	25	13		457	1482	1939	23·6	
1962	596	26	20	17		659	1715	2374	27·8	
1963	547	23	37	12		619	1699	2318	26·7	
1964	968	35	57	28		1088	1914	3002	36·2	
1965	1100	31	50	73		1254	1630	2884	43·5	
1966	1336	28	68	25		1457	1610	3067	47·5	
	6213	212	257	339		7021	15307	22328	31·4	
Women										
1958	533	52	—	43	628	1256	560	1816	69·2	34·6
1959	456	41	—	47	575	1119	564	1683	66·5	32·3
1960	628	65	—	38	514	1245	613	1858	67·0	39·3
1961	641	62	23	12	468	1206	612	1818	66·3	40·6
1962	1026	64	27	14	526	1657	823	2480	66·8	45·6
1963	1098	53	47	22	561	1781	807	2588	68·8	47·1
1964	1710	99	74	6	639	2528	887	3415	74·0	55·3
1965	1859	85	73	55	602	2674	820	3494	76·5	59·3
1966	2185	99	92	29	573	2978	908	3886	76·6	61·9
	10136	620	336	266	5086	16444	6594	23038	71·4	49·3

* See the note on page 210.

Table C.2. Wastage Rates of Clerical Officers by Age 1958–1966
(Voluntary losses expressed as percentage of mean number of staff in post)

Age	1958	1959	1960	1961	1962	1963	1964	1965	1966*
Men									
50–59	0·4	0·3	0·4	0·3	0·4	0·4	0·6	0·6	0·6
40–49	0·4	0·3	0·5	0·3	0·4	0·4	0·7	0·9	0·8
35–39	0·6	0·5	0·5	0·5	0·7	0·9	1·0	1·4	1·7
30–34	1·0	0·5	1·4	1·0	1·4	1·8	2·5	4·6	5·1
25–29	2·5	2·0	3·0	2·3	3·6	3·9	6·5	7·4	7·8
20–24	11·5	7·8	9·9	8·0	11·4	7·3	11·1	11·5	13·5
Under 20	6·9	7·5	9·1	5·9	6·2	5·9	9·9	9·4	11·1
Under 60	1·3	1·0	1·4	1·2	1·7	1·7	2·9	3·4	4·1
Women									
50–59	1·1	0·7	1·1	0·9	1·0	0·9	1·4	1·3	1·5
40–49	1·2	1·2	1·2	1·1	1·3	1·3	1·4	1·5	1·4
35–39	3·1	3·1	3·1	2·7	3·5	3·6	3·7	3·0	3·8
30–34	7·2	7·1	7·3	7·8	8·8	7·7	9·2	8·2	9·9
25–29	16·1	17·4	16·9	14·4	17·9	20·8	25·9	22·6	25·0
20–24	18·2	14·2	17·2	14·7	19·1	16·0	21·4	20·6	21·9
Under 20	10·0	6·1	8·3	6·1	7·1	7·7	9·3	11·8	12·1
Under 60	4·8	4·2	4·8	4·4	5·7	5·8	8·0	8·3	9·3

* Provisional—subject to correction

Table C.3. Wastage Survey: All Clerical Officers (including those not replying to the questionnaire): by Age

Age	Those replying to questionnaire				Those not replying			
	London		Elsewhere		London		Elsewhere	
	Men	Women	Men	Women	Men	Women	Men	Women
50–59 years ...	4	2	6	5	—	—	—	—
40–49 years ...	3	3	4	1	—	—	—	—
35–39 years ...	4	—	5	3	1	—	—	1
30–34 years ...	4	3	5	6	2	2	1	2
25–29 years ...	21	5	15	18	2	—	3	2
22–24 years ...	20	7	25	43	6	1	—	6
20–21 years ...	29	6	35	25	4	1	5	3
18–19 years ...	25	10	28	23	2	2	3	1
Under 18 ...	2	1	3	—	—	—	3	—
Total ...	112	37	126	124	17	6	15	16

Table C.4. Wastage Survey: Clerical Officers: Seniority in grade of those replying to questionnaire

Seniority	London		Elsewhere	
	Men	Women	Men	Women
15 years or over	—	—	7	3
10-years	4	2	3	5
7-years	2	2	13	25
5-years	17	3	14	21
4-years	14	10	13	15
2-years	26	6	26	16
1-year	23	8	31	20
6-months	17	4	10	10
Under 6 months	9	2	9	9
Total	112	37	126	124

Table C.5. Wastage Survey: Clerical Officers: Overall grading for qualities and performance of duties in present grade of those replying to questionnaire

Grading	Men	Women
Outstanding	1	—
Very able and effective Officer	27	25
Well up to standard	136	100
Rather below standard	29	18
Unsatisfactory	3	—
None given	42*	18†
Total	238	161

* 14 have less than six months' service, 8 less than 1 year and 15 less than 2 years.

† 6 have less than six months, 5 less than 1 year and 4 less than 2 years.

Table C.6. Wastage Survey: Clerical Officers: Items given as being of major importance in decision to leave Civil Service

MEN	Reasons: Family or domestic circumstances	Job outside	Both outside job and Family or dom. circs.	Full-time Education	Both full-time Education and family or dom. circs.	Others	Total
Generally satisfied with Civil Service							
Aged 30 years and over		7	1	6		1	15
20–29 years	4	24	7	21		1	57
Under 20 years	2	13	3	4			22
All	6	44	11	31		2	94
Generally dissatisfied with Civil Service							
Aged 30 years and over		6	1	6		1	14
20–29 years	3	49	6	11	1	1	71
Under 20 years	1	18	6	4	1	1	31
All	4	73	13	21	2	3	116
Expressing no views							
All	1	12	4	9	1	1	28
Total	11	129	28	61	3	6	238

Table C.6. Wastage Survey: Clerical Officers: Items given as being of major importance in decision to leave Civil Service

WOMEN	Reasons: Family or domestic circumstances	Job outside	Both outside job and family or dom. circs.	Full-time education	Both full-time education and family or dom. circs.	Others	Total
Generally satisfied with Civil Service							
Aged 30 years and over	9	1				6	16
20–29 years	58	6	7	5		1	77
Under 20 years	6	10	2	8		1	27
All	73	17	9	13		8	120
Generally dissatisfied with Civil Service							
Aged 30 years and over	1	3				2	6
20–29 years	9	5	1	3			18
Under 20 years	1	5	1				7
All	11	13	2	3		2	31
Expressing no views							
All	5		1	1	1	2	10
Total	89	30	12	17	1	12	161

Table C.7. Wastage Survey: Clerical Officer: Reasons given by grading

Men	Reasons						
Grading	Family or domestic circumstances	Job outside	Both outside job and family or dom. circs.	Full-time education	Both full-time education and family or dom. circs.	Others	Total
Generally satisfied							
Outstanding		1					1
Very able and effective	1	3	3	3			10
Well up to standard	3	29	4	18			54
Rather below standard	1	4	1	3			9
Unsatisfactory		1		1			2
None given	1	6	3	6		2	18
Total	6	44	11	31		2	94
Generally dissatisfied							
Outstanding							
Very able and effective		9		1		2	12
Well up to standard	2	47	6	13	1	1	70
Rather below standard	1	7	3	3			14
Unsatisfactory		1					1
None given	1	9	4	4	1		19
Total	4	73	13	21	2	3	116
All (including those expressing no views)							
Outstanding		1					1
Very able and effective	1	14	4	5		2	26
Well up to standard	5	82	11	35	2	2	137
Rather below standard	3	13	5	7			28
Unsatisfactory		2		1			3
None given	2	17	8	13	1	2	43
Total	11	129	28	61	3	6	238

Table C.7. Wastage Survey: Clerical Officers: Reasons given by grading

Women	Reasons						
Grading	Family or domestic circumstances	Job outside	Both outside job and family or dom. circs.	Full-time education	Both full-time education and family or dom. circs.	Others	Total
Generally satisfied							
Outstanding							
Very able and effective	15		1	2			18
Well up to standard	45	11	5	9		4	74
Rather below standard	7	3	1	1		2	14
Unsatisfactory							
None given	6	3	2	1		2	14
Total	73	17	9	13		8	120
Generally dissatisfied							
Outstanding							
Very able and effective	3	1					4
Well up to standard	5	10	2	3		1	21
Rather below standard	1					1	2
Unsatisfactory							
None given	2	2					4
Total	11	13	2	3		2	31
All (including those expressing no views)							
Outstanding							
Very able and effective	21	1	1	2			25
Well up to standard	51	21	8	13	1	6	100
Rather below standard	9	3	1	1		4	18
Unsatisfactory							
None given	8	5	2	1		2	18
Total	89	30	12	17	1	12	161

Table C.8. Wastage Survey: Clerical Officers: Family or Domestic Reasons given for leaving

Items listed	London			Elsewhere		
	Generally satisfied	Generally dissatisfied	All	Generally satisfied	Generally dissatisfied	All
Men						
Family leaving district	—	1	1	—	—	—
Returning to work near home	8	5	15	3	6	9
Moving for health or personal reasons	1	1	2	—	1	2
Travelling difficulties	1	3	4	2	4	6
Cost of accommodation	—	—	—	1	1	3
Emigration	—	—	—	1	2	3
Other	—	—	1	2	—	2
All items	10	10	23	9	14	25
Total men answering	8	8	20	9	11	22
Women						
Family leaving district	1	—	1	4	1	5
Returning to work near home	2	—	4	1	—	2
Moving for health or personal reasons	1	1	2	2	2	5
Marriage	5	2	7	23	2	26
Pregnancy	2	—	2	30	5	36
Husband leaving district	—	—	—	5	1	7
Travelling difficulties	5	1	7	9	2	13
Cost of accommodation	—	—	—	5	—	5
Emigration	—	—	—	1	—	1
Other	—	—	—	2	—	2
All items	16	4	23	82	13	102
Total women answering	12	3	16	70	10	86

Table C.9. Wastage Survey: Clerical Officers taking jobs outside

Attractions of outside job	London			Elsewhere		
	Generally satisfied	Generally dissatisfied	All	Generally satisfied	Generally dissatisfied	All
Men						
Higher Pay	18	40	64	18	34	60
Better prospects	18	37	61	17	35	58
More scope, more interesting or to broaden experience	14	34	52	17	38	63
Better suited	12	25	40	11	22	35
Better conditions of employment	7	15	25	1	8	11
Total attractions	69	151	242	64	137	227
Total men answering	26	41	75	29	45	82
Women						
Higher pay	9	5	14	6	4	10
Better prospects	5	3	8	6	4	10
More scope, more interesting or to broaden experience	7	4	11	11	8	20
Better suited	2	2	4	7	6	14
Better conditions of employment	4	1	5	3	3	6
Total attractions	27	15	42	33	25	60
Total women answering	11	6	17	15	9	25

Table C.10. Wastage Survey: Clerical Officers going to Full-time education

	Generally satisfied with Civil Service	Generally dissatisfied with Civil Service	All (incl. those expressing no views on Civil Service)
1. *By sex*			
Men	31	22	63
Women	13	3	18
Total	44	25	81
2. *By place of education*			
University	9	7	18
College of Education (no. of women in brackets)	28(11)	14(2)	49(14)
Other Place	7	4	14
3. *By subject studied*			
Arts subjects	12	11	26
Social sciences	2	2	5
Pure or applied science	1	—	3
Nursing	1	—	1
Professional training	7	3	10
Teaching	2	4	6
Other subjects	6	1	9
Not known	13	4	21
4. *By anticipated job*			
School teacher	14	13	29
Other teaching (lecturing)	1	1	3
Armed Forces	1	—	2
Legal work	5	—	5
Commerce	—	2	2
Civil Service	2	—	2
Other	6	3	12
Undecided	1	1	3
Not stated	14	5	23

Table C.11. Wastage Survey: Clerical Officers: Attitudes towards various aspects of the work

Men

Aspects	94 generally satisfied with Civil Service						116 generally dissatisfied with Civil Service						All (238)					
	Very good	Good	Ade-quate	Poor	Very poor	Not stated	Very good	Good	Ade-quate	Poor	Very poor	Not stated	Very good	Good	Ade-quete	Poor	Very poor	Not stated
Pay	3	8	44	30	7	2	1	7	18	60	28	2	5	18	70	99	42	4
Conditions of employment (hours, leave, etc.)	25	49	16	2	—	2	17	51	37	9	1	1	44	114	63	13	1	3
Career prospects	4	16	44	18	11	1	1	1	29	56	27	2	5	18	82	86	44	3
Interest of work	6	21	49	16	2	—	3	15	40	40	18	—	11	37	100	67	23	—
Use made of abilities " To the full " to " not at all "	1	11	17	55	10	—	3	10	14	57	32	—	4	24	34	129	47	—
Departmental training courses	12	21	31	17	7	6	10	14	29	22	25	16	22	38	72	46	37	23
" On the job " training	14	15	48	13	3	1	7	22	39	23	20	5	22	39	102	42	26	7
Departmental posting to give experience and development	5	20	41	17	5	6	2	4	33	45	24	8	7	27	83	73	33	15
Interest taken in personal progress	16	18	31	18	9	2	3	14	25	34	36	4	19	38	64	59	51	7
Superiors " good " or " difficult " to work for	34	42	16	1	—	1	13	33	41	17	9	3	51	84	67	22	9	5
Whether others are " good " or " difficult " colleagues	48	34	10	1	1	1	31	66	15	2	—	1	92	111	29	3	1	2
Office accommodation	16	34	32	5	6	1	6	23	42	22	22	1	25	63	84	29	35	2
	Far too much	Too much	About right	Too little	Far too little	Not stated	Far too much	Too much	About right	Too little	Far too little	Not stated	Far too much	Too much	About right	Too little	Far too little	Not stated
Responsibility	1	—	64	25	4	—	2	11	41	38	23	1	4	13	119	68	32	2
Work	3	7	65	17	2	—	16	32	39	19	7	3	22	43	121	38	10	4

Table C.11—continued

Women

Aspects	120 generally satisfied with Civil Service						131 generally dissatisfied with Civil Service						All (161)					
	Very good	Good	Ade-quate	Poor	Very Poor	Not stated	Very good	Good	Ade-quate	Poor	Very poor	Not stated	Very good	Good	Ade-quate	Poor	Very poor	Not stated
Pay	13	59	39	7	1	1	2	12	9	7	1	—	16	73	52	17	2	1
Conditions of employment (hours, leave, etc.)	26	54	34	4	—	2	3	18	8	2	—	—	30	77	45	7	—	2
Career prospects	7	25	52	30	5	1	—	2	10	12	7	—	7	28	67	45	12	2
Interest of work	7	42	63	6	1	1	—	2	10	13	4	2	7	45	80	20	5	4
Use made of abilities (" To the full " to " not at all ")	1	27	50	41	1	—	1	1	4	19	4	2	2	29	58	63	6	3
Departmental training courses	8	42	34	22	7	7	1	3	9	9	5	4	9	48	45	33	12	14
" On the job " training	3	33	43	33	7	1	—	21	14	10	3	2	3	36	60	48	10	4
Departmental posting to give experience and development	—	15	61	33	6	5	—	1	11	12	3	4	—	16	77	48	9	11
Interest taken in personal progress	22	20	38	28	11	1	1	3	7	7	12	1	26	24	47	36	24	4
Superiors " good " or " difficult " to work for	20	55	34	9	—	2	—	13	16	1	—	1	21	73	53	10	—	4
Whether others are " good " or " difficult " colleagues	37	69	12	1	—	1	10	17	4	—	—	—	49	91	17	2	—	2
Office accommodation	10	34	45	18	12	1	1	5	11	5	9	—	12	42	58	23	24	2
	Far too much	Too much	About right	Too little	Far too little	Not stated	Far too much	Too much	About right	Too little	Far too little	Not stated	Far too much	Too much	About right	Too little	Far too little	Not stated
Responsibility	—	8	93	18	—	1	1	1	44	9	4	2	2	10	112	29	4	4
Work	2	27	79	10	—	2	3	6	16	3	2	1	7	34	100	14	2	4

Appendix 1

General Description of the Wastage Survey

1. The Wastage Survey covered established Executive and Clerical Officers in the general Executive and Clerical Classes and all the statistics in this report relating to Executive and Clerical Officers refer to the general service grades. The Ministry of Labour Departmental Class was also included in the Survey, but the numbers of officers leaving that Department in the first four months of the currency of the Survey were not large enough to warrant separate statistical treatment and they have not been included in the tables relating to the general service class.

2. The form issued to those leaving (Form 1 of Appendix 2) stated that the information they provided would be used solely for statistical purposes and otherwise would be treated in the strictest confidence and would in no way reflect on them or form part of their personal records. It was suggested to Departments that they should ask an officer to complete the form immediately after he had handed in his notice and before he actually left the Civil Service. They were asked to arrange for a senior officer to explain personally to the officer concerned the reasons for the enquiry and to ask for his co-operation. In explaining the purpose of the enquiry Departments were asked to emphasise the fact that replies would be treated as confidential and to make it clear that there was no question of the answers being revealed to other people in the Department or forming part of the personal papers of the officer concerned. It was suggested that the form should be accompanied by an envelope for its return with the title of the enquiry and the officer's name on the outside so that the Departments could easily link the form completed by the officer leaving with the complementary form (Form 2 of Appendix 2) which they completed. Departments were asked to be careful not to discuss the question or answers with respondents.

3. The questionnaire issued to officers leaving the Civil Service was designed to cover the main reasons which they were likely to give for leaving. It first asked them to indicate what factors were of major importance in their decision to leave. The factors were divided into main groups: those which could be regarded as primarily family or domestic circumstances, and those which were primarily external to the home or to the Civil Service, e.g. the attractions of another job or undertaking full-time education or training. These sections were not designed to be mutually exclusive. Those leaving were then asked to state whether they were generally satisfied or generally dissatisfied with the Civil Service. Irrespective of whether they were satisfied they were asked to complete the section of the questionnaire dealing with attitudes towards certain aspects of work in the Civil Service. Finally respondents were asked to indicate which of all the reasons mentioned on the form they regarded as the most important motive for changing their job. They were asked to give up to three reasons.

4. Although respondents were given an opportunity to write-in additional reasons for leaving, over and above those listed on the form, the questionnaire was designed with a view to its being completed with a minimum of effort largely

by means of circling the appropriate numbers. It was necessary to strike a balance between a long and complicated document which some leavers might be unwilling to complete and a very short, and apparently simple form, to which no one could object. Such a form would however have relied much more heavily on the person setting out his reasons in writing and the detail and scope of such replies would vary enormously and be very difficult to analyse satisfactorily. In the event it was not found that officers leaving were reluctant to complete the form (in the first four months 89 per cent completed the questionnaire).

5. Officers who died, or who retired at or above the normal age, or for reasons of ill health, or who were dismissed for misconduct, inefficiency or redundancy were not included in the Survey. Although women leaving the Service on marriage were included, Departments were asked not to issue the questionnaire to such women who resigned on marriage, but continued to serve in an unestablished capacity without break of service. Details of those who left the Service under these headings in the four months ending 31st December 1966 are to be found in the following table:

All Departments

Total Losses from the Civil Service during the period 1st September to 31st December 1966 showing cause of leaving

Cause of loss	Executive Officers		Clerical Officers	
	Men	Women	Men	Women
(*a*) Retirements at or above the normal age	77	36	397	246
(*b*) Death	34	5	85	26
(*c*) Ill health	8	10	63	56
(*d*) Dismissals for misconduct, inefficiency or redundancy	2	—	9	1
(*e*) Women resigning on marriage, but re-employed in an unestablished capacity	—	25	—	206
Total (*a* to *e*)	121	76	554	535
(*f*) Other reasons				
(i) included in Wastage Survey sample	97	154	270	183
(ii) not included in Wastage Survey sample (see para. 8)	—	—	383	943
Total (*a* to *f*)	218	230	1,207	1,661

6. Departments were asked to include those who actually left in the year beginning 1st September 1966, including any who had already handed in their notices before the questionnaire and forms were issued to Departments, together with notes on procedure, in late July 1966.

7. As already mentioned, the whole wastage survey will relate to the 12 month period starting on 1st September 1966 but the figures included in this report relate only to the four month period from 1st September to the end of 1966. It will only be possible to assess with certainty the extent to which seasonal factors have affected the results when statistics for the full period are available. It

seems likely, however, that in the four-month period under review a disproportionate number left to take up full-time education. This is discussed in Sections 4 and 5.

8. All Executive Officers who left for " other reasons " were included in the Wastage Survey but, because of the larger numbers involved, only a sample of the Clerical Officers. The sample of Clerical Officers was random and was designed to comprise 50 per cent of the men and 20 per cent of the women which should give adequate numbers during a full year. Departments were given a choice of methods to select the sample to suit the form of their own records and in practice the realised sample fell slightly short of the expected proportions in that it included 41 per cent of the men and 16 per cent of the women.

Appendix 2

FORM 1

Reasons for leaving the Civil Service

Executive and Clerical Officers Enquiry

Serial Number .... NAME ....

GRADE ....

We are trying to find out exactly why people leave the Civil Service. We would be grateful if you could help by indicating on this document why you are leaving. For convenience it has been set out so that you should normally be able to give your reasons for leaving and attitudes towards work in the Civil Service by circling the appropriate numbers, but if you are leaving for a reason not listed then please say what it is in Section E (question 26).

The information you provide will be used solely for statistical purposes and otherwise will be treated in the STRICTEST CONFIDENCE and will in no way reflect on you or form part of your personal records.

Please circle the numbers on the left hand side of the form of any of the following items in Sections A and B which have been of major importance in your decision to leave the Department.

A. 1 My family is leaving the district

2 I am returning to work near my home

3 I wish to move to another district for health or similar personal reasons

For women only:

4 Marriage, recent or pending

5 Pregnancy

6 My husband is leaving the district

7 I am leaving because of travelling difficulties

8 Other reasons relating to family or domestic circumstances: specify

....

B. 9 I am taking a job outside the Civil Service. If this answer (9) applies, please indicate which of the reasons in 1–5 applies in your case by circling the appropriate number.

I am doing this because I believe that:

(1) I shall receive higher pay

(2) I shall have better prospects

(3) I shall have more scope, or more interesting work, or will be broadening my experience

(4) I shall be better suited to it

(5) I shall have better conditions of employment (hours, holidays and fringe benefits)

10 I shall be undertaking full-time education or training in (please circle as appropriate)

(1) A University or College of Advanced Technology

(2) A College of Education

(3) Elsewhere please specify...

....

(4) Please enter the subject you will be studying....................................

....

(5) Please indicate the job which you eventually hope to undertake

....

Irrespective of the answers you may have given in Sections A and B we would now like you to go on and answer Sections C and D.

C. Please circle the number of whichever of the following statements applies:

i. I have been generally satisfied with my Civil Service job and am leaving for reasons already indicated in Sections A and B.

ii. Quite apart from any reasons for leaving indicated above, I am generally dissatisfied with the Civil Service for reasons mentioned in Section D.

In either case please complete Section D by circling the number (1, 2, 3, 4 *or* 5) *in each of the statements below which best indicates your feelings.* If 25 applies please circle the number of the question.

D. My attitude towards certain aspects of the work is as follows:

	1	2	3	4	5
11 The pay is	Very good	Good	Adequate	Rather poor	Very poor

12	The conditions of employment (hours, leave etc.) are:	1 Very good	2 Good	3 Adequate	4 Rather poor	5 Very poor
13	I think my career prospects, if I were going to stay in the Civil Service, are:	1 Very good indeed	2 Good	3 Reasonable	4 Poor	5 Very poor indeed
14	I think the amount of responsibility I am expected to take in my work is:	1 Far too much	2 Too much	3 About right	4 Too little	5 Far too little
15	I think my work is:	1 Interesting all the time	2 Interesting most of the time	3 Partly interesting Partly boring	4 Boring most of the time	5 Boring all of the time
16	I think the amount of work we are expected to do is:	1 Far too much	2 Rather too much	3 About right	4 Rather too little	5 Far too little
17	I think my work uses my abilities:	1 To the full	2 Reasonably fully	3 Adequately	4 Not enough	5 Not at all
18	I think that the training courses provided by the department, both those as a background to the work of the department and those on more general subjects, are:	1 Very good indeed	2 Good	3 Adequate	4 Poor	5 Very poor indeed

		1	2	3	4	5
19	I think that from the point of view of enabling me to do my job as well as possible the training provided " on the job " is:	Very good indeed	Good	Adequate	Poor	Very poor indeed
20	I think that in my department posting to give staff the experience required for full use and development of their abilities is arranged:	Very well indeed	Well	Adequately	Badly	Very badly indeed
21	I think that the interest taken in my personal progress and development has been:	Considerable and sustained	Marked from time to time	Adequate	Sporadic	Negligible
22	I think that my superiors are:	Very good to work for	Good to work for	Not particularly good or difficult to work for	Rather difficult to work for	Very difficult to work for
23	I think that the other people with whom I work are:	All good colleagues	With one or two exceptions, good colleagues	Some good, some difficult colleagues	With one or two exceptions difficult colleagues	All difficult colleagues

24 I think that the office accommodation is:	1 Very good indeed	2 Good	3 Not particularly good or bad	4 Bad	5 Very bad indeed

25 My main reason for dissatisfaction is that I am threatened with transfer to another district or department.

E. 26 Another reason for dissatisfaction (not mentioned in any of the sections on this form) is:

F. We should now like to know which of all the reasons mentioned in sections A, B and D above (1–26) you regard as the most important motives for your changing your employment. You may, if you wish, give up to three reasons.

Please give the numbers below in order of importance

First ☐

Second ☐

Third ☐

FORM 2

Reasons for Wastage of Established General Service Executive and Clerical Officers

(*to be completed by the Department*)

Serial Number...
(for completion by E.M. (Stats.))

Delete inapplicable items in this section

Surname.................................Initials ....

Single woman (1)/
Married woman (2)/
Man (7)/

Month and year (enter as e.g. 3/40) of

(*a*) Birth ....

Grade: EO(0339)/CO(5121)

(*b*) Entry to Grade ....

Entering Grade by:

(*c*) Entry to Department ....

promotion (1)/
competition other than limited (3)/
limited competition (4)/
nomination or other means (9)

(*d*) Leaving the Department ....

Complete according to the codes in the Central Staff Record Handbook

Department (It. 1) ....

Location (It. 24) ....

This officer has left this Department and the Civil Service for a reason other than death, retirement at or above the normal age, premature retirement through ill health or dismissal for misconduct, inefficiency or redundancy.

He has completed Form 1—attached } delete whichever is
He was unwilling to complete Form 1 } inapplicable

On the basis of the last Annual Report available his assessment was:—

G. *Overall grading for qualities and performance of duties in present grade (Please circle the appropriate numbers)*

Outstanding	5
A very able and effective officer	4
Well up to standard	3
Rather below standard	2
Unsatisfactory	1

H. *Fitness for Promotion (Please circle the appropriate numbers)*

This officer is now capable of performing the duties of the next higher grade	Exceptionally well	5
	Very well	4
	Satisfactorily	3
This officer is not now capable of performing the duties of of the next higher grade. He is	Likely to qualify in time	2
	Unlikely to qualify	1

MEMORANDUM No. 8

submitted by

HER MAJESTY'S TREASURY

December, 1967

Study of Ability, Efficiency and Job Satisfaction among Executive and Clerical Officers

Contents

Introduction

1. This report relates to a survey of the ability, efficiency and job-satisfaction of a sample of Executive Officers and Clerical Officers employed within eleven Government Departments falling within one of two different categories. The first category (comprising five departments) is offices with large concentrations of staff doing similar work under the same management; the second category (comprising six departments) is offices containing staff in small sub-groups each engaged on a different kind of work but all subject to the same management. 1,507 Executive Officers and 1,982 Clerical Officers participated in the survey.

2. In April, 1965, a Working Party was set up, under the aegis of the Civil Service Efficiency Committee, to obtain factual evidence of the extent of the success which attends the policies and practices adopted in the recruitment and management of Executive Officers and Clerical Officers. The Working Party comprised members of the Establishments Management Divisions 1 and 2, the Establishments Management Statistics Division, the Welfare Branch and the Management Services (General) Division of the Treasury and, on a personal basis, the General Secretaries of the Society of Civil Servants and the Civil Service Clerical Association. It was decided to approach the task by exploring the factors which affect the ability, the efficiency and the attitudes to their employment of individual officers in these grades. The survey was possible only as a result of the ready co-operation of Management and Staff Side representatives at all levels in the departments concerned. We are grateful for this co-operation as well as that of individual officers who completed job-satisfaction questionnaires.

3. The study involved the collection of material of four kinds about each officer: none of the material bore the officer's name, a serial number being used to relate different documents for the same officer:

(*a*) From assessment forms (Appendix 1) completed independently by each officer's immediate supervisor and the latter's supervisor, appraisals of:

  (i) the level of ability the officer would be capable of developing given appropriate training and encouragement in the type of work for which he was best suited, i.e. whether he would be:

    (*a*) very much above, much above or above the standard required for the grade;
    (*b*) of the standard required for the grade; or
    (*c*) below, much below or very much below the standard required for the grade.

  In the analyses which follow, these assessments are referred to as " above standard ", " standard " or " below standard "; and

  (ii) his suitability for his job, i.e. whether he was suited only to his present work or as well suited to other types of work or better suited only to other types of work.

If the two assessments agreed within narrow limits, they formed the basis of ability and suitability markings in subsequent statistical analyses: but if the two assessments differed appreciably the officer was excluded from this part of the study but not from others;

(*b*) his efficiency as recorded in the latest staff annual report, i.e. whether his performance on his present duties was (*a*) outstanding or very good;

(*b*) good; or (*c*) fair or unsatisfactory. In our analyses these efficiency ratings are referred to as " above standard ", " standard " or " below standard ";

(*c*) facts about the officer's age, health and career—extracted from his personal file and sickness record; and

(*d*) his attitude to his employment and to a variety of different aspects to it, recorded in answers to a questionnaire completed by the officer himself.

4. In preparing the forms used for this study, we sought expert advice outside the Civil Service. We are grateful to those who assisted us in this way. Specimens of the three forms used for the collection of this material are at Appendices 1, 2 and 3.

5. The material was processed with the help of punched card equipment and analyses of the results made in order to explore the importance of factors affecting respectively:

(*a*) ability;

(*b*) efficiency; and

(*c*) job-satisfaction.

In addition, the relationship between efficiency and job-satisfaction was examined.

6. Because of the age of the officer or the shortness of his service in the grade or branch, a current Civil Service annual report (which includes an assessment of efficiency) was not always available for each participant. Such officers have had to be excluded from the analyses we have made on factors affecting efficiency but they have been included in that part of this report that relates to job-satisfaction. Furthermore, our total population varies because some analyses relate to:

(*a*) officers who were appraised for ability and suitability;

(*b*) officers who completed the job-satisfaction questionnaire; and

(*c*) officers who were common to both groups.

In about 10 per cent of cases it was necessary to exclude officers from some analyses because there were significant differences between the assessments of their two supervisors. Each of the officers for whom assessment forms were completed was invited to complete a job-satisfaction questionnaire (Appendix 3) and 86 per cent did so.

Recruitment and promotion procedure within the Civil Service

7. Recruitment to the Executive Class is from:

(*a*) Open competition by interview conducted by the Civil Service Commission for candidates between 17½–28 years of age who have two passes at the advanced level of the General Certificate of Education or an equivalent qualification.

(*b*) A competition conducted by the Civil Service Commission open to candidates who are serving in H.M. Forces or who completed a period of service within the previous 2 years.

(*c*) A competition conducted by the Civil Service Commission limited to officers in the clerical class between 19–24 years of age.

(*d*) Promotion by departmental selection from among established members of the clerical class aged 25 and over.

8. Recruitment to the clerical class is by direct recruitment and by the promotion of clerical assistants. In addition there is an annual limited competition among subordinate sub-clerical and non-clerical grades. The main avenue of direct recruitment is departmental selection of suitable candidates with five " O " level passes in the General Certificate of Education (or equivalent). The age limits are 15–59. For posts in London and certain other shortage areas the Civil Service Commission recruits direct to established posts by written examinations and on the strength of G.C.E. qualifications. Regular competitions are also held for ex-members of H.M. Forces.

9. Within the Civil Service promotions of E.Os and C.Os are made departmentally on the advice of a Promotion Board consisting of a number of selected senior officers. Promotions are made according to merit and not purely by seniority. The Board takes into account staff reports and may interview, from the agreed field of selection, a number of the most likely candidates for promotion. The annual staff report is an important factor in determining the suitability of an officer for promotion. Reports on all staff within the field of selection are examined and a special report may be called for if there is reason to believe that the latest one does not give a true up-to-date assessment.

10. In addition and in order to reduce disparities between departments, promotion pooling arrangements are promulgated each year. Under these arrangements the ratio of promotions to staff in the grade below is calculated for the preceding three calendar years and departments with promotion ratios above that of the Service as a whole contribute a specified quota of vacancies to the year's Pool. Departments with lower promotion ratios nominate corresponding quotas of suitable officers to be tested by the Pool Promotion Board, selected for promotion and transferred to fill the vacancies.

Ability

11. Appendix 4 sets out particulars of the distributions of ability amongst sub-populations. It must be borne in mind that the samples included only those who were of the Executive Officer or Clerical Officer grade at the time of the survey and did not include those who had passed through these grades but had since left the Service or had been promoted. Thus comparisons between levels of ability of young and older officers must be treated with reserve since the former, unlike the latter, are not likely to have lost any appreciable numbers through promotions.

12. The survey has shown that both Executive Officers and Clerical Officers are, almost without exception, up to the standard of ability required and not infrequently capable of developing a standard above that demanded for their grade. The number of E.Os and C.Os below standard ability is very small—1·1 per cent of our sample (0·9 per cent in the case of E.Os and 1·2 per cent for C.Os).

13. 41 per cent of male E.Os and 33 per cent of female E.Os are assessed as being capable of developing above standard ability, nearly one-half of both men and women under the age of 40 being so assessed. Amongst C.Os, 34 per cent of the men and 26 per cent of the women are capable of a standard of ability above that required of their grade.

14. The survey has suggested relationships between ability and the following:
(*a*) method of entry to the Civil Service;
(*b*) grade of entry to the Civil Service;
(*c*) method of entry to the grade; and
(*d*) educational attainment.
These are discussed in the 6 paragraphs which follow.

Method of entry to the Civil Service (Appendix 5A and B)

15. The analysis of the levels of ability amongst established entrants to the Civil Service by open competition (direct entrants to the E.O. or C.O. grade) and by local recruitment (officers originally recruited by departments into sub-clerical or non-clerical grades) suggests that both sources provide officers who again, almost without exception, are up to the standard of ability required for their grade. (Only 1·3 per cent of those who were locally recruited fail to measure up to this standard.) Amongst E.Os in age-groups where comparisons are justified, the figures suggest that higher proportions of staff capable of developing above standard ability are to be found amongst competition entrants. Thus, for example, amongst male E.Os aged 25–39 and 40–49, 51 per cent of competition entrants are so assessed compared with 37 per cent for locally recruited personnel. In the case of C.Os, there is nothing to choose between the two sources as providers of staff of above standard ability; amongst men and women aged under 40, 35 per cent of competition entrants are assessed as capable of above standard ability against 31 per cent of locally recruited staff.

Grade of entry to the Civil Service (Appendix 6A and B)

16. The tables at appendices 6A and 6B show the distributions of ability analysed by recruitment grade, and suggest that promotion into both the executive and clerical officer grades from other classes provides officers who, almost always, are up to the standard of ability required for the grade and, not infrequently, are capable of above standard ability. The figures do not suggest that higher proportions of staff capable of above standard ability are necessarily found amongst direct entrants to the grade. For example, amongst men and women E.Os aged under 40, 54 per cent of the direct recruits to the grade are assessed as capable of above standard ability against 52 per cent of those who entered the Service as a clerical officer; amongst men and women C.Os aged under 40, 37 per cent of the direct recruits to the grade are assessed as capable of above standard ability against 30 per cent of those who started as established clerical assistants and 31 per cent of those who started as temporary clerical assistants. It could well be that this finding is affected by the fact that direct entrants to a grade tend to obtain promotion to a higher grade at an earlier age than other entrants; and it is noticeable that amongst older E.Os, higher proportions of staff capable of above standard ability are found amongst those who started as clerical officers compared with those who started in lower classes. For example, amongst male E.Os aged 40 and over, 48 per cent of those who

entered the Service as Clerical Officers are assessed as capable of above standard ability, against 38 per cent of those who started as temporary clerical assistants and 25 per cent of those who started as Post Office manipulatives.

Method of entry to the Grade (Appendix 7A and B)

17. An analysis of the levels of ability amongst entrants to the grade by open competition, limited competition and by promotion suggests that, amongst E.Os in the 25–39 age group where the comparison may be made, there is little to choose between open competition entrants and those Clerical Officers who secure admittance to the grade through the limited E.O. examination. But the proportion of promotees to the grade who are assessed as capable of above standard ability is significantly smaller than the proportion of competition entrants so assessed.

Educational attainment (Appendix 8A and B)

18. The tables might suggest that the level of educational attainment is irrelevant to the question whether E.Os and C.Os are of the standard of ability required for the grade and, furthermore, may not be an important factor bearing on the development of above standard ability. Amongst male E.Os in the 25–39 age group, 53 per cent of those with 2 or more " A " levels are assessed as capable of above standard ability (against 46 per cent with 5 or more " O " levels and 39 per cent with less than 5 " O " levels) and there is little difference between the proportions of older male E.Os with 5 or more " O " levels and those with less than 5 " O " levels who are so assessed. Amongst all women E.Os aged 40 and over, 27 per cent of those with 5 or more " O " levels, are assessed as capable of above standard ability as against 24 per cent of those with less than 5 "O" levels.

19. Amongst C.Os under 40, the difference between the distributions by ability within each educational category again does not quite reach significance. (Comparisons for C.Os over 40 cannot usefully be drawn as less than 14 per cent of the sample have 5 or more " O " levels.)

20. As in para. 16 however, these findings may be affected by the fact that direct entrants to a grade (i.e. usually those with the higher educational attainment) tend to obtain promotion to a higher grade at an earlier age than other entrants. Moreover, the analyses demonstrate a downward pattern in each case and although differences do not reach statistical significance, we cannot conclude that educational attainment has no relevance to assessments of ability.

Efficiency

21. The table at Appendix 9 shows distributions of efficiency amongst our subpopulations. The analysis reveals that about two-thirds of the total staff are of standard efficiency. Amongst E.Os, some 26 per cent are of above standard efficiency and 7 per cent work at below standard efficiency. The proportion for C.Os is 20 and 12 per cent respectively. The proportion of officers in some age groups, particularly amongst Clerical Officers, who are working at below standard efficiency is large enough to raise the question whether there is something which could and should be done to reduce the proportion. Conversely, and again amongst Clerical Officers, the proportion of officers in some age groups who are of above standard efficiency is small enough to point to a need to increase the

proportion. We comment further on these problems in the next three sub-sections of this report dealing with:

(*a*) health;
(*b*) experience; and
(*c*) suitability.

Health (Appendices 10–11)

22. We have analysed the sickness records of our total population according to a formula based on advice received from the Treasury Medical Adviser. We find that 6·2 per cent of the total staff can be regarded as not enjoying satisfactory health (the proportion varies from 4·6 per cent in the case of male Executive Officers to 8·6 per cent for women Clerical Officers). A summary of the figures at Appendix 10A and B reveals the following:

Category	*No.*	*Above standard* %	*Standard efficiency* %	*Below standard* %
Executive Officers				
Men—				
Of good health	766	29	66	5
Of doubtful health	37	24	65	11
Women—				
Of good health	350	23	68	9
Of doubtful health	21	14	72	14
Clerical Officers				
Men—				
Of good health	620	21	68	11
Of doubtful health	41	17	61	22
Women—				
Of good health	560	20	68	12
Of doubtful health	53	11	66	23
All men—				
Of good health	1,386	25	67	8
Of doubtful health	78	20	63	17
All women—				
Of good health	910	21	68	11
Of doubtful health	74	12	68	20
Total men and women				
Of good health	2,296	24	67	9
Of doubtful health	152	16	65	18

23. The number of staff of doubtful health is small but the pattern does suggest an association between health and efficiency ratings.

24. Over 80 per cent of our sample took 2 days or less uncertificated sick leave per annum over the past 5 years; the proportion who took 4 days or more was 6 per cent. The tables at Appendix 11 have been produced to determine

whether the amount of uncertificated sick leave taken bears any relationship to an officer's efficiency. A summary of the figures shows the following:

Efficiency	*No.*	*Average number of days uncertificated sick leave p.a. over past 5 years*
Men—		
Above standard	369	1·08
Standard	976	1·18
Below standard	122	1·24
Women—		
Above standard	199	1·44
Standard	676	1·64
Below standard	112	1·52
All Staff—		
Above standard	568	1·20
Standard	1,652	1·37
Below standard	234	1·37

25. Although there is some suggestion (especially in the case of men) of a correlation between level of efficiency and uncertificated sick leave, the differences are not large enough to be statistically significant. With uncertificated sick leave in particular, there is also the problem of cause and effect in the relationship with efficiency. (See also para. 49—uncertificated sick leave and job-satisfaction; and para. 88—job-satisfaction and efficiency).

Experience

26. Analysis of efficiency ratings by length of service in the grade reveals the following:

Length of service in the grade	*No.*	*Above standard* %	*Standard efficiency* %	*Below standard* %
Executive Officers				
Under 2 years	182	15	77	8
2 ,,	132	18	74	8
3 ,,	118	19	75	6
4 ,,	95	24	76	—
5 ,,	188	29	67	4
7 ,,	138	37	57	6
10 ,,	113	28	59	12
15 years and over	175	28	59	13
Clerical Officers				
Under 2 years	147	10	81	10
2 ,,	167	13	75	12
3 ,,	104	18	77	5
4 ,,	65	25	66	9
5 ,,	145	22	68	10
7 ,,	161	20	66	14
10 ,,	159	21	63	16
15 years and over	285	28	58	14

27. Inexperience of the grade is an obvious factor in preventing or delaying the achievement of a high performance. For example, amongst E.Os, 31 per cent of those with over 7 years service in the grade are working at above standard efficiency as compared with 17 per cent of those with under 4 years' service.

28. Analysis of efficiency ratings by length of service in the branch reveals the following:

Length of service in the branch	*No.*	*Above standard* %	*Standard efficiency* %	*Below standard* %
Executive Officers				
Under 1 year	118	25	68	7
1 years	217	18	70	12
2 ,,	180	23	68	9
3 ,,	102	24	71	4
4 ,,	95	26	71	3
5 ,,	127	28	66	6
7 ,,	117	29	68	3
10 years and over	203	32	62	6
Clerical Officers				
Under 1 year	100	16	74	10
1 years	211	19	69	11
2 ,,	202	11	79	10
3 ,,	89	25	63	12
4 ,,	114	25	70	5
5 ,,	106	23	70	8
7 ,,	153	22	65	13
10 ,,	85	28	62	9
15 years and over	194	23	56	21

29. The association between efficiency ratings and length of service in the branch is not absolutely clear cut but, in the case of C.Os, retention on the same (or similar) work for over 15 years is associated with a greater number working at below standard efficiency. 21 per cent of C.Os with over 15 years service in the same branch are working at below standard efficiency as compared with 10 per cent of those with less than 15 years service in the same branch.

Suitability

30. Out of a total of 1,487 E.Os, 14·7 per cent were assessed as either suited to their present duties but better suited to other work or not suited to their present work but suited to other work. The proportion for 1,594 C.Os was 13·7 per cent.

31. We have carried this analysis further in an attempt to discover whether there is any relationship between efficiency and suitability for the work. Our analyses give the following results:

	No.	Suited only to own job %	Suited to own and to other work %	Better suited to other work %	Not suited to own job but suited to other work %
Executive Officers					
Above standard	302	6	88	6	—
Standard efficiency	760	11	74	15	1
Below standard	79	16	35	24	24
Clerical Officers					
Above standard	250	6	83	11	—
Standard efficiency	851	17	71	11	1
Below standard	140	25	41	25	9

32. The evidence suggests an association between efficiency ratings and assessments of suitability for the work. We do no overlook the fact that the assessments on suitability may, at times, be wrong, e.g. a supervisor reporting on an officer who performs on his present post at a level of efficiency below that of standard for the grade may easily assume that the officer must be better suited or suited only to other work. Nevertheless we regard these results as significant.

33. We recognise that because assessments of ability were based on potential for the type of work for which the officer was judged most suitable and that assessments of efficiency were based on performance on his present job, any comparisons between the two assessments would present difficulties of interpretation. We have, nevertheless, found it of interest to examine the data relating to each of those officers assessed as capable of developing above standard ability but presently working only at the standard level of efficiency.

34. Of 217 E.Os assessed as capable of developing above standard ability (but with a standard efficiency rating);

(*a*) 84 (39 per cent) are assessed as better suited or suited only to other work;
(*b*) 31 (14 per cent) dislike the job or are indifferent to it;
(*c*) 30 (14 per cent) are dissatisfied with the scope of the work and feel that it makes insufficient demands upon them;
(*d*) 9 (4 per cent) find lack of training, particularly desk training, a strong source of dissatisfaction; and
(*e*) 6 (3 per cent) feel that departmental postings to work which would fully employ their capabilities are inadequate.

35. Of 203 C.Os assessed as capable of developing above standard ability (but with a standard efficiency rating):

(*a*) 57 (28 per cent) are assessed as better suited or suited only to other work;
(*b*) 26 (13 per cent) dislike the job or are indifferent to it;
(*c*) 39 (19 per cent) are dissatisfied with the scope of the work;
(*d*) 8 (4 per cent) are not pleased with training arrangements; and
(*e*) 7 (3 per cent) are dissatisfied with the departmental posting policy.

36. For the reasons given in para. 33, no firm conclusions can be drawn from the above but we cannot help surmising that a large proportion of those officers of potentially above standard ability who perform at a standard level

of efficiency might well benefit from a change of duties, if, in fact, a change to other work is practicable.

Job-satisfaction

37. Part of the survey was devoted to considering the extent of job-satisfaction and the influence of factors affecting it. The principal ones are as follows:

Attitude towards the Civil Service (Appendix 12A and B)

38. High proportions of young officers say that they are not pleased at having joined the Civil Service. The proportions are:

E.Os under 25	–	25 per cent
,, 25–39	–	26 ,, ,,
C.Os under 25	–	29 ,, ,,
,, 25–39	–	12 ,, ,,

The appendices show that the proportions are clearly lower for officers aged 40 or over and in particular, older women are pleased at having joined the service. This may stem in part from dissatisfied officers resigning in their early years of service.

39. The influence of previous employment elsewhere on attitudes towards joining the Civil Service is not consistent between the different age groups. Generally speaking however, older officers with previous employment tend to be more pleased at having joined the service than their older colleagues with no previous outside employment. The reverse is the case for the few younger officers with previous outside employment extending to at least 2 years.

Attitude to the job (Appendix 13A and B)

40. It seemed likely that individuals' attitudes to the job might vary from time to time but answers to questionnaires indicate that only a minority of the respondents thought that any significant variations occurred.

41. About two-thirds (69 per cent) of all E.Os like the job; one-fifth (21 per cent) are indifferent to it and 10 per cent dislike it.

42. Young C.Os are more critical of the job than their executive colleagues; of the C.Os aged under 25, only about one-half like the job whilst nearly a third are indifferent to it and a sixth positively dislike it. The views of male C.Os aged 25–39 and 40–49 are similar to those of their executive colleagues but amongst male C.Os aged 50 and over and women C.Os aged 25 and over, more than three-quarters like the job and less than a quarter are either indifferent to or dislike it.

43. We have made a comparative study of the job attitudes of those employed in offices with large concentrations of staff doing the same work and those employed in offices of the " Whitehall " type and find no significant difference between them, except in the case of E.Os aged under 40 where, of those employed in offices with large concentrations of staff doing the same work, only 46 per cent like the job compared with 71 per cent of those employed in the " Whitehall " type of office.

44. The survey has suggested the following relationship of various factors to job attitudes:

Method of entry to the Service

45. We have analysed the job attitudes of entrants to the Civil Service by open competition and by local recruitment. The views of women E.Os and older C.Os within these two categories are closely similar. But amongst male E.Os aged 25 and over and C.Os under 40 higher proportions of officers originally recruited by departments into sub-clerical or non-clerical grades like the job compared with their colleagues who were direct entrants to the grade through open competitions.

Length of service in the grade

46. An analysis of the attitude to the job of all male officers aged 25 or over, with 3 years service or more in the grade reveals the following:

Length of service in the grade	*No.*	*Attitude to the job* Like %	Indifference %	*Dislike* %
Executive Officers				
3 years	137	75	19	6
5 ,,	242	70	22	8
10 ,,	50	70	20	10
15 years and over	39	69	21	10
Clerical Officers				
3 years	51	76	16	8
5 ,,	110	70	16	14
10 ,,	68	57	29	14
15 years and over	167	57	29	14

47. The views of E.Os are closely similar but, in the case of C.Os, there is a striking decrease in the liking for the job of those with 10 years or more service in the grade.

Health

48. The survey has produced no evidence to suggest that poor health has any bearing on job attitudes.

49. We have attempted to explore whether the amount of uncertificated sick leave taken is any guide to the attitude towards the job of individual officers. A summary of the tables at Appendix 14A and B produces the following results:

Job attitude	*No.*	*Average no. of days taken per annum over past 5 years*
Executive Officers		
Men—		
Like	629	0·95
Indifference and dislike	295	1·17
Women—		
Like	271	1·28
Indifference and dislike	126	1·55

Job attitude	*No.*	*Average no. of days taken per annum over past 5 years*
Clerical Officers		
Men—		
Like	442	1·27
Indifference and dislike	305	1·49
Single women—		
Like	319	1·46
Indifference and dislike	154	1·92
Married women—		
Like	158	1·61
Indifference and dislike	53	1·94

50. Differences are significant and the analysis thus suggests that there is a tendency for officers who are indifferent to or dislike the job, to take more uncertificated sick leave than their colleagues who like the job. (See paragraph 25—efficiency and uncertificated sick leave.)

Type of work

51. The work content of the job performed by each of the male E.Os included in our sample broadly falls into one of the three following categories:

(*a*) work demanding literate qualities (paper work not requiring an aptitude for figures);

(*b*) work demanding both literate and numerate qualities (paper work requiring an aptitude for figures); and

(*c*) organisation and management of work and control of junior staff.

An analysis of job attitudes to work content reveals the following:

Male E.Os	*% liking the job employed on* Category (*a*)	Category (*b*)	Category (*c*)
40 and over—			
With 5 or more " O " levels	75	61	61
With less than 5 " O " levels	74	65	80
25–39—			
With 2 or more " A " levels	57	67	50
With 5 or more " O " levels	72	63	46
With less than 5 " O " levels	64	70	69
Under 25—			
2 or more " A " levels—literate	74	57	—
2 or more " A " levels—literate and numerate	77	56	—

52. The samples are too small for the differences between the proportions liking the job to be regarded as significant and we would not be justified in attempting to draw any conclusions from the overall pattern.

53. We have, however, analysed the job attitude of each respondent (irrespective of the type of work performed) against the assessments by supervisors of

his suitability for the work. The analysis has produced the following distributions:

Attitude to the Job	*No.*	*Suited only to own job* %	*Suited to own and to other work* %	*Better suited or suited only to other work* %
Executive Officers				
Men—				
Like	629	8	78	14
Indifference	202	8	73	18
Dislike	87	3	63	33
Women—				
Like	264	10	78	11
Indifference	81	14	69	17
Dislike	41	5	66	29
Clerical Officers				
Men—				
Like	427	14	76	10
Indifference	188	9	70	22
Dislike	114	10	67	24
Women—				
Like	466	17	71	12
Indifference	136	13	76	11
Dislike	65	12	60	28

54. Dislike of the job may be either a cause or an effect of a feeling that the work does not suit one's capabilities but the figures point to a relation between job attitude and suitability for the work.

Main aspects of employment as causes of satisfaction and dissatisfaction

55. The last question in the job satisfaction questionnaire grouped together factors into 13 " main aspects " of employment. Respondents were asked to indicate up to two aspects causing satisfaction and up to two aspects causing dissatisfaction and, in each case to arrange them in order of importance. Values of 3 and 2 were given to each individual's first and second choice and the population of each age group brought to a common base of 100 to determine the comparative strength of feeling of each group towards each of the 13 aspects. The results are tabulated at Appendix 15A and B.

56. Our analyses show the current pay and conditions of service when viewed as a whole (pay, leave, hours of work, superannuation and security of employment) to be a source of satisfaction to women. Generally speaking for women, it can be regarded as a strong source of satisfaction except that in London only women aged 40 and over regard it as such. It is also a source of satisfaction to some

older male officers working in the provinces but is a source of dissatisfaction to some young male C.Os under 25.

57. Satisfaction with promotion and career prospects is limited to male E.Os under 25. Men and single women aged 40 and over find promotion prospects a source of dissatisfaction. Married women, although feeling that their prospects are poor, are not unduly influenced towards job dissatisfaction by this.

58. Except in one department, the social atmosphere of the office gives satisfaction to young men and women. Older officers do not tend to include this aspect among their two choices of satisfaction but neither do they indicate it as a source of dissatisfaction.

59. In 4 of our 6 typical " Whitehall " departments, the scope of the work affords some satisfaction to E.Os but not to C.Os. But the scope of the work dissatisfies most young men and women (E.Os and C.Os) employed in departments with large concentrations of staff doing similar work; also within these departments, lack of recognition of the individual is a source of dissatisfaction to young women and to male C.Os aged 40 and over (in the latter case possibly allied to their feelings about career prospects).

60. A comparative study of the views of the under 25 age groups and older age groups reveals that young women are more dissatisfied with lack of recognition of the individual; young men are more satisfied with supervision and with career prospects; young E.Os are more dissatisfied with training arrangements and young C.Os with the scope of the work; and, finally, all young people are more dissatisfied with those aspects grouped under " personal convenience " and with working conditions but more satisfied with the social atmosphere of the office than are their older colleagues.

Satisfaction and Dissatisfaction: a more detailed examination

61. We have analysed the replies to questions 14 to 51 in the job satisfaction questionnaire and have assessed the influence which each aspect has on the individuals' job attitude. (Detailed analyses are too voluminous to be reporduced as appendices to this report.)

Pay and Conditions of Service viewed as a whole (Q. 14)

62. Majorities in all age groups think that pay and conditions of service—viewed as a whole—are either " much the same " or " better " than those in other jobs of comparable responsibility which they might have gone in for. A majority of women think that pay and conditions of service are better than those obtainable elsewhere and are influenced towards job satisfaction by this. On the other hand, about one-third of male E.Os under 40 and male C.Os under 25 think that pay and conditions of service are worse than those outside the Civil Service and this influences them towards job-dissatisfaction. (From the " write-ins " we received it appears that dissatisfaction springs from feelings that the starting pay is too low and that incremental scales are too long; the inadequacy of London weighting was also commented upon[1]).

[1] The Prices and Incomes Board have recommended increases in London Weighting; their report is at present (December 1967) under consideration.

Promotion and career prospects (*Qs. 15–17*)

63. Whilst, in general, E.Os under 50 and C.Os under 40 are satisfied with career prospects, officers aged under 40 tend to be dissatisfied with too much weight being given to seniority. Older officers, although feeling their career prospects are poor, are not unduly influenced towards job dissatisfaction by this attitude and are generally of the opinion that merit and seniority are properly balanced in promotions.

64. Two-fifths of our respondents think that the system of regulating advancement within the Service gives poor protection against unfair influence. Criticism is more strong amongst older officers; for example, one-half of all C.Os aged 40 and over hold this view. (" Write-ins " showed that dissatisfaction with the " system " is often coupled with criticism of the inequality of promotion opportunity between different departments and the lack of opportunity for inter-departmental transfers. Married women and older single women also commented upon an apparent " anti-feminine " atttitude held in some quarters.)

Amount of work (*Q. 18*)

65. About one-half of our total population think that the amount of work they are expected to do is about right; two-fifths that the amount is too much and one-tenth that it is too little. (Many " write-ins " referred to unfair distributions of work, i.e. constant pressure in some parts of the office with " easy " branches elsewhere and, in some places, insufficient staff coverage for holiday periods and sick leave. Criticism of " too much work " came mainly from officers employed in establishments with large concentrations of staff doing the same or similar work.)

The scope of the work (*Qs. 19–22*)

66. In general, E.Os find their work interesting most of the time but C.Os find it " partly interesting and partly boring ". In all establishments surveyed, many officers aged under 40 feel that they are given too little responsibility and that the work neither extends them nor makes full use of their abilities. Among E.Os the proportion holding to these views ranges from 34 per cent to 52 per cent; among C.Os the proportion ranges from 40 per cent to 61 per cent. Older officers are less critical but one-third of E.Os and two-fifths of C.Os aged 40 and over think the work makes little use of their abilities and are influenced towards job-dissatisfaction by this.

67. Within 6 of the establishments surveyed (4 typical " Whitehall " offices and 2 others), disenchantment with the work is more strong amongst officers with 2 or more " A " levels and/or 5 or more " O " levels and the scope of the work tends to influence such officers towards job dissatisfaction more strongly than it does officers with no " O " levels. This suggests an inverse correlation between educational attainment and satisfaction with the work but the evidence is uncorroborated by our findings in the five remaining departments.

Other aspects of the work (*Qs. 23–25*)

68. A majority of our total population thinks that the variety of jobs which they may be called upon to do is neither more nor less than they like; but one-third of all C.Os and one-third of E.Os aged under 25 think that the variety is

less than they would like and this influences them towards job-dissatisfaction. The proportion is reduced to one-quarter in the case of E.Os aged 25 and over.

69. All age-groups have mixed feelings about other people's attitude to their jobs as Civil Servants. In general, one-third think that people respect it, one-third that people are indifferent to it and one-third that they look down on it. Three quarters of our respondents however indicate that their feelings on this subject neither influence them towards job-satisfaction nor towards job-dissatisfaction.

Recognition of the individual (Qs. 26–27)

70. Two-fifths of E.Os think that good work is acknowledged only sometimes by someone other than their immediate supervisor and a further two-fifths that good work is rarely, if ever, acknowledged. Among C.Os, one-third think that it is sometimes acknowledged and one-half that it is rarely acknowledged. Young people holding this view are influenced towards job-dissatisfaction but this tendency is not so apparent in the case of older officers.

71. Two-thirds of men aged 40 and over but only one-half of men under 40 and one-half of all women think that those above them (other than their immediate supervisor) know them well or fairly well. Officers who think that those above them do not know them very well are not, however, influenced towards job-dissatisfaction by this.

Supervision (Qs. 28–32)

72. Over 80 per cent of our respondents think that office discipline is about right; that the supervisor is generally helpful in solving problems which arise in the work and that he is generally fair and considerate in his treatment of the staff. All these factors influence a majority of the total population in all age groups towards job-satisfaction.

Training (Qs. 33–34)

73. Apart from young people, a majority of all officers think that the training courses provided by the Department are adequate. Nearly one-half of officers aged under 25 however, think that the courses are poor or very poor indeed, and young men, but not all young women are influenced towards job-dissatisfaction by this.

74. Two-thirds of our respondents think that training " on the job " is adequate to good whilst a third think it poor. Young people, but not older officers, who hold to the latter opinion indicate that it influences them towards job-dissatisfaction.

Management (Qs. 35–38)

75. Two-fifths of officers aged 40 and over and one-half of those under 40 think that posting by the Department to give staff the experience required for full use and development of their abilities is badly arranged and this opinion influences them towards job-dissatisfaction.

76. On other aspects of management, however, large majorities in all age groups think that staff suggestions about methods or organisation of work are encouraged; that arrangements for consultation between management and staff

representatives to solve local problems are all right; and that the machinery for making available to the staff information about changes in policy, procedure, conditions of service, etc., is adequate to good. None of these three factors, however, influence the staff towards job satisfaction.

Working conditions and amenities (Qs. 39–41)

77. Less than one-half of young women think that the office accommodation is good or " not particularly good or bad ". The proportion holding to this view increases to three-fifths in the case of men under 40 and to two-thirds for men and women aged 40 and over. Most officers who think that the accommodation is bad (one-third of those aged 40 and over rising to one-half of women under 25) find this aspect a source of job-dissatisfaction.

78. Staff are less critical about the provision of canteen facilities. Less than one-quarter of officers aged 25 and over consider these to be bad. Young people are again the most critical (two-fifths consider canteen facilities to be bad) but less than one-third indicate it as a source of job-dissatisfaction.

79. On the other hand, majorities in all age-groups think that the facilities available for social activities, sport, etc. are good or very good indeed. One-third of all young people find this tends to influence them towards job satisfaction but the majority in all age groups indicate that this aspect has little effect on job-satisfaction.

The social atmosphere of the office (Qs. 42–43)

80. Over 80 per cent of our respondents find that the people with whom they work are " good colleagues " and that the social climate in the office as a whole is pleasant or very pleasant indeed. Large majorities in all age-groups indicate that this influences them towards job-satisfaction.

Welfare (Qs. 44–45)

81. The provision of welfare facilities is commented upon favourably (less than 10 per cent of our sample think that welfare services are bad) although this factor has little effect on job-satisfaction. But over three-quarters of those respondents (about a quarter of our total population) who had had personal knowledge of the help available found the Welfare Officer to be helpful or very helpful indeed and over one-half of these, in acknowledging this help, indicate that it influences them towards job-satisfaction.

Personal convenience (Qs. 46–51)

82. Nearly 100 per cent of our total population think that the office hours are reasonable and/or suit them well. Large majorities in all age groups regard this as a source of job-satisfaction. Most officers working in the provinces regard their journey to work as easy or not particularly burdensome but a third of those working in London regard it as burdensome. The latter do not, however, all regard it as a factor causing job-dissatisfaction.

83. In only 2 of the 11 establishments surveyed is severe criticism levelled at the situation of the office. Over the remainder of our sample, about two-thirds regard the location of the office (and the opportunities to use the lunch hour usefully or pleasantly) as good or " not particularly good or bad ". There is little

difference in attitude between men and women or between young and older officers on this subject and it is not a factor affecting job-satisfaction.

84. About a fifth of our young people indicated that the location of the office forced them to live away from home. Of these, 70 per cent say that they either like living away from home or do not mind one way or the other. This opinion does not, however, influence them towards job-satisfaction. On the other hand, most of those who would rather live at home regard this aspect as a source of job-dissatisfaction.

85. Slightly more than half of our respondents regard their chances of being moved to another job in another part of the country as acceptable; one-third of the young people regard their chances as less than they would like but an equal proportion of older officers regard their chances as greater than they would like. Both viewpoints tend to influence the holder towards job-dissatisfaction.

86. The last question in this section referred to liability to transfer on promotion. Over three-quarters of male E.Os under 25 say that they would probably accept promotion even if it meant moving from home. The proportion decreases to two-thirds for male E.Os aged 25–39 and to less than one-half for men aged 50 and over. In the case of male C.Os the proportion ranges from two-thirds (under 25) to one-third (50 and over). One half of single women E.Os under 40, but only one third of single women C.Os in this age group would accept promotion if it meant moving home—a further one-third might accept or might reject it. About one-half of single women aged 40 and over and one-half of all married women would refuse promotion if it entailed moving house. The aspect has little effect on job-satisfaction, however; large majorities of respondents in all age groups indicate that their opinion influences them neither towards job-satisfaction nor job-dissatisfaction.

Attitudes of Indifference or Dislike

87. We have examined, separately, the replies from those who are indifferent to or dislike the job and find that they are more critical than their colleagues of the scope of the work, lack of variety and departmental posting. Whilst, in some instances but not in all, they also express greater dissatisfaction with acknowledgement and recognition and with training, it would seem from their responses that their opinion of the quality of the work is mainly responsible for job attitudes of indifference or dislike.

Job Satisfaction and Efficiency

88. Common sense would seem to suggest that an officer satisfied with his job is more likely to perform well on it. Research by others in this direction by no means supports this hypothesis although some work suggests that the higher the level of skill required by a job, the higher the probability of a correlation between job satisfaction and performance. But even this probability is without much support. We have had the advantage of conducting a sample survey within two grades of the Civil Service, one immediately above the other. When officers with less than 5 years service in the grade (for whom inexperience may be the dominant factor in delaying achievement of a level of efficiency above that of standard) are exluded from our analyses, a positive correlation between job

satisfaction and efficiency is revealed. The relationship can be seen by the following distributions:

	Efficiency rating	*No.*	*Percentages who like the job*
Executive Officers	Above standard	207	75
	Standard	341	71
	Below standard	45	49
Clerical Officers	Above standard	175	72
	Standard	436	68
	Below standard	97	58

89. There is a negligible difference between staff who are of above standard and of standard efficiency but it is noticeable that it is those who are of below standard efficiency whose distribution differs significantly from the others.

Main Conclusions

90. It is a feature of the report that the Executive and Clerical recruiting and grading systems, in terms of securing the minimum ability required for the tasks allocated to Executive and Clerical officers, seem to have worked well. The number of staff who lack the required ability is small (1·1 per cent of our sample) and one-third are capable of developing a standard of ability above that required of the grade.

91. About two-thirds of the total staff are of standard efficiency. Among E.Os some 26 per cent work at above standard efficiency as do 20 per cent of C.Os. But the proportions of officers who are working at below standard efficiency (7 per cent of E.Os and 12 per cent of C.Os) are high enough to point to the need for an effort to reduce the proportions.

92. Inexperience is a factor which is obviously playing a large part in preventing or delaying the achievement of good performance. It is for consideration whether the weakness here may not lie in any inadequacies of centralised training courses but rather in immediate post-training care and supervision. There may also well be a link between inadequate performance through inexperience and the dissatisfaction of a good number of younger officers with the job.

93. Amongst C.Os who have been working for over 15 years on the same (or similar) work there was a greater number working below standard efficiency. Active encouragement of staff to accept that it is in their own interests to transfer to other work may be part of the remedy especially where transfer may mean inconvenience to them. Where the character of the work within individual departments provides little scope for a change of work, inter-departmental transfers within the same town or city may be worth considering to avoid a situation in which the abilities of some officers become dulled through too long an association with the same work.

94. The report also suggests that a poor performance may be associated with poor health. When an officer is not rendering regular and efficient service, and his sick record seems excessive, the advice of the Treasury Medical Adviser should be sought at the earliest possible stage. Anything extra that can be done should be done to prevent officers from drifting into a state of chronic ill-health.

95. There is some evidence of an association between efficiency ratings and suitability for the work. Incompatibility between individual aptitudes and the demands of the work may, therefore, be a further factor in the prevention of a good performance. If assessments by Supervisors are right, 15 per cent of the E.Os and 14 per cent of the C.Os might perform better if they could be transferred to work more suited to their capabilities. This suggests that some further effort might be justified in fitting people into types of duty for which they are suited or at least keeping them out of types of duty for which they are palpably not suited.

96. Two-thirds of the total population sampled like their job. The most satisfying elements in it are the existence of good supervision, the hours of work, relations with colleagues and the social atmosphere of the office. Existing pay and conditions of service (viewed as a whole) is also a source of satisfaction to most women.

97. On the other hand, one third of all officers either dislike their job or are indifferent to it. The report provides evidence that satisfaction with the job and efficiency in performing it are related. A good performance may be either a cause or effect of job satisfaction but the best way of attacking this circle may well be through an attack on the " dissatisfying " factors.

98. Dissatisfying elements for young people include lack of recognition of the individual, training and working conditions; some young men also cite pay and conditions of service. Older officers feel that the system of securing advancement within the Civil Service is often unfair and they think more might be done to equalise promotion opportunity between different departments and provide easier opportunity for inter-departmental transfers.

99. But of prime importance is the belief, particularly among staff aged under 40, that the work does not fully employ their capabilities or enable them to develop their potential, 46 per cent of E.Os and 53 per cent of the C.Os under 40 hold this view. It would seem that many officers and, in some departments, particularly those with 2 or more " A " levels and/or 5 or more " O " levels, feel little sense of self-fulfilment in their work; the feeling that the work makes insufficient demands upon them is, in the main, responsible for job attitudes of indifference or dislike.

100. The relative dullness and frustration of much office work at junior levels is well recognised. The Civil Service has a vast range of work which is difficult enough to need intellectual ability but which, at the same time, cannot offer great variety or inherent interest. A good number of young Executive Officers, in particular, find these tasks frustrating whereas they give a more uniform measure of satisfaction to promoted people over the age of 40. One possible moral is that it is important not to overgrade work so that it is manned by staff who do not find it sufficiently satisfying intellectually. Secondly, either the range of work or the opportunities for transfer to other establishments ought to be sufficient to give proper scope to open Executive entrants. If this cannot be achieved, management may need to consider carefully whether it is right to employ them on the particular work. The evidence of the survey on this point is worth bearing in mind in any consideration of the grading and structure of the Clerical and Executive classes.

Appendix 1

Name..

STUDY OF ABILITY AND EFFICIENCY—ASSESSMENT FORM

Assessed Officer's Serial No.

Note:—Please base your answers on your assessment of the officer's *potential*: ignore his *actual performance* on his present job.

1. *TIME UNDER YOUR SUPERVISION* ....yrs ....months

2. *YOUR GRADE* ....

3. *POTENTIAL SUITABILITY*—Please tick as many of the following types of work as you think the officer could carry out *up to the standard expected* of his present grade:—

Paper work not involving an aptitude for figures		Work requiring an aptitude for figures		Regular personal contacts with the public and/or commerce		Organisation and Management of work and control of junior staff		Not suitable for any of types of work 1–4 available in the Civil Service	
	1		2		3		4		5

Please say which, if any, of types of work 1–4 the officer would be *most* suited to ....

4. *ASSESSED LEVEL OF ABILITY*—Now tick the most appropriate box below to show the officer's potential for the type of work for which you judge him most suitable (If you tick box 5 in Q.3 you must tick 5, 6 or 7 here).

Very much above standard required for the grade		1
Much above standard required for the grade		2
Above standard required for the grade		3
Of standard required for the grade		4
Below standard required for the grade		5
Much below standard required for the grade		6
Very much below standard required for the grade		7

5. *MENTAL SUITABILITY FOR PRESENT DUTIES*—Bearing in mind the answers you have given to questions 3 and 4 tick the most appropriate box below:—
The officer's mental proficiency and aptitudes are:—

Suited to his present duties and would *not* be *as well suited* to any other type of work appropriate to his grade		1
Suited to his present duties but would be *as well suited* to one or more of the other types of work appropriate to his grade		2
Suited to his present duties but would be *better suited* to one or more of the other types of work appropriate to his grade		3
Not suited to his present duties but would be *suited* to one or more of the other types of work appropriate to his grade		4
Not suited to his present duties and would *not be suited* to any other type of work appropriate to his grade		5

6. *PERSONAL QUALITIES* (*OTHER THAN MENTAL PROFICIENCY AND APTITUDES*)
Tick the most appropriate box:—

The officer's personal qualities are suitable for his present duties		1
The officer has personal qualities which detract from his suitability		2

Appendix 2

Name ....

STUDY OF ABILITY AND EFFICIENCY—DATA FORM

Serial No. .... [1–6]

[7]
1. *Potential Suitability* — 1, 2, 3, 4

[8]
2. *Assessed Level of Ability* — 1, 2, 3

[9]
3. *Mental Suitability* — 1, 2, 3, 4, 5

[10]
4. *Personal Qualities* — 1, 2

[11]
5. Single Male 1
   Married Male 2
   Single Female 3
   Married Female 4

[12]
6. Established E.O. 1
   Unestablished E.O. 2
   Established C.O. 3
   Unestablished C.O. 4
   Temporary C.O. 5

[13]
7. *Sickness Record*

Uncertified

61	62	63	64	65

[14]
Certified

61	62	63	64	65

1
2

8. *Length of Service*

	(*a*) In Dept.	(*b*) In Branch	(*c*) In Civil Service	(*d*) In Grade
	[15]	[16]	[17]	[18]
Under 6 months	0	0	0	0
6–12 months	1	1	1	1
1–2 years	2	2	2	2
2–3 years	3	3	3	3
3–4 years	4	4	4	4
4–5 years	5	5	5	5
5–7 years	6	6	6	6
7–10 years	7	7	7	7
10–15 years	8	8	8	8
Over 15 years	9	9	9	9

[19]
9. *Year of Birth*
   1916 or before 1
   1917–1926 2
   1927–1936 3
   1937–1941 4
   1942–1946 5
   1947 or later 6

[20]
10. *Method of Entry to Grade*
   0 School Leavers open }
   1 School Leavers G.C.E. }
   2 G.C.E. up to to 23 yrs. }
   3 Recon. Open } 1
   4 Recon. Limited }
   5 Limited (Normal) } 2
   6 Ex-National Service }
   7 Ex-Regular } 3
   8 Graduate 4
   9 Overseas C.S. 5
   10 On promotion 6
   11 Not Known 7

[21]
11. *Overall grading for qualities and performance on present duties*
   1. Outstanding 1
   2. Very Good
   3. Good 2
   4. Fair
   5. Unsatisfactory 3

[22]
12. *Grade of Entry*
   E.O. 0
   C.O. 1
   T.C.O. 2
   P.O. Manipulative 3
   Typist 4
   C.A. 5
   T.C.A. 6
   Minor and Manipulative 7
   Otherwise 8
   Not Known 9

[23]
13. *Method of Entry to Civil Service*
   0 Recon. Open }
   1 School Leavers Open }
   2 School Leavers G.C.E. } 1
   3 G.C.E. up to 23 yrs. }
   4 Ex-National Service }
   5 Ex-Regular } 2
   6 Graduate 3
   7 Overseas C.S. 4
   8 Local Recruitment 5
   9 Not Known 6

[24]
14. *Promotion Rating*
   Exceptionally well fitted 1
   Very well fitted 2
   Satisfactorily fitted 3
   Likely to qualify in time 4
   Unlikely to qualify 5

Appendix 3

1–6		7
Serial No.	For use in analysing the forms only	1
		2
		3
		4

In each of the questions on this page tick the answer which is applicable to you.

Question	Answer		Col.	Code
1. I am		Male	8	1
		Female		2
2. I am		Single	9	1
		Married		2
3. I have	Dependants at home		10	1
	No dependants at home			2
4. I was born in	1906 or before		11	1
	1907–1916			
	1917–1926			2
	1927–1931			3
	1932–1936			4
	1937–1941			5
	1942–1944			
	1945–1946			6
	1947–1948			
	1949–1950			7
5. I have been in the Civil Service for a total of	Under 6 months			12
	6–12 months			1
	1–2 years			2
	2–3 years			
	3–4 years			
	4–5 years			
	5–7 years			
	7–10 years			
	10–15 years			
	Over 15 years			

5(*a*). I entered the Civil Service by
(i) Open Competition............... (ii) Ex-Forces Competition...............
(iii) Local Recruitment (i.e. everything other than competitive written examinations)..........

5(*b*). My grade of entry to the Service was ....

6. This section is intended to find out what sort of subjects you may have done well at. If you have passed the G.C.E. or one of its equivalents tick the appropriate column below, adding in at the bottom any subject in which you have a pass but which is not listed. It is important that you tick both columns if you have " O " and " A " level passes in any particular subject.
If you have passed examinations other than the General Certificate of Education please *see the Appendix* on Educational Qualifications. If the exam you have passed is not mentioned in the appendix then you should complete question 7 instead.

I have passed examinations (at the level ticked in the appropriate column) in the following subjects:	G.C.E. "O" level	G.C.E. "A" level	Degree level	
English Language				13
English Literature				1
History				
Latin				2
Greek				
Spanish				3
German				
French				4
Russian				
Politics				
British Constitution				
Religious Knowledge				
Geography				14
Economics				1
Biology				
Botany				2
Zoology				
Physiology				3
Horticultural Science				
Agricultural Science				4
Geology				
Commerce				
Accounting				
Mathematics				
Applied Mathematics				
Mechanics				
Applied Mechanics				
Statistics				
Physics with Chemistry				
General Science				
Chemistry				
Physics				
Building Science				
Engineering				
Engineering Drawing				
Technical Drawing				

7. If you have any other qualifications or have passed any other examinations not covered by question 6 please give below the fullest possible details of the subjects passed, and the level at which you passed each subject.

For all the other questions on this page put a tick in the appropriate box.

8. Had you had any jobs before you joined the Civil Service?

	15	
Yes	1	
No	2	

9. Are you pleased that you joined the Civil Service?

	16	
Yes	1	
No	2	

10. How many different jobs (i.e. different types of work like finance, accounts, establishments, contracts, counter work or specialist duties) have you had in the Civil Service?

	17
1	
2	
3	
4	
5 or more	

11. Do you think that the jobs that you have had in the Civil Service have been the right kinds for you (i.e. the kind which you could make the most of your abilities and experience)?

	18	
Yes, in every case	1	
Yes—most but not all jobs	2	
Yes—but only in a minority of cases	3	
No, never	4	

12. Please tick the box appropriate to your attitude to your present job.

	19	
I like it very much	1	
I like it a good deal	2	
I like it	3	
I like it a little	4	
I am indifferent to it	5	
On the whole I don't like it	6	
I dislike it	7	
I dislike it very much	8	

13. Your attitude to the job may change from time to time. Please tick the item in each of the two following lists which best describes the way your feelings change.

How much they change

	20	
Very much	1	
Quite a lot	2	
A fair amount	3	
A little	4	
Not at all	5	

How often they change

	21	
From day to day	1	
From week to week	2	
From month to month	3	
Hardly change at all	4	

The following questions 14–51, ask for your opinions on a number of subjects relating to your job. Would you please tick whichever one of the boxes in the left-hand column is appropriate to your answer? We also want to know how important the point is for you in influencing your views about your job generally; and so we ask you to tell us this as well by putting a tick in the appropriate box in the right-hand column. If you do not know the answer to any of the items, or it is not applicable to you, or you do not want to give it, please cross through that particular question.

PAY AND CONDITIONS OF SERVICE

14. Compare Civil Servants' conditions of service (pay, leave, hours of work, superannuation and security of employment) with those in other jobs of comparable responsibility which you might have gone in for.

I think ours are generally—

	22	
Very much better	1	
Better	2	
Much the same	3	
Worse	4	
Very much worse	5	

The fact that I hold this opinion—

	23	
Is a strong influence towards satisfaction with my job	1	
Is a mild influence towards satisfaction with my job	2	
Influences my feelings towards my job neither way	3	
Is a mild influence towards dissatisfaction with my job	4	
Is a strong influence towards dissatisfaction with my job	5	

PROMOTION AND CAREER PROSPECTS

15. The degree of fairness and unfairness in the system of regulating advancement in the Civil Service.

I think our system—

	24	
Leaves no room for unfair influence	1	
Gives good protection against unfair influence	2	
Has no merit or demerit either way	3	
Gives poor protection against unfair influence	4	
Fosters unfair influence	5	

The fact that I hold this opinion—

	25	
Is a strong influence towards satisfaction with my job	1	
Is a mild influence towards satisfaction with my job	2	
Influences my feelings towards my job neither way	3	
Is a mild influence towards dissatisfaction with my job	4	
Is a strong influence towards dissatisfaction with my job	5	

16. The importance of seniority and merit in promotions in your Department.

I think that in our promotion system—	26		The fact that I hold this opinion—	27	
Seniority weighs far too much	1		Is a strong influence towards satisfaction with my job	1	
Seniority weighs rather too much	2		Is a mild influence towards satisfaction with my job	2	
The two are properly balanced	3		Influences my feelings towards my job neither way	3	
Merit weighs rather too much	4		Is a mild influence towards dissatisfaction with my job	4	
Merit weighs far too much	5		Is a strong influence towards dissatisfaction with my job	5	

17. Your career prospects (i.e. promotion prospects in the short and long term)

I think my career prospects are—	28		The fact that I hold this opinion—	29	
Very good indeed	1		Is a strong influence towards satisfaction with my job	1	
Good	2		Is a mild influence towards satisfaction with my job	2	
Reasonable	3		Influences my feelings towards my job neither way	3	
Poor	4		Is a mild influence towards dissatisfaction with my job	4	
Very poor indeed	5		Is a strong influence towards dissatisfaction with my job	5	

YOUR WORK (a) THE AMOUNT OF WORK

18. The amount of work.

I think the amount of work we are expected to do is—	30		The fact that I hold this opinion—	31	
Far too much	1		Is a strong influence towards satisfaction with my job	1	
Rather too much	2		Is a mild influence towards satisfaction with my job	2	
About right	3		Influences my feelings towards my job neither way	3	
Rather too little	4		Is a mild influence towards dissatisfaction with my job	4	
Far too little	5		Is a strong influence towards dissatisfaction with my job	5	

YOUR WORK (b) THE SCOPE OF YOUR WORK

19. The amount of interest you find in your work.

I think my work is—

	32	
Interesting all the time	1	
Interesting most of the time	2	
Partly interesting partly boring	3	
Boring most of the time	4	
Boring all of the time	5	

The fact that I hold this opinion—

	33	
Is a strong influence towards satisfaction with my job	1	
Is a mild influence towards satisfaction with my job	2	
Influences my feelings towards my job neither way	3	
Is a mild influence towards dissatisfaction with my job	4	
Is a strong influence towards dissatisfaction with my job	5	

20. The extent to which your work extends you and makes full use of your abilities.

I think my work uses my abilities—

	34	
To the full	1	
Reasonably fully	2	
Adequately	3	
Not enough	4	
Not at all	5	

The fact that I hold this opinion—

	35	
Is a strong influence towards satisfaction with my job	1	
Is a mild influence towards satisfaction with my job	2	
Influences my feelings towards my job neither way	3	
Is a mild influence towards dissatisfaction with my job	4	
Is a strong influence towards dissatisfaction with my job	5	

21. The extent of your responsibility.

I think that the amount of responsibility that I am expected to take in my work is—

	36	
Far too much	1	
Too much	2	
About right	3	
Too little	4	
Far too little	5	

The fact that I hold this opinion—

	37	
Is a strong influence towards satisfaction with my job	1	
Is a mild influence towards satisfaction with my job	2	
Influences my feelings towards my job neither way	3	
Is a mild influence towards dissatisfaction with my job	4	
Is a strong influence towards dissatisfaction with my job	5	

22. The extent to which you are able to use your initiative in carrying out your work.

I am able to use my initiative—	38		The fact that I hold this opinion—	39	
All the time	1		Is a strong influence towards satisfaction with my job	1	
Frequently	2		Is a mild influence towards satisfaction with my job	2	
Sometimes	3		Influences my feelings towards my job neither way	3	
Rarely	4		Is a mild influence towards dissatisfaction with my job	4	
Never	5		Is a strong influence towards dissatisfaction with my job	5	

YOUR WORK (c) OTHER ASPECTS

23. The variety of jobs in your Department which you may be called on to do (e.g. finance, accounts, establishments, contracts, counterwork, or specialist duties).

I think that the variety of jobs which I may be called on to do is—	40		The fact that I hold this opinion—	41	
Very much more than I like	1		Is a strong influence towards satisfaction with my job	1	
More than I like	2		Is a mild influence towards satisfaction with my job	2	
Neither more nor less than I like	3		Influences my feelings towards my job neither way	3	
Less than I like	4		Is a mild influence towards dissatisfaction with my job	4	
Very much less than I like	5		Is a strong influence towards dissatisfaction with my job	5	

24. Other people's attitude to your job as a Civil Servant.

I think—	42		The fact that I hold this opinion—	43	
They respect it very highly	1		Is a strong influence towards satisfaction with my job	1	
They have some respect for it	2		Is a mild influence towards satisfaction with my job	2	
They are indifferent to it	3		Influences my feelings towards my job neither way	3	
They tend to look down on it	4		Is a mild influence towards dissatisfaction with my job	4	
They despise it	5		Is a strong influence towards dissatisfaction with my job	5	

25. How does your work suit your health?

I think my work suits my health—	44		The fact that I hold this opinion—	45	
Very well indeed	1		Is a strong influence towards satisfaction with my job	1	
Well	2		Is a mild influence towards satisfaction with my job	2	
Adequately	3		Influences my feelings towards my job neither way	3	
Badly	4		Is a mild influence towards dissatisfaction with my job	4	
Very badly indeed	5		Is a strong influence towards dissatisfaction with my job	5	

RECOGNITION OF THE INDIVIDUAL

26. Acknowledgement of your work by someone other than your immediate supervisor.

I think good work is acknowledged—	46		The fact that I hold this opinion—	47	
Always	1		Is a strong influence towards satisfaction with my job	1	
Frequently	2		Is a mild influence towards satisfaction with my job	2	
Sometimes	3		Influences my feelings towards my job neither way	3	
Rarely	4		Is a mild influence towards dissatisfaction with my job	4	
Never	5		Is a strong influence towards dissatisfaction with my job	5	

27. Recognition of you as a person by someone other than your immediate supervisor.

I think that those above me—	48		The fact that I hold this opinion—	49	
Know me very well	1		Is a strong influence towards satisfaction with my job	1	
Know me well	2		Is a mild influence towards satisfaction with my job	2	
Know me fairly well	3		Influences my feelings towards my job neither way	3	
Do not know me very well	4		Is a mild influence towards dissatisfaction with my job	4	
Do not know me at all	5		Is a strong influence towards dissatisfaction with my job	5	

SUPERVISION

28. Discipline in your office (e.g. time-keeping)

I think that the discipline is—	50	The fact that I hold this opinion—	51
Far too strict	1	Is a strong influence towards satisfaction with my job	1
Rather strict	2	Is a mild influence towards satisfaction with my job	2
About right	3	Influences my feelings towards my job neither way	3
Rather lax	4	Is a mild influence towards dissatisfaction with my job	4
Far too lax	5	Is a strong influence towards dissatisfaction with my job	5

29. How good is your supervisor at helping you with the problems which arise in your work? Consider here only the technical application of knowledge of the work, not treatment of staff (for which see 31/32 below).

I think that in the terms of the work I do my supervisor is—	52	The fact that I hold this opinion—	53
Very helpful indeed	1	Is a strong influence towards satisfaction with my job	1
Helpful	2	Is a mild influence towards satisfaction with my job	2
Neither particularly helpful or unhelpful	3	Influences my feelings towards my job neither way	3
Unhelpful	4	Is a mild influence towards dissatisfaction with my job	4
Very unhelpful indeed	5	Is a strong influence towards dissatisfaction with my job	5

30. How good is your supervisor at organising the work?

I think my supervisor does it—	54	The fact that I hold this opinion—	55
Very well indeed	1	Is a strong influence towards satisfaction with my job	1
Well	2	Is a mild influence towards satisfaction with my job	2
Not particularly well or badly	3	Influences my feelings towards my job neither way	3
Badly	4	Is a mild influence towards dissatisfaction with my job	4
Very badly indeed	5	Is a strong influence towards dissatisfaction with my job	5

31. How considerate is your supervisor in his treatment of his staff?

I think my supervisor is—	56		The fact that I hold this opinion—	57	
Very considerate indeed	1		Is a strong influence towards satisfaction with my job	1	
Considerate	2		Is a mild influence towards satisfaction with my job	2	
Not particularly considerate or inconsiderate	3		Influences my feelings towards my job neither way	3	
Inconsiderate	4		Is a mild influence towards dissatisfaction with my job	4	
Very inconsiderate indeed	5		Is a strong influence towards dissatisfaction with my job	5	

32. How fair is your supervisor in his treatment of his staff?

I think that in his treatment of individual members of his staff my supervisor is—	58		The fact that I hold this opinion—	59	
Always scrupulously fair	1		Is a strong influence towards satisfaction with my job	1	
Generally fair	2		Is a mild influence towards satisfaction with my job	2	
Not particularly fair or unfair	3		Influences my feelings towards my job neither way	3	
Often unfair	4		Is a mild influence towards dissatisfaction with my job	4	
Always unfair	5		Is a strong influence towards dissatisfaction with my job	5	

TRAINING

33. Training courses provided by the Department

I think that the courses, both those as a background to the work of the Department and those on more general subjects, are—	8		The fact that I hold this opinion—	9	
Very good indeed	1		Is a strong influence towards satisfaction with my job	1	
Good	2		Is a mild influence towards satisfaction with my job	2	
Adequate	3		Influences my feelings towards my job neither way	3	
Poor	4		Is a mild influence towards dissatisfaction with my job	4	
Very poor indeed	5		Is a strong influence towards dissatisfaction with my job	5	

34. Training at your desk

I think that, from the point of view of enabling me to do my job as well as possible, the training provided " on the job " is—

	10	
Very good indeed	1	
Good	2	
Adequate	3	
Poor	4	
Very poor indeed	5	

The fact that I hold this opinion—

	11	
Is a strong influence towards satisfaction with my job	1	
Is a mild influence towards satisfaction with my job	2	
Influences my feelings towards my job neither way	3	
Is a mild influence towards dissatisfaction with my job	4	
Is a strong influence towards dissatisfaction with my job	5	

MANAGEMENT

35. Posting by your Department to give staff the experience required for full use and development of their abilities.

I think that in my Department posting is arranged—

	12	
Very well indeed	1	
Well	2	
Adequately	3	
Badly	4	
Very badly indeed	5	

The fact that I hold this opinion—

	13	
Is a strong influence towards satisfaction with my job	1	
Is a mild influence towards satisfaction with my job	2	
Influences my feelings towards my job neither way	3	
Is a mild influence towards dissatisfaction with my job	4	
Is a strong influence towards dissatisfaction with my job	5	

36. Notice taken of staff suggestions

I think that suggestions from the staff about methods or organisation of the work are—

	14	
Very much encouraged	1	
Encouraged	2	
Not sought but considered if offered	3	
Not encouraged	4	
Resented	5	

The fact that I hold this opinion—

	15	
Is a strong influence towards satisfaction with my job	1	
Is a mild influence towards satisfaction with my job	2	
Influences my feelings towards my job neither way	3	
Is a mild influence towards dissatisfaction with my job	4	
Is a strong influence towards dissatisfaction with my job	5	

37. The Whitley machinery for joint consultation

I think that the arrangements for consultation between the management and staff representatives to solve local problems are—

	16	
Very satisfactory	1	
Satisfactory	2	
All right	3	
Unsatisfactory	4	
Very unsatisfactory	5	

The fact that I hold this opinion—

	17	
Is a strong influence towards satisfaction with my job	1	
Is a mild influence towards satisfaction with my job	2	
Influences my feelings towards my job neither way	3	
Is a mild influence towards dissatisfaction with my job	4	
Is a strong influence towards dissatisfaction with my job	5	

38. Information to the staff about changes in policy, procedure, conditions of service and the like

I think that the machinery for making information available to the staff is—

	18	
Very good indeed	1	
Good	2	
Adequate	3	
Bad	4	
Very bad indeed	5	

The fact that I hold this opinion—

	19	
Is a strong influence towards satisfaction with my job	1	
Is a mild influence towards satisfaction with my job	2	
Influences my feelings towards my job neither way	3	
Is a mild influence towards dissatisfaction with my job	4	
Is a strong influence towards dissatisfaction with my job	5	

PHYSICAL WORKING CONDITIONS AND AMENITIES

39. The office and accommodation including furniture, lighting, heating, ventilation etc.

I think that the office accommodation is—

	20	
Very good indeed	1	
Good	2	
Not particularly good or bad	3	
Bad	4	
Very bad indeed	5	

The fact that I hold this opinion—

	21	
Is a strong influence towards satisfaction with my job	1	
Is a mild influence towards satisfaction with my job	2	
Influences my feelings towards my job neither way	3	
Is a mild influence towards dissatisfaction with my job	4	
Is a strong influence towards dissatisfaction with my job	5	

40. Amenities for social activities, sport etc.

I think that the facilities available are—

	22	
Very good indeed	1	
Good	2	
Not particularly good or bad	3	
Bad	4	
Very bad indeed	5	

The fact that I hold this opinion—

	23	
Is a strong influence towards satisfaction with my job	1	
Is a mild influence towards satisfaction with my job	2	
Influences my feelings towards my job neither way	3	
Is a mild influence towards dissatisfaction with my job	4	
Is a strong influence towards dissatisfaction with my job	5	

41. The canteen facilities provided by the Department

I think that, taking account of prices, menus and accommodation, the canteen facilities are generally—

	24	
Very good indeed	1	
Good	2	
Not particularly good or bad	3	
Bad	4	
Very bad indeed	5	

The fact that I hold this opinion—

	25	
Is a strong influence towards satisfaction with my job	1	
Is a mild influence towards satisfaction with my job	2	
Influences my feelings towards my job neither way	3	
Is a mild influence towards dissatisfaction with my job	4	
Is a strong influence towards dissatisfaction with my job	5	

THE SOCIAL ATMOSPHERE OF THE OFFICE

42. Relations with the other people with whom you work day by day

I think that the other people with whom I work are—

	26	
All good colleagues	1	
With one or two exceptions, good colleagues	2	
Some good, some difficult colleagues	3	
With one or two exceptions, difficult colleagues	4	
All difficult colleagues	5	

The fact that I hold this opinion—

	27	
Is a strong influence towards satisfaction with my job	1	
Is a mild influence towards satisfaction with my job	2	
Influences my feelings towards my job neither way	3	
Is a mild influence towards dissatisfaction with my job	4	
Is a strong influence towards dissatisfaction with my job	5	

43. The social climate in the office as a whole

I think that the social climate in the office as a whole is—

	28	
Very pleasant indeed	1	
Pleasant	2	
Not particularly pleasant or unpleasant	3	
Unpleasant	4	
Very unpleasant indeed	5	

The fact that I hold this opinion—

	29	
Is a strong influence towards satisfaction with my job	1	
Is a mild influence towards satisfaction with my job	2	
Influences my feelings towards my job neither way	3	
Is a mild influence towards dissatisfaction with my job	4	
Is a strong influence towards dissatisfaction with my job	5	

WELFARE

44. Welfare facilities provided by the Department (help given to staff over personal difficulties)

I think that my Department provides for staff welfare services—	30	
Very well indeed	1	
Well	2	
Not particularly well or badly	3	
Badly	4	
Very badly indeed	5	

The fact that I hold this opinion—	31	
Is a strong influence towards satisfaction with my job	1	
Is a mild influence towards satisfaction with my job	2	
Influences my feelings towards my job neither way	3	
Is a mild influence towards dissatisfaction with my job	4	
Is a strong influence towards dissatisfaction with my job	5	

45. Personal knowledge of the help available—to be answered only if you, *yourself*, have had occasion to make use of the welfare arrangements

I found that the welfare officer was—	32	
Very helpful indeed	1	
Helpful	2	
Not very helpful nor completely disinterested	3	
Unhelpful	4	
Very unhelpful indeed	5	

The fact that I hold this opinion—	33	
Is a strong influence towards satisfaction with my job	1	
Is a mild influence towards satisfaction with my job	2	
Influences my feelings towards my job neither way	3	
Is a mild influence towards dissatisfaction with my job	4	
Is a strong influence towards dissatisfaction with my job	5	

PERSONAL CONVENIENCE

46. Journey to work

I regard the journey between my home and work as—	34		The fact that I hold this opinion—	35	
No trouble at all	1		Is a strong influence towards satisfaction with my job	1	
Reasonably easy	2		Is a mild influence towards satisfaction with my job	2	
Not particularly easy or burdensome	3		Influences my feelings towards my job neither way	3	
Burdensome	4		Is a mild influence towards dissatisfaction with my job	4	
Very burdensome indeed	5		Is a strong influence towards dissatisfaction with my job	5	

47. Office hours

The times at which I go to and leave the office—	36		The fact that I hold this opinion—	37	
Suit me very well	1		Is a strong influence towards satisfaction with my job	1	
Suit me well	2		Is a mild influence towards satisfaction with my job	2	
Are reasonable	3		Influences my feelings towards my job neither way	3	
Do not suit me	4		Is a mild influence towards dissatisfaction with my job	4	
Suit me very badly	5		Is a strong influence towards dissatisfaction with my job	5	

48. Where you live—to be answered only if the location of the office forces you to live away from home.

I—

	38	
Very much like living away from home	1	
Like living away from home	2	
Do not mind one way or the other	3	
Would rather live at home	4	
Very much dislike not living at home	5	

The fact that I hold this opinion—

	39	
Is a strong influence towards satisfaction with my job	1	
Is a mild influence towards satisfaction with my job	2	
Influences my feelings towards my job neither way	3	
Is a mild influence towards dissatisfaction with my job	4	
Is a strong influence towards dissatisfaction with my job	5	

49. Situation of the office—opportunities for using the lunch hour usefully or pleasantly

I think that the opportunities are—

	40	
Very good indeed	1	
Good	2	
Not particularly good or bad	3	
Bad	4	
Very bad indeed	5	

The fact that I hold this opinion—

	41	
Is a strong influence towards satisfaction with my job.	1	
Is a mild influence towards satisfaction with my job	2	
Influences my feelings towards my job neither way	3	
Is a mild influence towards dissatisfaction with my job	4	
Is a strong influence towards dissatisfaction with my job	5	

50. Change of job: liability to transfer

I regard the chances of being moved to a different job in another part of the country (or abroad where applicable) as—	42		The fact that I hold this opinion—	43	
Very much greater than I like	1		Is a strong influence towards satisfaction with my job	1	
Greater than I like	2		Is a mild influence towards satisfaction with my job	2	
Acceptable	3		Influences my feelings towards my job neither way	3	
Less than I like	4		Is a mild influence towards dissatisfaction with my job	4	
Much less than I like	5		Is a strong influence towards dissatisfaction with my job	5	

51. Liability to transfer on promotion

If promotion meant moving my home I—	44		The fact that I hold this opinion—	45	
Would still accept it readily	1		Is a strong influence towards satisfaction with my job	1	
Would probably accept it	2		Is a mild influence towards satisfaction with my job	2	
Might accept it or refuse it	3		Influences my feelings towards my job neither way	3	
Would probably refuse it	4		Is a mild influence towards dissatisfaction with my job	4	
Would definitely refuse it	5		Is a strong influence towards dissatisfaction with my job	5	

52. Please show against the list below which aspects of your employment cause you the most satisfaction and the most dissatisfaction, as follows:—

Put a tick against *not more* than two aspects which cause you the most satisfaction. Your alternatives are to put no ticks, if nothing gives you any satisfaction; to enter a single tick in column one, if only one aspect gives you any satisfaction; or to enter one tick in column one against the most satisfying aspect and a second tick in column two against the next most satisfying aspect.

Similarly, put a cross or crosses against up to two aspects which cause you dissatisfaction. Thus, your alternatives are to enter no crosses at all; to enter a single cross in column three against the only aspect causing you dissatisfaction; or to enter one cross in column three against the aspect causing you most dissatisfaction and a second cross in column four against the next most dissatisfying aspect.

If, however, nothing causes you satisfaction or dissatisfaction or you do not want to answer the question please cross through it.

Aspect		Satisfaction		Dissatisfaction	
		Col. 1 First tick	Col. 2 Second tick	Col. 3 First cross	Col. 4 Second cross
		46–47	48–49	50–51	52–53
Pay and conditions of service (question 14)	01				
Promotion and career prospects (questions 15–17)	02				
Your Work (*a*) The amount (question 18)	03				
Your Work (*b*) The scope of your work (questions 19–22)	04				
Your Work (*c*) Other aspects (questions 23–25)	05				
Recognition of the individual (questions 26–27)	06				
Supervision (questions 28–32)	07				
Training (questions 33–34)	08				
Management (questions 35–38)	09				
Physical working conditions and amenities (questions 39–41)	10				
Social atmosphere of the office (questions 42–43)	11				
Welfare (questions 44–45)	12				
Personal convenience (questions 46–51)	13				

53. If there is anything about your work or conditions of service not covered above which contributes to the satisfaction or dissatisfaction you get from your job please tell us about it in the appropriate box below or, if necessary on a separate sheet:—

Satisfaction
Dissatisfaction

That is all; please return the form as quickly as possible in the envelope provided. Thank you very much for your co-operation.

Appendix

Educational Qualifications

(see question 6)

The following are the broad examination equivalents of the General Certificate of Education.

1. *Examinations equivalent to Ordinary (" O ") Level*

(i) Northern Ireland General Certificate of Education
(ii) Lower Grade of Scottish Certificate of Education
(iii) Lower Grade of Scottish Leaving Certificate
(iv) Lower grade Scottish Universities Preliminary Examination
(v) Credit passes *only* in any of the following:—
  (*a*) School Certificate
  (*b*) Forces Preliminary Examination
  (*c*) Army Special Certificate of Education
  (*d*) First Class Certificate in the Admiralty Higher Education Test
(vi) A pass in a matriculation examination of a British University

If you have obtained passes in any of the above you should place a tick against the appropriate subject or subjects in the first column of question 6.

2. *Examinations equivalent to Advanced ("A ") Level*

(i) Northern Ireland Senior Certificate
(ii) Higher Grade Scottish Certificate of Education
(iii) Higher Grade Scottish Leaving Certificate
(iv) Higher Grade Scottish Universities Preliminary Examination
(v) Higher School Certificate
(vi) A pass in an intermediate examination of a British University.

If you have obtained passes in any of the examinations listed above you should place a tick against the appropriate subject or subjects in the second column of question 6.

Appendix 4

Distributions of ability amongst significant sub-populations

Grade	Sex	Age group	No.	Above Standard ability %	Standard ability %	Below Standard ability %
Executive Officer	Men	under 25	172	55·2	43·6	1·1
		25–39	195	44·1	55·8	—
		40–49	380	40·5	58·9	0·5
		50 and over	213	27·6	69·9	2·3
	Single Women	under 25	99	52·5	47·5	—
		25–39	54	37·0	63·0	—
		40–49	126	24·6	75·3	—
		50 and over	80	23·7	72·5	3·7
	Married Women	40 and over	53	30·1	67·9	1·8
Clerical Officer	Men	under 25	293	33·7	65·8	0·3
		25–39	100	45·0	54·0	1·0
		40–49	157	42·6	56·0	1·2
		50 and over	254	23·6	72·8	3·5
	Single Women	under 25	234	28·2	71·7	—
		25–39	74	31·0	68·9	—
		40–49	80	33·7	66·2	—
		50 and over	121	14·0	84·2	1·6
	Married Women	25–39	49	40·8	59·1	—
		40–49	74	21·6	77·0	1·3
		50 and over	97	20·6	76·3	3·1

Appendix 5A

Established Executive Officers

Distributions of ability by method of entry to Civil Service

Sex	Age group	Ability	Method of entry to Civil Service: Open examination No.	%	Ex-forces No.	%	Local recruitment No.	%
Men	Under 25	Above Standard	94	56			1	
		Standard	73	43			2	
		Below Standard	1	1			1	
	25–39	Above Standard	51	50	5	36	29	37
		Standard	51	50	9	64	49	63
		Below Standard	—		—		—	
	40–49	Above Standard	32	53	9	45	112	38
		Standard	28	47	11	55	184	62
		Below Standard	—		—		2	1
	50 and over	Above Standard	5	25	6	27	41	26
		Standard	15	75	15	68	115	72
		Below Standard	—		1	5	3	2
Single Women	Under 25	Above Standard	49	52			2	
		Standard	46	48			1	
		Below Standard	—				—	
	25–39	Above Standard	12	43	—		6	26
		Standard	16	57	1		17	74
		Below Standard	—		—		—	
	40–49	Above Standard	5	22			26	25
		Standard	18	78			77	75
		Below Standard	—				—	
	50 and over	Above Standard	2	12			17	27
		Standard	15	88			43	68
		Below Standard	—				3	5
Married Women	40 and over	Above Standard	2				14	30
		Standard	4				32	68
		Below Standard	—				1	2

Appendix 5B

Established Clerical Officers

Distributions of ability by method of entry to Civil Service

Sex	Age group	Ability	Method of entry to Civil Service					
			Open examination		Ex-forces		Local recruitment	
			No.	%	No.	%	No.	%
Men	Under 25	Above Standard	67	36			32	30
		Standard	117	63			76	70
		Below Standard	1	1			—	
	25–39	Above Standard	16	47	2		27	44
		Standard	17	50	2		35	56
		Below Standard	1	3	—		—	
	40–49	Above Standard	3		3		61	42
		Standard	4		2		82	57
		Below Standard	1		—		1	1
	50 and over	Above Standard	5	19	2		53	24
		Standard	19	73	7		159	73
		Below Standard	2	8			7	3
Single Women	Under 25	Above Standard	51	29			15	25
		Standard	124	71			44	75
		Below Standard	—				—	
	25–39	Above Standard	9	45			14	26
		Standard	11	55			40	74
		Below Standard	—				—	
	40–49	Above Standard	—				27	36
		Standard	4				49	64
		Below Standard	—				—	
	50 and over	Above Standard	2		—		15	13
		Standard	5		1		96	85
		Below Standard	—		—		2	2
Married Women	25–39	Above Standard	9	56			11	33
		Standard	7	44			22	67
		Below Standard	—				—	
	40–49	Above Standard	2				14	20
		Standard	3				54	78
		Below Standard	—				1	2
	50 and over	Above Standard	2				18	19
		Standard	2				72	77
		Below Standard	—				3	3

Appendix 6A

Established Executive Officers

Distributions of ability by grade of entry to Civil Service

Sex	Age group	Ability	Grade of entry to Civil Service											
			E.O.		C.O.		P.O. Manip.		Typist		C.A.		Temp. C.A.	
			No.	%	No.	%	No.	%	No.	%	No.	%	No.	%
Men	Under 25	Above Standard	65	55	27	61	1				—		—	
		Standard	53	44	17	39	—				2		2	
		Below Standard	1	1	—		—				—		1	
	25–39	Above Standard	15	60	42	46	5	25	1				19	38
		Standard	10	40	49	54	15	75	—				31	62
		Below Standard	—		—		—		—				—	
	40–49	Above Standard	1		41	53	26	30	1		1		75	41
		Standard	1		36	47	62	70	1		2		108	58
		Below Standard	—		—		—		—		—		2	1
	50 and over	Above Standard	4	31	13	37	8	16	—		—		30	32
		Standard	8	62	22	63	41	80	1		2		63	67
		Below Standard	1	7	—		2	4	—		—		1	1
Single Women	Under 25	Above Standard	37	51	13	54							1	
		Standard	35	49	11	46							1	
		Below Standard	—		—								—	
	25–39	Above Standard	5	42	8	53	—		1		1		4	27
		Standard	7	58	7	47	2		4		2		11	73
		Below Standard	—		—		—		—		—		—	
	40–49	Above Standard			1		5	45	8	29	3	10	12	25
		Standard			3		6	55	20	71	28	90	36	75
		Below Standard			—		—		—		—		—	
	50 and over	Above Standard			1		—		8	29	2	10	7	39
		Standard			2		8		19	68	19	90	9	50
		Below Standard			—		—		1	3	—		2	11
Married Women	40 and over	Above Standard			—		4		2		4		5	21
		Standard			3		3		6		4		18	75
		Below Standard			—		—		—		—		1	4

Appendix 6B

Established Clerical Officers

Distributions of ability by grade of entry to Civil Service

Sex	Age group	Ability	Grade of entry to Civil Service: C.O. No.	C.O. %	P.O. Manip. No.	P.O. Manip. %	Typist No.	Typist %	C.A. No.	C.A. %	Temp. C.A. No.	Temp. C.A. %	Minor and Manip. No.	Minor and Manip. %
Men	Under 25	Above Standard	51	37	1				31	31	15	30	1	
		Standard	88	63	2				68	68	35	70	—	
		Below Standard	—		—				1	1	—		—	
	25–39	Above Standard	18	45	6	60	—		2		17	53	2	18
		Standard	21	53	4	40	1		2		15	47	9	82
		Below Standard	1	2	—		—		—		—		—	
	40–49	Above Standard	6	50	15	56	1		—		41	39	3	
		Standard	5	42	12	44	1		2		62	60	4	
		Below Standard	1	8	—		—		—		1	1	—	
	50 and over	Above Standard	8	22	9	30	1		—		40	24	2	11
		Standard	26	72	21	70	—		2		119	73	15	79
		Below Standard	2	6	—		—		—		5	3	2	11
Single Women	Under 25	Above Standard	45	34					14	22	7	19	—	
		Standard	89	66					49	78	29	81	1	
		Below Standard	—						—		—		—	
	25–39	Above Standard	7	47			2		5	38	5	20	4	33
		Standard	8	53			7		8	62	20	80	8	67
		Below Standard	—				—		—		—		—	
	40–49	Above Standard	—		5		5	50	—		16	31	—	
		Standard	1		2		5	50	7		35	69	3	
		Below Standard	—		—		—		—		—		—	
	50 and over	Above Standard	2		—	—	2	13	—		13	18	—	
		Standard	3		15	94	14	87	5		60	81	5	
		Below Standard	—		1	6	—		—		1	1	—	
Married Women	25–39	Above Standard	7	54			1		4		7	32	1	
		Standard	6	46			—		4		15	68	4	
		Below Standard	—				—		—		—		—	
	40–49	Above Standard	1		—		2		1		12	30	—	
		Standard	4		8		6		4		27	68	8	
		Below Standard	—		—		—		—		1	2	—	
	50 and over	Above Standard	2		2		2	20	—		12	18	2	
		Standard	2		4		8	80	2		54	81	4	
		Below Standard	—		2		—		—		1	1	—	

Appendix 7A

Established Executive Officers

Distributions of ability by method of entry to grade

Sex	Age group	Ability	Method of entry to grade					
			Open examination		Limited examination		On promotion	
			No.	%	No.	%	No.	%
Men	Under 25	Above Standard	88	55	5		2	
		Standard	71	44	2		2	
		Below Standard	2	1	—		—	
	25–39	Above Standard	24	60	17	52	39	34
		Standard	16	40	16	48	75	66
		Below Standard	—		—		—	
	40–49	Above Standard	1		3		150	41
		Standard	4		1		218	59
		Below Standard	—				2	1
	50 and over	Above Standard	—		5	45	51	26
		Standard	2		6	55	138	71
		Below Standard	—				5	3
Single Women	Under 25	Above Standard	51	53	1			
		Standard	46	47	1			
		Below Standard	—		—			
	25–39	Above Standard	5	42	5	50	8	28
		Standard	7	58	5	50	21	72
		Below Standard	—		—		—	
	40–49	Above Standard			1		30	24
		Standard					95	76
		Below Standard			—		—	
	50 and over	Above Standard			1		18	23
		Standard			—		58	73
		Below Standard			—		3	4
Married Women	40 and over	Above Standard	—				16	31
		Standard	1				34	67
		Below Standard	—				1	2

Appendix 7B

Established Clerical Officers

Distributions of ability by method of entry to grade

Sex	Age group	Ability	Method of entry to grade					
			Open examination		Limited examination		On promotion	
			No.	%	No.	%	No.	%
Men	Under 25	Above Standard	72	35	4	15	23	36
		Standard	130	64	22	85	41	64
		Below Standard	1	1	—		—	
	25–39	Above Standard	21	50	13	42	8	38
		Standard	20	48	18	58	13	62
		Below Standard	1	2	—		—	
	40–49	Above Standard	8	57	40	46	16	31
		Standard	6	43	45	52	36	69
		Below Standard	—		2	2	—	
	50 and over	Above Standard	5	17	38	30	17	19
		Standard	22	76	87	68	70	78
		Below Standard	2	7	3	2	3	3
Single Women	Under 25	Above Standard	55	30	1		10	25
		Standard	131	70	7		30	75
		Below Standard	—		—		—	
	25–39	Above Standard	8	38	2		13	27
		Standard	13	62	3		35	73
		Below Standard	—		—		—	
	40–49	Above Standard	—		14	64	13	24
		Standard	3		8	36	42	76
		Below Standard	—		—		—	
	50 and over	Above Standard	2		9	21	5	7
		Standard	3		33	79	65	90
		Below Standard	—		—		2	3
Married Women	25–39	Above Standard	7	54	3		10	34
		Standard	6	46	4		19	66
		Below Standard	—		—		—	
	40–49	Above Standard	2		2	20	12	21
		Standard	3		8	80	45	77
		Below Standard	—		—		1	2
	50 and over	Above Standard	3		8	30	9	14
		Standard	2		19	70	53	81
		Below Standard	—		—		3	5

Appendix 8A

Established Executive Officers

Distributions of ability by educational attainment

Sex	Age group	Ability	Educational attainment							
			" A " levels				5 or more " O " levels		Less than 5 " O " levels	
			Literate		Literate and numerate					
			No.	%	No.	%	No.	%	No.	%
Men	Under 25	Above Standard	47	55	35	55	1		1	
		Standard	38	44	28	44	—		—	
		Below Standard	1	1	1	1	—		—	
	25–39	Above Standard	18	58	6	43	31	46	28	39
		Standard	13	42	8	57	37	54	44	61
		Below Standard	—		—		—		—	
	40–49	Above Standard	2		6		50	43	92	38
		Standard	3		2		67	57	145	61
		Below Standard	—		—		—		2	1
	50 and over	Above Standard	3		2		11	27	43	27
		Standard	—		4		29	71	114	71
		Below Standard	—		—		1	2	3	2
Single Women	Under 25	Above Standard	36	54	12	46	1		1	
		Standard	31	46	14	54	—		—	
		Below Standard	—		—		—		—	
	25–39	Above Standard	7	54	1		8	40	2	14
		Standard	6	46	1		12	60	12	86
		Below Standard	—		—		—		—	
	40–49	Above Standard	—		1		6	17	20	27
		Standard	4		1		29	83	55	73
		Below Standard	—		—				—	
	50 and over	Above Standard	3				6	27	10	20
		Standard	3				16	73	36	73
		Below Standard	—				—		3	6
Married Women	40 and over	Above Standard	—				9	45	7	23
		Standard	1				11	55	23	74
		Below Standard	—				—		1	3

Appendix 8B

Established Clerical Officers

Distribution of ability by educational attainment

Sex	Age group	Ability	Educational attainment			
			5 or more "O" levels		Less than 5 "O" levels	
			No.	%	No.	%
Men	Under 25	Above Standard	46	37	37	29
		Standard	78	63	88	70
		Below Standard	—		1	1
	25–39	Above Standard	17	53	22	42
		Standard	15	47	29	56
		Below Standard	—		1	2
	40–49	Above Standard	10	36	51	44
		Standard	17	61	64	55
		Below Standard	1	3	1	1
	50 and over	Above Standard	5	19	49	25
		Standard	19	73	145	73
		Below Standard	2	8	5	2
Single Women	Under 25	Above Standard	43	31	19	24
		Standard	96	69	59	76
		Below Standard	—		—	
	25–39	Above Standard	9	33	9	25
		Standard	18	67	27	75
		Below Standard	—		—	
	40–49	Above Standard	5	38	18	32
		Standard	8	62	38	68
		Below Standard	—		—	
	50 and over	Above Standard	4		12	13
		Standard	5		80	85
		Below Standard	—		2	2
Married Women	25–39	Above Standard	9	60	9	30
		Standard	6	40	21	70
		Below Standard	—		—	
	40–49	Above Standard	3		12	22
		Standard	6		41	76
		Below Standard	—		1	2
	50 and over	Above Standard	4		13	19
		Standard	5		53	77
		Below Standard	—		3	4

Appendix 9

Distributions of efficiency amongst significant sub-populations

Grade	Sex	Age group	No.	Above standard %	Standard efficiency %	Below standard %
Executive Officer	Men	under 25	120	24·2	70·9	5·0
		25–39	162	31·4	60·5	8·0
		40–49	336	31·0	65·7	3·2
		50 and over	188	23·4	68·1	8·5
	Single Women	under 25	71	23·9	66·2	9·8
		25–39	47	21·2	72·3	6·3
		40–49	122	23·8	68·9	7·3
		50 and over	81	23·4	64·2	12·3
	Married Women	40 and over	50	18·0	72·0	10·0
Clerical Officer	Men	under 25	197	15·8	76·7	7·6
		25–39	85	21·2	65·9	12·9
		40–49	144	29·2	59·0	11·8
		50 and over	236	21·6	64·9	13·6
	Single Women	under 25	148	15·6	77·7	6·8
		25–39	65	33·8	56·9	9·2
		40–49	82	20·7	62·2	17·1
		50 and over	117	11·1	73·5	15·4
	Married Women	25–39	41	29·2	63·4	7·3
		40–49	70	18·6	60·0	21·4
		50 and over	91	16·5	72·5	11·0

Appendix 10A

Established Executive Officers

Distributions of efficiency by health record

Sex	Age group	Health	No.	Efficiency: Above standard %	Efficiency: Standard %	Efficiency: Below standard %
Men	Under 25	Of good health	119	24	71	5
		Of doubtful health	1	—	100	—
	25–39	Of good health	159	32	60	8
		Of doubtful health	3	—	67	33
	40–49	Of good health	317	32	66	3
		Of doubtful health	18	22	67	11
	50 and over	Of good health	171	23	69	8
		Of doubtful health	15	33	60	7
Single Women	Under 25	Of good health	69	25	65	10
		Of doubtful health	2	—	100	—
	25–39	Of good health	42	21	74	5
		Of doubtful health	5	20	60	20
	40–49	Of good health	116	24	70	6
		Of doubtful health	6	17	50	33
	50 and over	Of good health	77	23	64	13
		Of doubtful health	4	25	75	—
Married Women	40 and over	Of good health	46	20	70	11
		Of doubtful health	4	—	100	—

Appendix 10B

Established Clerical Officers

Distributions of efficiency by health record

Sex	Age group	Health	No.	Efficiency: Above standard %	Efficiency: Standard %	Efficiency: Below standard %
Men	Under 25	Of good health	191	15	77	7
		Of doubtful health	5	20	60	20
	25–39	Of good health	80	21	66	13
		Of doubtful health	5	20	60	20
	40–49	Of good health	130	30	58	12
		Of doubtful health	13	23	62	15
	50 and over	Of good health	219	22	65	12
		Of doubtful health	18	11	61	28
Single Women	Under 25	Of good health	139	16	78	6
		Of doubtful health	5	20	60	20
	25–39	Of good health	61	34	57	8
		Of doubtful health	4	25	50	25
	40–49	Of good health	74	23	59	18
		Of doubtful health	10	10	70	20
	50 and over	Of good health	109	11	74	15
		Of doubtful health	9	11	56	33
Married Women	25–39	Of good health	38	32	63	5
		Of doubtful health	3	—	67	33
	40–49	Of good health	63	21	59	21
		Of doubtful health	7	—	71	29
	50 and over	Of good health	76	17	72	11
		Of doubtful health	15	13	73	13

Appendix 11A

Established Executive Officers

Distributions of efficiency by uncertificated sick leave

Sex	Age group	Efficiency	No.	Average No. of days taken per annum over past five years					
				0	1	2	3	4	5
				%	%	%	%	%	%
Men	Under 25	Above Standard	29	48	17	14	17	3	—
		Standard	85	42	25	14	9	7	2
		Below Standard	6	17	—	50	33	—	—
	25–39	Above Standard	51	29	37	20	12	2	—
		Standard	98	25	40	20	7	4	4
		Below Standard	13	38	15	23	15	8	—
	40–49	Above Standard	104	47	32	14	5	1	1
		Standard	220	40	39	15	5	1	—
		Below Standard	11	36	45	18	—	—	—
	50 and over	Above Standard	44	45	32	14	7	2	—
		Standard	127	44	36	12	6	1	1
		Below Standard	16	56	44	—	—	—	—
Single Women	Under 25	Above Standard	17	35	29	12	—	18	6
		Standard	47	23	17	21	19	17	2
		Below Standard	7	14	57	29	—	—	—
	25–39	Above Standard	10	20	20	40	20	—	—
		Standard	34	15	32	41	6	3	3
		Below Standard	3	—	33	33	—	33	—
	40–49	Above Standard	29	34	38	14	14	—	—
		Standard	84	26	36	21	11	6	—
		Below Standard	9	44	44	11	—	—	—
	50 and over	Above Standard	19	37	32	26	—	—	5
		Standard	52	33	31	27	6	4	—
		Below Standard	10	40	20	10	30	—	—
Married Women	40 and over	Above Standard	9	22	22	11	33	11	—
		Standard	36	22	19	22	25	11	—
		Below Standard	5	20	40	20	—	20	—

Appendix 11B

Established Clerical Officers

Distributions of efficiency by uncertificated sick leave

Sex	Age	Efficiency	No.	Average No. of days taken per annum over past five years					
				0	1	2	3	4	5
				%	%	%	%	%	%
Men	Under 25	Above Standard	30	3	47	33	10	7	—
		Standard	151	26	29	20	16	7	3
		Below Standard	15	7	40	13	27	—	13
	25–39	Above Standard	18	22	33	28	11	6	—
		Standard	56	21	25	29	16	7	2
		Below Standard	11	45	18	27	—	—	9
	40–49	Above Standard	42	33	31	21	12	2	—
		Standard	85	32	36	15	8	8	—
		Below Standard	18	17	38	28	11	6	—
	50 and over	Above Standard	51	33	33	24	10	—	—
		Standard	154	32	39	19	6	3	1
		Below Standard	32	25	47	22	6	—	—
Single Women	Under 25	Above Standard	23	13	22	30	17	13	4
		Standard	115	17	24	24	24	7	3
		Below Standard	10		30	30	30	10	—
	25–39	Above Standard	22	27	23	18	27	5	—
		Standard	37	19	32	30	11	5	3
		Below Standard	6	—	50	33	17	—	—
	40–49	Above Standard	17	29	59	6	6	—	—
		Standard	51	22	27	20	23	6	2
		Below Standard	15	20	27	33	13	7	—
	50 and over	Above Standard	13	23	46	8	15	—	8
		Standard	86	24	30	28	9	7	1
		Below Standard	19	26	47	11	16	—	—
Married Women	25–39	Above Standard	12		8	42	25	8	17	—
		Standard	26	15	23	23	23	12	4
		Below Standard	3	—	—	—	33	67	—
	40–49	Above Standard	13	23	38	31	8	—	—
		Standard	42	19	29	29	14	7	2
		Below Standard	15	20	20	47	7	—	7
	50 and over	Above Standard	15	27	20	47	7	—	—
		Standard	66	17	29	32	17	3	3
		Below Standard	10	20	50	10	10	10	—

Appendix 12A

Established Executive Officers

Attitude towards joining the Civil Service

Sex	Age group	Are you pleased that you joined the Civil Service? Answer	No.	% of Age Group
Men	Under 25	Yes	122	77
		No	37	23
		Total	159	
	25–39	Yes	141	73
		No	52	27
		Total	193	
	40–49	Yes	333	85
		No	58	15
		Total	391	
	50 and over	Yes	215	87
		No	31	13
		Total	246	
Single Women	Under 25	Yes	66	73
		No	25	27
		Total	91	
	25–39	Yes	40	77
		No	12	23
		Total	52	
	40–49	Yes	104	87
		No	16	13
		Total	120	
	50 and over	Yes	70	82
		No	15	18
		Total	85	
Married Women	40 and over	Yes	49	91
		No	5	9
		Total	54	

Appendix 12B

Established Clerical Officers

Attitude towards joining the Civil Service

Sex	Age group	Are you pleased that you joined the Civil Service?		
		Answer	No.	% of Age Group
Men	Under 25	Yes No	187 88	68 32
		Total	275	
	25–39	Yes No	91 11	89 11
		Total	102	
	40–49	Yes No	145 44	77 23
		Total	189	
	50 and over	Yes No	311 47	87 13
		Total	358	
Single Women	Under 25	Yes No	167 59	74 26
		Total	226	
	25–39	Yes No	60 9	87 13
		Total	69	
	40–49	Yes No	70 13	84 16
		Total	83	
	50 and over	Yes No	120 11	92 8
		Total	131	
Married Women	25–39	Yes No	47 3	94 6
		Total	50	
	40–49	Yes No	74 7	91 9
		Total	81	
	50 and over	Yes No	112 3	97 3
		Total	115	

Appendix 13A

Established Executive Officers

Attitude to job

Sex	Age group	Attitude to the job	No.	% of age group
Men	Under 25	Like	101	63
		Indifference	39	24
		Dislike	21	13
	25–39	Like	127	65
		Indifference	43	22
		Dislike	24	12
	40–49	Like	272	69
		Indifference	89	23
		Dislike	31	8
	50 and over	Like	183	74
		Indifference	45	18
		Dislike	19	8
Single Women	Under 25	Like	49	53
		Indifference	28	30
		Dislike	15	16
	25–39	Like	38	73
		Indifference	8	15
		Dislike	6	12
	40–49	Like	86	71
		Indifference	23	19
		Dislike	12	10
	50 and over	Like	61	72
		Indifference	17	20
		Dislike	7	8
Married Women	40 and over	Like	42	78
		Indifference	6	11
		Dislike	6	11

Appendix 13B

Established Clerical Officers

Attitude to the job

Sex	Age group	Attitude to the job	No.	% of age group
Men	Under 25	Like	145	51
		Indifference	83	29
		Dislike	55	19
	25–39	Like	68	67
		Indifference	25	24
		Dislike	9	9
	40–49	Like	122	65
		Indifference	43	23
		Dislike	24	12
	50 and over	Like	267	74
		Indifference	60	17
		Dislike	32	9
Single Women	Under 25	Like	125	55
		Indifference	69	30
		Dislike	33	15
	25–39	Like	53	77
		Indifference	12	17
		Dislike	4	6
	40–49	Like	65	77
		Indifference	13	15
		Dislike	6	7
	50 and over	Like	104	79
		Indifference	21	16
		Dislike	7	5
Married Women	25–39	Like	38	70
		Indifference	11	20
		Dislike	5	9
	40–49	Like	59	73
		Indifference	9	11
		Dislike	13	16
	50 and over	Like	99	85
		Indifference	13	11
		Dislike	4	3

Appendix 14A

Established Executive Officers

Attitude towards the job by uncertificated sick leave

Sex	Age group	Job attitude	No.	Average No. of days taken per annum over past five years					
				0	1	2	3	4	5
				%	%	%	%	%	%
Men	Under 25	Like	97	52	22	17	5	4	—
		Indifference	39	44	26	15	5	8	3
		Dislike	17	41	23	12	18	—	6
	25–39	Like	120	24	42	17	11	4	2
		Indifference	42	31	21	36	7	2	2
		Dislike	24	21	42	25	12	—	—
	40–49	Like	260	42	38	14	5	1	—
		Indifference	83	36	31	19	8	4	1
		Dislike	30	37	27	20	10	3	3
	50 and over	Like	152	45	37	9	8	1	—
		Indifference	42	40	38	12	7	2	—
		Dislike	18	33	50	11	6	—	—
Single Women	Under 25	Like	50	42	28	10	6	12	2
		Indifference	29	31	24	28	7	10	—
		Dislike	14	29	21	21	14	14	—
	25–39	Like	38	11	39	37	8	3	3
		Indifference	8	25	25	37	13	—	—
		Dislike	6	17	33	33	17	—	—
	40–49	Like	85	33	39	13	13	2	—
		Indifference	23	13	35	30	9	13	—
		Dislike	12	25	42	17	17	—	—
	50 and over	Like	58	31	38	22	7	—	2
		Indifference	15	33	33	33	—	—	—
		Dislike	7	14	—	29	43	14	—
Married Women	40 and over	Like	40	22	28	22	20	8	—
		Indifference	6	17	17	33	17	17	—
		Dislike	6	17	33	33	17	—	—

Appendix 14B

Established Clerical Officers

Attitude towards the job by uncertificated sick leave

Sex	Age group	Job attitude	No.	Average No. of days taken per annum over past five years					
				0	1	2	3	4	5
				%	%	%	%	%	%
Men	Under 25	Like	135	29	30	24	12	4	1
		Indifference	81	22	31	22	16	6	2
		Dislike	52	13	25	35	15	2	10
	25–39	Like	54	20	32	32	9	6	2
		Indifference	24	29	29	21	17	4	—
		Dislike	9	11	22	44	22	—	—
	40–49	Like	86	33	35	19	12	2	—
		Indifference	38	18	37	21	8	16	—
		Dislike	24	29	37	25	4	4	—
	50 and over	Like	167	32	38	19	8	4	1
		Indifference	47	36	34	23	4	2	—
		Dislike	30	27	47	17	3	7	—
Single Women	Under 25	Like	119	29	23	24	15	7	2
		Indifference	64	9	23	38	19	6	5
		Dislike	31	16	19	32	26	6	—
	25–39	Like	52	19	33	27	15	6	—
		Indifference	11	9	27	45	18	—	—
		Dislike	5	20	20	—	20	40	—
	40–49	Like	60	25	38	18	13	5	—
		Indifference	13	8	31	23	38	—	—
		Dislike	4	25	—	25	25	—	25
	50 and over	Like	88	22	43	19	10	3	2
		Indifference	20	30	25	20	20	5	—
		Dislike	6	17	17	33	—	33	—
Married Women	25–39	Like	32	3	28	41	13	9	6
		Indifference	10	10	20	10	40	20	—
		Dislike	5	20	20	20	—	40	—
	40–49	Like	50	28	32	26	10	4	—
		Indifference	9	—	33	44	—	11	11
		Dislike	12	—	25	58	17	—	—
	50 and over	Like	76	20	26	38	11	3	3
		Indifference	13	15	46	15	23	—	—
		Dislike	4	—	50	50	—	—	—

Appendix 15A

Established Executive Officers

Main aspects of satisfaction and dissatisfaction

Main aspect	Men				Single women				Married women
	Under 25	25–39	40–49	50 and over	Under 25	25–39	40–49	50 and over	40 and over
Satisfaction									
Pay and conditions	51	64	96	97	89	94	136	162	167
Career prospects	66	49	19	8	20	25	12	2	13
Amount of work	7	11	11	13	5	13	2	—	6
Scope of the work	80	79	67	66	74	81	115	71	89
Other aspects of the work	2	6	7	9	—	6	9	8	19
Recognition	8	7	10	11	16	21	14	2	11
Supervision	30	23	22	19	15	37	23	14	43
Training	2	1	7	8	11	6	7	5	9
Management	—	1	5	4	—	—	—	—	—
Working conditions	6	10	13	19	11	10	3	9	7
Social atmosphere	81	68	51	46	99	73	46	36	41
Welfare	2	3	2	4	2	4	3	7	4
Personal convenience	20	38	56	54	30	21	35	46	31
Dissatisfaction									
Pay and conditions	60	76	37	28	34	12	4	2	6
Career prospects	59	61	74	82	51	48	60	71	49
Amount of work	35	32	30	17	60	39	45	41	33
Scope of the work	43	46	32	22	53	41	18	24	33
Other aspects of the work	1	7	9	6	4	—	2	2	4
Recognition	35	33	32	32	46	33	49	34	43
Supervision	11	16	7	9	11	21	14	2	4
Training	48	34	13	13	29	21	10	4	26
Management	7	7	15	11	9	21	15	6	26
Working conditions	31	35	34	24	72	19	44	41	22
Social atmosphere	—	—	1	1	—	4	2	2	6
Welfare	—	4	1	—	—	10	5	—	6
Personal convenience	22	35	16	17	31	23	24	11	31
Pay and conditions									
London based staff:									
Satisfaction	37	44	86	89	60	80	138	151	164
Dissatisfaction	56	77	57	32	49	10	3	—	10
Provincial based staff:									
Satisfaction	64	85	103	101	132	115	135	176	169
Dissatisfaction	65	76	28	26	11	14	5	5	—

Appendix 15B

Established Clerical Officers

Main aspects of satisfaction and dissatisfaction

	Men				Single women				Married women		
Main aspect	Under 25	25–39	40–49	50 and over	Under 25	25–39	40–49	50 and over	25–39	40–49	50 and over
Satisfaction											
Pay and conditions	36	68	87	94	129	123	156	151	104	181	153
Career prospects	43	33	8	5	15	20	5	8	9	9	12
Amount of work	15	16	9	18	6	10	7	9	6	12	10
Scope of the work	33	49	39	45	29	38	35	42	26	35	54
Other aspects of the work	3	6	8	13	1	—	4	9	6	11	5
Recognition	6	23	8	19	4	—	6	16	15	9	9
Supervision	30	15	19	19	19	17	19	6	28	23	10
Training	7	9	3	5	5	6	—	3	4	—	—
Management	4	—	3	4	—	4	—	2	—	6	—
Working conditions	25	24	23	22	8	6	20	11	7	6	6
Social atmosphere	89	55	48	46	110	59	54	33	48	41	34
Welfare	3	17	8	8	9	14	12	7	—	20	6
Personal convenience	43	48	42	50	38	17	26	42	74	51	32
Dissatisfaction											
Pay and conditions	94	61	43	28	25	17	2	8	7	6	3
Career prospects	66	89	117	105	35	45	92	67	50	43	54
Amount of work	20	22	20	23	30	45	20	14	24	32	20
Scope of the work	58	24	31	24	72	46	26	17	35	32	18
Other aspects of the work	2	13	4	3	4	6	5	—	7	10	3
Recognition	39	41	53	42	56	29	32	45	20	36	50
Supervision	7	10	7	8	14	6	23	16	17	26	7
Training	18	15	20	9	16	20	19	11	24	19	11
Management	5	12	11	8	7	7	9	6	7	25	5
Working conditions	35	16	11	19	46	21	30	35	39	48	41
Social atmosphere	6	6	2	2	7	—	—	—	3	5	3
Welfare	1	4	2	1	—	4	—	2	3	4	3
Personal convenience	16	6	10	2	32	4	13	14	24	17	5
Pay and conditions											
London based staff:											
Satisfaction	31	52	88	76	48	104	123	127	63	156	135
Dissatisfaction	110	63	43	43	50	44	7	15	11	7	5
Provincial based staff:											
Satisfaction	38	80	86	104	150	131	174	176	126	207	171
Dissatisfaction	86	59	44	19	18	—	—	—	6	5	—

MEMORANDUM No. 9

submitted by

THE PSYCHOLOGICAL RESEARCH CENTRE

June, 1967

The Recruitment of Graduates to the Civil Service: Survey of Student Attitudes

Table of Contents

List of Tables

List of Figures

Preface

By ALEC RODGER

Professor of Occupational Psychology in the University of London at Birkbeck College

Pitfalls abound in the field of attitude surveying. Those who planned and carried out the enquiry reported here evidently knew about them. They would not claim to have kept clear of every hazard, but it seems to me that they have done an important and exciting job very competently. They have handled their sampling problem with patience. They have formulated their questions with relevance and plied them with skill. They have drawn their conclusions with care.

Their opening gambit, What ideas do you have about what you would like to do once you graduate ?, illustrates the sensitiveness and elegance of their approach. Over the years, I have heard many interviews of the careers guidance kind spoiled irretrievably at the outset by the brisk (and sometimes brusque) question, Have you decided what you are going to do . . . ? The word " decided " (or perhaps the way it is uttered) commonly produces a defensive response which seems to say, Apparently I *should* have decided. The upshot has been that the applicant for advice has been made to feel rather guilty, and the conversation has lost its chance of becoming easy, frank, wide-ranging.

Discrepancies will be found—or at least seem to be found—between conclusions reported here and some presented elsewhere. The diehards and the sceptics will no doubt seize on these and say they show the uselessness of surveys. It would be unfortunate if these people had their reactionary way. Discrepant findings often provide, in science as in law, the starting-point for a major advance. They should be used to stimulate curiosity, not to encourage complacency or cynicism.

In any event, it is becoming fairly obvious to most of us that what is needed by recruiters is more, not less, attitude surveying. Technological change is accompanied by occupational change; and occupational change is accompanied by organisational change. We cannot hope to fit men to jobs and jobs to men in the leisurely styles of old. One of the conditions of our success in coping with these increasingly pressing problems will be foreknowledge of what people are going to think. Nothing short of the continuous " monitoring " of attitudes, performed with all the skill and discretion we can muster, will do. Only is this way will major employers in the public and private sectors of the economy be able to do their manpower planning well enough.

Of course, there is much that can be done immediately. It is worth noting the observation (on p. 361): " If the Scientific Civil Service fails to attract sufficient candidates it is perhaps because students are ignorant of the opportunities and possibilities rather than that an unfavourable image deters them. " I must confess that I have often been worried by the tendency of Civil Service " handouts " to go into great detail about conditions of employment and say next to nothing about the work to be done. Indeed, the same tendency spills over into interviews. I sympathised with the young graduate who, after twenty minutes of talk and interrogation by the chairman of a selection panel (with a brief intervention by the head of the branch concerned, who was particularly anxious to know when the young man might be able to start), was invited to say whether he himself had any questions. Taking a rather cool look at the chairman, he asked, What exactly *is* this job? What would I have to *do*?

Another step towards parity is suggested by Table XIII (on p. 359), which shows how the attractions of university links stand out when an interesting adaptation of Henry A. Murray's " theory of personality " is applied to the problem. Rapid progress is being made in the strengthening of ties between universities and Government research institutions. Why should not Civil Servants in non-research appointments be roped in too, for their own benefit and that of their employers? There are precedents. Currently in my own department at Birkbeck we have a dozen or so civil servants (in various classes, including the administrative) who are taking, on a part-time basis, higher degrees in manpower studies or occupational psychology. (Let me add, though the point is not directly relevant here, that part-time first degree courses have provided a considerable number of self-starting Civil Servants with qualifications leading them from general or departmental classes to undermanned specialist classes. There could be more.)

It will be a great day—hastened, I think, by the publication of this report—when public and private organisations, large and small, recognise the limitations of attempts to solve their recruitment problems by changing their " image " and give at least equal attention to the task of changing themselves.

Acknowledgements

Our thanks are due to the various authorities of the universities concerned for their permission to carry out the study and to the staff of the Registrars' departments and Appointments Boards for their very considerable assistance in giving access to records and in providing interviewing facilities.

We are especially grateful to those Appointments Boards who commented on sections of the interview schedule, in particular C. E. Escritt and G. C. Francis of Oxford University Appointments Committee, J. G. W. Davies of the University of Cambridge Appointments Board, E. H. K. Dibden and his colleagues of the University of London Appointments Board and to P. C. Hordern of the University of Birmingham Appointments Board.

Not least we are indebted to the undergraduates who devoted so much of their time to taking part in this survey.

D. C. Collins
Director
The Psychological Research Centre

Introductory Note

The following report is based on a study of undergraduate attitudes to employment in the Civil Service. It sets out those results of the enquiry thought most relevant to the work of the Fulton Committee.

The data is derived from interviews with a random sample of 2031 Arts, Social Studies, Pure and Applied Science students from fifteen Universities in England, Scotland and Wales. Interviews were conducted in the Summer Term of 1966. Brief descriptions of the method and the sample are given in Appendices I & II respectively.

Where conclusions are drawn from the differences between sub-samples the level of statistical significance is given in a footnote. Statements referring to there being no difference mean no statistically significant difference. Tests of significance have not been applied to differences where it is judged that no meaningful conclusion can be drawn.

Percentages are rounded to the nearest whole number; responses totalling less than 0·5% are indicated by an asterisk. The total for all categories on multiple response questions may exceed 100%.

Since this analysis relates only to selected questions in the interview the schedule is not reproduced in full, instead the relevant questions head each sub-section.

Statement of Objectives

This study sought to discover the ways in which undergraduates consider and assess opportunities in the Civil Service.

The specific objectives were to investigate:

1. Students' attitudes towards the Civil Service in terms of:
   - (i) their knowledge of its structure and function;
   - (ii) their conceptions of the jobs available;
   - (iii) their ideas of what working for the Civil Service would be like;
   - (iv) their perceptions of certain aspects as attractions or deterrents to a Civil Service career.
2. The role played by Civil Service and other selection procedures in career decision-making.
3. Students' assessment of the Civil Service in the competitive situation posed by the appeals of other employment and of further study.

Summary of Findings

(The summary follows the order of the text, i.e. the findings are not listed in order of importance.)

1.1. *Career Ideas*

17% of the sample from all academic years were considering Public Service. Nearly a quarter of those reading Arts and Social Studies subjects had this in mind compared with about one-tenth of those reading Pure Science and Applied Science. The reverse trend is observed for those considering Industry where the proportion increases sharply as we pass from Arts and Social Studies to Pure and Applied Science. Overall a greater proportion of women students than men students are interested in Public Service and a lesser proportion of women students interested in industry/commerce. (Pp. 331–333.)

1.2. *Job Types Considered*

15% of final year students in their last term had not considered applying for any specific job type. A fifth had not considered applying to any specific employer. There is a tendency for women to consider more job types and more possible employers than men do. A substantial minority, 30%, of male Pure Scientists were considering applying for administrative jobs in industry but only 10% were considering similar jobs in Public Service. Both Pure and Applied Science man-students show a marked preference for research and development work in industry over comparable work in the public service. (Pp. 333–335.)

2.1. *Timing of Job Considerations*

Apart from those choosing vocations such as teaching and social work most students did not give serious consideration to a specific job until some time during their university course, mainly in their final year. This was particularly true of students wanting to do administration or research and development, of whom 49% and 63% respectively decided upon this in their last academic year. (Pp. 339–340.)

2.2. *The Timing of Consideration of the Civil Service as a Career*

45% of the students who were considering a job with the Civil Service first had the idea before entering University. School teaching was the only other job to which a greater proportion gave early consideration;

57% of those wishing to teach had this in mind before coming up to University. Of those interested in industry and commerce, two-thirds did not consider these employers until some time during their university course; nearly a half not until their final year. (Pp. 341–342.)

3.1. *Employer Image*

When the Civil Service and industry are compared as competitors for the graduate manpower pool it is clear that government bureaucracies are perceived differently from industrial ones. It is not so much that industry is favoured as that the Civil Service fails to arouse interest. This appears to be due to some of the poorer aspects of its image. When the images of the two categories of employer are contrasted we find two fairly well defined image syndromes.

The image of the Civil Service is more favourable than that of industry in terms of the congeniality of colleagues, the interest of the work and its greater importance: a much larger proportion of students held unfavourable attitudes towards the value of work in industry compared to that of the Civil Service. Openings related to the student's degree subject were seen as being much more limited in industry (as exemplified by some major industrial employers) than in the Civil Service. But more applied scientists considered research and development in industry rather than similar work in the Civil Service.

The stereotyped image of the Civil Service was most clearly demonstrated in the student's perception of " dull, routine, dead-end " type of jobs. Further, nearly a third of the sample mentioned strict supervision and lack of scope for initiative. The disadvantages of major industry, on the other hand, were expressed in terms of impersonality and the " rat-race " image.

Although industry was rated higher than the Civil Service in terms of future salary prospects, the difference is not great. But it appears that the Scientific Civil Service had made little impact on students as offering promotion prospects.

Comparisons between the Civil Service and major industry give the general impression that students' perceptions of these employers did not differ greatly, and point to considerable lack of specific knowledge of career possibilities. However, the Civil Service was favoured in terms of perceived openings for work relevant to students' degree subjects, and was referred to favourably by a higher proportion of students than any other single employer. (Pp. 345–348.)

3.2. *Working in the Civil Service*

Students' conceptions of working in the Civil Service were generally expressed in favourable terms although many thought there would be low scope for initiative and strict supervision. The Civil Service was seen as offering better chances of working with congenial colleagues and doing more important work than industry. (Pp. 348–352.)

3.3. *Students' Perceptions of Employers along Specified Dimensions*

(*a*) Employers examined along single dimensions.

The Scientific Civil Service and University teaching rank highest in terms of the prospect of professional training to a high standard. Both the Administrative and Scientific Civil Service were rated lower than the private sector in the ease with which one might be able to transfer from one job to another or one employer to another. The Administrative and Scientific Civil Service were thought to involve work less conducive to bringing out the best in you than University teaching or industry and commerce. The administrative class was rated high in terms of directing the activities of others.

In this strictly comparative context industry and commerce were rated more highly than the two branches of the Civil Service for salary prospects, both early and in twenty years time.

Career advancement in the private sector and teaching at University is judged as being more likely to be based on performance rather than age than it is in the Civil Service although the Scientific is rated higher than the Administrative and Diplomatic Service.

(*b*) Employers examined in terms of needs and values.

An attempt was made to group attributes of different employers into larger categories. Looked at in this way University teaching was seen by students as most likely to satisfy their needs for achievement, affiliation, autonomy, dominance, understanding (knowledge), exhibition (recognition) compared with the scientific and administrative branches of the Civil Service and industry or commerce as represented by large organisations.

In terms of intrinsic work rewards and satisfaction of the need for security all four employer types are perceived alike and achieve high mean ratings. In terms of novelty, however, all except industry and commerce (large organisations) are rated low.

Industry and commerce are perceived as more likely to provide organisational flexibility than either the Civil Service or University teaching. (Pp. 352–364.)

4.1. *The Students' Knowledge of the Structure and Function of the Civil Service*

Perceptions of suitable job opportunities are dependent to a considerable extent on the student's knowledge of the structure and function of the employer. Knowledge of the function of the Civil Service was generally sound and expressed in fairly broad terms; structure was not so well perceived. In neither case was knowledge sufficiently detailed for most students to be able to gauge fully what openings there might be for their own subject or interest. (Pp. 367–368.)

4.2. *Students' Conceptions of Job Possibilities in the Civil Service*

Two-thirds of the students mentioned administration as a possible opening for graduates but their other responses indicated that they had limited ideas about specific jobs available. There was no increase in ideas about job possibilities between first and middle and final year students. (Pp. 368–369.)

4.3. *Job Preferences in the Civil Service*

Nearly 60% of all students were able to cite three possible Civil Service classes for which they might apply if considering a job in the Civil Service. The range of choice obviously varies according to faculty in terms of both eligibility and interest. In general, those reading Social Studies as a group displayed the widest range of choices of classes because of the heterogeneity of the faculty. Arts students confined themselves largely to the administrative class (71%) as a first choice. Though most scientists (63%) put scientific officer as first choice, a considerable number (11%) made the administrative class their first choice. The most substantial difference among the University groups is the Oxbridge choice of the administrative class—48% compared with 29% for all others.

There is no significant difference between students with first or upper second class degrees and those obtaining lower degree classes in respect of the Civil Service class to which they would apply.

Further academic study was a competing claim on half of those who expressed a preference for the administrative class and on nearly three-quarters of those who preferred scientific officer class. (Pp. 369–374.)

4.4. *Job Expectations*

Choice of job in the Civil Service centres on the intrinsic interest of the work and the opportunity of putting one's degree knowledge to good use. Interest of the work maintains a high level of response with each successive choice of job within the Civil Service made by students. (Pp. 374–375.)

4.5. *Selected Feature of Jobs and their Relationship to the Civil Service as a Choice of Career*

(1) Specialist and Managerial Jobs

Two-thirds of the sample, if they were to enter the Civil Service as specialists, thought they might want to move into management eventually. The same proportion thought that the transition from specialist to management work could be made without too much difficulty. This level was maintained by scientists. There were no differences between University groups. (Pp. 376–378.)

(2) Formal Training

Students expressed a preference for formal training to learning on the job in the proportions 55% to 29% respectively. Of those students who had accepted or intended to accept a job, over half will overgo a formal training period, two-thirds preferring a scheme lasting more than six months. No significant differences emerge from analysis by faculty. (Pp. 378–380.)

(3) Working in London

Two-thirds of the students irrespective of University group preferred to work in London all their working career, and many stipulated that they would not be willing to work outside London even for a few years only. (Pp. 380–381.)

(4) Short Term Contracts
Well over half the students thought the idea of working in the Civil Service on a short term contract was an interesting possibility, although it is not clear how many of them knew at the time of the interview that employment on short-term contracts was already possible in a number of classes. Applied scientists in particular favoured short-term contracts. (Pp. 381–382.)

(5) Pension Schemes
Three quarters of those who had accepted, or intended to accept jobs stated that they would be under a pension scheme. When asked which feature of a pension scheme rated most important, 71% of students gave a preference for transferability. (Pp. 382–383.)

4.6. *Attitudes to Methods I and II Selection Procedures*

Very few students had actual knowledge of Method I or Method II but with this reservation in mind, taking all students together, half preferred Method II and over one-third preferred Method I. There were no significant differences between University groups. When responses from those choosing the administrative class were analysed separately, 61% preferred Method II. (Pp. 383–386.)

4.7. *Biographical and Academic Differences between those considering the Civil Service, Further Study and Research and Other Employment*

An examination of final year students according to the type of career they were considering showed that the groups considering the Civil Service and academic careers contained a higher proportion of women than the group considering only industry or commerce. They also contained a higher proportion of those reading Arts and Social Studies than the industry/commerce group, where the proportion of applied scientists was greater. The make up of the three groups by type of University attended was markedly similar and there were no significant differences in respect of social class and type of secondary school attended. But there was a tendency for the children of graduate parents to consider a Civil Service or academic career rather than one in industry or commerce. (Pp. 386–392.)

4.8. *Students' Assessment of their Chances of Entry into the Civil Service*

Only a few students thought their chances of gaining admission to the Civil Service were low; however, the question as phrased did not refer to any specific grade. Nevertheless, a third of the sample did not know what their chances were. A large proportion of the sample thought that Oxbridge students stood a better chance of getting into the Civil Service than did students from other Universities. There was no difference between those who obtained firsts or upper seconds, and other degree classes, in rating their chances of obtaining a job in the Civil Service.

In explanation of their confidence in obtaining a job in the Civil Service, four reasons given by students seem relevant:

(i) The need for graduates facilitates entry.
(ii) Expectation of a good degree result.
(iii) There are many vacancies for graduates in subjects studied.
(iv) Self judged ability to pass entrance exams and interviews. (Pp. 392–394.)

5.1. 5.5 *Sources of Information*

Parents and such advisers as teachers and University Appointments Boards (U.A.B.'s) head the list of sources of information. Careers literature and the various kinds of career talks have a relatively low ranking, as do the several varieties of work experience. U.A.B.'s were visited by 66% of all finalists and about half (45%) of them making their first visit to their U.A.B.'s during their final year. Four-fifths of the students who visited U.A.B.'s attended advisory interviews. Reactions were more often favourable when seeking information about jobs but more often unfavourable when seeking new ideas about careers. Careers talks were poorly attended. Similarly, few students had met employers' representatives (about one-eighth of all finalists), and few had made formal visits to potential employers (16%).

Most formal visits left the student with an unchanged or more favourable attitude to the host. Over a quarter of the students making government office visits increased their already favourable disposition towards the Civil Service as an employer. This is particularly true of Oxbridge students. Though most vacation work similarly left students with an unchanged or more favourable attitude to the employer, a slightly larger number of people were discouraged by vacation work than by formal visits. (Pp. 397–408.)

Section 1

1.1. Career Ideas
1.2. Job Types Considered

1.1. Career Ideas

17% of the sample were considering Public Service. Nearly a quarter of those reading Arts and Social Studies subjects were considering the Public Service compared with about one-tenth of those reading Pure Science and Applied Science. The reverse trend is observed for those considering Industry where the proportion increases sharply as we pass from Arts and Social Studies to Pure and Applied Science. Overall a greater proportion of women students than men students are interested in Public Service and a lesser proportion of women students interested in Industry/Commerce.

Question asked: " What ideas do you have about what you would like to do once you graduate? "

Responses to this question have been grouped into a limited number of categories and are tabulated below in Table I. Some students were, of course, considering more than one career. Roughly speaking, nearly a fifth of the sample considered going into Public Service and just over two-fifths into Industry, a quarter into teaching, a quarter into further study and academic research, and others opted for the professions, cultural pursuits and so forth.

Table I. Students' Ideas about their Future Careers (By Faculty)

BASE: STUDENTS OF ALL YEARS	All 2031	Arts 609	Social Studies 423	Pure Science 614	Applied Science 385
	%	%	%	%	%
Public Service*	17	23	22	10	11
Academic Study or Further Research	25	24	24	34	16
Teaching and Other Education	26	41	22	25	10
Industry and Commerce including Nationalised Industries and Research in Industry	42	26	31	48	68
Professional†	15	18	27	4	6
Arts, Entertainment, Broadcasting and Cultural Organisations	3	4	1	—	*
Armed Services	2	1	1	1	3
All others	13	9	12	20	18
No distinct career ideas	5	4	7	5	2

* Includes Civil Service, Local Government Authorities, Hospital Service, Town and Country Planning and Social Services.

† Includes Accountancy, Architecture, Law, Politics, Publishing and Journalism.

It should be noted that Table I refers to students of all academic years and career ideas are not expected to match exactly what students eventually do after graduation. The UGC[1] statistics for 1965/6 show that of the total population of first degree graduates (excluding students from overseas and former Colleges of Advanced Technology) only one-quarter actually entered industry or commerce and 6% public service.

Sixty-six per cent of the students gave one, 23% gave two and 7% gave three or

[1] First Employment of University Graduates. 1965/6 H.M.S.O., 1967.

Fig. 1. Students Considering Public Service and Commerce and Industry

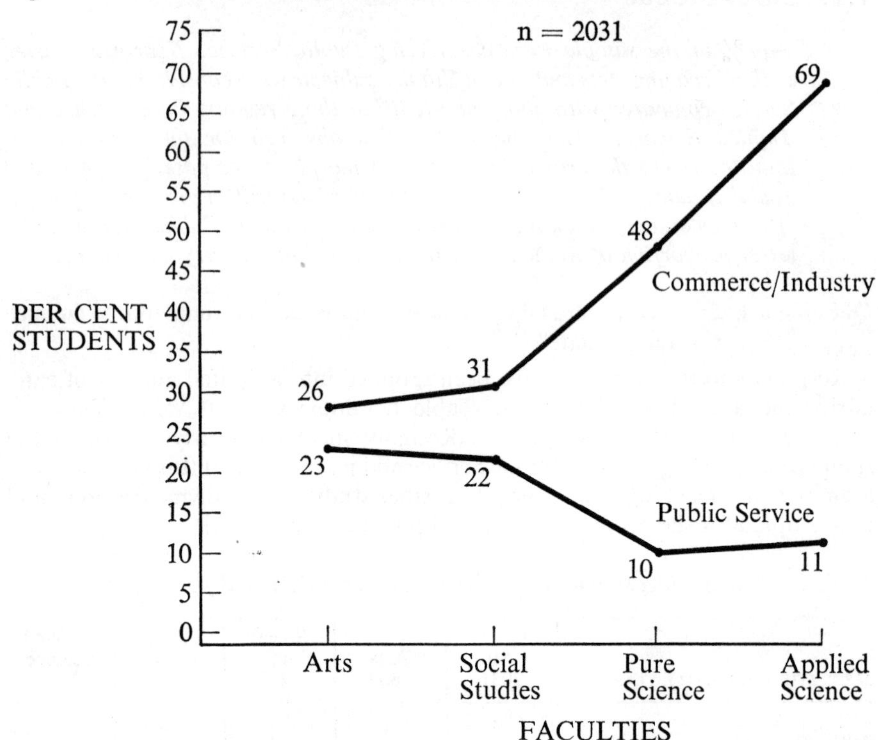

more ideas on what they would like to do on graduation. As will be seen on p. 334, the range of jobs ever considered by students is much greater.

It can be seen from Fig. 1 that for both sexes combined, interest in Public Service decreases as we pass from Arts to Applied Science whereas the reverse trend may be observed for Industry. The only departure from this when the sexes are examined separately is the high proportion of women Social Studies students considering Public Service (Table II). It will be observed

Table II. Faculty Differences between Students Considering Public Service and Industry/Commerce (by Faculty)

BASE: STUDENTS OF ALL YEARS CONSIDERING PUBLIC SERVICE AND INDUSTRY	Total		Arts		Social Studies		Pure Science		Applied Science	
	M	W	M	W	M	W	M	W	M	W
	1474	557	363	246	295	128	484	130	332	53
	%	%	%	%	%	%	%	%	%	%
Public Service including the Civil Service, Local Government, Hospital Service, Town and Country, and Social Services	11	30	17	31	11	50	8	13	10	20
	17		23		22		10		11	
Industry/Commerce including Nationalised industry and Research in industry	48	27	29	21	37	19	51	35	71	57
	42		26		31		48		69	

that overall a greater proportion of women than men are interested in Public Service and a smaller proportion of women than men in Industry/Commerce.

Although the numbers will be pruned according to degree result a quarter of the total sample of all years were considering post-graduate study; slightly more London and Oxbridge students than Civic and Scottish and Welsh were so minded. There is also a notable difference between Pure and Applied science men, 62% and 45% respectively. Interest in the subject and increased professionalism is the predominant motivation for further study although material rewards are not unnoticed; 13% prospects of higher salary and 11% prospects of further promotion. 55% would wish to continue their studies at their present University. Only 10% would consider the possibility of studying overseas although 54% of the total sample thought they might want to work overseas for some period of their career; 45% 2–6 years, 33% less than 2 years, 13% career largely overseas, 9% did not know. United States was the country of first choice for 28%, Canada 16%, Australia 13%, and New Zealand 7%.

1.2. Types of Job Considered

15% of final year students in their last term had not considered applying for any specific job type. A fifth had not considered applying to any specific employer. There is a tendency for women to consider more job types and more possible employers than men do. A substantial minority, 30%, of male Pure Scientists were considering applying for administrative jobs in industry but only 10% were considering similar jobs in public service. Both Pure and Applied Science men-students show a marked preference for research and development work in industry over comparable work in the public service.

Question asked: " Before discussing in detail any application you might have made would you tell me all the types of jobs and employers to whom you have considered applying? "

Responses to this question relating to job types considered were collapsed into a limited number of categories briefly described as follows:

(i) Job strictly related to student's degree subject.
(ii) Research or further academic study.
(iii) Research and Development.
(iv) Administration, Management, Planning, etc.
(v) Teaching, including Teacher training.
(vi) Social/Welfare work.
(vii) Operations Research, Computer Programming, etc.
(viii) Sales, Marketing, Advertising, Market Research, etc.
(ix) Broadcasting, Journalism, etc.
(x) Other, including Secretarial, Librarianship, etc.
(xi) No specific job type in mind.

The number of different job types for which men and women had considered applying is shown in Table III.

Table III. Number of Specific Job Types for which Students had Considered Applying (by Sex)

BASE: STUDENTS OF ALL YEARS	All 2031	Men 1474	Women 557
Number of Job types considered:	%	%	%
One	38	40	32
Two	22	21	24
Three	12	12	13
Four	3	3	4
Five plus	1	1	1
No specific job type mentioned	23	23	25
Total	100	100	100

There is a tendency for more women to consider more than one type of job, but the greater spread of this group is not significant. Although these figures relate to students of all years the pattern does not change to any marked extent when finalists are examined separately except that the group who had not con-considered applying for any specific job type reduces to 13% for men and 15% for women in their final year.

The three categories of administration, job strictly related to degree, and research and development form the largest single groups of work activity mentioned by students in terms of response frequencies. These categories are compared for public service and industry in Table IV. The categories, of course, are not mutually exclusive.

Table IV. Students Considering Selected Categories of Jobs in Public Service and Industry/Commerce (by Faculty)

		Total		Arts		Social Studies		Pure Science		Applied Science	
	All	M	W	M	W	M	W	M	W	M	W
BASE: ALL STUDENTS	2031	1474	557	363	246	295	128	484	130	332	53
	%	%	%	%	%	%	%	%	%	%	%
Administrative, Managerial											
Public Service*	8	7	10	13	16	14	12	10	2	2	—
Industry	25	30	12	28	15	42	15	30	10	25	—
Job related to degree											
Public Service	5	5	6	3	4	7	5	16	6	6	9
Industry	20	24	11	1	2	12	3	16	20	71	47
Research and Development											
Public Service	3	3	4	2	2	1	5	19	8	3	—
Industry	20	25	9	1	1	3	—	49	35	37	—

* Public Service includes Local Government, Town and Country Planning and Social Services in addition to the Civil Service.

The table shows that whereas women considered management positions in both industry and the public services equally (except for Pure Scientists), men did not. It may well be that the image of the Civil Service (see Section 3) and the student's perceptions of salary and promotion prospects are major determinants of the men's attitudes.

Another interesting feature of Table IV is that the same proportion of men Pure Science students would consider jobs in industry and the public services provided the work was related to their degree subjects.

Women Applied Scientists considered neither managerial nor research positions in either industry or public service unless they were related to their degree subjects. Substantially more men students of Applied Sciences considered job openings related to their degree subjects in industry (71 %) than did so in the public services (6 %).[1]

Two more observations seem worth making; both refer to the science faculties. Firstly, a substantial minority want managerial jobs in industry. Secondly, they show a marked preference for research and development work in industry rather than in the public services. As we shall show in Table VII students made more favourable comments about the Civil Service than about industry (represented by certain large industrial organisations) and less often saw limited opportunities in the Civil Service than they did in industry. Thus there is an inconsistency between their expressed attitudes towards the Civil Service and their job-seeking behaviour.

Table V. Number of Specific Employers to whom Finalists had Considered Applying (by sex)

BASE: FINALISTS ONLY	All 1088	Men 752	Women 336
Number of employers	%	%	%
One	23	19	33
Two	15	13	21
Three	11	11	10
Four	8	8	7
Five	7	8	4
Six	5	7	1
Seven	4	5	1
Eight or more	6	8	2
No specific employer	20	20	20
Total	100	100	100

Table V shows that a greater proportion of women cast their net over at least two individual employers. This may reflect their anxiety about possible openings. The high figure among women for one employer is largely due to the high number entering the teaching profession. Men on the other hand show extremes with 8 % considering eight or more applications to specific employers.

[1] Percentage difference statistically significant at 0·001 level.

Section 2

2.1. Timing of Job Considerations

2.2. Timing of Consideration of the Civil Service as a Career

2.1. Timing of Job Considerations

Apart from those choosing vocations such as teaching and social work, most students did not give serious consideration to a specific choice of job until some time during their University course, mainly in their final year. This was particularly true of students wanting to do administration or research and development of whom 49% and 63% respectively decided upon this in their last academic year.

Question asked: " When did you come to consider these job possibilities? "

The point in time of career decision-making is of course subject to a number of factors not solely related to degree subject. Attitudes to careers and University as a stepping stone are, to some extent, influenced by socio-economic background and secondary education. Many students with a public school background, of which Oxbridge has the highest proportion, tend to consider the University as one stage in a total career function. By contrast, others tend to be educationally and emotionally exhausted by the act of achieving University and initially put aside the question of an ultimate career.

Table VI sets out the stages in the student's history when the three selected types of jobs discussed in section 1.2 were considered. Section 2.2 examines the timing of consideration of the Civil Service as an employer.

Table VI. Stages in Student History when Job Possibilities Considered

BASE: STUDENTS HAVING MENTIONED SPECIFIC JOB POSSIBILITIES	Pre-University	University	Dont' know	Total
	%	%	%	%
1. Administration, Management n=560	22	76	2	100
2. Research and Development n=465	19	79	1	100
3. Job strictly related to degree subject n=529	38	62	*	100

It can be seen that the main decision points in all three cases occurred during the students' University course; the proportion of students who made up their minds in their final year is shown below:

	Career Considered in final year
	%
Administration, Management	49
Research and Development	63
Job related to degree subject	32

A substantial number of those opting for a career strictly related to their degree had made up their minds whilst still at school. This is not surprising when one considers the student's level of commitment to his chosen subjects in the sixth form. A change at this stage is seldom possible due to " A " level obligations.

This kind of argument may account for differences in the other career categories. Only a fifth of those who decided on an administrative career did so at school. The talents required are both more general and more specific. A wide variety of academic studies are suitable training grounds for administrators but on the other hand a choice of employer must depend (among other things) on level of performance. The final year is a more reliable time at which to assess one's class rating.

This is perhaps most obviously true for those contemplating a career in research in which only the most able performers have the opportunity.

Most students in fact, appear to pass through distinctive stages in their thinking which can be related to their university history.

Stage 1

The typical student enters University with well defined but ill-informed ideas about his future career. He includes romantic and stereotyped notions and sees himself as an adviser or consultant or academic researcher in his chosen subject. Only 7% of first year men compared with 3% of men finalists had no career ideas.

These ideas are usually based on parental and teachers' influence. The roles taken by these early sources of influence are to inspire and ensure attendance at University; only rarely are specific employers referred to. Industry at this stage often tends to be rejected because its image does not live up to the picture which the student has of himself. Industrial and material values have yet to be reconciled with self-concepts. The Civil Service in some respects is more in keeping with the students' personal values as we shall see under Employer Image Section 3.

Stage II

By the time the student enters his second year, his ideas and aspirations tend to become blurred and open-minded. He appraises his ambitions in relation to his performance and relative to his fellow students. He may pass into a stage of inertia with respect to his future career.

Vacations are often seen as a time to make money, rather than as a period for individual academic work.

Stage III

By the third year there is some differentiation according to abilities and a more realistic appraisal of opportunities. Inertia gives way to information-seeking activities. For some there is the realisation that university life will come to an end and something must be done. For the keenly ambitious or for the anxious there may be extensive information-gathering about the various employers and the prospects which they hold.

Among the procrastinators, reluctant to accept the need for making a decision, must be numbered some students showing superior abilities who tend to procrastinate by entering academic research.

If an active/passive index based on the number of sources of information used by students seeking information about jobs is constructed, using the eight sources rated as being most important, an index of 4·23 for those men students considering industry/commerce is found compared with 0·93 for those considering academic research.

2.2. The Timing of Consideration of the Civil Service as a Career

45% of the students who were considering a job with the Civil Service first had the idea before entering University. School teaching was the only other job to which a greater proportion gave early consideration; 57% of those wishing to teach had this in mind before coming up to University.

Of those interested in industry and commerce two thirds did not consider these employers until some time during their University course; nearly a half not until their final year.

Question asked: " When did you come to consider these employers? "

The periods in the students' academic career when the Civil Service was considered by finalists in relation to other important categories of employer is depicted in Fig. 2.

Fig. 2. Timing of Students Consideration of the Civil Service in Relation to Other Employers.

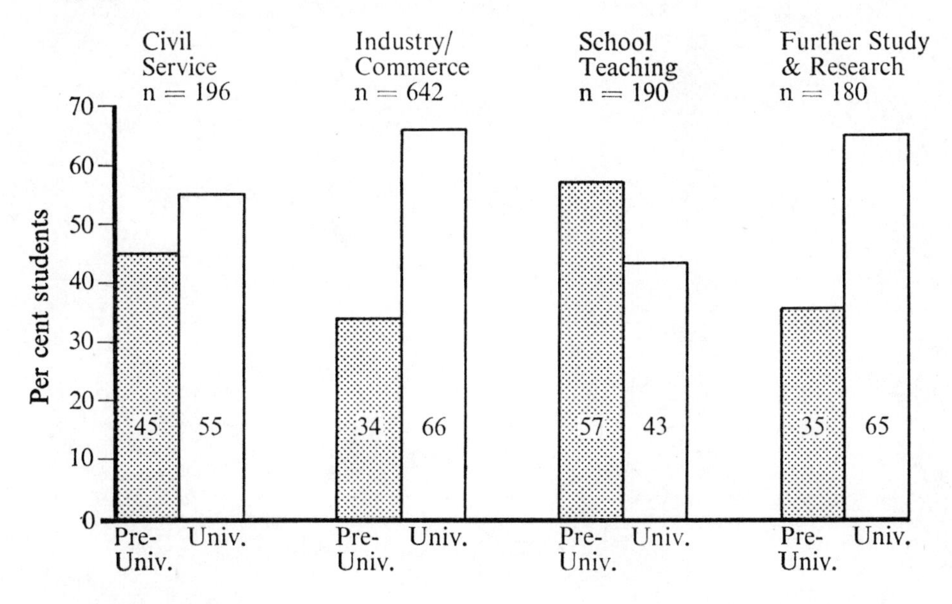

It will be observed that further study and research and industry/commerce present similar patterns. The late serious consideration by those aspiring to further study is probably because they are aware that this is dependent on their degree result which can only be realistically assessed in the terminal stages of their academic career.

The industry and commerce group, however, contains a large proportion of students who had left their career-seeking activities until their final year, many of them previously having scant ideas about their future destiny as responses to the following question reveal.

Question asked: " How did you come to consider these employers? "

The way in which students learn about different jobs and employers is dealt with in detail in Section 5, Sources of Information. Here it is sufficient to say that consideration of openings in industry were generated largely by the Appointments Boards whereas the sources of information and influence of those interested in the Civil Service were more diverse some of them operating earlier in the students' academic history, although, as we shall see, the Appointments Boards play an important role for this group too. The pattern of timing of Civil Service consideration is, however, very different from that of industry.

Section 3

3.1. Employer Image

3.2. Working in the Civil Service

3.3. Students' Perceptions of Employers along Specified Dimensions

(*a*) Employers examined along single dimensions

(*b*) Employers examined in terms of needs and values

3.1. Employer Image

When the Civil Service and industry are compared as competitors for the graduate manpower pool it is clear that government bureaucracies are perceived differently from industrial ones. It is not so much that industry is favoured as that the Civil Service fails to arouse interest. This appears to be due to some of the poorer aspects of its image. When the images of the two categories of employer are contrasted we find two fairly well defined image syndromes.

The image of the Civil Service is more favourable than that of industry in terms of the congeniality of colleagues, the interest of the work and its greater importance: a much larger proportion of students held unfavourable attitudes towards the value of work in industry compared to that of the Civil Service. Openings related to the student's degree subject were seen as being much more limited in industry (as exemplified by some major industrial employers) than in the Civil Service. But more Applied scientists considered research and development in industry rather than similar work in the Civil Service.

The stereotyped image of the Civil Service was most clearly demonstrated in the student's perception of " dull, routine, dead-end " type of jobs. Further, nearly a third of the sample mentioned strict supervision and lack of scope for initiative. The disadvantages of major industry, on the other hand, were expressed in terms of impersonality and the " rat-race " image.

Although industry was rated higher than the Civil Service in terms of future salary prospects, the difference is not great. But it appears that the Scientific Civil Service had made little impact on students as offering promotion prospects. Comparisons between the Civil Service and major industry give the general impression that student's perceptions of these employers did not differ greatly, and point to considerable lack of specificity as to career possibilities. However, the Civil Service was favoured in terms of perceived openings for work relevant to students' degree subjects, and was referred to favourably by a higher proportion of students than any other single employer.

After students had been given an opportunity of discussing their career ideas and the sorts of jobs they had considered, the interviewer mentioned certain employers, provided that the students had not already done so themselves. The attitudes, spontaneous responses, of students to the Civil Service and to major industry (as exemplified by several large and diverse industrial and commercial organisations) are given in Table VII.

The two most interesting items have been boxed in. Twice as many students felt that openings for their subject were limited in the industrial firms as held a similar view of the Civil Service. Of the two groups of students—those who had not considered the Civil Service, those who had not considered the companies—the first group made more favourable references to the Civil Service as a potential employer than did the other group about the industrial organisations.

The overriding impression is that industry is not so much favoured as that the Civil Service fails to arouse interest. Quite a high proportion of students are discouraged by aspects of the Civil Service image, notably those shown at 6 and 8 of Table VII.

Table VII. Reasons for not having considered the Civil Service or Major Industry

BASE: STUDENTS NOT HAVING SPONTANEOUSLY CITED THE CIVIL SERVICE OR COMPANIES X, Y AND Z AS POSSIBLE EMPLOYERS	Civil Service 1750	Weighted mean responses in respect of companies 1862
	%	%
1. No interest in Civil Service or in companies mentioned	27	13
2. No interest in industry	—	16
3. Openings for students subject felt to be limited	10	20
4. Competition for entry too great	7	4
5. Too large, loss of individuality	—	7
6. Deterred by hierarchical structure	13	—
7. Dislikes " big business " image	—	6
8. Stereotyped image, prejudice	10	7
9. Inadequate information about jobs with these employers	7	6
10. Inadequate information about the employer (conditions, etc.)	4	3
11. Favourable references (as an employer)	21	11
12. No definite career ideas	7	10
13. Don't know	7	12

Apart from the students', probably inaccurate, ideas about possible openings for their subject, a small minority have inadequate knowledge about these particular employers and the career opportunities they provide. The Civil Service and these industrial employers may well have " lost " favourable responses because of the students' lack of knowledge. Since all of the employers under consideration employ a wide range of graduates there appears to be as much a problem of satisfying information needs as there is in bringing about attitude change.

Question asked: " What do you see as (i) the main advantages (ii) the main disadvantages of working with each of these employers? " (i.e., Civil Service, Scientific Civil Service, Companies X, Y, and Z).

Advantages

Table VIII represents some of the advantages brought to light in the responses to this question in a manner which enables comparisons to be made between the Civil Service and the industrial organisations. Note that only Arts and Social Studies students were asked this question about the Civil Service, and only Pure and Applied Scientists about the Scientific Civil Service.

Security obviously figures largely in the perceptions of students when considering career possibilities—at least with these employers. Favourable work facilities and conditions were more often associated with Civil Service careers, especially the Scientific Civil Service, than with jobs in the industrial firms and so were stimulating work, 12% for the Scientific Civil Service and high status, which was less than 0·5% for industry.

Wide variety of work is notably low for the Scientific Civil Service, less than 0·5%, compared with 8% for the Civil Service and 10% for industry.

Favourably salary prospects for the Civil Service are rated nearly as high as for industry, 15% and 18%. The Scientific Civil Service suffers in this respect. Similarly the Civil Service does not lag far behind industry in promotion prospects, 9% and 14% respectively.

Table VIII. Perceived Main Advantages of a Career in the Civil Service and Major Industry

BASE: STUDENTS OF ALL YEARS	Civil Service Arts and Social Studies 1032	Scientific Civil Service Pure and Applied Science 999	Weighted mean responses in respect of companies 2031
	%	%	%
Advantages associated with a large organisation, security, fringe benefits, etc.	48	37	31
Favourable salary prospects	15	9	18
Favourable promotion prospects	9	*	14
Opportunities for travel	5	3	20
Wide variety of work	8	*	10
Favourable work facilities, laboratories, equipment, etc.	12	16	6
Stimulating work	4	12	*
Good training scheme	*	*	3
High status	4	3	*
No distinct advantages perceived and don't know	20	33	36

Table IX. Perceived Main Disadvantages of a Career in the Civil Service and Major Industry[1]

BASE: STUDENTS OF ALL YEARS	Civil Service Arts and Social Studies 1032	Scientific Civil Service Pure and Applied Science 999	Weighted mean responses in respect of companies 2031
	%	%	%
Dislike of large organisation, loss of individuality, impersonal, etc.	15	8	32
Unfavourable salary prospects	8	14	*
Openings for student's subject felt to be limited	4	4	11
Routine job, red tape, etc.	38	20	*
Feels personally unsuited to pace of work in industry, " rat race " etc.	*	*	11
Dead end job	18	15	*
Too strong competition for advancement	*	*	5
Job may depend on consumer market fluctuations, insecure	*	*	2
Others, dislike possibility of going overseas, would not want to work in London, etc.	10	10	7
No distinct disadvantages perceived and don't know	12	23	36

[1] A number of categories earning few responses have been omitted.

Disadvantages

Table IX compares the students' perceptions of the main disadvantages of careers with these employers. The high " Don't know " rate in the case of the Scientific Civil Service and, more particularly industry compared with the Civil Service should be noted.

There are some interesting differences. If some aspects associated with bureaucratic type organisations were seen as advantages (e.g. security), others were viewed as disadvantages (e.g. routine work, dead-end job, etc.). However, government bureaucracies were perceived differently from industrial ones. For example, although industry did not evoke responses like " routine work " or " dead-end job " they, more than the Civil Service, were considered too large and impersonal, 32%, and they alone were associated with the " rat race ", by 11% of the sample.

The general tone of the students' responses suggest that students have a stereotyped image of both categories of employer. This will be examined in more detail later in this section when students' rating of a number of important employer attributes are looked at.

The differences in response between Table VII and Tables VIII/IX is due to the different kind of question being asked. In this latter exercise students were specifically being requested to bring to mind possible advantages and disadvantages.

3.2. Working in the Civil Service

Students' conceptions of working in the Civil Service were generally expressed in favourable terms although many thought there would be low scope for initiative and strict supervision. The Civil Service was seen as offering better chances of working with congenial colleagues and doing more important work than industry.

Question asked: " What do you think it would be like working in the Civil Service department which is most appropriate to you? "

Spontaneous responses were classified into the following main categories:

(i) conditions of work
(ii) type of colleague
(iii) interest of the work
(iv) importance of the work
(v) variety of the work
(vi) extent of supervision
(vii) extent of anonymity
(viii) scope for initiative
(ix) inability to pursue political ambitions

Men students' conceptions of some of the above aspects of working in the Civil Service are set out in Fig. 3 and Table X. It can be seen that responses were generally favourable. Exceptions centre on scope for initiative where 30% thought there was good or average scope and 31% thought little initiative was possible, and on supervision which was thought to be strict by 30%.

Variety of work did not evoke many responses (cf. Table VIII only 8% spontaneous mentions); just over one quarter of the students thought it would be either very varied or of average variety. Similarly extent of anonymity was commented on by only half the students.

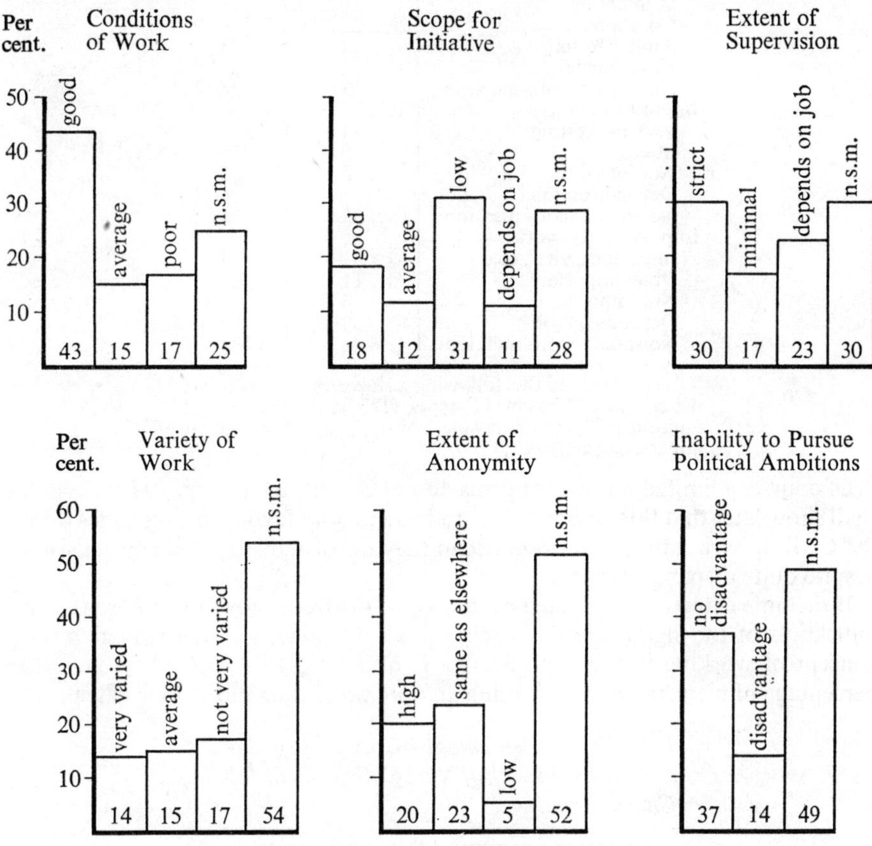

Fig. 3. Men Students' Expectations of Certain Aspects of Working in the Civil Service. n = 1474

n.s.m. = no spontaneous mention

Students' expectations of the Civil Service and industry (as reflected by their expectations of major industries) are compared in some other respects in Table X.

The Civil Service was seen by students as offering better chances for meeting congenial colleagues than industry and the work was also seen as more interesting.

If it is assumed that people will regard as worthwhile that which they think is important (although, of course, the reverse is not necessarily true) it is legitimate to equate the two concepts. Thus students saw greater value in the work of the Civil Service than they did in industrial work. Not only did the modal point to their favourable attitudes shift downwards (i.e. from very worthwhile to worthwhile) in the case of industry; there was a much greater proportion of students who held unfavourable attitudes towards the value of work in industry compared to that of the Civil Service.

Table X. Students' Expectations about Working in the Civil Service and Industry

BASE: MEN STUDENTS ONLY	Civil Service 1474	Industry 1474
	%	%
Type of colleague:		
Stimulating	10	11
Congenial	21	8
Similar to self	24	24
Uncongenial	22	21*
No spontaneous mention	23	36
Interest of work:		
Very interesting	14	10
Interesting	30	20
Not interesting	18	20
Depends on job	6	14
No spontaneous mention	32	36
Importance of work:		
Important, vital, etc.	31	9
Quite important	11	29
Not important	4	21
Depends on job	8	9
No spontaneous mention	46	32

* The sum of the following categories: competitive, materialistic " business " types (11%); limited outside interests (4%); uninteresting, boring, unintelligent (5%); impersonal, aloof (1%).

Of course, a limited number of firms do not constitute industry. However, we shall show later that this tendency for students to hold favourable attitudes about the Civil Service rather more often than they do of industry is fairly consistent despite quite disparate contexts.

If the nine categories are listed according to the frequency of response then an indication of the significance of each one's contribution to the student's total concept of working in the Civil Service is obtained. Table XI below gives the percentage of men students expressing an opinion in each of the nine categories.

Table XI. Percentage of Students giving a Response in each of Nine Categories of Job Characteristics

BASE: MEN STUDENTS (n=1474) Prompted response category:	Percentage responding
Type of colleague	77
Conditions of work	75
Scope for initiative	72
Extent of supervision	70
Interest of the work	68
Importance of the work	54
Inability to pursue political ambitions	51
Extent of anonymity	48
Variety of the work	46

In Section 4.3 students' preferences for jobs are examined along with the reasons for their preferences but here it can be said that most students gave as their main reasons either that their choice was because the work was intrinsically interesting or was related to their field of study (see Table XII).

Table XII. Appeal of Job Possibilities Considered

BASE: STUDENTS HAVING MENTIONED SPECIFIC JOB POSSIBILITIES	Men and women combined 1139
	%
Intrinsic interest of the work	77
Salary, fringe benefits	20
Promotion prospects	19
Opportunity of putting degree knowledge to good use	17
Importance of the work	9
Freedom to work on own initiative	5
Intellectual climate	4
Leadership, responsibility	4
Status attached to job	1
Others: location, travel, easy entry, etc.	23
Don't know, no special appeal	4

Four-fifths of the sample seek " intrinsic interest of the work " in their career and 17% expect " the opportunity of putting their degree knowledge to good use " and similar proportions expect both good salary conditions and promotion prospects. In contrast only 4% mentioned " intellectual climate " though there is good reason to suppose this is implicit in the intrinsic interest expectation. Table XII also shows that " importance of the work " in the context of this question was cited by only 9% of the sample.

Although attractions are not expectations one can reasonably argue that they are closely interdependent. That is to say if a student says that a job appeals to him because the work is intrinsically interesting we can fairly safely assume that he expects that particular job to be interesting.

Throughout this section reference has been made to a variety of features which either attract or deter students from considering a career in the Civil Service.

To conclude we shall bring the more important of these features together so that comparisons can be made with industry.

Attention has been drawn to the students' views of bureaucracy which were far more unfavourable towards the Civil Service than was the case with the industrial organisations.

The appropriate items from Table VII are reproduced below:

	Civil Service 1750	Industry 1862
	%	%
Too large, loss of individuality	—	7
Deterred by hierarchical structure	13	—
Stereotyped image, prejudice	10	7

What needs to be examined here is how differently the two bureaucracies—a government department and a large industrial complex—are perceived by students. It could very well be that their image of " red tape ", " routine boring work ", and " no scope for initiative " overflow into other attitude areas, e.g. that relating to organisational structure.

This may account also for the larger proportion of students admitting to the influence of a bad image of the Civil Service compared with those who claimed to dislike the " big business " image of industry.

The range of students' responses reinforce this line of argument. Reference to " red tape ", " dead-end job ", " low scope for initiative ", " restricting, frustrating work ", were common and account for half the number of comments made by students when discussing the disadvantages of the Civil Service. The picture for the Scientific Civil Service is similar but a new image appears—" lack of job flexibility "—which reflects students' concern with getting stuck in a rut.

In the case of industry, however, half the comments referred either to the impersonal nature of large scale organisations or to their competitive character; the " rat race " was mentioned by a tenth of those responding to this part of the interview schedule.

When the proportion of students who mentioned favourable salary prospects are combined with those citing favourable promotion prospects industry comes off better than the Civil Service although the differences are not great.

The interesting point to note is that less than 0·5 % of science students mentioned promotion prospects when discussing the advantages of the Scientific Civil Service. In contrast, when discussing the disadvantages students mentioned poor prospects for both the administrative and scientific sections of the Civil Service whereas no student referred to them in the context of industrial organisations. Students of the Humanities and Sciences regarded the Civil Service as offering poor promotion prospects in about equal proportions (19 % and 15 % respectively) but twice as many Science as Humanities students mentioned unfavourable salary prospects (14 % and 7 % referring to the scientific and administrative sections of the Civil Service respectively).

3.3. Students' Perceptions of Employers along Specified Dimensions

(*a*) *Employers examined along single dimensions.*

The Scientific Civil Service and University Teaching rank highest in terms of the prospect of professional training to a high standard. Both the administrative and the Scientific Civil Service were rated lower than the private sector in the ease with which one might be able to transfer from one job to another or one employer to another. The Administrative and Scientific Civil Service were thought to involve work less conducive to bringing out the best in you than University teaching or industry and commerce. The administrative class was rated high in terms of the likelihood of directing the activities of others.

In this strictly comparative context industry and commerce were rated more highly than the two branches of the Civil Service or University teaching for salary prospects both early and in twenty years time.

Career advancement in the private sector and teaching at University is judged as being more likely to be based on performance rather than age than it is in the Civil Service although the Scientific is rated higher than the administrative or diplomatic service.

Question asked: " The following is a list of job characteristics some of which you may associate more closely with one type of employer than another. Here is a list of the employers I would like you to consider. Would you please indicate (on the rating scales provided) the extent to which you associate each employer with each characteristic? "

Fig. 4(i). Early Salary Prospects

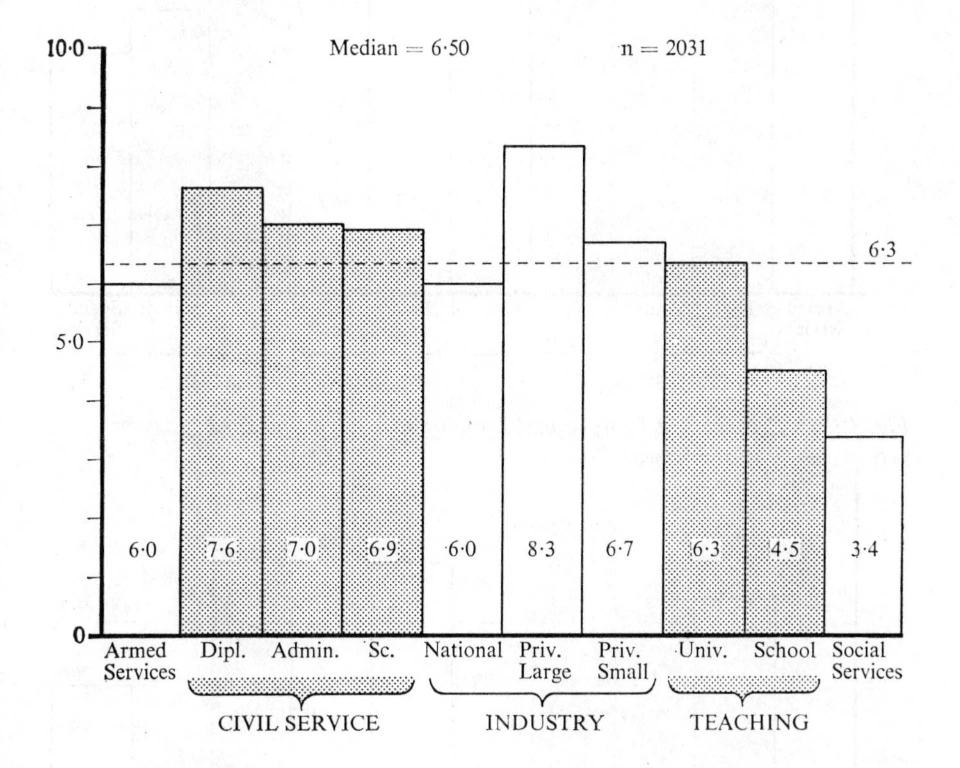

The ratings of attributes represent perceptions students of all years (n = 2031) have of different categories of employer; the latter are compared with one another for each of the 28 attributes. These ratings are of considerable interest in their own right, of course, but they also provide indirect evidence of underlying motivations guiding or influencing students' perceptions of employer types.

In the first instance a limited number of employer attributes thought to be of particular interest to the Civil Service are examined singly. They are shown in Figs. 4.i to 4.viii. (See also Appendix III.)

Fig. 4(ii). Salary Prospects in 20 years time

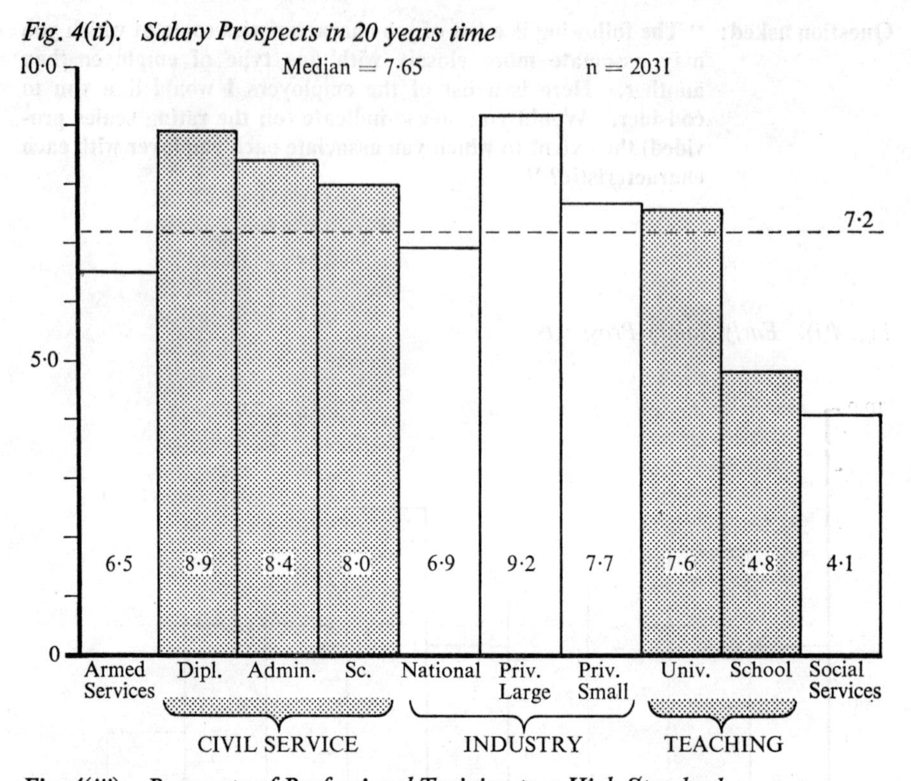

Fig. 4(iii). Prospects of Professional Training to a High Standard

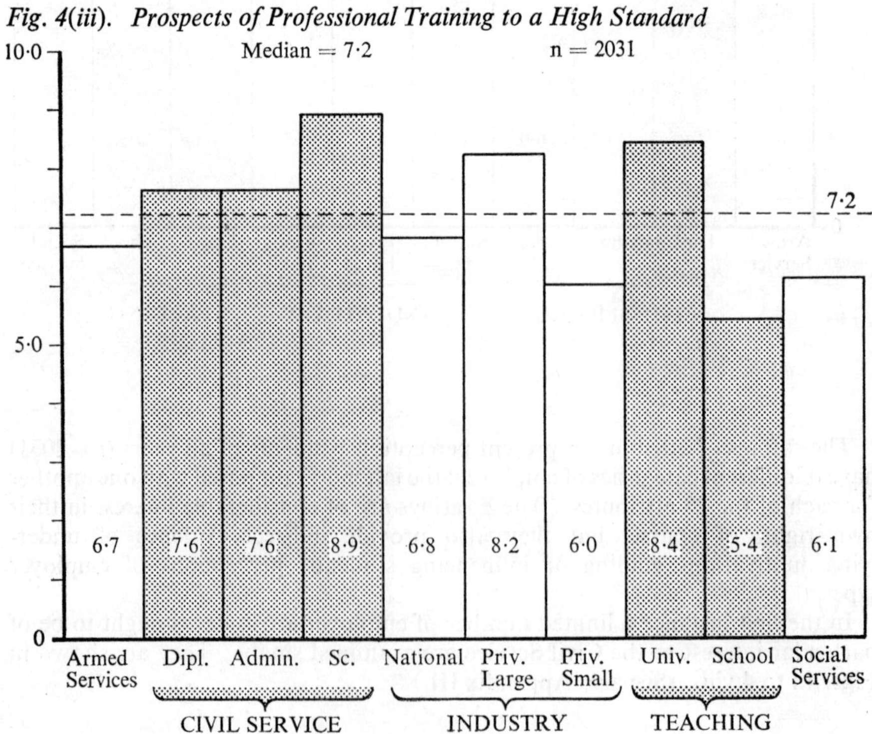

Fig. 4(iv). Work Conducive to Bringing Out the Best in You

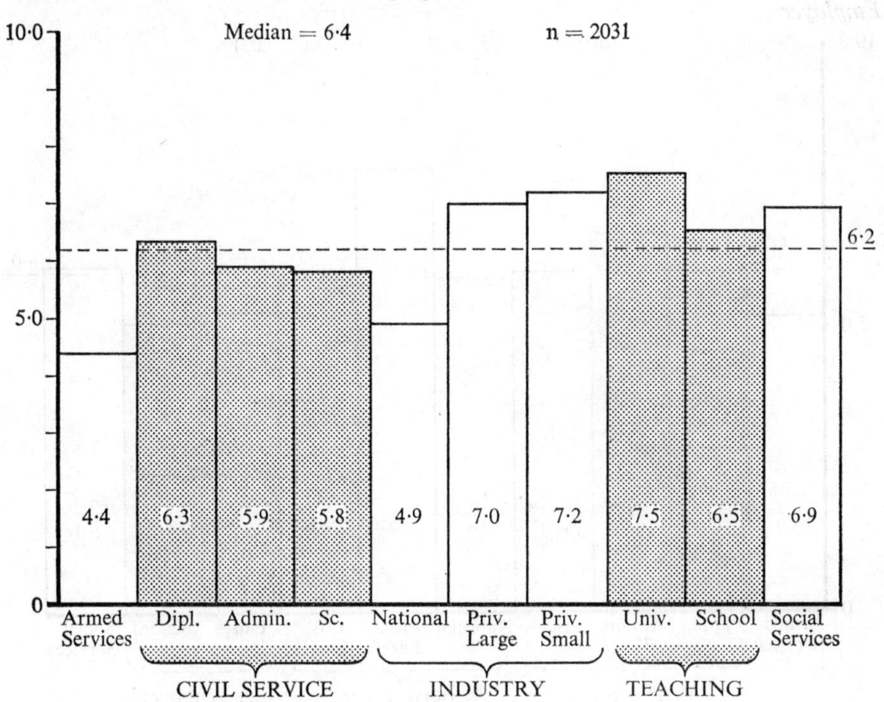

Fig. 4(v). Career Advancement based on Performance rather than Age

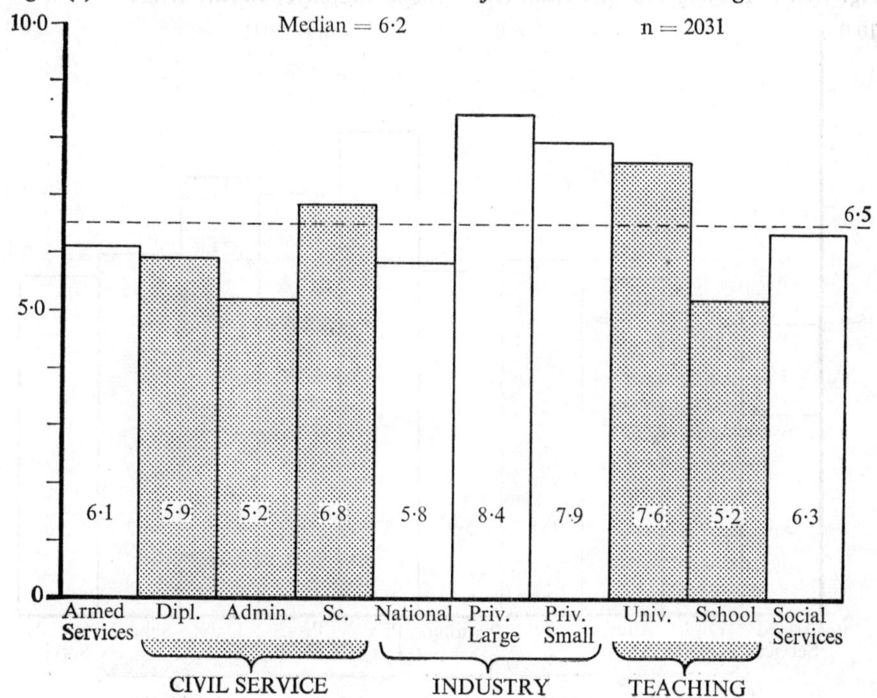

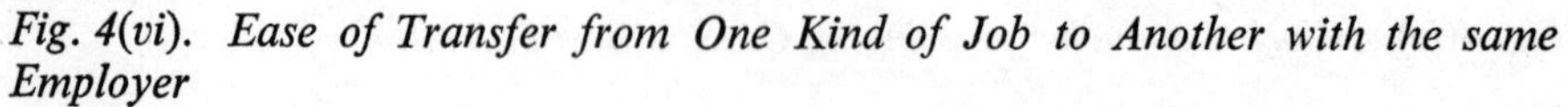

Fig. 4(vi). Ease of Transfer from One Kind of Job to Another with the same Employer

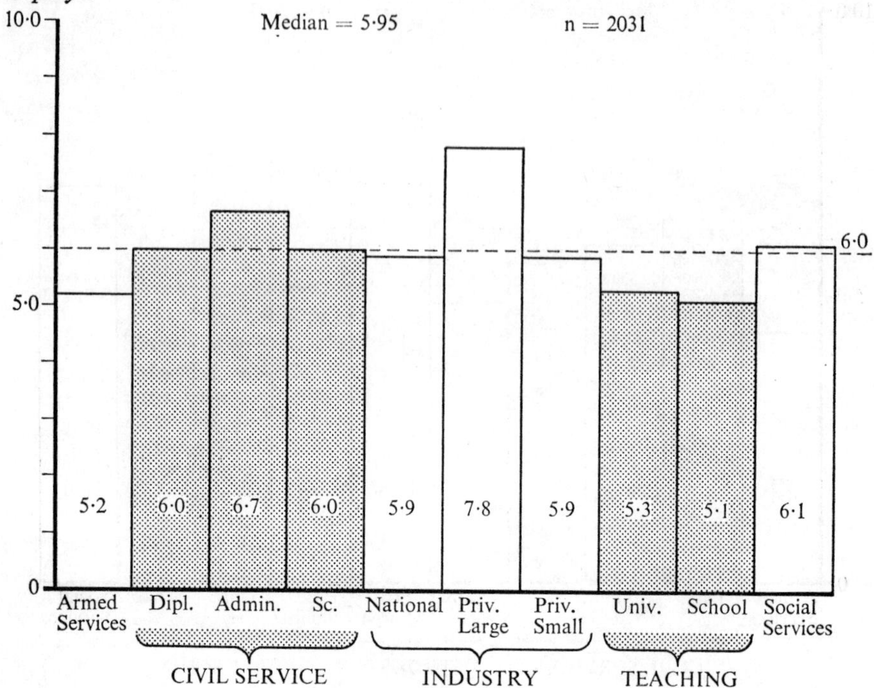

Fig. 4(vii). Ease of Transfer from One Type of Employer to Any Other

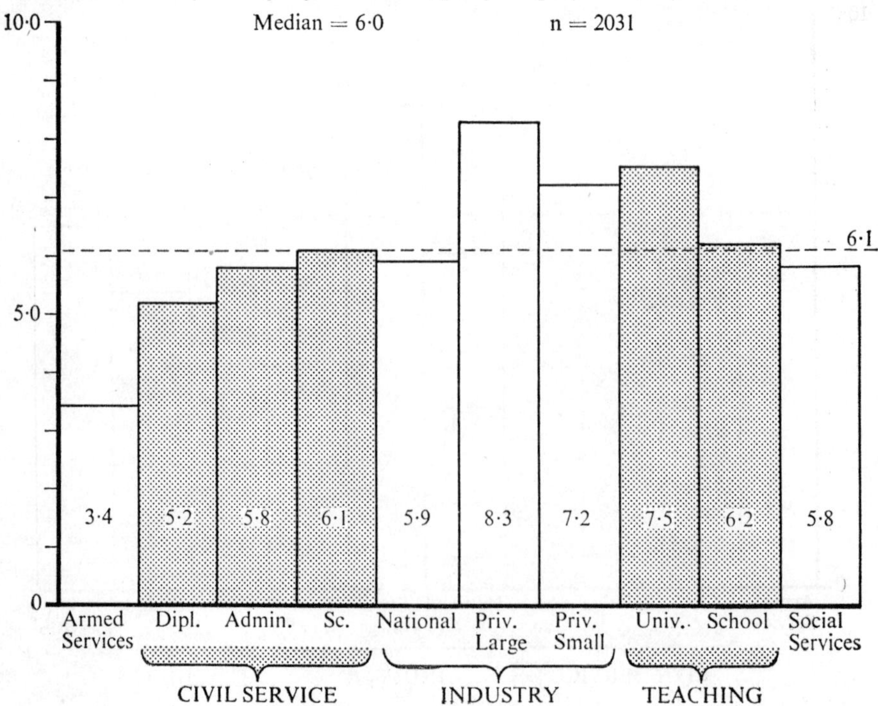

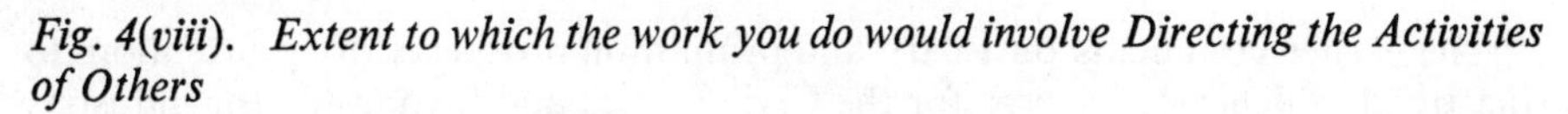

Fig. 4(viii). Extent to which the work you do would involve Directing the Activities of Others

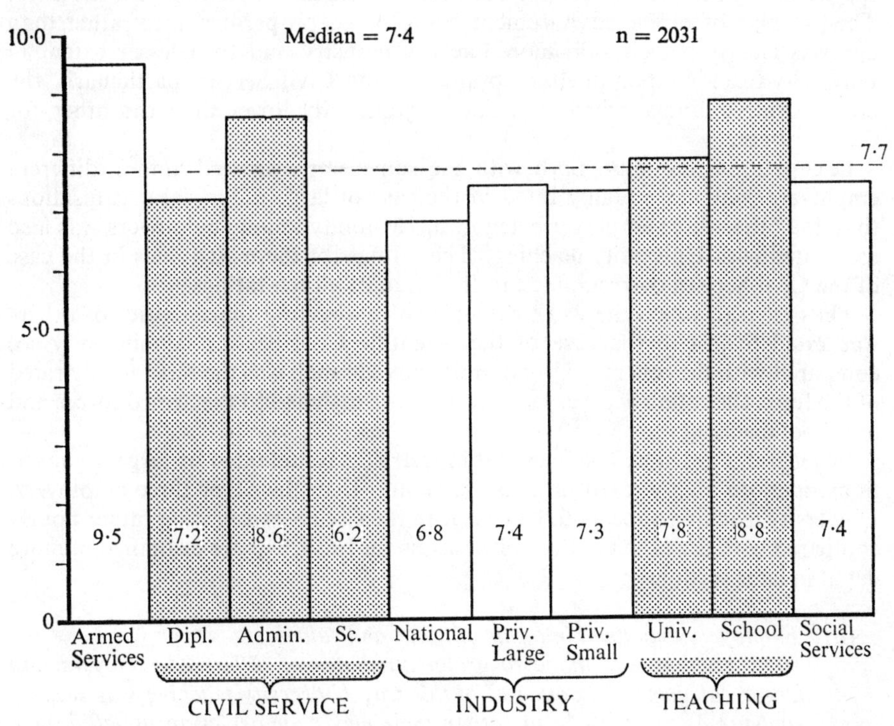

Industry and commerce were rated more highly than either the two branches of the Civil Service or University teaching for salary prospects both early and in twenty years time. Among these four employers this difference is significant.

Earlier the students perceptions of the advantages and disadvantages of working in the Civil Service and in certain large, industrial organisations were examined. In connection with the ratings it is interesting to note that though unfavourable salary and promotion prospects were spontaneously mentioned in connection with all branches of the Civil Service students did not cite either when citing the disadvantages of working in industry. On the other hand, when mentioning advantages, favourable salary and promotion prospects were cited less often in connection with the Civil Service than with industry and significantly so in the case of the scientific branch of the Civil Service.

The prospect of professional training to a high standard was less highly rated for the administrative Civil Service than for the other three employers; the scientific Civil Service and University teaching rank highest. These tendencies are those one would expect and support the analysis in section 4 of attitudes towards formal training.

University teaching was rated highest for work conducive to bringing out the best in the individual followed by industry and commerce. Both earned ratings above the mean ratings for all ten employer categories used in the survey whereas both branches of the Civil Service were slightly below the mean though not significantly so.

The earlier comments on salary and promotion prospects drew attention to the trend which was adverse for the Civil Service and favourable for industry. The prospect of career advancement being based on performance rather than age was clearly perceived as more likely in industry and to a lesser extent in university teaching than in either branch of the Civil Service particularly the administrative branch which was rated significantly lower than the other for this attribute.

Occupational mobility, both with the same employer and among different employers, was more highly rated in the case of large industrial organisations than the other three employer categories. Mobility among employers was also associated with University teaching. The ratings for these attributes in the case of the Civil Service corresponded to the mean of all ten ratings.

The extent to which the work would involve directing the activities of others was rated lowest in the case of the Scientific Civil Service (significantly so) compared with the others. The administrative branch was the most highly rated of the four; the rating was very similar to those assigned to the armed forces and to school teaching.

In general, then, it can be seen that industry (as represented by large organisations) is more highly rated on these attributes than the other three employers. University teaching appears to be next with the Civil Service rating rather poorly compared with the others. Possible reasons for this trend are examined in more detail in later sections.

(*b*) *Employers examined in terms of needs and values*

An attempt was made to group attributes of different employers into larger categories. Looked at in this way University teaching was seen by students as most likely to satisfy their needs for achievement, affiliation, autonomy, dominance, understanding (knowledge), exhibition (recognition) compared with the scientific and administrative branches of the Civil Service and Industry or Commerce as represented by large organisations.

In terms of intrinsic work rewards and satisfaction of the need for security all four employer types are perceived alike and achieve high mean ratings. In terms of novelty, however, all except Industry and Commerce (large organisations) are rated low.

Industry and Commerce are perceived as more likely to provide organisational flexibility than either the Civil Service or University teaching.

In the second form of analysis twelve concepts have been used derived from personality theorists and social psychologists whose work has proved particularly useful in recent psychological and sociological studies of occupations. Other and perhaps equally useful constructs might have been used.

Seven of Murray's twenty needs have been adopted for use in the following analysis of the ratings of attributes—achievement, affiliation, autonomy, dominance, understanding, exhibition and succourance.[1] To add to this list one more has been devised—the need for novelty. Following Rosenberg[2] three sets of values influencing occupational choice—people-oriented values, intrinsic work

---

[1] For definitions see p. 362.

[2] Rosenberg, Morris. Factors influencing change of occupational choice in The Language of Social Research. Free Press, Glencoe, Illinois, 1957.

rewards, and self-expression—have been distinguished, since it is likely that ratings of employer attributes will be partly determined by the predominant values held by students. A final residual category refers to organisational flexibility.

These twelve categories permit a grouping of the various attributes into psychologically meaningful clusters and thus the derivation of a set of indices with which to compare types of employers, as perceived by the students, in terms of these constructs. For example, one may ask whether the Civil Service tends to be perceived as more or less able to satisfy the student's need for achievement compared with industry or commerce?

For the purposes of this analysis only four employer types were selected—the Administrative Civil Service, the Scientific Civil Service, industry and commerce (large organisations), and University teaching.

The attributes which referred to achievement (using Murray's definition of the latter) were selected and arranged in order of their contribution to achievement satisfaction as judged by a team of psychologists. This subjective assessment then formed the basis of a weighting factor for each of the attributes forming the achievement cluster. This procedure was adopted for each need.[1]

The ratings (each multiplied by the weighting factor) were then summed and divided by the total weighting to give an index. As can be seen in Table XIII University teaching secured the highest achievement index, 8·16; then industry and commerce with 7·39; the Scientific Civil Service follows with an index of 7·04 and finally the Administrative Civil Service at 6·28.

Table XIII. Indices of Various Needs and Values Derived from Ratings of Employer Attributes.

BASE: ALL STUDENTS (n=2031)	Administrative Civil Service	Scientific Civil Service	Industry and Commerce	University Teaching
Achievement	6·28	7·04	7·39	8·16
Affiliation	6·90	7·13	6·63	9·09
Autonomy (independence)	5·28	5·66	6·81	7·10
Dominance	7·17	6·57	6·90	8·73
Understanding	4·53	8·30	5·97	10·03
Exhibition (recognition)	5·37	6·97	6·03	9·87
Succourance (security)	8·25	7·92	7·79	7·51
Novelty	4·85	5·22	6·75	5·16
People oriented values	7·04	6·70	6·66	8·52
Intrinsic work reward values	7·40	7·33	7·97	7·38
Self expression	5·58	7·00	6·70	9·48
Organisational flexibility	4·72	5·61	7·20	5·47

As a rough guide any difference between rows or columns greater than 1·2 is statistically significant at 95% level. Estimated standard error is less than 0·3.

If the attributes listed on p. 362 refer to achievement and were preceived so by students then it can be said that students perceived University teaching most favourably for this quality and the Administrative Civil Service least favourably;

[1] For clusters of attributes comprising each " need " see p. 362.

the Scientific Civil Service and industry and commerce shared the middle place.

Both University teaching and industry and commerce were perceived as offering more autonomy (independence) than either branch of the Civil Service. As one might expect the Scientific Civil Service and University teaching were perceived alike as far as understanding is concerned and much more favourably so than industry and commerce or the Administrative Civil Service. The same trend is seen in the case of exhibition (recognition). That is to say the student tended to see his thirst for knowledge and his need to be seen and heard and listened to as more likely to be satisfied in University teaching or the Scientific Civil Service than in industry and commerce or the administrative Civil Service.

Dominance and affiliation need satisfaction were most strongly associated with university teaching but the differences among the two indices for the other three employer types is not very great.

Most modern theories of perception take account of the need for novelty the existence of which is supported by considerable and varied evidence. Industry and commerce earned the highest index for this characteristic; the other three employer categories do not differ very much from each other. Since novelty has been closely tied to occupational mobility this result is perhaps understandable.

When the three value clusters are analysed by type of employer it can be seen that University teaching was most highly regarded for people-orientation; the other three employer categories do not differ very much. All four employer types were perceived similarly so far as intrinsic work rewards are concerned. In self-expression, however, University teaching was the most highly rated and the Administrative Civil Service the least; the Scientific Civil Service and industry and commerce occupied the middle position.

The Scientific Civil Service being concerned with research and having a pronounced technological flavour might well be judged as less people-oriented than University teaching which, despite the substantial research element, does involve extensive contact with others. What is surprising is that the Administrative Civil Service was perceived no differently (in this respect) from the scientific branch. The fact that it was not provides further evidence of the stereotyped views students have of the Civil Service in general.

There was a slight tendency to associate intrinsic work rewards (e.g. money, position, status, security) more with industry and commerce than with the others but the difference is negligible. Whether this means that students genuinely were unable to distinguish between employer types where intrinsic rewards were concerned or whether they considered other values were more important is not clear. In absolute terms both people-oriented values and self-expression earned a much higher rating for University teaching than for the other three employer types, and so the trend of these ratings may reflect the idealism of youth rather than a lack of concern about money and so forth.

Self-expression echoes the pattern seen in exhibition. Admittedly both have one attribute in common—opportunity for publishing work—but obviously this cannot explain the similarity. A possible explanation is that an environment which is perceived as sufficiently sympathetic to the student as to listen to him may also allow him to develop his own ideas and to be himself. The similarity between the profiles of understanding and recognition already alluded to offer some support for this view.

All except industry and commerce received low ratings for organisational flexibility. In both branches of the Civil Service this trend has important consequences for recruitment. In the first place do students want and expect organisational flexibility? The numbers requiring a move from their specialism into management suggests that to some extent they do. (See p. 376 et seq.) If this is so then clearly the image of the Civil Service is in need of repair, especially the administrative branch. The latter fares particularly badly on responsiveness to new ideas and neither side of the Civil Service does as well as industry and commerce on career mobility, nor to a lesser extent on job mobility.

To summarise the above analysis of the indices derived from the ratings of employer attributes, it is evident that, in general university teaching is perceived most favourably. The difficulty of interpretation is that students are probably more sympathetic to, and perceptive of, the details of university life and that the favourable attitude springs as much from this intimate association as from a more objective assessment.

The administrative Civil Service tends on the whole to earn lower mean ratings in the twelve clusters. The Scientific Civil Service and industry tend to be perceived alike. This is of interest because its general image is apparently no more (or less) off-putting than industry's. If the Scientific Civil Service fails to attract sufficient candidates it is perhaps because students are ignorant of the opportunities and possibilities rather than that an unfavourable image deters them.

Table XIV summarises the information provided by the indices. High is scored 5, middle 3 and low 1. University teaching scores 50, industry and commerce 36, and Scientific Civil Service 35, and the Administrative Civil Service 26. It is apparent that the latter's image (in terms of students' perceptions of the extent to which certain needs and values are likely to be satisfied) is relatively poor.

*Table XIV. Comparison of Four Employer Categories in Terms of Summed Scores Derived from Indices on Needs and Values**

BASE: ALL STUDENTS (n=2031)	Scientific Civil Service	Administrative Civil Service	Industry and Commerce	University Teaching
Achievement	M 3	L 1	M 3	H 5
Affiliation	M 3	M 3	M 3	H 5
Autonomy	L 1	L 1	M 3	M 3
Dominance	M 3	M 3	M 3	H 5
Understanding	H 5	L 1	L 1	H 5
Exhibition (recognition)	M 3	L 1	L 1	H 5
Succourance (security)	H 5	H 5	H 5	H 5
Novelty	L 1	L 1	M 3	L 1
People oriented values	M 3	M 3	M 3	H 5
Intrinsic work reward values	H 5	H 5	H 5	H 5
Self-expression	M 3	L 1	M 3	H 5
Organisational flexibility	L 1	L 1	M 3	L 1
Total	35	26	36	50

* For indices see Table XIII, p. 359.
L=Low; M=Medium; H=High.

Definitions and Attribute Clusters

Brief definitions of a selected number of Murray's needs[1] and the attribute clusters used in the analysis are given below.

ACHIEVEMENT—to accomplish something difficult. To master, manipulate, or organise physical objects, human beings, or ideas. To do this as rapidly and as independently as possible. To overcome obstacles and attain a high standard. To excel oneself. To rival and surpass others. To increase self-regard by the successful exercise of talent.

Attributes

Career advancement based on performance rather than age.
Career advancement based on performance rather than type and class of degree.
Extent to which you would expect to use your degree knowledge with such an employer.
Extent to which the work you would do would involve directing the activities of others.
High social status.
Chances of getting into a progressive position.
Prospect of professional training to a high standard.
Prospect of gaining further degree (higher degrees, diplomas).
Opportunity of publishing your work.
Work conducive to bringing out the best in you.
Opportunity to make a valuable contribution to society.
Opportunity to make a valuable contribution to human knowledge.

AFFILIATION—to draw near and enjoyably co-operate or reciprocate with an allied other (an other who resembles the subject or who likes the subject). To please and in affection of a cathected subject. To adhere and remain loyal to a friend.

Attributes

Congeniality of fellow workers.
Intellectual climate.
A job which involves working with others.
Extent to which you would associate with leaders in your field.

AUTONOMY—to get free, shake off restraint, break out of confinement. To resist coercion and restriction. To avoid or quit activities prescribed by domineering authorities. To be independent and free to act according to impulse. To be unattached, irresponsible. To defy convention.

Attributes

Freedom given in the way in which you would wish to do your work.
Extent to which your career is open to change if you join this employer.
Ease of transferring from one type of employer to any other.
Ease of transferring from one kind of job to another with the same employer.
Compatibility between the work to be done and your own moral code.
The opportunity to travel.

---

[1] Hall & Lindzey " Theories of Personality ", Wiley. 1957.

DOMINANCE—to control one's human environment. To influence or direct the behaviour of others by suggestion, seduction, persuasion, or command. To dissuade, restrain, or prohibit.

Attributes

Extent to which the work you would do would involve directing the activities of others.
Opportunity of publishing your work.

EXHIBITION—to make an impression. To be seen and heard. To excite, amaze, fascinate, entertain, shock, intrigue, amuse, or entice others.

Attributes

Extent to which you would associate with leaders in your field.
Opportunity of publishing your work.

SUCCOURANCE—to have one's needs gratified by the sympathetic aid of an allied object. To be nursed, supported, sustained, surrounded, protected, loved, advised, guided, indulged, forgiven, consoled. To remain close to a devoted protector. To always have a supporter.

Attributes

Favourable early salary prospects.
Job security.
Favourable salary prospects in 20 years time.
Likelihood of sound pension scheme.

UNDERSTANDING—to ask or answer general questions. To be interested in theory. To speculate, formulate, analyse, and generalise.

Attributes

Opportunity to make a valuable contribution to human knowledge.
Prospect of gaining further degree (higher degrees, diplomas).

NOVELTY

Attributes

Extent to which employees do a variety of jobs rather than specialising in one.
Flexibility of the organisation in adopting new ideas.
Extent to which your career is open to change if you join this employer.
The opportunity to travel.

PEOPLE ORIENTED VALUES

Attributes

A job which involves working with others.
Congeniality of fellow workers.
Extent to which the work you would do would involve directing the activities of others.
Opportunity to make a valuable contribution to society.
Extent to which you would associate with leaders in your field.

INTRINSIC WORK REWARD VALUES

Attributes

Favourable early salary prospects.
Favourable salary prospects in 20 years time.
High social status.
Career advancement based on performance rather than age.
Career advancement based on performance rather than type and class of degree.
Job security.

SELF-EXPRESSION

Attributes

Extent to which you would expect to use your degree knowledge with such an employer.
Opportunity of publishing your work.
Work conducive to bringing out the best in you.
Compatibility between the work to be done and your own moral code.

ORGANISATIONAL FLEXIBILITY

Attributes

Flexibility of the organisation in adopting new ideas.
Extent to which your career is open to change if you join this employer.
Ease of transferring from one kind of job to another with same employer.
Extent to which employees do a variety of jobs rather than specialising in one.

Section 4

4.1. Students' Knowledge of the Structure and Function of the Civil Service

4.2. Students' Conceptions of Job Possibilities in the Civil Service

4.3. Job Preferences in the Civil Service

4.4. Job Expectations

4.5. Selected Features of Jobs and their Relationship to the Civil Service as a Choice of Career.

- (i) Specialist and managerial jobs
- (ii) Formal training
- (iii) Working in London
- (iv) Short term contracts
- (v) Pension schemes

4.6. Attitudes to Method I and II Selection Procedures.

4.7. Biographical and Academic Differences between those Considering the Civil Service, Further Study and Research and Other Employment.

4.8. Students' Assessments of their Chances of Entry into the Civil Service.

4.1. Students' Knowledge of the Structure and Function of the Civil Service

Perception of suitable job opportunities is dependent to a considerable extent on the student's knowledge of the structure and function of the employer. Knowledge of the function of the Civil Service was generally sound and expressed in fairly broad terms; structure was not so well perceived. In neither case was knowledge sufficiently detailed for most students to be able to gauge fully what openings there might be for their own subject or interest.

Question asked: " What is the Civil Service? "

Job opportunities are considered within a general framework of knowledge about the way in which employing organisations are constituted, how the enterprise works, what the demands and characteristics of the employee's role are seen to be, and so forth.

In order to understand students' perceptions of career opportunities in the Civil Service it was first necessary to establish what sorts of concepts and ideas they had about the Service.

Students were asked how they would describe the Civil Service. Their spontaneous comments were classified into seventeen categories. In general the responses fall into two groups; those descriptions which relate to function and those relating mainly to structure.

Function was more often mentioned than structure, which is, perhaps, not surprising; whereas on average each student made one response related to function, nearly a quarter of the sample failed to mention structure at all.

Two thirds of the total sample of men students referred to the Civil Service as the administrative branch of government, (performs an administrative function; the organ for carrying out the government's decisions, etc.). Nearly one fifth named specific government departments and almost as many referred to the departmental structure of the Civil Service.

As might be expected references to organisational hierarchy and the occupational stratification by grade and class were more often mentioned by students of Social Studies than by others—52% compared with 25% for the three other faculties. Pure and Applied Scientists made fewer responses in this category (24% and 19% respectively), but they more often referred directly or indirectly to the Scientific Civil Service though the response frequencies are surprisingly small—17% and 13% respectively compared with 2% and 6% from Arts and Social Studies students. (Table XV).

Burns and Stalker[1] draw attention to the communication problems created by the hierarchy of positions experienced by scientists working in typical bureaucracies. Judging by the relatively few references by science students to the hierarchical structure of the service this does not appear to have filtered through to the student population.

There are no differences between University groups in the distribution of responses between or within the categories of function and structure with the exception of the high Oxbridge mentions of hierarchical structures—23% compared with 13% for all other Universities.

[1] Burns and Stalker. The Management of Innovation 1961.

Table XV. Conceptions of the Structure and Function of the Civil Service (Summarised) (by Faculty)

BASE: MEN STUDENTS OF ALL YEARS	Total 1474	Arts 363	Social Studies 295	Pure Science 484	Applied Science 332
	%	%	%	%	%
Function					
Administrative branch of government	67	72	71	65	61
Coordinates government policies	13	16	17	8	14
Others—Financial Management, Research Advisory Body, National/Local Government Services	22	18	25	21	21
Structure					
Specific government departments mentioned	19	17	15	21	20
Reference to departmental structure	18	20	20	14	18
Reference to hierarchical structure, pyramid of control	16	18	21	14	11
Mention of Administrative, Executive, Clerical grades	15	15	31	10	8
Mention of Scientific Civil Service	10	2	6	17	13
References to:					
Political impartiality, security, permanence, rule by civil servants, people working for government	38	38	38	35	40

Comparison by academic year of study shows a considerably uniformity of response. The static position of knowledge of function may be attributable to the relatively well informed ideas students have about this aspect of the Civil Service. On the other hand, one might have expected knowledge of structure to increase as the student gains information about job possibilities during his course. The absence of shift in position may be partly accounted for by the relatively low number of students seeking information about the Civil Service.

4.2. Students' Conception of Job Possibilities in the Civil Service

Two-thirds of the students mentioned Administration as a possible opening for graduates but their other responses indicated that they had limited ideas about specific jobs available. There was no increase in ideas about job possibilities between first, middle and final year students.

Question asked: " What do you think are the main sorts of jobs open to graduates in the Civil Service? "

Each male student gave an average of two responses. 65% of the sample referred to administrative or managerial posts as possible openings, including the Administrative Grade of the Diplomatic Service, ranging from 58% of Pure Scientists to 78% of Social Studies students (Table XVI).

The second point to emerge from the analysis of job possibilities by faculty concerns the relatively large number of references made by Arts (29%) and Social Studies students (41%) to jobs in the executive class, compared with Pure (13%)

and Applied Science (9 %)[1] students. Although the executive class is attracting more students than in former years (see page vii Sixth Report from the Estimates Committee, Session 1964–65) over 90 % of the outside entrants into this class are school leavers with two or more " A " level passes.

Table XVI. Conceptions of Main Jobs Open to Graduates in the Civil Service (Summarised) (by Faculty)

BASE: MEN STUDENTS OF ALL YEARS	Total 1474	Arts 363	Social Studies 295	Pure Science 484	Applied Science 332
	%	%	%	%	%
Administration*	65	67	78	58	61
Executive	22	29	41	13	9
Scientific and Experimental Officer	40	17	21	63	46
Professional/Specialist	20	14	26	14	29
Other Managerial (e.g. Tax Inspectorate, Ministry of Labour cadets—see Appendix III)	4	6	3	4	4
Reference to wide range of jobs (unspecified)	9	7	11	12	6
Others: Clerical, Overseas work, work in specific government departments, etc.	34	52	34	30	30
Don't know	7	8	6	7	7

* Includes Diplomatic Service (Administrative grade).

When analysed by sex there are differences in perceptions of job opportunities; 27 % of women compared with 22 % of men mentioned the executive class, and only 33 % compared with 40 % of men referred to the scientific and experimental officer openings.

Responses by academic year of study exhibit a similar pattern to that observed when knowledge of the structure and function was examined. There is no significant widening in ideas about possible jobs in the Civil Service with the passage of time. The mean number of responses per student for first, middle and third year is 1·9, 2·0 and 2·0.

The Oxbridge response in citing specific government departments is the only notable difference in the university group comparisons. 15 % of Oxbridge students specified individual Government Departments for job openings compared with 7 %[1] for the three other University groups.

4.3. Job Preferences in the Civil Service

Nearly 60 % of all students were able to cite three possible Civil Service classes for which they might apply if considering a job in the Civil Service. The range of choice obviously varies according to faculty in terms of both eligibility and interest. In general, Social Studies as a group displayed the widest range of choice of classes because of the heterogeneity of the faculty. Arts students confined themselves largely to the administrative class (71 %) as a first choice. Though most scientists (63 %) put scientific officer as first

[1] Percentage differences statistically significant at ·01 level.

choice, a considerable number (11%) made the administrative class their first choice. The most substantial difference among the University groups is the Oxbridge choice of the administrative class—48% compared with 29% for all others.

There is no significant difference between students with first or upper second class degrees and those obtaining lower degree classes in respect of the Civil Service Class to which they would apply.

Further academic study was a competing claim on half of those who expressed a preference for the administrative class and on nearly three-quarters of those who preferred scientific officer class.

Question asked: " Which of the classes described (on a card handed to the student—see Appendix I) would you apply for, in order of preference, if you were considering a career in the Civil Service? "

In the exercise described on page 368, students were asked without the help of a prompt card to cite the kinds of Civil Service job that might be open to a graduate. The mean response was two jobs per student; 65% gave the choice of administration although this was not necessarily defined in terms of the administrative class. In the prompted situation (i.e. the above question) each student was shown a list of the main types of Civil Service job and asked to say for which ones he would consider applying for. The mean number of responses per student increased to 2·7 and a wider range of jobs was named.

Men students' preferences for jobs in the Civil Service are shown in Fig. 5. The three categories of " Other Managerial " (see prompt card Appendix I) have been combined; so have " Professional Classes ", e.g. economists, lawyers, statisticians and engineers to form the professional/specialist category.

The distribution of first choices between the faculties varies according to the homogeneity of the discipline (see Table XVII).

The interests of Arts students are biased strongly towards the administrative class (71% choosing this class of which 35% mentioned the Diplomatic Service). The heterogeneity of the Social Studies faculty is reflected by the wider range of classes chosen (50% preferring the administrative class, 18% the legal and 10% the economist classes).

The majority of Pure Scientists (63%) expressed preference for the scientific officer class. This should be contrasted with the fairly low (17%) spontaneous mention of the Scientific Civil Service (Table XV) when questioned on the structure and function.

Altogether the pure science faculty considered mainly two classes—scientific officer and administrative. With regard to the 11% of Pure Scientists whose first choice was the administrative class it is worth noting that the Oxford Appointments Committee report for 1966 refers to the increasing interest among scientists in graduate business schools.

The Applied Scientists' choice was confined mainly to the professional and scientific officer classes (78% combined). 7% chose the administrative class.

Table XVIII represents the contribution each faculty makes to the total number of responses in favour of the most " popular " Civil Service classes. The position of a class in terms of being a " popular " choice is, in some cases, dependent upon the size of the faculty making the largest contribution. The first

Fig. 5. Types of Jobs Preferred by Students Interested in a Career in the Civil Service. n = 1474 (men only)

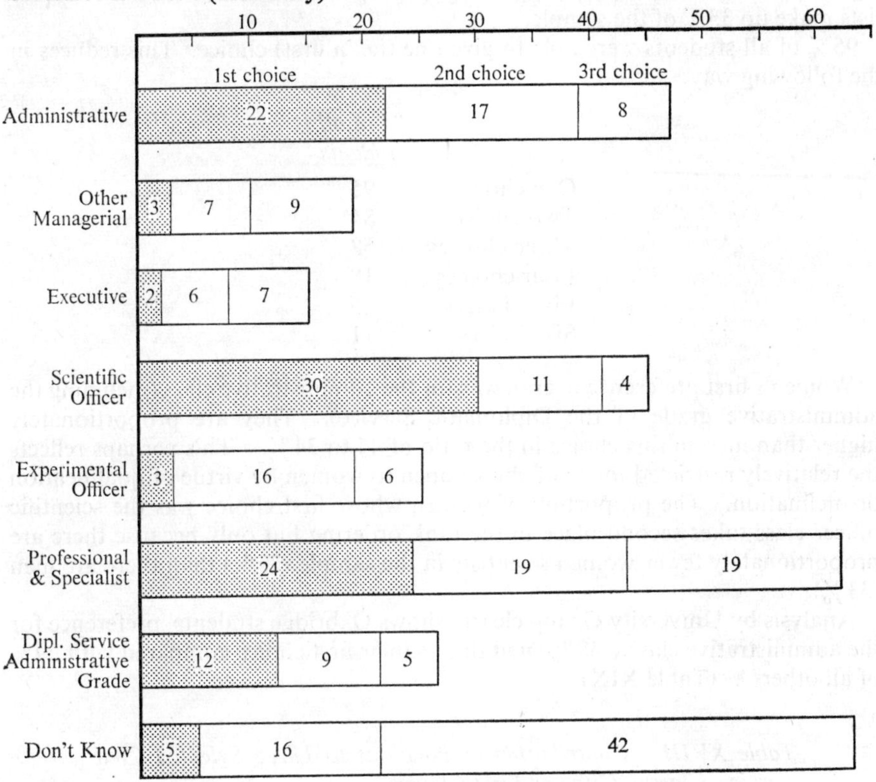

Table XVII. Students' First Choice of Civil Service Class (by Faculty)

BASE: MEN STUDENTS OF ALL YEARS	Arts 360	Social Studies 298	Pure Science 484	Applied Science 332
	%	%	%	%
Administrative	36	37	11	7
Diplomatic Service	35	13	2	3
Professional	9	5	5	42
Executive	3	3	1	1
Scientific Officer	3	4	63	36
Assistant Postal Controller	2	—	—	—
Ministry of Labour Cadet	2	1	—	1
Economist	2	10	*	*
Experimental Officer	1	2	5	3
Legal	1	18	—	—
Statistician	1	2	5	2
Tax Inspector	1	3	2	1
Don't know	5	3	6	4
Total	100	100	100	100

place of scientific officer, for example, obviously owes its position not only to the high number of Pure Scientists choosing it (63%) but to the fact that Pure Scientists make up 33% of the sample.

95% of all students were able to give one (i.e. a first) choice. This reduces in the following way:

	% of all students
One choice	95
Two choices	84
Three choices	58
Four choices	18
Five choices	5
Six choices	1

Women's first preference overall was for the administrative class (including the administrative grade of the Diplomatic Service). They are proportionately higher than men in this choice in the ratio of 44 to 34%.[1] This perhaps reflects the relatively restricted range of choice open to women by virtue of qualification or inclination. The proportion of women whose first choice was the scientific officer class takes second place in the rank ordering but only because there are proportionately fewer women scientists in the sample (23%) than there are men (33%).

Analysis by University Group clearly shows Oxbridge students' preference for the administrative class. 48% cited this as their first choice compared with 29% of all others.[2] (Table XIX)

Table XVIII. Contribution of Faculties to Three Selected Civil Service Classes Cited as First Choice

BASE: UNDERGRADUATE MEN	Scientific Officer Class 443	Professional Classes 349	Administrative Class 317
	%	%	%
Arts	2	16	41
Social Studies	3	7	34
Pure Science	69	12	17
Applied Science	27	65	8
Total	100	100	100

Likewise London's higher proportion of students eligible for the professional classes boosts this response category.

University group results here must be viewed in the light of their constituent faculties. The higher proportion of Arts undergraduates in Oxbridge (38% compared with 20% for the other groups) accounts to some extent for the higher preference for the administrative class. The effect is more marked when we examine the interest in classes which require a vocational degree. For example

[1] Percentage difference statistically significant at the 0·01 level.
[2] Percentage difference statistically significant at the 0·001 level.

the higher figures for London and Civic in respect of the choice of scientific officer (which, by its nature, is recruited from science faculties) is almost entirely dependent upon the differences in faculty size. Adjusted figures taking account of differences in faculty sizes give the following results for first choice of scientific officer.

London	Oxbridge	Civic	Scotland and Wales
33%	35%	37%	35%

Thus there is no significant difference between university groups.

The data by academic year (Table XX) show a slight increase in choice of administrative class by finalists. Although this is not statistically significant it is interesting to note that 49% of those final year students seriously considering administration as their future career decided on this in their last year (see page 339).

Though there was an apparent tendency for administrative class preference to increase with the passing of time, professional class preferences decrease significantly (from 26% for first and middle years combined to 21% in the final year[1]).

Table XIX. Students Choice of Class if Considering Job in the Civil Service (Summarised) (By University group)

BASE: MEN STUDENTS OF ALL YEARS	Total 1474	London 294	Oxbridge 374	Civic 550	Scotland and Wales 256
	%	%	%	%	%
Administration*	34	27	48	28	35
Executive	2	2	2	1	3
Scientific and Experimental Officer	33	33	26	37	33
Professional/Specialist	24	34	20	23	22
Other Managerial	3	2	2	4	4
Don't Know	5	3	3	7	4
Total	100	100	100	100	100

* Includes Diplomatic Service (Administrative Grade).

Table XX. Students Choice of Class if Considering Job in the Civil Service (Summarised) (By year)

BASE: MEN STUDENTS OF ALL YEARS	Total 1474	First 334	Middle 388	Final 752
	%	%	%	%
Administration*	34	32	33	36
Executive	2	1	2	2
Scientific and Experimental Officer	33	34	36	31
Professional/Specialist	24	29	24	21
Other Managerial	3	3	2	4
Don't Know	5	2	3	6
Total	100	100	100	100

* Includes Diplomatic Service (Administrative Grade).

[1] Percentage difference statistically significant at 0·05 level.

Since further academic study is the main competitor to employment particularly among the more coveted first and upper second class graduates a comparison of Civil Service class preference and consideration of further study is given in Table XXI. There are two notable items. First is the equal distribution of students choosing the administrative class among those who were and those who were not considering further study.

The second major difference is the strong competing claim of further study (71%) on those who might apply for the scientific officer class.

Analysing the first choice by class of degree shows that students obtaining firsts and upper seconds do not differ to any significant extent from the others in the proportions who would consider the various openings.

Since the standard of entry to the administrative, scientific officer, economist and statistician classes is a first or second class degree, some of the respondents will have overrated their chances of entry.

Table XXI. Students First Choice of Class in the Civil Service Analysed by Consideration of Further Study

BASE: MEN FINALISTS WHO GAVE THE FOLLOWING CLASSES AS FIRST CHOICE OF JOB	Further study considered	Further study not considered	Don't know	Number of students choosing each class 703
	%	%	%	
Administrative	50	50	—	171
Inspector of Taxes	20	80	—	17
Assistant Postal Controllers	—	100	—	5
Cadets in Ministry of Labour	33	67	—	6
Executive	40	60	—	13
Scientific Officer	71	27	2	206
Experimental Officer	50	50	—	25
Professional Classes	49	51	—	106
Economist	31	62	7	17
Legal	59	41	—	22
Statistician	42	50	7	16
Diplomatic Service Administrative Grade	37	58	5	99

4.4. Job Expectations

Choice of job in the Civil Service centres on the intrinsic interest of the work and the opportunity of putting one's degree knowledge to good use. Interest of the work remains a high level of response with each successive choice of job within the Civil Service made by students.

Students' perceptions of career opportunities within the Civil Service have already been dealt with earlier in this section; here the reasons given for their job preferences are examined.

Questions asked: " Which of the classes described (on a card handed to the student: see Appendix I) would you apply for, in order of

preference, if you were considering a career in the Civil Service ? Why? "

The students' reasons for choosing certain jobs were they to consider a Civil Service career are analysed in Fig. 6. It is clear that the majority of responses centre on one of two reasons—the use of the student's degree knowledge and intrinsic interest of the work.

In Fig. 3 and Table X the students' concepts of working in the Civil Service were analysed in terms of nine categories one of which referred to " Interest of the Work "; 44% expected the work to be interesting which is consistent with Fig. 6.

Fig. 6. Reasons given by Students for Preferring Certain Classes in the Civil Service

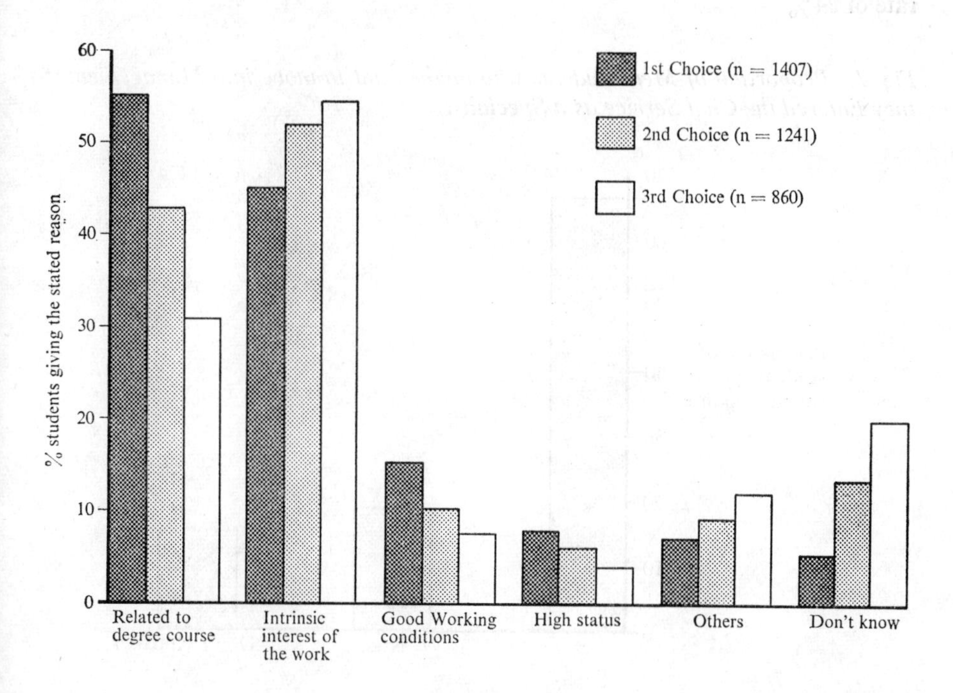

It is worthy of note that this major reason consistently maintains a high level of response for all three choices whereas the reason relating to degree knowledge drops markedly with each successive choice.

Not many students mentioned working conditions and even fewer referred to high status as reasons for their choice of class. This is interesting in view of their marked preference for jobs in administration and in the scientific officer class discussed in Section 1.

4.5. Selected Features of Jobs and their Relationship to the Civil Service as a Choice of Career

(1) *Specialist and Managerial jobs*

Two-thirds of the sample, if they were to enter the Civil Service as specialists, thought they might want to move into management eventually. The same proportion thought that the transition from specialist to management work could be made without too much difficulty. This level was maintained by scientists. There were no differences between university groups.

Question asked: " If you entered the Civil Service as a specialist do you think you might want to move to management during your career? "

Two-thirds of the men students would want to move into management eventually although there is a high " Don't know " rate (15%) (see Fig. 7). Among women 38% thought they might eventually wish to move, with a " Don't know " rate of 24%

Fig. 7. Proportion of Men Students who might want to move into Management if they Entered the Civil Service as a Specialist.

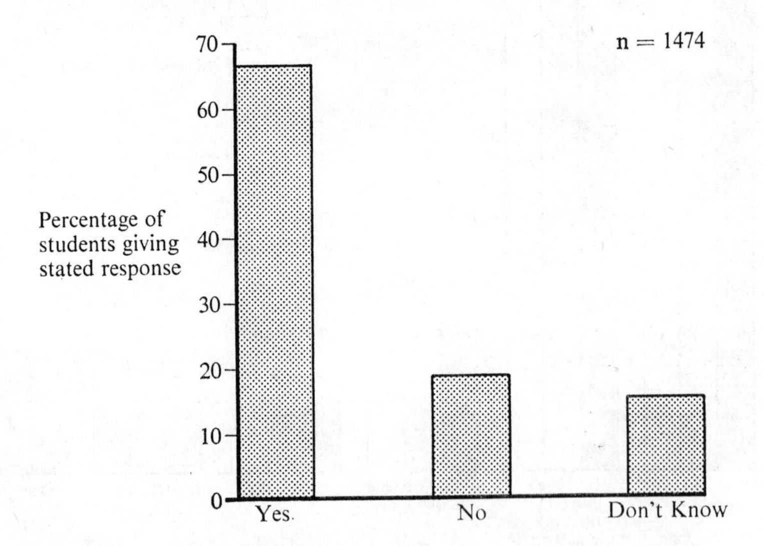

Question asked: " How easy do you think it would be to make this move? "

Two-thirds of the men and 56% of the women thought the move could be made without too much difficulty (see Fig. 8).

It is apparent that:

(i) few students wanted to remain indefinitely in the specialisation of their choice;

(ii) a substantial majority wanted to end up in management;

(iii) at least half of this majority thought the change would not be difficult.

Fig. 8. Men Students' Rating of Ease of Change from Specialist to Management Function.

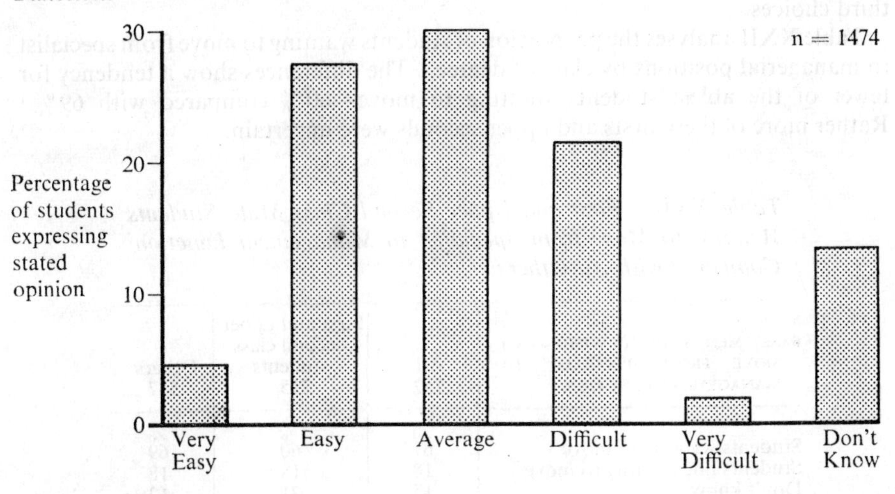

In order to provide a framework within which to analyse the above trend, the managerial classes—administrative, other managerial, executive and Diplomatic Service (administrative grade) were combined and the totals compared with the remainder, which thus constituted the specialisations—scientific officer, experimental officer, and the professional classes. The comparison is presented in Fig. 9.

Fig. 9. Men Students' Choice of Class if Considering a Job in the Civil Service Analysed by Specialist and Management Jobs n = 1474

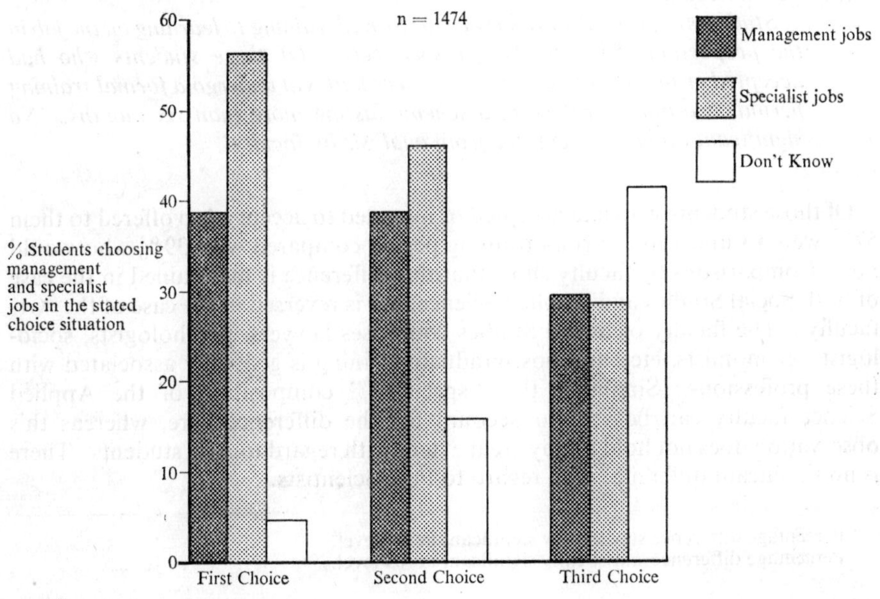

As can be seen specialist jobs were markedly preferred over managerial by students in their first choice but are more or less equally favoured in second and third choices.

Table XXII analyses the proportion of students wanting to move from specialist to managerial positions by class of degree. The differences show a tendency for fewer of the ablest students wanting to move—60% compared with 69%.[1] Rather more of these firsts and upper seconds were uncertain.

Table XXII. First and Upper Second Class Male Students Wanting to Move from Specialist to Management Function, Compared with All Others.

BASE: MEN STUDENTS WISHING TO MOVE FROM SPECIALIST TO MANAGEMENT FUNCTION	All 752	First and upper second class students 215	Others 537
	%	%	%
Students wanting to move	67	60	69
Students not wanting to move	18	18	18
Don't know	15	21	12
Total	100	100	100

Two points emerge from further analysis of the proportion of students wishing to move from specialist to management functions.

Secondly, the comparison of responses by faculty shows that of those who want a specialist job in the first place, slightly more Pure & Applied Science students (67%) than Arts students (60%)[2] want to move to management.

(2) *Formal Training*

Students expressed a preference for formal training to learning on the job in the proportions 55% to 29% respectively. Of those students who had accepted or intended to accept a job, over half will undergo a formal training period, two-thirds preferring a scheme lasting more than six months. No significant differences emerge from analysis by faculty.

Of those students who had accepted or intended to accept a job offered to them 57% were to undergo a formal training period compared with 39% who would not. Comparisons by faculty show that this difference is maintained in the case of both Social Studies and Applied Science, but is reversed in the case of the Arts faculty. The faculty of Social Studies comprises lawyers, psychologists, sociologists, economists, etc., and post-graduate training is generally associated with these professions. Similarly, the " specialist " composition of the Applied Science faculty can be said to account for the difference here, whereas this observation does not hold to any great extent with regard to Arts students. There is no significant difference with regard to Pure Scientists.

---

[1] Percentage difference statistically significant at ·05 level.
[2] Percentage difference statistically significant at ·05 level.

Table XXIII. Students Having Accepted or Intending to Accept Job Offered Analysed by Provision of Formal Training Schemes.

BASE: FINAL YEAR MEN	Total 262	Arts 35	Social Studies 60	Pure Science 72	Applied Science 95
	%	%	%	%	%
Students who will undergo formal training	57	46	63	47	65
Students who will not undergo formal training	39	54	32	49	32
Don't know	4	—	5	4	3
Total	100	100	100	100	100

Students preferred formal training to on-the-job learning in the proportions 55% to 29% respectively. 3% of students having accepted a job stated a preference for a combination of both systems, 12% either did not know or had no preference. The overall preference for formal training shows little change by faculty.

The following table presents students' conceptions of the length of formal training period.

Table XXIV. Preferred Duration of Formal Training Schemes.

BASE: MEN STUDENTS HAVING ACCEPTED OR INTENDING TO ACCEPT JOB OFFERED AND WHO PREFERRED FORMAL TRAINING SCHEME. n=144	
Duration:	%
One month or less	3
More than one month but less than three	10
Between three months and six months	17
More than six months	64
Don't know	7
Total	100

Table XXV. Students Preference for Formal Training Scheme Analysed by Class of Degree.

BASE: FINAL YEAR MEN HAVING ACCEPTED OR INTENDING TO ACCEPT JOB OFFERED	All 228	First and upper second class students 66	Others 162
	%	%	%
Formal training scheme preferred	58	44	64
On the job learning preferred	31	48	24
No preference	11	8	12
Total	100	100	100

It can be seen that the majority of students preferring formal training would choose a scheme lasting more than six months. Analysis by class of degree shows a tendency for first and upper second class students to prefer ' on the job learning ' to ' formal training '.[1] (Table XXV).

(3) *Working in London*

Two-thirds of the students irrespective of university group preferred to work in London all their working career, and many stipulated that they would not be willing to work outside London even for a few years only.

Fig. 10. Men Students prepared to Work in London Analysed by Duration of Stay.

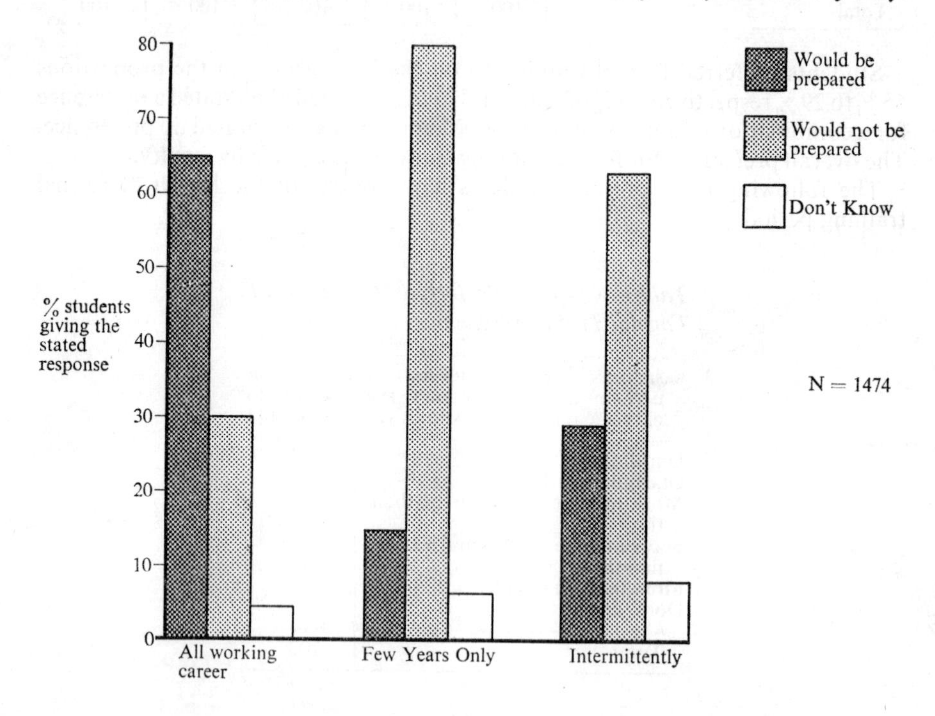

Question asked: " Would you object to working in London? "

An analysis of men students' responses, in terms of the duration they would wish to stay in London, is given in Fig. 10. As can be seen most students were not only prepared to work in London all their working career; they were not prepared to work outside it whether for a few years only or intermittently. This could reflect, of course, a preference for domestic stability just as much as a wish to remain in the capital.

There are no apparent differences in the results when they are analysed by University group.

---

[1] Percentage difference statistically significant at 0·01 level.

Question asked: " If you worked in the Civil Service what do you think the likelihood of working in London would be? High, medium or low? "

Fig. 11 analyses the findings. Only one-third of the students rated as high their chances of working in London all their working careers though one-half thought their chances were high for a working period of a few years only. As shown in Fig. 10 four-fifths of the sample would not be prepared to work in London for only a few years then to be moved elsewhere.

Fig. 11. Men Students' Assessments of their Likelihood of Working in London for Various Periods during their Working Career in the Civil Service.

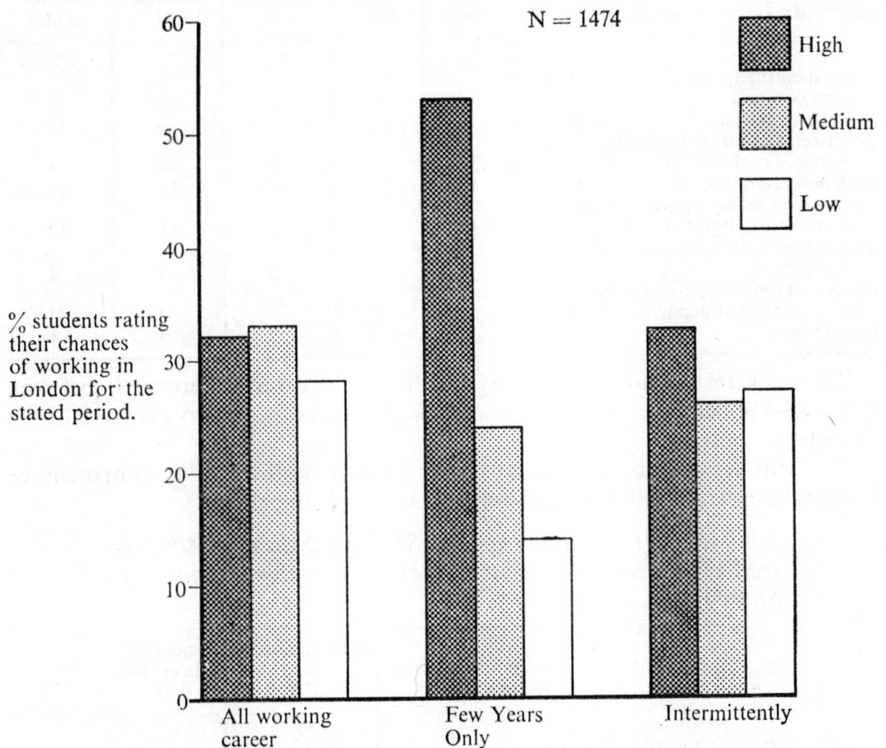

It seems reasonable to conclude from Figs. 10 and 11 that the perceived chances of working in London for the whole of his working life may be an important influence on the student's attitude towards a Civil Service career.

(4) *Short Term Contracts*

Well over half the students thought the idea of working in the Civil Service on a short-term contract was an interesting possibility, although it is not clear how many of them knew at the time of the interview that employment on short term contracts was already possible in a number of classes. Applied scientists in particular favoured short-term contracts.

Question asked: " How would you react to working for the Civil Service on a short term basis, say on a three year contract? "

The results for men students are condensed in Table XXVI. Well over half the students liked the idea; a further tenth were reserved though probably sympathetic. As one-fifth were not interested in the Civil Service at all this means that the majority of the remainder had favourable attitudes towards the notion as a hypothesis, though it does not follow that all or even many of them would in fact seriously consider entering the Civil Service on these terms.

Table XXVI. Students' Reaction to Working for the Civil Service on Short Term Basis (By Faculty).

BASE: MEN STUDENTS OF ALL YEAR	Total 1474	Arts 360	Social Studies 298	Pure Science 484	Applied Science 332
	%	%	%	%	%
Interesting idea, would consider short-term contract	47	42	46	46	54
Not interested in Civil Service career	19	24	21	16	14
Short-term contract considered waste of time—preference for settled career	16	21	14	14	8
Welcome chance of short-term contract	13	13	14	11	16
Depends on salary, conditions of work, alternative jobs available	10	7	11	12	12
Short-term contract considered impractical	4	4	5	5	2
Others: (Useful experience, depends on government department, etc.)	2	2	3	2	3
Don't know	2	3	*	3	1

When the results are analysed by faculty, the greatest difference is between Arts and Applied Science; the Applied Scientists asked were very in favour of the short term contract.

The attitudes of students to short-term contracts according to their first choice of the administrative and scientific officer class is given below.

Table XXVII. Proportion of Students Selecting Administrative and Scientific Officer Class Favourably Disposed to Short Term Contracts.

BASE: STUDENTS SELECTING ADMINISTRATIVE OR SCIENTIFIC OFFICER CLASS	Administrative class 320	Scientific officer class 440
	%	%
Favourably disposed to short term contracts	60	72
Unfavourably disposed to short term contracts	40	28
Total	100	100

(5) *Pension Schemes*

Three quarters of those who had accepted, or intended to accept jobs stated that they would be under a pension scheme. When asked which feature of a pension scheme rated most important, 71% of students gave a preference for transferability.

30 per cent of all final year students had accepted, or intended to accept, the job already offered to them. Table XXVIII shows that of the jobs accepted 68% had a pension scheme but 11% of the students who had accepted jobs did not know whether the latter had a pension scheme or not.

Table XXVIII. Students with Jobs Including a Pension Scheme

BASE: STUDENTS HAVING ACCEPTED OR INTENDING TO ACCEPT JOB OFFERED	All 317	Men 262	Women 55
	%	%	%
Job including pension scheme	68	70	56
Job without pension scheme	21	20	29
Don't know	11	10	15
Total	100	100	100

The students who had accepted or intended to accept jobs were then shown a card giving the four features of pension schemes shown in Table XXIX. It will be noted that although these features are not mutually exclusive, they were asked to state which single feature they considered the most important.

Table XXIX. Features of a Pension Scheme Rated First in Importance (By Faculty)

BASE: STUDENTS HAVING ACCEPTED OR INTENDING TO ACCEPT JOB OFFERED	Total 317	Arts 52	Social Studies 71	Pure Science 85	Applied Science 109
	%	%	%	%	%
Transferable from one employer to another	71	61	68	80	72
Ability to terminate and withdraw cash	12	17	11	5	15
In employee's own name	11	7	15	12	8
Non-contributory	7	15	6	3	5
Total	100	100	100	100	100

The table shows that 71% considered that transferability was the most important feature and 7% overall thought that it was most important that a scheme should be non-contributory. Analysis by faculty showed few differences except that more Art students than students in other faculties had rated the non-contributory feature as most important. (15% compared with 5%).[1]

4.6. Attitudes to Methods I and II Selection Procedures

Very few students had actual knowledge of Method I or Method II, but with this reservation in mind, taking all students together, half preferred Method II and over one-third preferred Method I. There were no significant differences between university groups. When responses from those choosing the administrative class were analysed separately, 61% preferred Method II.

Before commenting on students' attitudes towards Civil Service selection procedures it would be as well to establish how knowledgeable they were about Methods I and II.

[1] Percentage difference statistically significant at 0·05 level.

Questions asked: " Have you seen any specimen papers of the written qualifying examinations? "

" Do you think such papers are a fair eliminator (a) for you (b) for all candidates irrespective of their degree course? "

Only 106 students (7%) had seen specimen papers of the written qualifying examination which is a forerunner for both Method I and II candidates. The majority of this small number thought the papers were fair for all candidates irrespective of their degree course.

Question asked: " Have you seen the syllabus of the optional Method I academic papers? How do the optional Method I papers fit in with your degree course? "

An even smaller number of students were personally familiar with the syllabus of the optional Method I academic paper. Of these half thought the scope of the optional subjects was only partly related to their degree course.

Methods I and II

Question asked: " If you were applying for a job in the Civil Service would you choose the selection procedure outlined under Method I or Method II? " (See Card. Appendix I)

Since only a very small proportion of students in the sample had any familiarity with either Method I or II, one must interpret with caution the fact that taking the sample as a whole, half the students favoured Method II, whereas one third favoured Method I. 12% had no preference or didn't know. Reasons for the preferences are listed in Table XXX below. Most of the students who favoured Method I preferred examinations over extended interview methods which is perhaps not surprising since examination ' behaviour ' is prominent in students' lives. This accounts for the responses of one-third of the Method I group who found examinations easier and perhaps also for the 13% who thought they were fairer than interview assessments.

Table XXX. Reasons for Choosing Method I or II Selection Procedure

BASE: MEN STUDENTS STATING A PREFERENCE FOR METHOD I OR II

Method I (n=567)	%	Method II (n=734)	%
Exams preferred over interview	52	Better aptitude test than exams	35
Easier: recent exam experience	35	Better opportunity for assessing all candidates qualities	34
No administrative problem tests	16	Interviews preferred over exams	24
Consider exams fairer	13	More realistic estimates of ability	20
Dislike extensive testing methods	7	Objections to more exams	17

Conversely examinations were disliked by some Method II students just because of recent or impending examination experience. The interesting feature of this group's responses is the emphasis placed on assessing the candidate's practical all-round abilities and personal qualities.

Those students (n = 78) who considered selection by examination the least fair selection procedure felt that examinations (a) fail to take account of personal qualities (44%) (b) fail to indicate applicant's aptitude for the actual job (44%) and (c) consider degree a sufficient indicator of academic standard (13%).

If preference for Methods I and II selection procedures are tabulated (Table XXXI) according to those who would make the administrative class their first choice, Method II is clearly preferred. This is in keeping with expectations; administration aspirants would consider themselves fitted to contend with this type of selection situation.

Table XXXI. Preference for Method I or Method II Selection Procedure Analysed by Final Year Male Students Who Would Choose the Administrative Class as First Choice of Job

BASE: MEN STUDENT FINALISTS	Students choosing Administrative Class 270	Others 482
	%	%
Method I procedure preferred	32	38
Method II procedure preferred*	61	46
No preference	6	8
Don't know	1	8
Total	100	100

* Percentage difference statistically significant at 0·01 level.

Analysis of Method I and II selection procedure preference by university type attended shows there is no significant difference between university groups in the overall preference for Method II procedure.

In order to probe further into sex differences among attitudes towards Civil Service selection procedures, the reasons for choosing Method I are analysed separately for men and women in Table XXXII.

Question asked: " Why would you choose this particular method? (i.e. Method I or II) "

Table XXXII. Analysis by Sex of Reasons for Choosing Method I Selection Procedure (By Seniority)

BASE: STUDENTS GIVING PREFERENCE TO METHOD I SELECTION PROCEDURE	Men 567	Women 267
	%	%
1. General preference for exams over extended interview	52	56
2. Easier because of recent exam experience	35	27
3. No tests on administrative problems as in Method II	16	13
4. Fairer than subjective interviews	13	6
5. Dislike of extensive testing of Method II	7	14
6. Wide range of choice in examination paper	4	2
7. Exams more accurate assessment of ability	4	4
8. Others: e.g. sets more definite standards	2	2

It seems possible that the ambivalent attitude of women may reside in their greater anxiety about attending long interviews than men, a fact which might be inferred from combining items 1 and 5 in Table XXXII. 70% of women gave these responses compared with 59% men.

Question asked: " From your knowledge and experience, or judging by the description you have just read of Method I and Method II what do you think about such methods as selection procedures? "

The general impression gained is that Method I evokes more unfavourable responses (duplicates examinations, only suitable for academics, ignores personal qualities) and that Method II tends to attract favourable ones (takes personality into account, matches people to jobs, assesses practical abilities).

Two-thirds of the responses were of a rather global kind—both fair methods 34%, both too severe 26%, and so on. However, a more analytical approach is perhaps not to be expected when students had so little information at first hand either of the Civil Service as an employer or of the detailed methods of recruitment.

4.7. Biographical and Academic Differences Between Students According to the Employer Considered

An examination of final year students according to the type of career they were considering showed that the groups considering the Civil Service and academic careers contained a higher proportion of women than the group considering only industry or commerce. They also contained a higher proportion of those reading Arts and Social Studies than the industry/commerce group where the proportion of applied scientists was greater. The make up of the three groups by type of University attended was markedly similar and there were no significant differences in respect of social class and type of secondary school attended. But there was a tendency for the children of graduate parents to consider a Civil Service or academic career rather than one in industry or commerce.

Introduction

In this sub-section the 1088 students who were in their final year are examined in order to determine whether there are important differences among students willing to consider the Civil Service only, those prepared to consider both the Civil Service and industry and commerce, those who would consider a career in industry/commerce only, and finally those who favoured further study, academic research, teaching or the professions. Throughout this sub-section the four groups are referred to as:

I. Those giving consideration only to a career in the Civil Service.

II. Those giving consideration to both the Civil Service and to industrial and/or commercial concerns.[1]

III. Those giving consideration mainly to industrial and/or commercial concerns.

[1] Industry includes nationalised industries. Commerce includes cultural organisations.

IV. Those giving consideration mainly to further study and research or teaching. (This group includes the small number of students who were considering local authorities, private practice, and the armed services.)

For certain purposes Groups I and II are merged (and designated Group I/II). This enables comparisons to be made between students willing to consider the Civil Service and those who were not.

Group I/II accounts for about one-fifth of finalists, a further third make up Group IV. The remainder (about half) are in Group III.

The basic groups are examined in order to identify the similarities and differences between the groups in terms of the biographical, social and academic backgrounds of their members.

(*a*) *The Groups by Sex*

Table XXXIII shows the difference in distribution for men and women between Groups I, II, III and IV.

Table XXXIII. Distribution of First Degree Finalists Between Those Having Considered Employment and Those Having Considered Research, Further Study and Teaching

BASE: FINALISTS	All 1088	Men 752	Women 336
	%	%	%
I Civil Service only	7	5	11
II Civil Service and Industry/ Commerce	11	11	12
III Industry/Commerce	48	56	32
IV Academic Study, Teaching, etc.	34	28	46
Total	100	100	100

The association between sexes and groups considering employment are made more apparent if the figures are transformed to equalise the rows and columns.

By equalisation it is possible to see more clearly the association between the groups and the characteristics of its members. (i.e. whether they are more likely to be men or women, Oxbridge students or Arts students, etc.). Equalisation eliminates the effect of different row and column sizes. For each row and column a multiplier is found such that the final effect of the multiplications on columns and rows is to make the row totals the same and the column totals the same.

Students Considering Employment in the Various Categories (Equalised)

Groups		Men	Women
I	Civil Service	18	31
II	Civil Service and Industry/ Commerce	26	24
III	Industry/Commerce	35	16
IV	Further Study and Research	21	28

It will be seen that more men appear as we move from Group I to III whilst for women the trend is in the opposite direction.

(b) The Groups by University Type

The distribution by university type (Figs. 12 and 13) shows that finalists from each university group distribute their preferences more or less equally among the four employment categories.

Again, equalising the rows and columns, we obtain:

Fig. 12. Analysis of Employment Groups by University (Men)

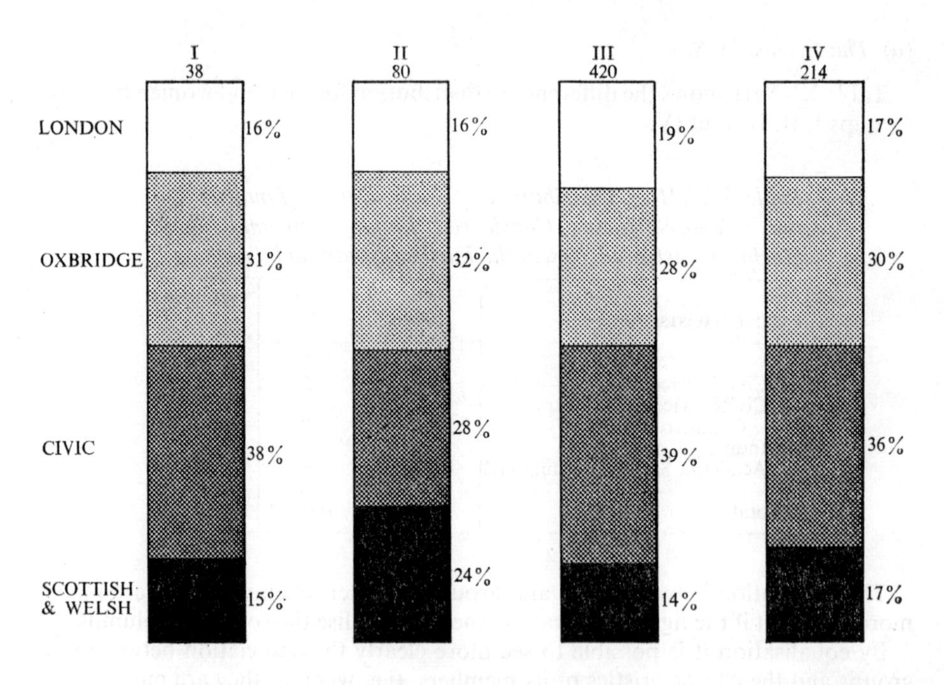

Analysis of Employment Groups by University (Equalised) Men

	I	II	III	IV
London	6·0	5·5	7·0	6·5
Oxbridge	7·0	6·2	5·8	6·0
Civic	6·8	5·0	7·2	6·2
Scottish and Welsh	5·2	8·3	5·0	6·3

There is only a slight association present in this table, which is not significant. The very low figure for Scottish and Welsh in Group I, and the high figure for Oxbridge may be noted. The " Equilibrium " for entries here is 6·25. If there were no association at all one would expect each cell to take this value.

Analysis of Employment Groups by University (Equalised) Women

	I	II	III	IV
London	4·0	6·0	8·5	6·5
Oxbridge	6·2	9·8	5·0	3·2
Civic	7·5	5·0	5·5	7·5
Scottish and Welsh	7·3	4·2	6·1	7·5

Fig. 13. Analysis of Employment Groups by University (Women)

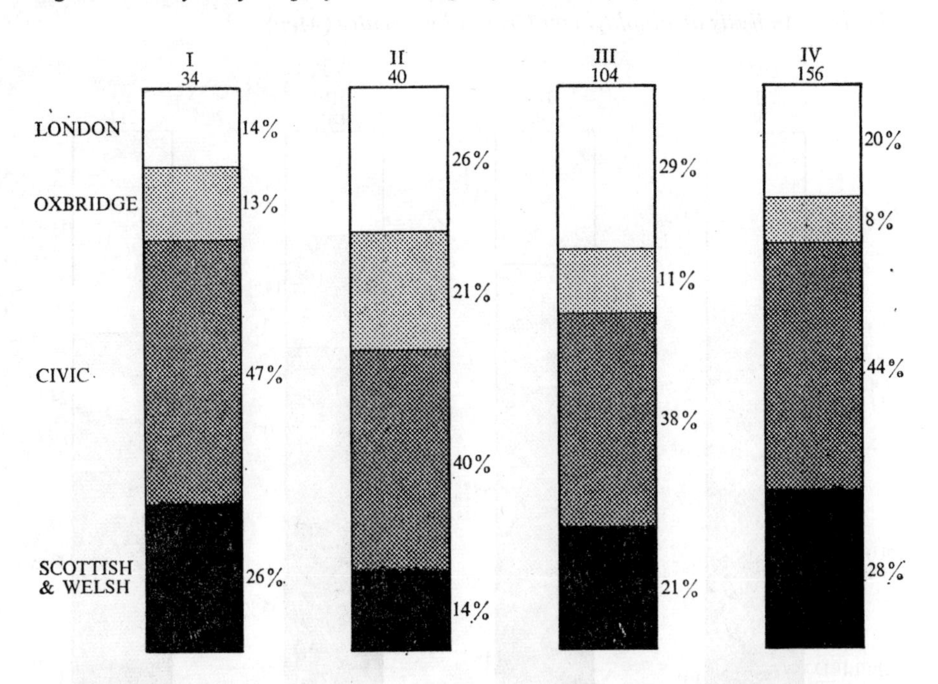

There is somewhat more association for the women than men. The overall pattern is slightly different; the low figure for London in Group I is contrasted by the high figure for Scottish and Welsh. The Oxbridge Group IV figure is very low. The association is that the ordering LONDON–SCOTTISH–CIVIC–OXBRIDGE tend to go with IV–III–II–I so that a person to the left of one ordering tends to be on the left of the other, e.g. a London woman is more likely to be group IV than group I.

(*c*) *By Faculty*

About one-fifth of finalists in the Arts, Social Studies and Pure Science faculties were willing to consider the Civil Service (Group I/II) compared with about one-tenth of those from Applied Science.

Students Considering the Civil Service Expressed as Percentages of Total Population of Finalists in each Faculty

	Arts	Social Studies	Pure Science	Applied Science
	%	%	%	%
Considering Civil Service (Group I/II)	22	19	18	11

Fig. 14. Analysis of Employment Groups by Faculty (Men)

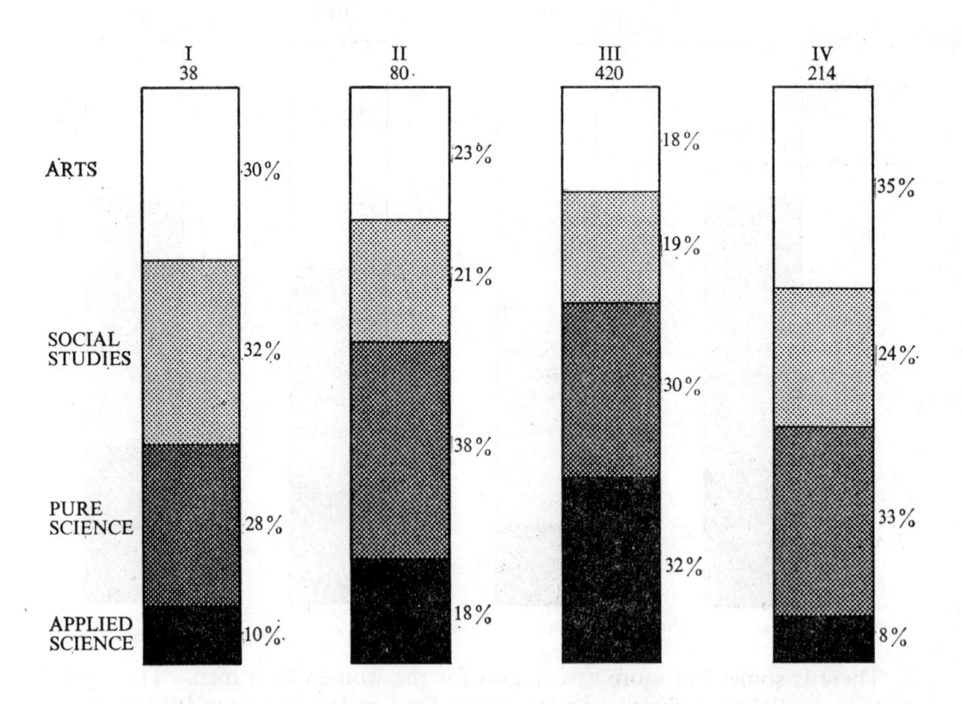

Pure Scientists may be expected to apply mainly for the scientific officer class, although there would appear to be an increasing interest among scientists in the administrative class as reported in Section 3. The relatively few applied scientists willing to consider a career in the Civil Service (Group I/II) may reflect ignorance of opportunities rather than antipathy towards the Civil Service. This point of view is examined later in this section.

The faculty representation in Group I/II closely approximates Group IV but differs from that of Group III, where the greater number of applied scientists compensates for the fewer Arts students willing to consider a career in industry or commerce only. (See Fig. 14). This supports the difference discussed above.

The pattern presented by equalised figures is as follows:

Distribution by Faculty (Equalised) Men

	I	II	III	IV
Arts	7·5	5·5	4·5	8·5
Social Studies	8·0	5·8	4·8	7·0
Pure Science	5·5	7·2	5·5	6·8
Applied Science	4·0	6·5	11·2	3·0

Fig. 15. Analysis of Employment Groups by Faculty (Women)

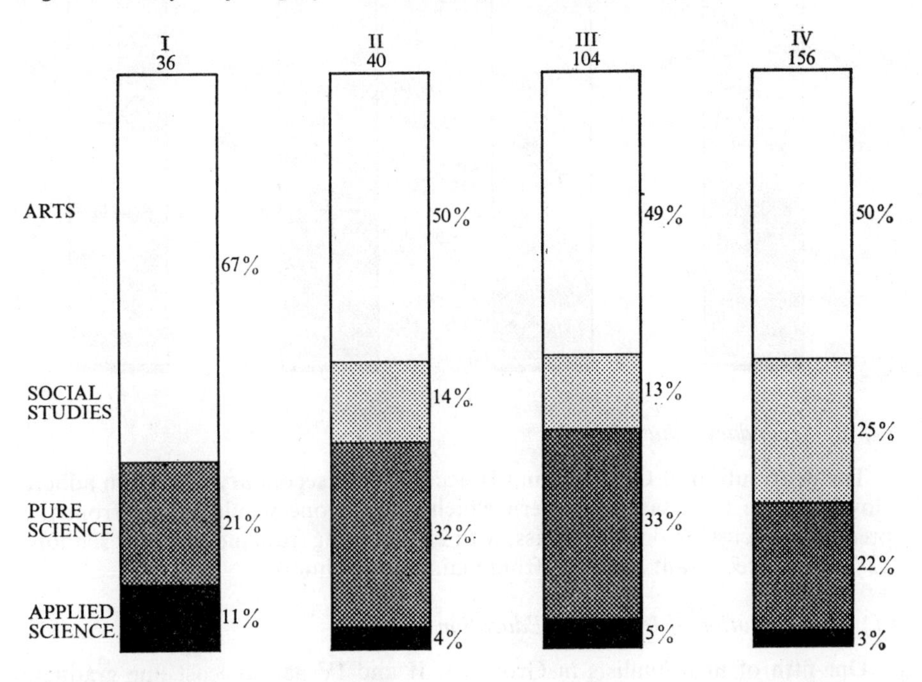

(*d*) *By Social Class*

The categories used are based on the Registrar General's Classification of Social Class (H.M.S.O. 1966). The distribution of those considering the Civil Service, Groups I and II, does not depart significantly from Groups III and IV (Fig. 16), although I/II is slightly closer to IV than it is to III.

Socio-Economic class	Group I/II %	III %	IV %
I	23	27	22
II	48	45	50
III	28	25	23
IV	1	2	3
V	1	1	1

Fig. 16. Analysis of Employment Groups and Administrative Class Applicants by Socio-Economic Class (Men and Women Combined)

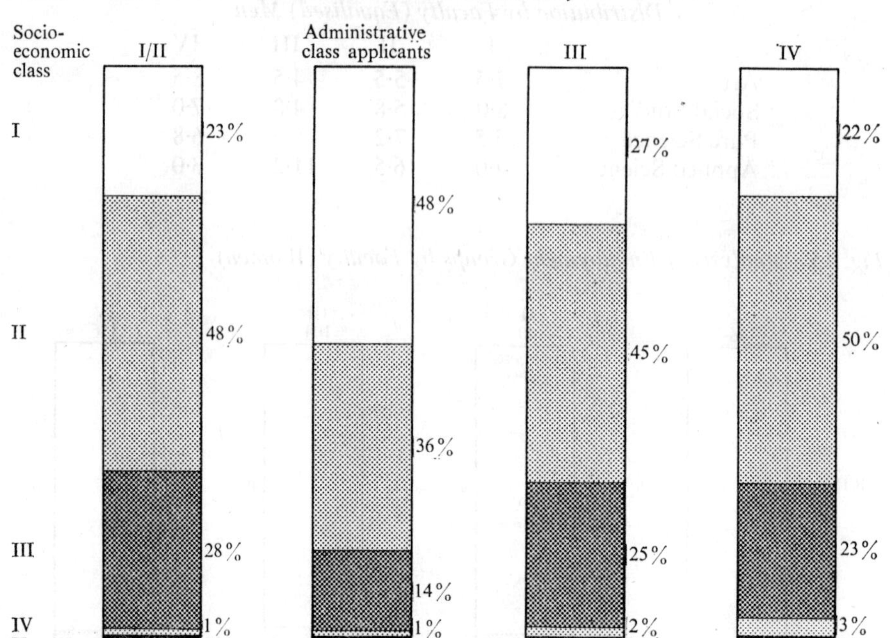

(*e*) *By Secondary Education*

The distribution of Groups I and II according to secondary education adhere closely to the total sample pattern which is what one would expect from the preceding discussion on social class, with 21% coming from independent schools, 12% from direct grant and 66% from maintained schools.

(*f*) *By Generation of University Education*

One-fifth of men finalists in Groups I, II and IV had at least one graduate parent. There is a tendency for sons of graduate parents to be more interested in a Civil Service or an academic career than one exclusively in industry or commerce.

The same pattern emerges among women students although there is a fall in the percentage of second generation students in Group IV. This may be accounted for by the higher number of women going into teaching whose parents may have a teacher's certificate rather than a degree.

4.8. Students' Assessments of their Chances of Entry into the Civil Service

Only a few students thought their chances of gaining admission to the Civil Service were low; however, the question as phrased did not refer to any specific grade. Nevertheless, a third of the sample did not know what their chances were. A large proportion of the sample thought that Oxbridge students stood a better chance of getting into the Civil Service than did students from other universities. There was no difference between those who obtained firsts or upper seconds, and other degree classes, in rating their chances of obtaining a job in the Civil Service.

In explanation of their confidence in obtaining a job in the Civil Service, four reasons given by students seem relevant:

(*i*) *The need for graduates facilitates entry.*
(*ii*) *Expectations of a good degree result.*
(*iii*) *There are many vacancies for graduates in subjects studied.*
(*iv*) *Self judged ability to pass entrance exams and interviews.*

Question asked: " If you were interested in getting a job with the Civil Service when you graduate, what would you think would be your chances of doing so: high, medium or low? "

As Table XXXIV shows most students thought they had a reasonable chance of getting a job in the Civil Service.

Table XXXIV. Students' Assessments of Chances of Entry into the Civil Service

BASE: ALL STUDENTS	Men (n=1474)	Women (n=557)
	%	%
High	40	31
Medium	42	47
Low	12	18
Don't know	6	4
Total	100	100

The reasons for their assessments are presented in Fig. 17. The optimists obviously place great faith in their degree, or in their general competence, or in the needs of the Civil Service (perceived or imagined) for graduates. The most frequent response of the pessimists referred to the difficulty or competitiveness of the entrance examinations. Very few students in this category referred to their university as a determining factor but students were immediately questioned on this point.

Question asked: " What do you think your chances are compared with graduates from other Universities? "

Two-thirds of all students consider that the chances of getting a job in the Civil Service are greater for Oxbridge students than for students from other universities. Further, Oxbridge students themselves rated their own chances higher.

If students' assessments of their chances of entry are analysed by their preferences for Method I or II selection procedures Table XXXV is obtained.

Students were more confident of getting a job with the Civil Service irrespective of class than with the major industrial firms selected as being representative of

Fig. 17. Reasons for Students' Self-ratings of Likelihood of Obtaining a Job in the Civil Service

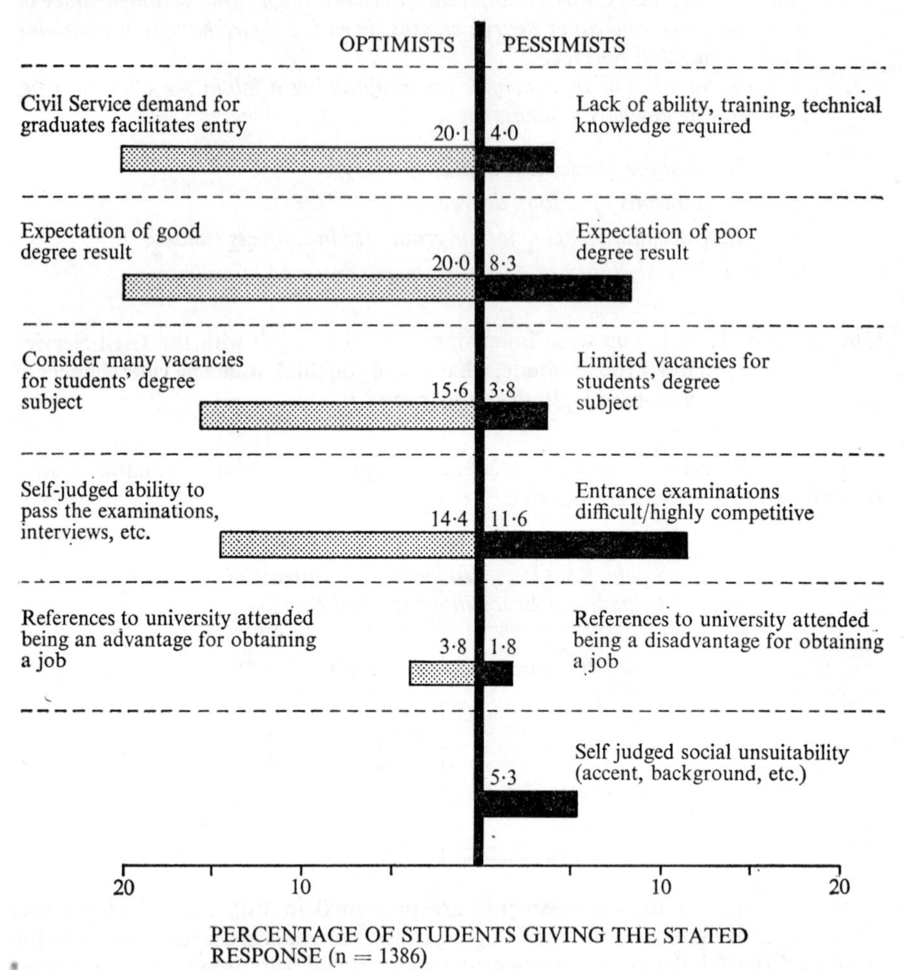

Table XXXV. Preferences for Methods I and II Selection Procedures Analysed by Students' Assessments of Chances of Getting a Job in the Civil Service

BASE: MEN STUDENTS (n=1474)	Method I	Method II	No preferences	Don't Know	Total
Rating of chance of getting a job in the Civil Service	%	%	%	%	%
High	41	49	5	5	100
Medium	39	51	8	2	100
Low	33	51	11	5	100
Don't know	37	47	8	9	100

industry. The differences between the proportions of men students who gave a self rating of "high" (40%) for the Civil Service and "high" (21%) for industry are significant at a very high level. (p is less than 0·005).

Section 5

5.1. Sources of Information
5.2. Social/Personal Sources of Information
5.3. University Teachers as Sources of Information
5.4. Visits to Possible Employers
5.5. Vacation Work Experience

5.1. Sources of Information

Parents and such advisers as teachers and University Appointments Boards (U.A.B.'s) head the list of sources of information. Careers literature and the various kinds of career talks have a relatively low ranking, as do the several varieties of work experience. U.A.B.'s were visited by 66% of all finalists and about half (45%) of them making their first visit to their U.A.B.'s during their final year. Four-fifths of the students who visited U.A.B.'s attended advisory interviews. Reactions were more often favourable when seeking information about jobs but more often unfavourable when seeking new ideas about careers. Careers talks were poorly attended. Similarly, few students had met employers' representatives (about one-eighth of all finalists), and few had made formal visits to potential employers (16%). Most formal visits left the student with an unchanged or more favourable attitude to the host. Over a quarter of the students making government office visits increased their already favourable disposition towards the Civil Service as an employer. This is particularly true of Oxbridge students. Though most vacation work similarly left students with an unchanged or more favourable attitude to the employer, a slightly larger number of people were discouraged by vacation work than by formal visits.

Introduction

This section deals not only with the use but the relative influence of different sources of information. Initially students were asked to cite, unaided, sources of information they had used. They were then provided with a prompt list of over thirty possible sources and asked if they had made use of any channels not so far spontaneously mentioned. Following this they named the source out of their spontaneous and prompted responses which to them was the first, second and third most important.

The differences between the sexes are not great and combined figures are given. In general women tend to use fewer sources of information than men.

Question asked: " Thinking back can you tell me how you came to learn about various jobs you've considered? "

Sources of information quoted by 10% or more of those students who had considered specific jobs are presented in Table XXXVI. These figures relate to students of all years. The picture for finalists alone, in respect of some of the more important sources of information, is examined later in this section. As might be expected, parents and advisers like academic staff and U.A.B.s. head the list; careers literature and the various kinds of career talks have a relatively low ranking; so do the several varieties of work experience.

Question asked: " Here is a list of the ways other students have said they have found out about jobs. Are there any you have used apart from the ones you have mentioned? "

In the prompted situation, students made one third more responses (3·3 per student compared with 2·5 spontaneous responses). In Table XXXVI prompted and spontaneous responses given by more than 10% of the students are set alongside each other.

Table XXXVI. Sources of Information about Jobs Mentioned by 10% or More of Students who had Considered Specific Jobs

BASE: STUDENTS OF ALL YEARS (n=1803)	Spontaneous (Mean: 2·5 responses/student)		Prompted (Mean 3·3 responses/student)	
	%	Rank	%	Rank
Academic staff	28	1	29	1
Parents	25	2	19	5
Advertisements	20	3½	20	4
University appointments board (U.A.B.)	20	3½	10	16½
Personal friends	19	5	21	3
Non-careers literature (e.g. newspapers)	17	6		
People in similar jobs	12	7		
School careers teachers	10	8½	10	16½
Personal interest	10	8½		
Employers' literature	9	10	17	6
Professional literature	7	12	13	12
Other relatives	7	12	11	15
School career talks	7	12	16	7½
Directory of opportunties for graduates (D.O.G)	6	14	26	2
Family friends	5	16	13	12
Vacation work	5	16	15	9
U.A.B. hand-outs	5	16	16	7½
Pre-University job experience	4	18½	14	10
Radio/T.V.	4	18½	13	12

The most interesting difference between the two sides of this table is the promotion of the Directory of Opportunities for Graduates to second place when a prompt list is used. Obviously this was an important source of information which, in the unaided recall situation, failed to evoke a response in competition with the more obvious sources. Work experience, both pre-university and vacation, also improved their relative positions in the prompted condition.

Table XXXVII combines both percentages into a single figure which then forms the basis of a new rank ordering. The extent to which computed ratings represent the relative priority of the sources in terms of their importance to students in aiding their career decisions can be seen when they are compared with the students' ranking of the three most important sources.

Question asked: " Could you tell me which of all the sources of information you have mentioned was the most important, the next most important and the third most important? "

The analysis of responses to this question forms the " Obtained Ranking " of Table XXXVI. It is evident that, but for two exceptions, there is no great difference between the rankings given by each method. School Careers talks, though ranked 9th in terms of combined spontaneous and prompted response frequency, did not fall within the twelve most important sources cited by students. Whilst they may suggest that schools' career talks made little impact on students, it is also possible that career ideas have changed since students' school days and that more recent influences would be considered more important by their association with these newer ideas.

Table XXXVII. Computed and Obtained Rankings of Sources of Information in Terms of their Importance to Students

BASE: STUDENTS OF ALL YEARS (n=1803)	Computed Ranking (Sum of spontaneous and combined responses derived from Table XXXVI)		Obtained Ranking*
	%	Rank	Rank
Academic staff	57	1	2
Parents	44	2	1
Personal friends	40	3½	3
Advertisements	40	3½	5
D.O.G.	32	5	6
U.A.B.	30	6	4
Employers' literature	26	7	7
Non-careers literature	25	8	8
School careers talks	23	9	—
U.A.B. hand-outs	21	10	10
School careers teachers	20	12	11
Vacation work	20	12	12
Professional literature	20	12	—
Pre-University work experience	18	15	9

* The obtained ranking is the sum of the scores for each category (first twelve only) when the first choice is given a score of three, the second a score of two, and the third a score of one.

The second difference is the changed ranking of pre-university work experience from 15th position on the computed ranking of spontaneous and prompted responses combined to 9th position of importance as a source of information.

Before discussing sources of information individually it is interesting to compare Table XXXVI with Table 20 of the Heyworth Report reproduced below as Table XXXVIII. The close correspondence between the two tables is noteworthy.

Table XXXVIII. Extract from Table 20 of the Heyworth Report on University Appointment Boards

BASE: FINAL YEAR STUDENTS (n=1596)	
Students who had had useful advice/ information from:	%
Academic staff	45
Own friends	33
Parents, relations, friends of family	31
Periodicals/Books	25
Advertisements	24
School teachers	17
Others	15

Source: University Appointments Boards. H.M.S.O. 1964.

5.2. Social/Personal Sources of Information

Question asked: " Have you sought advice from your parents about your future career? What did they advise? "
" Did you accept what your parents said? "

It has been seen that parents were ranked first in order of importance as a source of information although 42% of the sample with parents living (44% men and 37% women) did not seek advice, and of those who did, 23% chose not to accept it, at least, not completely.

Of those seeking advice from parents, 45% claimed that choice of career was left to the student himself to decide, and 8% received no helpful advice. 17% were advised to consider specific jobs, of whom 2% were advised to consider the Civil Service (see Table XXXIX).

Table XXXIX. Analysis of Advice Given To and Accepted By Students Who Discussed their Careers with Their Parents

BASE: STUDENTS SEEKING PARENTAL ADVICE	All 1126	M 787	W 399
	%	%	%
Choice left to student	45	45	44
Advised specific job	17	15	22
Endorsed career intentions	12	12	10
Advised further study	9	9	8
No helpful advice given	8	10	5
Advised Civil Service	2	2	4
Advised against students choice	7	7	6
Percentage accepting parental advice	77	77	76

89% of the 453 students in the sample who were either engaged or married had discussed their career intentions with their partners. As might have been predicted the most common advice was to follow the student's own inclinations (65%). Also predictable, perhaps, are the sex differences revealed. Men, it seems, are more inclined to be forthcoming with advice on what their partners should do.

It is clear that social/personal sources of information were seen as important by students, the majority accepting the advice given. In the main, advice appears to be a reinforcement of the students' choice.

5.3. University Teachers as Sources of Information

Question asked: " Have you discussed your future with any of the University Teaching Staff? "

It has been seen that academic staff were most often cited as a source of information and were considered second in importance in terms of their influence on career choice.

Half the sample had discussed their future with the staff and a substantial number had sought advice from more than one member. The proportion does not change to any great extent when analysed by sex or faculty but, as might be expected, it does by year of study. (Table XL).

Table XL. Analysis of Students who Discussed their Futures with University Teaching Staff (By year of study).

BASE: ALL STUDENTS								
All	Total		1st Year		Mid. Year		Final Year	
	M	W	M	W	M	W	M	W
2031	1474	557	334	104	308	117	752	336
49%	49%	50%	23%	22%	41%	40%	64%	62%

Question asked: " With which members of the staff have you discussed your career? "

The tutor was the main source of advice at Oxbridge, Civic and London Universities. Lecturers were hardly ever consulted by Oxbridge students but a third of them sought advice from their Heads of Departments. Students of Scottish and Welsh Universities appeared to use all members of the staff though Professors and lecturing staff rather more than tutors.

Civic and London students were very similar in their patterns of staff use, Heads of Departments being least preferred as advisers in both cases.

Question asked: " Were these discussions helpful to you in forming your ideas for your career? "

Paragraph 74 of the Heyworth Report[1] contains the following: " Where the appointments service is working well and on good terms with the academic staff, one would expect to find students going both to the academic staff and to the appointments service in fairly large numbers. Where there is, or is felt to be, any deficiency in the appointments service one would expect to find students going to the academic staff and not to the service. In other words, advice from the academic staff can either be complementary to advice from the appointments service or competitive with it, but the relationship is complex and subtle and we do not claim we have figures to illustrate it."

The Heyworth Report was based on data from final year students only. Table XLI compares the proportion of final year students who visited U.A.Bs. and who consulted their teachers as revealed by the two research projects.

Table XLI. Proportion of Students Who Attended their U.A.Bs. Compared with Proportion who Discussed their Future with University Teachers

BASE: FINAL YEAR STUDENTS	Present Survey 1965/6 (n=1088)	Heyworth Report 1962/3 (n=1596)
	%	%
Attended U.A.B.	66	66
Discussed career with Academic Staff	63	45

[1] University Appointments Boards. H.M.S.O. 1964.

As can be seen there is a substantial difference[1] in proportions of students seeking advice from teachers in the two enquiries. When the University Groups are compared (Table XLII) there are no great differences between the two rows of data with the exception of London where more than twice as many London men and women sought advice from university teaching staff as attended their appointments board or college careers office. There is also a slight tendency for Oxbridge men to discuss jobs with their teachers rather than their U.A.Bs. because of the close contact with tutors.

Table XLII. Proportion of Students who Attended their U.A.Bs. Compared with Proportion who Discussed their Future with University Teachers

		Total		London		Oxbridge		Civic		Scottish and Welsh	
BASE: ALL STUDENTS	All 2031	M 1474	W 557	M 294	W 112	M 374	W 69	M 550	W 233	M 256	W 143
	%	%	%	%	%	%	%	%	%	%	%
Attended U.A.Bs.	42	42	42	26	23	39	60	52	50	39	33
Consulted Teachers	49	49	50	56	50	49	59	48	49	41	47

A comparison of attitudes towards U.A.B.s. and teachers as careers advisors is shown in Table XLIII.

Although a smaller proportion of Scottish and Welsh students conferred with their teachers about careers a higher proportion of those who did accepted their advice.

An examination of Table XLIII suggests that students who thought highly of their teacher's advice also tended to speak favourably of U.A.Bs. Additional support comes from the proportions of those who expressed satisfaction. 30% of London students were unable to express any criticisms for various reasons, compared with about 20% of students from the other universities. London is atypical in its organisation of career advisory services which may explain the higher incidence of consultation with teachers.

When we come to consider faculty differences the Heyworth Report comments as follows:

" What does appear to be true is that on the scientific and technological side direct contact between employers and academic staff is commoner than on the arts side and no doubt leads to students getting jobs through that channel rather than through the appointments service ".[2]

Table XLIV shows some of the data from the current study analysed by faculty.

It does not lend support to the Heyworth hypothesis though it must be remembered that there were important differences in the ways in which the two samples of students were described in terms of faculties.

[1] Significant at the 5% level.

[2] *Op. cit.*

Table XLIII. Students' Assessments of U.A.Bs. and Teachers as Careers Advisers

		Total		London		Oxbridge		Civic		Scottish and Welsh	
BASE: ALL STUDENTS	All 2031	M 1474	W 557	M 294	W 112	M 374	W 69	M 550	W 233	M 256	W 143
		%	%	%	%	%	%	%	%	%	%
Criticism of U.A.Bs.											
No criticisms of U.A.Bs.	44	46	38	39	31	41	28	51	43	54	41
No opinion through lack of personal experience	13	13	13	17	20	14	13	12	11	9	10
Don't know	10	10	9	15	11	9	9	8	6	12	15
Suggestions for improving U.A.Bs. usefulness											30
Don't know. No specific suggestions	32	33	29	38	36	32	19	32	28	30	
Satisfied with U.A.B.	25	25	22	23	25	18	22	30	24	29	16

		Total		London		Oxbridge		Civic		Scottish and Welsh	
BASE: STUDENTS HAVING DISCUSSED FUTURE WITH ACADEMIC STAFF	All 994	M 716	W 278	M 182	W 102	M 147	W 76	M 227	W 74	M 160	W 26
Discussions with teachers helpful in forming careers ideas (n=994)	55	56	54	55	57	55	44	52	53	66	60

Table XLIV. Students' Use of U.A.Bs and University Teachers

	Arts		Social Studies		Pure Science		Applied Science	
BASE: ALL STUDENTS (n=2031)	M 363	W 246	M 295	W 128	M 484	W 130	M 332	W 53
	%	%	%	%	%	%	%	%
Visited U.A.B. (n=2031)	38	41	35	50	43	39	50	30
Consulted teachers (n=2031)	50	41	50	59	47	57	48	49
	Arts		Social Studies		Pure Science		Applied Science	
BASE: STUDENTS HAVING DISCUSSED FUTURE WITH ACADEMIC STAFF (n=994)	M 182	W 102	M 147	W 76	M 227	W 74	M 160	W 26
	%	%	%	%	%	%	%	%
Discussions with teachers helpful in forming career ideas (n=994)	59	53	53	46	57	51	53	88

When the usefulness of talks with teaching staff is examined according to the students' University (Table XLV) the only difference to attract attention is the higher rating of the Scottish and Welsh universities (65% compared with 53% for all other universities.)[1]

Table XLV. Students' Assessment of the Usefulness of Discussion with Teaching Staff (By University groups)

BASE: STUDENTS CONSULTING TEACHING STAFF	All (994)	London (221)	Oxbridge (223)	Civic (378)	Scottish and Welsh (172)
	%	%	%	%	%
Discussion helpful	55	56	53	52	65
Made no difference	34	34	34	38	27
Discussion unhelpful	10	10	13	10	10

Question asked: " When and how did you come to consider these (i.e. job/employer) possibilities and what was it about them that appealed to you? "

Analysis of the ways in which students came to consider various job possibilities shows that 16% of the group (n=1557) were prompted by the advice of U.A.Bs. and 6% on advice of teachers. The data is compared in Table XLVI and shows that pure scientists and to a lesser extent applied scientists rely more on U.A.Bs. This is surprising in view of the high number of applied scientists interested in industry.

Teachers are clearly an important source of information for, and powerful influence on, students' career decisions. However, whilst this study does not altogether refute the assumptions made in the Heyworth Report about the influence of university staff, in particular about their relative impact on students compared with that of the U.A.Bs., it certainly casts some doubt upon them.

[1] Percentage difference statistically significant at 0·01 level.

Table XLVI. Comparison of Use of U.A.Bs. and Careers Advice from Academic Staff

	All	Arts		Social Studies		Pure Science		Applied Science	
BASE: STUDENTS CONSIDERING SPECIFIC JOBS	1557	270	199	232	95	353	100	284	24
	%	%	%	%	%	%	%	%	%
Advice from U.A.Bs.	16	15	12	9	16	28	24	11	13
Advice from Academic staff	6	8	7	6	9	6	11	3	*

3.6. Use of University Appointment Boards

U.A.Bs. were ranked 4th in order of importance as sources of information by students of all years. 42% of the total sample from all years had visisted their U.A.B. or College Careers Office though, as might be expected, more students (65%) did so in their final year. In fact, two thirds of finalists who had used U.A.B.'s had made their first visit during their final year (i.e. about 45% of all finalists); thus in this respect there has not been much change since the Heyworth Report. However if we look more closely at those finalists (see also Section 4) who were mainly giving consideration to a career in industry then the importance of the U.A.B.'s is apparent. 76% of the men (n=420) and 68% of the women (n=104) who were interested exclusively in a career in commerce or industry, as opposed to further study, the Civil Service or teaching, attended their U.A.Bs. or C.C.O.'s for advice. To this must be credited the use made of A.B. Handouts by students interested in industry or commerce. When the rank order of the first twelve sources of information are set side by side for men finalists (Table XLVII) the relative importance of the sources to those exclusively considering industry and commerce and those exclusively considering further study or teaching of all types can be compared.

Table XLVII. Rank Order in Importance of Sources of Information.

BASE: MEN FINALISTS CONSIDERING THE CIVIL SERVICE, INDUSTRY/ COMMERCE OR FURTHER STUDY/ TEACHING (n=790)	Civil Service only n=76	Commerce/ Industry n=500	Further Study/ Teaching n=214
Academic staff	1	6½	1
A.B. staff	2	1	4
Friends	7	2	2
Parents	3	5	3
Advertisements	5½	4	5
A.B. handouts	8½	3	12
Employer literature	8½	8	10
D.O.G.	11	6½	11
Vacation work	10	9	9
Pre-University work	5½	12	7
Non-Careers literature	12	10½	6
Careers teachers	4	10½	8

Kendall's coefficient of concordance (W=0·626) is significant at the 0·01 level.

5.4. Visits to Possible Employers

7% of male students had visited a government office and 11% had been on at least one formal visit to other prospective employers. Here the effect such visits had on the student's inclination to apply for a job are examined. Table XLVIII compares (for men only) all visits combined with visits to government offices in terms of changes in students' attitudes towards taking a job with the organisation visited.

Question asked: " How did it (i.e. a formal visit) affect your attitude to taking a job with this employer? "

Table XLVIII. Effects of Formal Visits on Students' Attitudes to a Career with the Employers Visited

BASE: MEN STUDENTS EXPERIENCING A FORMAL VISIT	All visits combined 271		Govt. Office visit 100	
	%		%	
More favourably disposed	48	82	27	76
Unchanged	34		49	
Less favourably disposed	15		17	
Don't know	3		7	
Total	100		100	

If we make the reasonable assumption that most students who take the trouble to pay a formal visit are already fairly well disposed towards their hosts then the two categories " more favourably disposed " and " unchanged " may be merged into a single " sympathetic " category in opposition to " less favourably disposed ". It can be seen from the Table XLVIII that visits to government offices and all visits combined differ barely at all in their net general effect on attitudes. It appears, however, that visits to government offices more often meet students' expectations than do visits in general since the latter more often result in attitude changes than do the former (63% compared with 44%).

An interesting difference emerges when sympathetic attitudes are analysed by university groups. Table XLIX shows that 48% of Oxbridge students were more favourably disposed to consider a job with the Civil Service compared with only 11% of Scottish and Welsh students as a result of their visits.

Table XLIX. Effects of Formal Visits to Government Offices on Students' Attitudes to a Civil Service Career (by University groups)

BASE: MEN STUDENTS VISITING GOVERNMENT OFFICES	Total 100	Oxbridge 25	Civic 33	London 23	Scottish and Welsh 19
	%	%	%	%	%
More favourably disposed	27	48	27	17	11
Unchanged	49	40	61	52	37
	76	88	88	69	48
Don't know	24	12	12	31	52
Total	100	100	100	100	100

Combining the two categories into a single one as before the table shows clearly that Oxbridge and Civic universities lead in sympathetic attitudes. The poor showing of students from Scottish and Welsh universities must be considered in the light of a very high proportion of " Don't knows ", (52%)

A similar analysis by faculty shows that as a result of their visits students of Social Studies in general are slightly less sympathetic than students from other faculties but considerably less so after government office visits.

Table L. Effect of Formal Visits on Students' Attitudes to Careers with the Employers Visited

BASE: MEN STUDENTS EXPERIENCING FORMAL VISIT	Total 271	Arts	Social Studies	Pure Science	Applied Science
	%	%	%	%	%
All visits Combined (n=271)					
More favourably disposed	48	58	39	52	47
Unchanged	34	23	37	32	38
Sympathetic	82	81	76	84	85
Government Office visits (n=100)					
More favourably disposed	26	50	22	25	10
Unchanged	50	39	11	55	69
Sympathetic	76	89	33	80	79

5.5. Vacation Work Experience

In the section on Sources of Information it was shown that pre-university and vacation work experiences were highly rated by students as sources of information (9th and 12th in importance respectively). Many students expressed the view that both types of contact with firms provided opportunities for employers to assess their (the students') abilities.

35% of those with vacation work experience had been engaged in work related to their subject, career or course.

Question asked: " In what way did the experience influence your views on a career with this employer? "

Table LI. Comparison of Effects of Vacation Work Experience and Formal Visits on Students' Attitudes to Careers with Host Firms

BASE: MEN STUDENTS EXPERIENCING VACATION WORK AND FORMAL VISITS RELATED TO DEGREE COURSE	Vacation Work n=409	Formal Visits n=271
	%	%
More favourably disposed	30 } 61	48 } 82
Unchanged	31	34
Less favourably disposed	31	15
Don't know	9	3

The effect of vacation work on students' attitudes towards the vacation employer tends to be more evenly distributed among the three categories shown in Table LI.

Table LI compares the effects of vacation work experience and formal visits on students' attitudes towards the career possibilities with the employers concerned.

When these results are analysed by faculty it seems that fewer Arts students are discouraged from considering a job with vacation firms than is the case with students from other faculties.

Adopting the convention of the previous discussion of formal visits, Arts students are also the most " sympathetic " as Table LII shows.

Table LII. Comparison by Faculty of Effect of Vacation Work Experience on Students' Attitudes to Consideration of a Career with Vacation Employers

BASE: MEN STUDENTS EXPERIENCING VACATION WORK	Total 409	Arts 43	Social Studies 53	Pure Science 116	Applied Science 197
	%	%	%	%	%
More favourably disposed	30	33	26	36	26
Unchanged	31	44	36	24	30
Sympathetic	61	77	62	60	56

Students of Applied Science are more often discouraged than encouraged from considering a job with their vacation employers. (40% less favourably disposed as against 26% more so.[1])

A possible explanation of the first tendency is that over a third of Arts students had considered or were considering careers in education and the most frequently mentioned vacation work experience was teaching (quoted by 23% of male Arts students). Teaching is a career and presumably for most students that is the end of the matter. One employer is much like another. It is interesting to observe that 60% of Arts men had no suggestions to offer on ways in which vacation work might be made more useful.

The situation for Applied Scientists is rather different. 71% of these students had considered or were considering a job in industry or commerce that was " strictly related to degree subject ". This is no less a single minded view of a career than that hypothesised above for 36% of Arts men but the specific opportunities are much wider. One employer is not like another even within the same industry and Applied Scientists may therefore be inclined to shop around more. This is borne out by the analysis of responses made by students when they discussed the jobs for which they intended applying.

[1] Significant at the 5% level.

Appendices

Appendix I. Method

The following is an abbreviated description of the method used in the enquiry.

The sample was designed to be representative of the population of undergraduates in the Arts, Social Studies, Pure and Applied Science faculties of the fifteen Universtities listed under II The Sample. Medicine, Veterinary Science, Theology and Music were excluded for obvious reasons. A sample size of 2,500 was decided upon; an initial and up to three follow-up letters were sent requesting an interview. 2,031 interviews were achieved giving a response rate of 82 per cent. The study was planned so that final year students would be interviewed during their last term i.e. as near as possible to the point of taking up their careers, and the gain in information about the career decision-making of finalists more than compensated for the non-response. To compare respondents and non-respondents a postal questionnaire was sent to those students who did not attend the personal interview. This revealed no significant differences in biographical and academic characteristics between those personally interviewed and non-respondents. Non-attendance was in the main attributable to study pressures and examination commitments.

The survey was designed as a trend study and attempted to track the decision making process. Thus students from all years were sampled permitting comparisons to be made particularly in relation to the growth, development and crystallisation of career ideas. Since the final year student was likely to be of greater value in providing information on sources of interest, motivation and influence in job choice variable sampling fractions were used such that finalists compared with first and middle year students were sampled roughly in the ratio 2:1:1.

The frames used for the extraction of the sample were the lists of first degree home students provided by the Registrars departments of each of the Universities concerned in the study. Within each University the sample was stratified by sex and faculty. Selection was made with probability proportionate to size such that the number of students from each University was proportionate to the contribution of that University to the total population.

(i) The report deals only with those sections of relevance to the Civil Service. The study as a whole had a broader base which may be described briefly as:

(*a*) to investigate the reasoning, interests and motives of the student in seeking a career.

(*b*) to assess the importance of influences which effect students' attitudes towards careers and the timing of his career choice; in particular, home, school, university, past experience with employers and other sources of information.

(*c*) to determine the relative views which students hold of all career opportunities including the Civil Service, commerce, private and nationalised industries, the Armed Forces and professional private practice, particularly in relation to academic postgraduate studies and teaching as alternatives.

(*d*) to examine the information which students possess about different types of employment, and the images which they have formed of various employers.

(*e*) Dependent upon the subject of specialisation of the student and the type of career he is envisaging, an examination of:

(1) the attractiveness of management and other training schemes, for both arts and science students.

(2) attitudes towards postgraduate research at university compared with other research posts, for science students.

The study also obtained basic information on the students' social and educational background, extra-curricular activities, readership habits and so forth.

(ii) The present work is part of a longitudinal study and is to be followed by further research whose aim will be to discover the extent to which the aspirations and expectations of the student have been matched by actual work experience. It is planned to interview those of the original sample who are now in employment in order to:

(*a*) to assess the extent to which career intentions match actual choice of jobs.

(*b*) to obtain additional data on the way in which the final career decisions were arrived at.

(*c*) to examine the reasons why applicants rejected previously considered employers.

(*d*) to determine the degree to which the image of the employer, has been influenced by the graduate's subsequent work experience.

(*e*) to obtain feedback on the graduate's image of different employers and their selection and training procedures.

(*f*) to study the extent and reasons for job switching.

(*g*) to study the use made of graduates and the relationship between the job and his expectations.

The research will also be concerned with the graduate recruit's work activities and his attitudes to them and to his employer. An examination of the graduate's use of careers advice and information is included and finally the employer's point of view will be studied.

(iii) The data was collected by personal interview, each lasting 2–3 hours. Information for the main body of the enquiry was obtained by means of an interview schedule using open questions. The responses were recorded as nearly as possible verbatim.

Since the report related only to selected questions the interview schedule is not reproduced in full, instead the relevant questions head each sub-section of the text.

Certain open questions were followed by one in which a prompt card was used. Whenever this is so it is explicitly stated in the text.

For all but two cards their content is reproduced as a table with relevant responses against each item. The text of the two remaining cards is given below. In all cases the student was handed the card to read.

A. *Prompt Card used for Question on Civil Service Class to which Students would apply* (see p. 370)

Civic Service Class	*Duties*	*Salary range*[1]	*Key number*
Administrative	Advise on formation of policy; co-ordination and improvement of Government machinery; and general administration and control of public departments.	£926–8,600	1
Other Managerial Inspector of Taxes	Assessment of taxation, planning and management of the work of local offices.	£916–6,300	2
Assistant Postal Controllers	Responsible for organising the postal and counter services in their regions.	£889–3,520	3
Cadets in Ministry of Labour	Work leading to positions of higher responsibility in the management of the Ministry's regional organisation.	£890–3,500	4
Executive	Middle management, i.e. responsibility for the day to day conduct of Government business; responsibility for accounts and revenue collection; management of regional and local offices.	£685 (at 20) –4,000	5
Scientific Officer	Covers practically every field of pure and applied science, including fundamental research, applied research and advisory and inspectorial work.	£926–5,250 Some higher posts	6
Experimental Officer	Assistance to scientific officers on new investigations, particularly their organisation and execution; and responsibility for work applying established scientific principles.	£685 (at 20) –3,000	7
Professional Classes	Include engineers of all kinds, architects, surveyors, planners, valuers. Duties include advisory and consultant work; original design of schemes; managerial control of processes to translate schemes into action and direction of professional and other staff.	£807–7,200	8

[1] The salaries in this column were those current at the time of the survey.

Civil Service Class	*Duties*	*Salary Range*	*Key Number*
Economists	Analysis and interpretation of economic trends; advice on the economic aspect of departments' programmes. Play an important part of the formulation of policy.	£926–4,500	9
Legal	Advice on the legal implications of policy; drafting of legislation; litigation, conveyancing and advice on legal aspects of day to day administration.	£1,554–8,600	0
Statistician	Organising, directing and supervising statistical work and participation in formation of policy.	£926–5,250	X
Diplomatic Service Administrative Grade	Advice on the formulation of foreign policy. Representation of Britain abroad. Protection and promotion of British interests, in particular, trade.	£926–8,600	Y

B. *Prompt Card Used for Questions on Selection Procedures* (See p. 384).

Administrative Class Selection Procedures

METHOD I

Method I consists of a short general qualifying examination; an interview and an academic examination of honours degree standard in papers chosen by candidates from a wide range. The result is the total marks for interview and academic examination.

METHOD II

Method II has the same short general examination as Method I followed by two days of tests and interviews at the Civil Service Selection Board. An important part of these tests is a series of exercises both oral and written on administrative problems. Those who do not drop out at this stage go on to a final selection board which determines their result on the basis of their whole performance.

(iv) Seventy-eight interviewers, mainly graduate psychologists, took part in the investigation. The use of open questions has its hazards and extreme care was taken in the training and supervision of interviewing in order to minimise interviewer bias. The training programme included instruction, rehearsal, role reversal and interviews carried out under observation with students not included in the sample.

(v) Editing and coding of open questions was carried out in the office. The supervisor/coder ratio was high and there was a 100% check on schedules. Coding frames were generous in catering for a wide variety of responses and some collapsing of the data was executed at the presentation stage. Scalar data were punched directly from the questionnaires.

(vi) 18 eighty column punch cards per student were used to accommodate the data which was processed on a CDC 2300 computer by Scientific Control Systems Ltd.

The data from which the tables in the current report are extracted are reproduced separately in eight volumes.

(vii) The field work took place in the Summer term of 1966. The interviewing of students began in April and was completed by mid June. Most of the interviews were conducted in rooms provided by the Universities or by individual colleges in London and Oxbridge.

In all cases, except one (Southampton), the request for an interview was made direct to the student. The initial contact letter is reproduced below. Up to three follow-up letters or a personal call on the student were made in an effort to ensure attendance.

THE PSYCHOLOGICAL RESEARCH CENTRE

Research into Social, Occupational and Industrial Problems

85 PRINCE ALBERT ROAD,
REGENT'S PARK,
LONDON, N.W.8
Telephone: 01-722 1297

Dear Mr. . . . . . .,

I am writing to ask you for your help in a Survey of Undergraduates that we are carrying out for a number of Government Departments and Industrial Organisations. As part of this survey we are interviewing a sample of students from your University.

The purpose of the enquiry is to examine the ways in which career decisions are made by University students. We wish to emphasise that, although this study is being conducted with the permission of (name of University/College), the Psychological Research Centre is an entirely independent organisation.

The sample has been selected on a random basis and your name has come up in the selection. We hope that we may count on your co-operation because, as you know, the accuracy of the results obtained in a survey depends upon the co-operation of every member in the sample.

All the information you give will be treated as strictly confidential and under no circumstances will any information about you as an individual be passed on to anyone outside the staff of The Psychological Research Centre.

Yours sincerely,

(viii) Tests of significance were made where it was felt that meaningful conclusions could be drawn from the data. These are given as footnotes to the text. In the case of the significant differences in respect of the ratings of employer attributes (see Section 3.3) we may assume a sample of n persons rate two attributes a, b in groups from 1 to 11; group 0 will be " don't knows ". Let the probability of a person rating attribute " a " as group i be π_{ia}. For attribute " b " we shall write π_{ib} for the corresponding quantity. The ratings given will be assumed independent between both persons and attributes.

Suppose m_{ia} persons rate attribute " a " as group i; similarly m_{ib} persons rate attribute " b " as group i.

We want to know when the difference in mean ratings of " a " and " b " is different, i.e. when

$$D = \sum_{i=0}^{11} \frac{i}{n}(m_{ia} - m_{ib})$$

is significantly different from zero. We have

$$\sum_{i=0}^{11} m_{ia} = \sum_{i=0}^{11} m_{ib} = n. \sum_{i=0}^{11} \pi_{ia} = \sum_{i=0}^{11} \pi_{ib} = 1$$

Now, D will have an asymptotically normal distribution, and variance of

$$D = \text{var}\left(\sum \frac{i}{n} m_{ia}\right) + \text{var}\left(\sum \frac{i}{n} m_{ib}\right)$$

$$= \frac{1}{n}\left[\sum_{i=0}^{11} i^2 \pi_{ia} - \left(\sum_{i=0}^{11} i\pi_{ia}\right)^2\right] + \frac{1}{n}\left[\sum_{i=0}^{11} i^2 \pi_{ib} - \left(\sum_{i=0}^{11} i\pi_{ib}\right)^2\right]$$

One may estimate π_{ia}, π_{ib}, from m_{ia}, m_{ib}. In the absence of these details one may set an upper bound for var (D).

$$\text{Variance } D \leqslant \frac{2}{n} \cdot \frac{11^2}{4} = \frac{11^2}{2n}.$$

(ix) Weights were assigned to cater for variable sampling fractions within strata.

Appendix II. The Sample

(i) The population covered by the survey comprised first degree students who, at the time of the survey, were attending universities or university colleges at fifteen universities in England, Scotland and Wales. The universities were selected to meet the needs of the sponsors of the study. Students of Medicine, Music, Theology, Dentistry and Veterinary Science and occasional students were excluded.

(ii) Consideration of the information required and the resources available led to the decision to aim at a sample size of 2,500. This involved an overall sampling fraction of 1:25 with 1:12 for final year students, 1:39 for middle year students (2nd of a three year course and 2nd and 3rd of a four year course), and 1:47 for final year students.

(iii) The sample was drawn independently from each university and university college. At London and at Oxford and Cambridge the sample was drawn separately from each college. Names were selected by The Psychological Research Centre from lists supplied using a random start and thereafter a differing sampling interval according to academic year of study. This procedure had the effect of stratifying the sample.

(iv) The sampling fractions gave a selected sample of 2,488. The effective sample was 2,031 giving an overall 82% response rate. Response rates for each university are given below:

Edinburgh	86
London	84
Durham	84
Birmingham	83
Glasgow	83
Liverpool	83
Cambridge	82
Manchester	82
Nottingham	80
Oxford	79
Leeds	79
Sussex	79
Cardiff	78
St. Andrews	78
Southampton	71

(v) A postal questionnaire was sent to non-respondents to which there was a 72% reply. Non-respondents to personal interviews showed no significant differences in terms of their academic and biographic characteristics. Non-reponse was in the main a function of conducting the field work during the summer term in competition with the inroads made by examinations.

(vi) University Groups

The fifteen Universities are grouped as follows:

(i) London	
(ii) Oxbridge	Oxford Cambridge
(iii) Civic	Birmingham Durham Leeds Liverpool Manchester Nottingham Southampton Sussex
(iv) Scottish and Welsh	Cardiff Edinburgh Glasgow St. Andrews

Table 1. The Sample by University Group

	All		Men		Women	
	No.	%	No.	%	No.	%
London	406	20	294	20	112	20
Oxbridge	443	22	374	25	69	12
Civic	783	39	550	37	233	42
Scottish and Welsh	399	20	256	17	143	26
Total	2,031	100	1,474	100	557	100

(vii) Faculties

Faculty of Arts comprises students reading:

Archaeology
Art and Design
Classical Studies
Drama
Geography
History
Languages
Literature
Philosophy

Faculty of Social studies comprises students reading:

Accountancy
Anthropology and Social Anthropology
Business studies and Commerce
Economics
Law
Politics/Government/Public Administration
Psychology
Sociology

Faculty of Pure Science comprises students reading:

Biochemistry
Biology
Botany
Chemistry
Geology
Mathematics
Maths and Physics
Pharmacology
Physics
Physiology
Zoology

Faculty of Applied Science comprises students reading:

Aeronautical Engineering
Agriculture
Agricultural Biology
Architecture
Chemical Engineering
Civil Engineering
Electrical Engineering/Electronics
Mechanical/Automobile Engineering
Metallurgy
Mining
Pharmacy
Production Engineering
Town and Country Planning

The disciplines Medicine, Music, Theology, Dentistry and Veterinary Science were excluded.

Table II. The Sample by Faculty

	All		Men		Women	
	No.	%	No.	%	No.	%
Arts	609	30	363	25	246	44
Social Studies	423	21	295	20	128	23
Pure Science	614	30	484	33	130	23
Applied Science	385	19	332	23	53	10
Total	2,031	100	1,474	100	557	100

(viii) Year of Study

(*a*) Students repeating a year of their course were assigned to the group of the year they were in at the time of interviewing.

(*b*) The category " Middle Year " comprises students in the second year of a three-year course, students in the second or third year of a four-year course, and students in the second, third or fourth year of a five-year course.

Table III. The Sample by Year of Study

	All		Men		Women	
	No.	%	No.	%	No.	%
First	438	22	334	23	104	19
Middle	505	25	388	26	117	21
Final	1,088	54	752	51	336	60
Total	2,031	100	1,474	100	557	100

Note: Other biographical characteristics of the sample are given in Section 4.7 p. 386 *et seq.*

Appendix III. Ratings of employers in Terms of Job Characteristics

The following give the full list of ratings in respect of the four categories of employer used in the analysis in Section 3 on p. 358.

(i) *THE ADMINISTRATIVE CIVIL SERVICE*

Ranking	*Attribute*	*Rating*
1	Likelihood of a sound pension scheme	9·8
2	Job security	9·3
3 5	Extent to which the work you would do would involve directing the activities of others	8·6
4	Salary prospects in twenty years time	8·4
5	Social status	8·4
6	A job which involves working with others	7·8
7	Prospect of professional training to a high standard	7·6
8	Intellectual climate	7·3
9	Early salary prospects	7·0
10	Compatability between the work to be done and your own moral code	6·9
11	Ease of transfer from one kind of job to another with the same employer	6·7
12	Opportunity to make a valuable contribution to society	6·5
13	Congeniality of fellow workers	6·4
14	Career advancement based on performance rather than type and class of degree	6·1
15	Extent to which you would associate with leaders in your field	5·9
16	Work conducive to bringing out the best in you	5·9
17	Ease of transfer from one type of employer to any other	5·8
18	Prospect of gaining further degrees (higher degrees, diplomas)	5·8
19	Extent to which employees do a variety of jobs rather than specialise in one	5·8
20	Chances of getting into a progressive job	5·3
21	Career advancement based on performance rather than age	5·2
22	Opportunity for travel	5·2
23	Extent to which you would expect to use your degree knowledge with such an employer	5·2
24	Freedom given in the way in which you would wish to do your work	5·1
25	Opportunity of publishing work	4·3
26	Flexibility of the organisation in adopting new ideas	4·3
27	Opportunity to make a valuable contribution to human knowledge	3·9
28	Degree to which your career is open to change if you join this employer	3·6

(*ii*) *THE SCIENTIFIC CIVIL SERVICE*

Ranking	*Attribute*	*Rating*
1	Likelihood of a sound pension scheme	9·5
2	Prospect of professional training to a high standard	8·9
3	Job security	8·7
4	Opportunity to make a valuable contribution to human knowledge	8·6
5	Intellectual climate	8·3
6	Salary prospects in twenty years time	8·0
7	Social status	7·8
8	Prospect of gaining further degrees (higher degrees, diplomas)	7·7
9	Extent to which you would expect to use your degree knowledge with such an employer	7·7
10	Opportunity to make a valuable contribution to society	7·4
11	Opportunity of publishing work	7·3
12	Compatability between the work to be done and your own moral code	7·2
13	Early salary prospects	6·9
14	Flexibility of the organisation in adopting new ideas	6·9
15	Career advancement based on performance rather than age	6·8
16	Extent to which you would associate with leaders in your field	6·8
17	Congeniality of fellow workers	6·7
18	Chances of getting into a progressive job	6·6
19	A job which involves working with others	6·4
20	Extent to which the work you would do would involve directing the activities of others	6·2
21	Ease of transfer from one type of employer to any other	6·1
22	Freedom given in the way in which you would wish to do your work	6·1
23	Ease of transfer from one kind of job to another with the same employer	6·0
24	Career advancement based on performance rather than type and class of degree	5·8
25	Work conducive to bringing out the best in you	5·8
26	Opportunity for travel	5·5
27	Extent to which employees do a variety of jobs rather than specialise in one	4·5
28	Degree to which your career is open to change if you join this employer	4·0

(*iii*) *PRIVATE INDUSTRY/COMMERCE* (*LARGE ORGANISATIONS*)

Ranking	*Attribute*	*Rating*
1	Salary prospects in twenty years time	9·2
2	Career advancement based on performance rather than type and class of degree	8·5
3	Career advancement based on performance rather than age	8·4

Private Industry/Commerce (Large Organisations)—continued

Ranking	*Attribute*	*Rating*
4	Early salary prospects	8·3
5	Ease of transfer from one type of employer to any other	8·3
6	Likelihood of a sound pension scheme	8·3
7	Flexibility of the organisation in adopting new ideas	8·3
8	Prospect of professional training to a high standard	8·2
9	Opportunity for travel	7·8
10	Ease of transfer from one kind of job to another with the same employer	7·8
11	A job which involves working with others	7·6
12	Social status	7·4
13	Extent to which the work you would do would involve directing the activities of others	7·4
14	Extent to which you would expect to use your degree knowledge with such an employer	7·1
15	Work conducive to bringing out the best in you	7·0
16	Compatability between the work to be done and your own moral code	6·8
17	Congeniality of fellow workers	6·6
18	Prospect of gaining further degrees (higher degrees, diplomas)	6·3
19	Intellectual climate	6·2
20	Chances of getting into a progressive job	6·1
21	Extent to which you would associate with leaders in your field	6·1
22	Job security	6·0
23	Freedom given in the way in which you would wish to do your work	6·0
24	Opportunity of publishing work	5·9
25	Opportunity to make a valuable contribution to human knowledge	5·8
26	Extent to which employees do a variety of jobs rather than specialise in one	5·8
27	Degree to which your career is open to change if you join this employer	5·8
28	Opportunity to make a valuable contribution to society	5·6

(*iv*) *UNIVERSITY TEACHING*

Ranking	*Attribute*	*Rating*
1	Intellectual climate	10·6
	Opportunity of publishing work	10·6
3	Prospect of gaining further degrees (higher degrees, diplomas)	10·5
4	Extent to which you would expect to use your degree knowledge with such an employer	10·5
5	Opportunity to make a valuable contribution to human knowledge	9·8
6	Extent to which you would associate with leaders in your field	9·5
7	Freedom given in the way in which you would wish to do your work	9·5

University Teaching—continued

Ranking	*Attribute*	*Rating*
8	Social status	9·3
9	Compatibility between the work to be done and your own moral code	9·3
10	Opportunity to make a valuable contribution to society	9·1
11	Job security	9·1
12	Congeniality of fellow workers	8·6
13	Prospect of professional training to a high standard	8·4
14	Extent to which the work you would do would involve directing the activities of others	7·8
15	Salary prospects in twenty years time	7·6
16	Career advancement based on performance rather than age	7·6
17	A job which involves working with others	7·6
18	Ease of transfer from one type of employer to any other	7·5
19	Work conducive to bringing out the best in you	7·5
20	Likelihood of a sound pension scheme	7·4
21	Chances of getting into a progressive job	7·4
22	Opportunity for travel	7·2
23	Flexibility of the organisation in adopting new ideas	7·0
24	Early salary prospects	6·3
25	Ease of transfer from one kind of job to another with the same employer	5·3
26	Career advancement based on performance rather than type and class of degree	4·4
27	Degree to which your career is open to change if you join this employer	4·1
28	Extent to which employees do a variety of jobs rather than specialise in one	3·8

MEMORANDUM No. 10

submitted by

J. B. BOURN
(Ministry of Defence)

May, 1968

The Main Reports on The British Civil Service since the Northcote–Trevelyan Report[1]

I. Introduction

1. This essay is an account of the main reports that have been made on the British Civil Service since the Northcote–Trevelyan report of 1854. Its purpose is to describe the problems with which each of these reports were concerned, to outline the solutions they proposed and to detail the action that was taken upon them. It is not a comprehensive history of the Civil Service; developments which neither influenced nor originated from the report of a reviewing committee are either omitted or mentioned only in passing.

[1] I should like to thank Sir James Dunnett, who first suggested that I should undertake this study. His advice and encouragement have been invaluable throughout its writing. I also received most helpful comments from Dr. Norman Hunt, Mr. Robert Neild, and Mr. Richard Wilding.

II. The Northcote–Trevelyan Report

2. The Northcote–Trevelyan Report, published in 1854, is the most important report on the Civil Service and the source of the principles underlying its present structure. But the publication of the Report was not the first attempt to introduce reforms into the Service, and it would be wrong to ignore the developments that took place in the first half of the nineteenth century.

3. The origin of these changes is to be found in the disquiet occasioned by the revelations of government inefficiency during the War of American Independence, in such writings as Burke's " Plan for the better Security of the Independence of Parliament and the Economical Reformation of the Civil and Other Establishments ", and in the reports of various Commissions and Select Committees set up between 1780 and 1810 to inquire into public accounts and the emoluments of offices.[1] These and similar works exposed an administrative chaos of sinecure offices, many dating from the Tudor period and before; of the sale of offices; of appointments by patronage; of entirely different methods of office organization and practice between one department and another; and of a complete failure in account keeping and auditing some of which was still conducted in Latin.

4. Inefficiency and corruption were the obvious results of such a system, and the first reforms to be introduced were improvements in acccounting methods and the removal of some of the worst features of patronage. By the middle of the nineteenth century many sinecures had gone; a Superannuation Act had been passed and pensions were paid on the basis of salary and length of service; and, though patronage continued to be the method of appointment, there was an increasing reluctance to give posts to completely unsuitable persons and some form of qualifying examination had been introduced in many departments.

5. The impetus behind these changes was not so much an attack on privilege as a desire to achieve economy and efficiency and the belief, following the ideas of Bentham, that the utility of administrative practices and procedures should be openly examined and adjustments made as necessary.

6. But a great deal remained to be done. Although the Civil Service consisted of only about 16,000 people,[2] the departments still differed widely in conditions of service, pay, organization and methods of work. The age of entry to the Civil Service differed from one Department to another. Customs clerks, for example, might be engaged at any age between 16 and 40 but all started as equals in the junior division of the Department and promotion depended on seniority for all but the very ablest.[3] In some departments work had increased and changed its nature. For example, the duties of the Board of Trade were originally consultative, but in 1832 it was given the responsibility for collecting and publishing statistics and it was later charged with the administration of the Acts relating to the railways and to joint stock companies.

---

[1]See for example
- (*a*) Reports of the Commissioners on Public Accounts, appointed in 1780, 3 Volumes.
- (*b*) Report of the Select Committee on Finance of 1798. Reports from Committees of the House of Commons. Volumes XII and XIII.
- (*c*) Reports of the Commissioners Appointed to Inquire into the Fees, Perquisites and Emoluments received in Public Offices. Parliamentary Papers. 1806 vii.

[2] Northcote–Trevelyan Report. C.1713 of 1854.

[3] Trevelyan, Charles " Memorandum on the Examination and Probation of Candidates for Public Employment ". Papers on Emoluments in the Public Service, 1856.

7. In 1848 a Select Committee of the House of Commons on Miscellaneous Expenditure[1] took evidence from Sir Charles Trevelyan who put before them a scheme for reforming his own Department, the Treasury, by appointing men to posts on the basis of proven capacity and by reorganizing methods of work so as to eliminate unnecessary expense of the kind that resulted, for example, from the practice of employing men earning from £300–£1,000 a year on copying duties that could be done by clerks at 6/- a day.

8. If Trevelyan's criticisms were sound, they applied not only to the Treasury but also to other Departments of State and while the Select Committee "... were not prepared to express an opinion favourable to the suggestions submitted by Sir Charles Trevelyan "[2] successive Governments appointed a series of Committees, Select Committees and Commissions to investigate Government administration and, in particular, the organization of certain public offices. Sir Charles Trevelyan sat upon all the Committees on the English offices and Sir Stafford Northcote, who had been Gladstone's Private Secretary, was his colleague on eight of them.

9. In 1853 Northcote and Trevelyan were appointed by Gladstone, then Chancellor of the Exchequer, to report on the organization of the Civil Service as a whole. As Chapter I of the Fulton Report makes clear, Northcote and Trevelyan were much influenced by Macaulay, whose report on the examination of candidates for the Indian Civil Service was also published in 1854.

10. Trevelyan had himself spent four terms at Haileybury, founded in 1806 for the higher education of those who were to enter the service of the East India Company, and had served for 14 years in India, where he had met Macaulay and subsequently married Macaulay's sister. Indeed, Macaulay and Trevelyan had often discussed the reform of the Indian Civil Service, and Macaulay had shown the draft of his report on recruitment by competitive examination to Trevelyan.[3] Another influential figure in these discussion was Dr. Benjamin Jowett, who was keenly interested in the reform of the Indian and home Civil Services and, of course, in University Reform. He was a member of Macaulay's Committee on the examination of candidates and came into close touch with Trevelyan.

11. The common belief of these three influential men and their supporters in the value of competitive examinations as a test of character and capacity, led, when it was finally accepted, to a system under which individuals who could acquit themselves well in examinations administered by the Universities were appointed to responsible and relatively well paid positions in the public services at home and abroad. But the initial result of their collaboration was the Report of the Organisation of the Permanent Civil Service, which was published in 1854, together with a letter from Jowett outlining a scheme of examinations in which he proposed that the subjects to be set should include political economy, law, modern languages, modern history and physical science as well as classics and mathematics.[4]

12. The Northcote–Trevelyan report is published in full as an Appendix to the

---

[1] See Parliamentary Papers 1847–48, xviii.
[2] Ibid.
[3] Trevelyan, G. O., " Life and Letters of Lord Macaulay " (1876), Vol. II, p. 372.
[4] Parliamentary Papers, 1854, xxvii.

Fulton Committee report so there is no need to summarize it here beyond a statement of its main principles, viz:

(*a*) recruitment should be by competitive examinations rather than by patronage and these examinations should be conducted by a central and independent body of examiners;

(*b*) a division should be made between intellectual and mechanical work and officers should be recruited specifically for these different tasks;

(*c*) promotion should be by merit;

(*d*) the unity of the Civil Service should be fostered by placing first appointments on the same basis throughout the Service, by providing opportunities for those in the higher grades to secure promotion in other departments, and by redeploying lower staff between departments as required by the state of public busines.

13. These principles now seem unexceptionable. But at the time they were published they were regarded as extreme. The criticisms made of them may be divided into a number of groups. The first group was concerned with the idea of competitive examinations. Some claimed that the public service did not require the intellectual capacities that would be provided by a system of competitive examinations. The Chairman of the Emigration Board is recorded as saying " unusual intellectual attainments are not the first requisite for a clerk in a public office ".[1] Allied with this was a fear that competitive examinations would bring into the Civil Service men who were clever but socially and hence morally undesirable. The Secretary to the Board of Trade said " The tendency of your system gradually to fill the public offices with a lower class of man, I consider one of the strongest objections to it. The lower you descend in the social scale the less is the probability that the candidate for the Civil Service will possess those moral qualifications which I have already insisted on as being more important than the intellectual ones in the practical business of official life ".[2] But there were others, including John Stuart Mill, who claimed that there was no reason to believe that the higher orders of society would prove themselves less capable of passing these examinations than the lower classes.[3]

14. The second group of objections was concerned with the subjects to be set in the examinations. The scheme proposed by Jowett had placed heavy weight, though not exclusive emphasis, on the classical subjects taught in middle class schools and at the older Universities. And this was also true of the Macaulay report, so far as the scheme of examination was concerned, though the Committee also suggested that young men entering the Indian Service should be given instruction in such subjects as Indian history and languages, in law and in financial and commercial subjects such as accounts, the principles of banking, public finance and matters of taxation; in short in political economy. Yet as this instruction was to be given after the entrance examination had been passed, many agreed with Edwin Chadwick that " A strictly academical examination would have admitted the gentleman who is, par excellence, an instructor in the abstract sciences and who wrote articles in the Reviews to show the impracticability of steam navigation across the Atlantic, and it would have excluded

[1] Parliamentary Papers 1854, 15, xx, p. 327.
[2] Ibid. p. 133.
[3] Ibid. p. 94.

those who accomplished the feat ".[1] Nevertheless, John Stuart Mill provided a strong counter argument when he said " To test a candidate to ascertain whether he has been well educated, he must be interrogated in the things which he is likely to know if he has been well educated, even though not directly pertinent to the work to which he is to be appointed. Will those who object to his being questioned in classics and mathematics in a country where the only things regularly taught are classics and mathematics tell us what they would have him questioned in ? "[2]

15. A third group of criticisms centred on the proposal to divide the work into the intellectual and the routine and to recruit separately for each. Many feared that even if promotion was by merit those who entered the Civil Service at the lowest levels would be precluded from the most senior posts. This view was held by some senior Civil Servants who had themselves entered at the lowest level. For example, Sir Alexander Spearman, who had held the posts of Assistant Secretary in the Treasury and Comptroller of the Debt Office, said " It is upwards of 46 years since I first entered the Civil Service of the Crown in its humblest ranks, and I speak from practical and personal knowledge, when I express my opinion that such a system would be injurious as well as unjust ".[3] And he defended this view with the argument that the requisite knowledge of a department could be gained only by working right through it, and so to prevent those with the opportunity of acquiring such experience from reaching the highest positions would be damaging to the Service. It was also argued that if the best posts were reserved for those who entered with a University education the general body of Civil Servants would be disheartened and decline in quality.

16. The final group of criticisms was concerned with the proposal to unify the Service—and to extend Treasury control over it. As might be expected, it was argued that the differences between the work of the various Departments was so great that it would be against the interests of the public service to transfer men between them. Northcote and Trevelyan replied to this by stating that " We have nowhere suggested or even hinted at the idea of transferring men from one office to another in cases where the business is not of a cognate character ".[4]

III. Developments from 1854–1874

17. The Northcote–Trevelyan Report received a generally cool reception, but wind was put into the sails of reform by the outbreak of the Crimean War and the subsequent revelations, particularly in the despatches from " The Times " correspondent, W. H. Russell, of the mismanagement and incompetence in the British military administration. An Administrative Reform Association was founded in May 1855 and meetings were organised up and down the country. Summaries of the Northcote–Trevelyan Report were included in its publications.

18. Lord Palmerston's Government, anxious to take some steps to meet the reformers without offending those interested in preserving the existing order, appointed by Order in Council on the 21st March 1855 a Civil Service Commission

[1] Ibid. pp. 165–6.
[2] John Stuart Mill, " Representative Government ", 1861.
[3] Parliamentary Papers 1854–5, xx, p. 400.
[4] Ibid. p. 421.

consisting of three Commissioners, the Right Honourable Sir Edward Ryan, Assistant Comptroller-General of the Exchequer, J. G. Shaw-Lefevre, Clerk Assistant to the House of Lords, and Edward Romilly, Chairman of the Board of Audit. The task of the Commissioners was to satisfy themselves that the candidates nominated for admission to the Civil Service were within the age limits, satisfied prescribed conditions of health and good character, and that they had the requisite knowledge to perform their duties. The determination of what the requisite knowledge should be was the task of the Commissioners in consultation with the heads of those Departments for which they were examining. A six months probationary period was instituted for newly appointed officers.

19. The effect of this order was to transfer to the Commissioners the responsibility for conducting such examinations and inquiries into candidates as had previously been undertaken by the Departments. It gave to an impartial rather than an interested body the task of assessing the competence of candidates, but the system of private nomination and appointment by patronage continued undisturbed. The Order in Council said nothing about the question of division of labour in government offices or about promotion by merit. Neither did it deal with other aspects of the Northcote–Trevelyan report.

20. The Commission did valuable work in drawing attention in its reports to the low standard of those nominated for Government appointments. It showed that people were not put forward because their sponsors believed they would make an effective contribution to the public service but as a reward for private or political services or in recognition of a personal or family obligation. Those interested in the reform of the Civil Service had therefore still to fight the main battle to secure appointment on the basis of open competition, and determined defensive actions were mounted by many Departments who, although willing to observe the form of the new regulations, usually tried to circumvent their effective operation. In their reports, for example, the Commissioners complained about the low standard set in examinations, about the unwillingness to have competition between nominees and of the almost universal preference for testing particular candidates for individual posts.

21. In 1859 the Commissioners' powers were strengthened by the Superannuation Act of that year which stated that pensions should be paid only to those who held the Commissioners' certificate, except for those who held their appointments directly from the Crown. This considerably reduced the attraction of uncertificated appointments, and so brought more candidates within the purview of the Commissioners' examinations.

22. In 1860 a resolution was carried in Parliament for the appointment of a Select Committee to enquire into " the existing methods of nominating and appointing candidates for junior appointments in the Civil Service, with a view to ascertaining whether greater facility may not be afforded for the admission of properly qualified persons ".[1] Sir Stafford Northcote opposed this motion in the Commons, contending that such an enquiry would be premature. Nevertheless, the Select Committe on Civil Service Appointments was set up and included among

[1] Parliamentary Debates, 3rd Series, Volume 156 (1860), p. 1194.

its members Sir Stafford Northcote, Robert Lowe, John Bright and two former Patronage Secretaries of the Treasury, Sir William Hayter and Sir William Jolliffe. The Committee found that the system of competitive examinations as it existed was " a delusion on the public, and a fertile source of abuse ".[1]

23. Nevertheless, in spite of such strictures and their conclusion that the present arrangements were inadequate, the Committee made no proposals for comprehensive reform. But they did say that open competitive examinations were the best way of recruiting junior clerks and they advocated limited competitions among small numbers of nominated candidates for senior places rather than the examination of single nominees. They suggested that experiments should be undertaken in open competitions for appointments to these higher posts, so as to build up a sufficient body of knowledge for a comparison to be made between the results of limited and open competitions. They also said that a preliminary test should be set to those who intended to compete in limited competitions so as to eliminate the weakest candidates. Although the Select Committee's proposals were so reserved, its endorsement of the principle of competition was significant in view of its membership.

24. However, little action resulted from the Committee's report. There was a modification in the regulations for recruitment to posts within the patronage of the Treasury, which included the revenue collecting offices. Under this change, nominees were required to pass a qualifying examination before entering for limited competitions. But this did not apply to those Departments where patronage lay in other hands.

25. The next stage in the reform of the Civil Service began in 1869 with the appointment of Robert Lowe as Chancellor of the Exchequer. Lowe was a firm supporter of Civil Service reform, and believed especially in the virtues of open competitive examinations. But, while Gladstone supported him, other important Ministers were less interested. Gladstone's solution was to avoid any further detailed inquiry, and to issue an Order in Council in 1870 which laid down that, except for the Foreign Office and the Home Office, all vacancies should be filled by open competitive examination,

26. These examinations were to be of two kinds; examinations designed to recruit University graduates for the higher posts and examinations for the lower ranks of the Service. This Order in Council was of the highest importance, since it established that recruitment should be by open competition, rather than by the examination of nominees or limited competition among nominees, and it laid down that men of educational standards should be recruited for different kinds of work. By abolishing patronage recruitment the Order in Council opened the way to other reforms to which Northcote–Trevelyan had attached importance in their report. Places in the Civil Service were valuable gifts so long as their recipients could remain undisturbed by any re-organisation of work or by the promotion of the able and industrious. So long as patronage existed, therefore, pressure was maintained to preserve the value of the patron's gifts. But when the power to make these gifts was removed, a good deal of the opposition to further reforms was also removed, and it became somewhat easier to make

[1] Report from the Select Committee on Civil Service appointments, Parliamentary Papers 1860, ix, p. 13.

progress with the reorganisation of work, and the institution of promotion by merit.

27. Lowe thought it would be necessary to ensure that the Heads of Departments, who had previously exercised patronage, did not resurrect it through their power to make temporary appointments. He therefore arranged for the issue of an Order in Council in 1871 which defined the terms on which temporary or unestablished clerks might be employed. These terms were deliberately made unattractive; the temporary clerks, who were to be known as writers, were to be paid at the rate of 10d an hour and would lose their privileges of sick pay and leave. Writers who had been given certificates by the Civil Service Commissioners and had served for a certain period were to be retained at the same rate of wages they received in June 1870. Others were given the choice of accepting lower rates of pay or a gratuity and retirement.

28. These temporary clerks were vital to the Civil Service of the time because they did most of the work of copying documents. The Northcote–Trevelyan Report had endorsed the employment of unestablished clerks for this kind of work, as part of their general plan for the division of labour within the Civil Service. And while most Departments had recruited temporary staff, each had done so under different arrangements and in different ways, though all had obtained Treasury sanction for their particular schemes. Under these schemes, some of the clerks were enjoying progressive rates of pay which rose to a maximum of £3 a week. The advocates of this practice said that progressive rates were needed as an inducement to good work. Others thought that good copying and simple arithmetic could be procured without providing such incentives, and it was this argument which carried the day and was reflected in the scheme that was introduced.

29. The Order in Council of 1871 naturally caused much indignation among the unestablished clerks, who formed an association to protect their interests. This was one of the first examples of organised staff activity in the Civil Service. A Member of Parliament, Mr. Otway moved a resolution for an inquiry into the Writer's difficulties and in 1873 he was himself appointed as a Chairman of a Select Committee to " inquire whether Writers appointed before August 1871 suffered any injustice by the cessation of progressive payment ". As a result of this inquiry, and the agitation on which it was founded, the Writers did extremely well. Two-thirds of them received permanent and pensionable posts and the rest secured higher wages. But these events underlined the difficulties of re-organising staff in the Civil Service and of introducing a system of merit promotion. Following an enquiry into Civil Service expenditure by a Select Committee of 1873, whose recommendations were generally unhelpful to the cause of reform, a Commission was appointed in 1874 under the Chairmanship of Mr. Lyon Playfair[1] to enquire into the Civil Service.

[1] Lyon Playfair, first Baron Playfair of St. Andrews (1818–1898). Studied chemistry at Glasgow, Edinburgh, London and in Germany; carried out research on nitroprussides, on hydrated salts and on blast furnace gases. F.R.S. 1848; President of the Chemical Society 1857–59; President of the British Association 1885. Special Commissioner and member of the executive committee of the Great Exhibition 1851; Secretary for Science in the Department of Science and Art from 1853 to 1855 and Secretary of the Department from 1855–1858. Professor of Chemistry at Edinburgh from 1858–1869. Liberal M.P. from 1868, Postmaster General 1873–74, Vice-President of the Council 1886.

IV. The Playfair Commission 1874–75

30. The Commission began its work at a time when the work and responsibilities of the central government were increasing. Education, for example, which cost the central government only £250,000 in 1853, was estimated to cost £1,400,000 for the year 1873/4. The Local Government Board, which started work in 1869, doubled its expediture in the first five years of its existence. And the duties of the Board of Trade continued to increase, as did those of the Home Office which was by now responsible for factory inspection on a large scale. Yet the Civil Service was still organised on a departmental basis. Conditions of service and pay rates differed between offices, and there was little scope for transferring a man from one to another. The Exchequer and Audit Act of 1866 required that all Departments should prepare their accounts on the same basis and to ensure this was done a Treasury Officer worked in conjunction with each Department. But this extension of Treasury control was purely financial. The Treasury had none of the additional powers of co-ordination such as it possesses today.

31. The Playfair Commission was unusual in that 6 of its 8 members were Civil Service Heads of Departments and the other two were Members of Parliament, the Chairman being one of these. It was also unusual in that it took evidence from Associations of Civil Servants—an early example of a practice followed by later inquiries.

32. The Commission decided[1] on the basis of its survey that the Civil Service could be divided into four groups of officials. The first group was of senior officers, described as Staff Officers, who had been promoted from the lower classes or recruited from outside the public service usually without any examination. The second group consisted of those recruited by the examination established by the Order in Council of 1870 for men with a University training. The third group of officials were those recruited under this Order in Council by the examinations for the lower offices, and the fourth group were the Writers which have been described above.

33. The Commission found that these four groups were in no sense service-wide grades. Work of a kind that was given to a university graduate in one Department was performed in others by entrants from the lower examination. And the steady expansion of the quantity of work had been met by the recruitment of temporary staff who were often given work of a kind that should have been carried out by more highly qualified officials.

34. The Commissioners therefore returned to the principle of labour division advocated by Northcote and Trevelyan. They emphasized the need to classify the different kinds of work to be done in the Civil Service and to recruit differently qualified people for each kind of work. They recommended that this classification of work should be carried out for the Service as a whole, and that each Department should employ the various kinds of staff in proportion to its needs. One department, for example, might need relatively few men of high quality but large numbers of the lower grades; another might have these proportions reversed.

35. Another problem studied by the Commission arose from the fact that, under the existing system, all Civil Servants felt they had a right to promotion, though

---

[1] The Commission issued two reports; C. 1113 and C. 1226 both of 1875.

few had any prospects of rising very far. The Commissioners said that it was wrong to meet this demand by granting promotions to inferior officers and so paying more than was necessary for the kind of work they could do. They proposed that the lower class of work should be entrusted to people who were specially recruited for it, with few prospects of advancement, and paid a salary which to them would be an acceptable reward for their labours. In this way the Commissioners hoped that there would not only be greater efficiency in the Civil Service, by men doing the work for which they were best fitted, but that there would also be greater contentment. Men of capacity would be recruited for interesting work and given a reasonable chance of promotion, whereas those with lesser abilities would be happy to undertake the more routine work on salaries which for them would be attractive compared with the alternatives that might be available to them.

36. In detail, the Playfair Commission proposed the organisation of the Service in four groups or divisions. These divisions were not markedly dissimilar from those in which they found the Service to be organised already, but the divisions were to represent real differences in the capacity of officers and the kind of work they did in all Departments. The scheme was as follows: first, there should be administrative or Staff Officers chosen by merit from within the Service or recruited from outside if necessary; secondly, there should be a higher division with " Remuneration . . . such as would attract men of a liberal education who would otherwise go into the open professions ".[1] The administrative officers and the higher division would not be very large in number and the great bulk of the work of the Service would be carried out by the third group, the lower division. This should be recruited by a competitive examination in " Subjects included in an ordinary commercial education " to be open to men between the ages of 17–20 years. The Commission added that " To each of these grades, certain standard rates of pay should be attached throughout the public service, and persons should be appointed on the distinct understanding that they have no claim to go beyond the maximum salary of the grade in which they are placed, and that any further advancement must depend on special official aptitude ".[2] The fourth group of Civil Servants were to be boys on temporary engagements. These were to be recruited by a competitive examination " of a very limited character " and were to undertake such copying as would still be necessary when the Commissions' recommendation that copying presses should be used in all departments had been carried out. Some places in the lower division would be reserved for boy clerks to compete for at the age of 19. Those who failed to win these places would be discharged. This seems a harsh prescription, but the Commission hoped that the need for these boys would be temporary, as they believed that, in a few years, presses would be used for all copying and they recommended that the rest of the work should in any case be carried out by the lower division.

37. Although the Commission supported promotion by merit at the highest levels of the Service, and said that administrative or staff officers should be promoted solely on this basis, and not on seniority, they were also anxious to ensure that, below these levels, promotion between grades should be possible but exceptional. They proposed that promotions between grades should receive

[1] C. 1113 p. 15.
[2] C. 1113 p. 14.

approval from the Head of the Department, the Treasury and the Civil Service Commissioners. They saw the higher division as requiring qualifications of a different order from those necessary in the lower division and they also believed that " the work in the inferior grades will rarely be calculated to develop superior capacity ".

38. So far as entry to the higher division was concerned, the Commission said that " The variety and range of duties in this Division of the Civil Service (after those committed to the Lower Division are eliminated) are so great that no one examination will by itself adequately test the various capacities required ".[1] The Commission therefore proposed a flexible scheme of recruitment under which a preliminary qualifying examination would be open to all men above the age of 17 years. Those successful would take a further competitive examination of a character to suit young men " adequately trained at Public School, good Private School or University and aged between 18–23 years " and those successful would form a panel of persons eligible for appointment but having no claim to a job. Heads of Departments would choose from this panel those candidates who they thought would fit their particular needs and, as a quid pro quo, candidates could refuse such offers if they preferred to wait in the hope of receiving one from a Department they preferred, though if they had not taken a post by the age of 25 their candidacy would lapse.

39. The Commissioners believed that this scheme would not only cater for those entering the ordinary work of the higher division, but also provide candidates for appointments of a professional or technical nature, or, as they put it, " cases in which qualifications are required which are wholly or in part professional or otherwise peculiar and not ordinarily to be acquired in the public service ".

40. Nothing came of this scheme, nor indeed was there any fruit from another of the Commission's suggestions that the lack of co-ordination between Departments should be overcome by strengthening the position of the Treasury. The Commission said that " the position of that Department in relation to other Departments should be made as strong as possible: that it ought to have the means of making itself accurately acquainted with the wants and conditions of other Departments; that it should thus, whilst acquiring their confidence, be able to exercise an efficient and intelligent control ". Again, little came of the recommendation that there should be more transfers between departments. The Commission recommended that liability to transfer should be one of the conditions of service in the Lower Division, and that transfers were also desirable in the early years of service in the Higher Division, though they recognised that there is " a great deal of work in public offices special in its character, and requiring much study and care to master, the performance of which would therefore be seriously embarrassed by frequent transfers ".[2]

41. The Playfair Commission was the first inquiry to consider the position of women in the Civil Service. Women Civil Servants had appeared for the first time when the Post Office took over the staff of the telegraph system, and the Commission thought that women clerks would be useful for the lower levels of clerical

[1] C. 1113 p. 11.
[2] Ibid. p. 19.

work in other Departments as well, especially as they could be obtained for lower wage rates than men.

42. The recommendations of the Playfair Commission were not fully implemented. Gladstone's Government fell before the Commission had finished its work and Sir Stafford Northcote, who was Chancellor of the Exchequer, in its Conservative successor, was unwilling to implement the Report in full. The only reforms that stemmed from the Commission's work were those set out in an Order in Council of 1876. This Order led to the creation of the lower division of the Civil Service. Recruitment was to be by open competition for boys between 15 and 17 and for men between the ages of 17 and 20, and they were liable to serve in or be transferred to any Department. None of the boys who were recruited were to be retained after the age of 19 but they were to be allowed to compete for a small number of permanent places. Two rates of pay were proposed. For officers working six hours a day, the scale was £80 per year rising by triennial £15 increments to £200; for officers working seven hours a day, £90 rising in similar increments to £250. Extra pay for special duties not exceeding £100 a year was also introduced. Beneath this lower division, provision was made for the employment of men or boy writers for copying, preferably at piece-rates. The Order in Council endorsed the Commission's proposal that there should be limited opportunities for promotion from the Lower Division, though it was stipulated that no-one should be promoted without ten years' Service.

43. The principal result of the Playfair Commission, therefore, was the creation of the first truly Service-wide grade, the lower division. This was the effective start of the abolition of the rigid departmentalism that had been condemmed by Northcote and Trevelyan. It is therefore significant that the Commission which brought it about was mainly composed of Heads of Departments.

V. The Royal Commission on Civil Establishments 1886–1890

44. The inauguration of a Service-wide lower division led to the growth of a corporate spirit among its members. Social and athletic clubs were founded and the Civil Service Supply Association, which began in the Post Office, extended its services to Civil Servants in other Departments. Staff Associations began to press more strongly for improvements in pay and conditions and, in 1887, the lower division clerks organised a protest meeting and were able to persuade 200 Members of Parliament to attend.

45. This kind of activity caused senior officials a good deal of surprise and annoyance. In evidence to the Royal Commission of 1886–90, for example, the Permanent Secretary to the Treasury, Sir Reginald Welby, even proposed splitting the Lower Division so as to weaken its Staff Association. The particular grievance of the lower division was that, in spite of the changes that had been made in the Civil Service organisation, there were still a number of men in the higher division doing work appropriate to the lower division. The lower division naturally resented this, and they also believed that it reduced their scope for promotion to the higher division. Another problem arose from the fact that the copyists, the need for whom the Playfair Commission had expected to disappear as the copying-press was introduced, still continued to be employed in substantial

numbers. In 1887, there were still over 1,200 of them, a third of them being employed on work of higher quality than copying. The copyists were naturally discontented and sent complaints to the Treasury who appointed a Committee of Inquiry "to consider the Memorial of the Civil Service Copyists". This reported in 1877[1] and recommended that the copyists should either be abolished or completely reorganised. In the meantime, no further copyists were to be recruited.

46. In addition to the problems connected with the Lower Division and the copyists, the Civil Service faced other difficulties at this time. The Playfair Commission had recommended that the scale of pay for the higher division should be £100 to £400 a year with opportunities for extra or duty pay from between £50 to £200 per annum. This scale had not been universally adopted as the Treasury and certain other departments continued to appoint officers at salaries beginning at over £200 a year and rising as high as £1,200. The Treasury favoured the introduction of the Upper Division as recommended by the Playfair Commission into other Departments, although they had rejected it for themselves.

47. For all these reasons, and particularly to deal with the agitation from the Lower Division for greater opportunities for promotion, the Government appointed the first Royal Commission on the Civil Service, under the Chairmanship of Sir Matthew White Ridley[2], to enquire into the civil establishments of the different offices of State. Meanwhile the Government decided that no promotions should be made from the lower to the higher division until 1890, thus giving time for the Commission to report.

48. The Commission issued four reports,[3] three of which dealt with particular Departments; the first with the War Office and Admiralty, the third with the question whether the Customs and Inland Revenue should be amalgamated, and the fourth with the Foreign Office and Diplomatic Services. The second report dealt with general questions.

49. In this report, published in 1888, the Committee once again underlined the importance of the division of labour in the Service and the need to determine which work required capacities of a high order and which could be done by those with lesser attainments. They found that, in spite of the strictures of previous Commissions and Committees, the Civil Service was not organised properly and that a large number of men in the higher division were doing work that could be done properly by lower division Officers. They said that the line between the higher and lower Divisions was drawn too low, and they recommended that the upper Division should consists of three grades with the following pay scales: £200 to £500, £600 to £800 and £800 to £1,000. They also recommended that Duty Pay should be abolished.

50. They recommended that recruitment to the upper division should be by open competitive examination and, on the subject of the examination, they said

---

[1] Parliamentary Papers 1887, lxvi.

[2] Sir Matthew White Ridley, fifth baronet and first Viscount Ridley (1842–1904) was a Conservative M.P. from 1868 to 1885 and from 1886 to 1900. He was Home Secretary from 1895 to 1900. He was a Northumberland landowner and had extensive interests in the North East, including the chairmanship of the North Eastern railway from 1902.

[3] C. 5226 of 1887, C. 5545 of 1888, C. 5748 of 1889, C. 6172 of 1890.

" We are disposed to doubt whether undue weight is not now given in the examination for the Upper Division, to extensive information, as distinguished from accurate knowledge, and we suggest that the subjects for examination should be grouped in some such manner as they are in the Final Schools at the Universities, and that no candidate should be admitted to more than two groups at most ".[1] This was clearly a criticism of an examination system under which people could acquire a smattering of a large number of subjects and attain a respectable total of marks distributed over a wide variety of subjects.

51. The Commission concluded that the present higher division was too large, and they said that there were a number of offices in which it would not be necessary to employ such officers at all; " The Upper Division, however, should be very much smaller than at present, and in some offices need not exist at all." [2] Those joning the upper division should be under strict probation for two years and any who showed that they had no capacity for the work should be discharged. " This condition is absolutely necessary in order to guard the Public Service against the introduction of men who have no other aptitude than that of being able to succeed in a literary examination ".[3]

52. The Committee condemned the practice of the Treasury and some other Departments of appointing upper division clerks at higher salaries than those obtaining in other Departments. They recommended that the scales for the upper division should be the same throughout the Civil Service, and that the higher salaries in the Treasury and the Departments of the Secretaries of State should be reduced for those newly appointed to such departments.

53. As for the lower division, the Committee approved the existing regulations about age and examinations although they suggested the addition of shorthand and a foreign language as optional subjects. They recommended an initial salary of £70 per annum rising eventually to £350 with efficiency bars at £100 and £190. Duty pay should be abolished for this division also. Promotion from the lower division to the upper division should be available to those of exceptional merit.

54. The Committee devoted their main attention to the higher and lower divisions, and the division of work between them. They did not pay a great deal of attention to appointments to technical posts, but said that there was a need for certain special appointments requiring professional or technical knowledge which cannot be satisfactorily filled by open competition; " they recommended that these should be scheduled, with age limits quoted for each appointment.

55. On the vexed question of copying, the Committee proposed that such work that could not be done by mechanical means should be done by Junior Clerks in the Second division and by boys between the ages of 15 and 19. Such boys were to be able to compete for a larger number of places in the second division than before, but those who were unsuccessful were to be discharged.

56. The Committee also accepted and supported the idea of Treasury control over Civil establishments. It proposals on this matter are worth quoting at length.

---

[1] C. 5545 para. 55.
[2] Ibid. para. 53.
[3] Ibid. para. 57.

CONTROL OVER CIVIL ESTABLISHMENTS

15. This brings us to a consideration of the question as to what should be the authority which should directly control the Establishments of the Civil Service. At present, no increase either in the numbers of clerks in an office, or in the scale of any salary, can be made without the consent of the Treasury. If any such unauthorised increase were attempted, the Comptroller and Auditor-General, who is furnished with all the authorised scales, would call attention to the first payment made in excess, the Treasury would be in a position to direct the Paymaster-General to make no further payment of the kind, and the Comptroller and Auditor-General would disallow the payment already made. So far the Treasury control is sufficient, and occasion rarely arises to put it in force, because the Departments now hardly ever neglect to observe the rule of coming to the Treasury to sanction proposed changes before they are made. If the changes proposed are of an extensive character, the common course is, for the Treasury to nominate one of its own principal officers, with a principal officer of the Department concerned, and perhaps a third independent and experienced officer, to form a Committee of Inquiry, and to report to the Treasury. No doubt, a good deal of friction is apt to arise before a decision is arrived at, and it will be seen that, in this process, no initiative rests with the Treasury, but that its decision is confined to each individual case as it arises.

16. With a view of improving this state of things, and of bringing the Treasury into more harmonious and efficient relations with the other Government departments, as well as of instituting a more satisfactory control over establishments, we are of opinion that it would be desirable, in the first instance, to embody general regulations for the organization of the Civil Service, in an Order in Council.

17. That every department should then be called upon to formulate its normal establishment in accordance with the general directions of such Order in Council.

18. That the establishments so formulated should be referred to a Permanent Consultative Committee, which we propose should be constituted, and that the best method of effecting gradually the necessary changes should be then determined, and, as far as possible, upon uniform lines.

19. That this Committee should have power to entertain all questions affecting establishments, including pensions, and all proposals for increased expenditure, and that it should also be required to review periodically all offices, with the object of ascertaining whether any reductions can be made in the number of the staff, or other economies effected, its recommendations and proceedings being officially recorded.

20. We think that this Committee should be composed of a principal Treasury officer, and (say) four other permanent officers, one of whom should represent the Civil Service Commission, and another, one of the great Revenue Departments.

21. It might be desirable to change the composition of this Committee periodically, retaining always the representation of the Treasury, the Civil Service Commission, and one of the great Revenue Departments.

22. Such a body would, of course, report to the Treasury, and the final authority would continue to belong to the Government, but we believe that it would be of great value in securing uniformity of regulations, in suggesting reforms, in facilitating transfers, and, not least, in bringing about harmonious action between the Treasury and the other departments.

23. Some demands would, no doubt, and especially in the first instance, be made upon the time of the permanent officers appointed to such a Committee, but we are persuaded that the requisite time will be cheerfully given, and we attach great importance to the co-operation and mutual knowledge which we believe would by this means be brought about.

24. We reject the idea of constituting a special separate body for this purpose, in the first place because we are reluctant to make any recommendations that are likely to lead to an increase in the number of public officers, and secondly because we are of opinion that it would be difficult to find permanent adequate employment for such a separate body, whilst it is obvious that a step of this nature would have no tendency to encourage departmental co-operation. Our object is to carry the heads of departments along with the Treasury in determining, and regulating their respective staffs, and not to subject them to a fresh and independent authority.

57. On the question of transfers between Departments, the Committee recommended that all those entering the Civil Service should have the liability

to work in other Departments besides the one to which they were first assigned, and they said that experience in more than one Department was valuable, especially in the early years of service. At the same time, they recognised the difficulties of transferring officers from one department to another, especially at a time when reorganisation was rendering many officers redundant.

58. The Committee also proposed that the names upper and lower divisions should be superseded by the names first and second division.

59. Another point dealt with by the Committe was the conduct of Civil Servants. In the nineteenth century it was not uncommon for Civil Servants to interest themselves directly in commercial concerns. In 1882, for example, the name of the Comptroller of the National Debt appeared in advertisements in connection with an issue of bonds for a business venture in Texas. Although a number of attempts had been made to restrict such activities, they had not been completely successful and the Royal Commission advocated a firm rule that Civil Servants should not take part in any way in the management of commercial concerns other than these exclusively concerned with the welfare of the Civil Servants. This recommendation was not accepted at the time, but in the long run it was adopted.

60. The main action taken on the Ridley Report[1] was embodied in two Orders in Council, dated 21st March 1890 and 15th August 1890. The first Order dealt with the second division, which was the new name given to the lower division in accordance with the Commission's recommendation. The Second Order dealt with the higher division plus all other officers of a rank superior to those of the second division.

There was thus no order dealing with the higher division as such.

61. So far as the second division was concerned, the Order divided it into lower and higher grades, the first with an upper salary of £250 per annum and the second, to be filled by those promoted from below, with an upper salary of £350. The two Orders of Council also generally accepted the Commission's recommendations for the regulation and control of the Civil Service. They prescribed a 7-hour day throughout the Service and laid down general rules for sick-leave, annual-leave and Bank Holidays. Duty pay was abolished, and rules were made for periods of probation. So far as the higher division was concerned, the Government accepted the reorganisation of the examination but did not accept the proposals for re-organising the higher division into three grades, or for renaming it the first division. Again, they did not specify that each Department should have the same salary scales for its higher division clerks, and this was not finally achieved until 1919. No action was taken immediately to reduce the numbers in the higher division, although an Order in Council of 1898 enjoined a reduction in its size and prescribed that no work suitable for the second division should be allocated to the higher division. The Consultative Committee that the Committee had proposed was set up but had no success. Finally, no action was taken to deal with the problem of transferability.

62. In the later 1890's, and early part of the twentieth century, further Orders were made for the organisation of the Civil Service and finally, in June 1910,

---

[1] See "Papers showing the manner in which the Recommendations of the Royal Commission with the respect to the Civil Service have been dealt with". P.P. 1893–94 lxxi.

an amending and consolidating Order in Council was made which repealed all Orders then in force and became, in effect, a Civil Service code of regulations.

VI. The Royal Commission on the Civil Service 1912–1915

63. The next investigation of the Civil Service was the Royal Commission of 1912–1915, under the Chairmanship of Lord MacDonnell.[1] This Commission made a very detailed investigation of its subject and its Reports,[2] its Minutes of Evidence and the papers submitted to it, constitute a most interesting review of the Civil Service and of the opinions of those at the Universities and of other authoritative people on its working. Nearly all the questions with which the present Committee is concerned are dealt with by the MacDonnell Report in one way and another. Indeed, the Committee's papers are a rich source of information not only about the Civil Service but also on many aspects of British society at the turn of the century.

64. The Terms of Reference of the Commission were:

"To inquire into and report on the methods of making appointments to and promotions in the Civil Service, including the Diplomatic and Consular Services and the Legal Departments; to investigate the working and efficiency of the system of competitive examinations for such appointments, and to make recommendations for any alterations or improvements in that system which may appear to be advisable; and to consider whether the existing scheme of organisation meets the requirements of the Public Service, and to suggest any modifications which may be needed therein."

65. The Commission decided not to deal with what would now be called industrial Civil Servants, such as those employed in the Dockyards, at Woolwich Arsenal and other manufacturing establishments, and they also omitted any consideration of the General Post Office as a Select Committee of the House of Commons was enquiring into conditions of employment in that Department at the same time. They also excluded from their examination Departments not maintained by the Exchequer, such as the India Office, and the Ecclesiastical Commission. The total number of persons with whose employment they were concerned was therefore about 60,000, employed in some 80 Departments or sub Departments of State.

66. The Commission issued a general invitation to the public and, in particular, to serving or retired Civil Servants, to submit any evidence that they wished to put forward. They also received witnesses or written evidence from the various Staff Associations, from all the Universities of the United Kingdom, and from a number of industrial and commercial undertakings including the Bank of England, the Alliance Insurance Company, some of the Railway Companies and Messrs. Cadbury's. They also compiled information about the organisation of the government and civil services in the self-governing Dominions and some foreign countries.

---

[1] Antony Patrick MacDonnell, Baron Macdonnell of Swinford (1844–1925). Indian Civil Servant; Lieutenant Governor of the United Provinces from 1895–1901; Permanent Under Secretary at Dublin Castle from 1902–1908.

[2] Cds. 6209, 6534, 6739, 7338, 7748, 7832.

67. The Commission's main report was their Fourth Report, which was published in 1914.[1] There was published at the same time a minority report, some details of which will be given later in this essay. The majority report began with a historical survey of the Civil Service from 1853 to 1912. It then described the methods of appointment to the Civil Service. The first was Open Competitive Examination and the Commission were able to say that this method was used to recruit about 20,000 of the 60,000 appointments with which they were concerned. The second method of entry was the Limited Competition, but here the Commission noted that this was no longer a method of testing the competence of personal nominees but related to competitions for which candidates were required to possess certain qualifications. They were therefore really Open Competitions and the Commission recommended they should be so called.

68. The third method of appointment was nomination followed by qualifying examination. This method was used for about 8,500 of the lower posts, such as Prison Warders, Office Keepers and Messengers. The fourth method was direct appointment by the Crown; there were about 250 posts to which appointment was made by this method including the Permanent Heads of Departments, the Inspectors of Schools and some of the more important Constabulary Officers.

69. The next two methods of appointment were under Clause 7 of the Order in Council of 1910 and Section IV of the Superannuation Act of 1859 which provided for the appointment of officers whose qualifications were " wholly or in part professional or otherwise peculiar and not ordinarily to be acquired in the Civil Service ".[2] Many posts were recruited in this way, requiring knowledge of a specialist or technical nature such as law, medicine, engineering, architecture, surveying or natural science.

70. Finally, some 25,000 officers, mainly temporary, were recruited under Schedule B of the Order in Council of 1910, under which it was possible to make appointments without applying the ordinary rules for competition.

71. Having described the various methods by which the Civil Service was recruited, the Commission went on to classify the various types of officials. Leaving aside those employed on manual or mechanical work and those engaged on a temporary basis, the Commission distinguished three groups of officials; the clerical classes, the executive or departmental, and the professional and technical.

72. The clerical classes were six in number. The first consisted of the Secretaries, Assistant Secretaries, Heads and Sub-Heads of Divisions; in short all non-professional posts carrying a salary of £600 a year or more. They were recruited almost exclusively from the first division. The second class, or the first division, was a small class recruited by the examination at university level from candidates between the ages of 22 and 24. The third class was designated the intermediate class, by which was meant officers recruited by the Intermediate Examination. This class was a relatively new development at the time of the MacDonnell Report, and it was designed to recruit to posts for which the qualifications of the first division were too high and those for the second division too low. It was divided into three grades and its salaries ran from £100–£700. The fourth class was the second division, recruited by competitive examination, open to candidates

[1] Cd. 7338 of 1914.
[2] Clause 7 of the Order in Council, using language modelled on that of Section IV of the Act.

between the ages of 17 and 20 and offering salaries from £70–£300 and, on promotion, to £700. The Commission noted that during the 20 years from 1892 to 1911, the the total number of promotions from the second to the first division had been 73, which gave an average of 3·65 per annum. The next class was the assistant clerks—which numbered over 3,000. These were recruited from boy clerks and their salary rose from £45 per annum to £150, with supervisory posts at a salary of £220 per annum and a possibility of promotion to the Second Division. The final class was the Boy Clerks, of which there were some 2,500 employed. They entered by a simple examination between the ages of 15 and 16 and were discharged at the age of 18 unless they had succeeded in obtaining a place by open competition as an assistant clerk or in some other capacity. In addition to these classes, the Commission also drew attention to the Permanent Heads of the major Departments, most of whom came from the class of Secretaries and held their appointments directly from the Crown.

73. The second group of classes were the departmental or executive by which the Commission meant those officers recruited specifically for service in a given department, such as the officers of Customs and Excise. Finally, the Commission distinguished the professional and technical Civil Service (including inspectorates), by which they meant the officers who were members of the specialist professions, such as law, medicine, engineering or teaching, and who were usually recruited at a more mature age than the clerical staff.

74. After describing the structure of the Service, the Commission formulated its recommendations. Their principle theme was that the organisation of the Service should be based on the division of labour. As they said " This principle had been laid down by every important Commission or Committee which has inquired into the subject and we desire to reaffirm its soundness at the outset of our recommendations. With the lapse of time the principle has become not less, but, if possible, more cogent, because the importance of the Civil Service has increased in recent years in a manner which calls for special remark ".[1] The point to which the Commission thus drew attention was the increasing number of Acts of Parliament, often of extreme complexity, which not only imposed upon Departments the responsibility for administering laws on the lines laid down by Parliament but also for interpreting the general principles of legislation and making schemes for their implementation. As the Commission said, " the Civil Service is now being called upon to take a larger share in carrying out the policy of the legislature than has been usual in the past, the burden of administration is certainly heavier now that it has ever been before in the history of this country".[2]

75. To deal with the tasks it had described the MacDonnell Report recommended the setting up of three classes common to the Service in the administrative-clerical sphere:

(*a*) a junior clerical class recruited from boys at about the age of 16;
(*b*) a senior clerical class recruited from boys at about the age of 18;
(*c*) an administrative class recruited in the main from University entrants.

76. On the question of recruitment to the Civil Service the Commission commended " the broad principle of gathering the natural fruits of the educational

[1] Cd. 7338, Chapter III, para. 3.
[2] Ibid. para. 4.

system of the country in its various stages as they mature "[1] and they laid down that examinations should be devised accordingly. The Commission devoted much attention to securing greater co-ordination between the educational system and the Civil Service examination system. Of particular interest, perhaps, was their consideration of the recruitment to their proposed administrative class.

77. The Commission received a good deal of evidence to the effect that the existing examination was unfair because it gave those who had read classics at Oxford and Cambridge a better chance of success than those who had read other subjects or who had read classics at other Universities. To quote from the evidence submitted by the University of London " The result of the present arrangement is that the State is practically deprived of the services of men who have not had a classical, mathematical, or an historical training and there is a comparative neglect of such subjects as Political Science, Law and certain of the natural Sciences—subjects which may be of greater or at least of equal importance to persons about to undertake important administrative duties ".[2]

78. They also received evidence that it would be valuable to bring into the administrative class people who had experience of other walks of life. Professor Vertheimer of Bristol said, " . . . I am not by any means certain that it is altogether wise that these men should be chosen as they are at present, practically immediately after they have left the university and before they have had any outside experience of life. I am inclined to think that it tends somewhat—with respect to the Civil Service, many members of which I know and whose friendship I value—to make a class of " mandarins " who have not had sufficient experience in the outside world; and in some cases I think it leads to a certain amount of want of touch between the public and the high officials of the Civil Service ".[3]

79. The Commission treated this evidence very seriously. They reaffirmed that competitive examinations were the best method of securing candidates " giving the greatest promise of administrative capacity "[4] and that " the best education taken in conjunction with the training and formative influence of University life produces the best type of public servant ".[5] But they were anxious that entrants to the administrative class should not predominantly be students of history, classics and mathematics nor should they come mainly from Oxford and Cambridge. They looked forward to recruits from many disciplines, and from Scottish, Irish, English and Welsh Universities. They said that the predominance of Oxford and Cambridge might well be due to the fact that many of the ablest boys from Elementary Schools were attracted to these rather than other Universities, and pointed out that in a recent Honours List at Cambridge consisting of thirteen names, eight were those of men who had received their first education at public elementary schools. This was " a striking illustration of the fact that the candidates from Oxford and Cambridge include young men brought up under a great variety of educational and social conditions ".[6] They also thought that the predominance of Oxford and Cambridge was the result of the tradition of entering

---

[1] Cd. 7338, Chapter III, para. 6.
[2] Parliamentary Papers, 1914, XVI, p. 983.
[3] Ibid. p. 476.
[4] Cd. 7338, Chapter III, para. 42.
[5] Ibid.
[6] Ibid. para. 48.

the public service which existed in these Universities. Scottish Universities, on the other hand, showed a distinct preference for the professions of medicine, teaching and the Ministry. In the other English Universities, there was a greater emphasis on the study of professional subjects and of applied science, and the Commission looked forward to the time when more people with knowledge of these subjects would enter the Civil Service.

80. On the particular assertion that the examinations for the administrative class were biased against those who had not read classics at the older Universities, the Commission recommended that this matter should be immediately investigated by a special Committee and the Government should adjust the examination if they found the charge to be justified.

81. The Commission seemed to regard professional and technical Civil Servants as outside the main stream of Departmental work, and their recommendations concentrated on conditions of entry. They suggested that where competitive examinations were impracticable by reason of the standing of the candidates or their age, then the procedure to be followed should provide for the public notification of vacancies, the submission of all applications to a Departmental Committee on which the Civil Service Commissioners should be represented, and a final choice to be made in such a way as to make it clear that the best man had been chosen for the job, and that the persons with special connections or inside knowledge had received no undue preference.

82. The Commission's report had a section on the comparison of Civil Service procedure with business methods.[1] They noted that there were wide differences between the work of the public service and private business, arising from such factors as the detailed and continuous investigation of the Civil Service by Parliament, the need to deal fairly with all persons having dealings with the Government, and the higher level of working expenses that arose because " It is an accepted principle with all parties that the Government should be a ' model employer '."[2] The Commission recommended that there were certain areas where the Civil Service might adapt some business practices e.g. in the Post Office and the manufacturing establishments of the Admiralty and the War Office. But for the rest they suggested that the most businesslike method of conducting public affairs under the limiting conditions which they had described were:

> " 1. To establish effective control over the Civil Service in order that the activities of all its members may be wisely directed, and fully and economically utilized to the best advantage in the public interests;
>
> 2. To differentiate duties in order that the more highly educated and paid officers may not be employed on duties for which a less highly educated and paid agency will suffice;
>
> 3. To promote officers of exceptional capacity to situations to which higher responsibilities and emoluments are attached."[3]

83. Another subject dealt with by the Commission was Treasury control over the Civil Serivce. They noted from evidence given by senior Treasury officials

---

[1] Cd. 7338, Chapter IX, Part II.
[2] Ibid. para. 87.
[3] Ibid. para. 89.

that the basis of the Treasury's control was financial and that, while the Treasury could seek to persuade other Departments to follow their advice on matters of organisation, there was no means by which the Treasury could compel them to do so. The Commission concluded that the Treasury should be strengthened for the purpose of establishing a more effective control over the organisation of the Civil Service. They recommended that a special section should be set up with the following duties:

"(i) To watch over the general condition and activities of the Civil Service, with a view to its effective and economical employment; and to make of its own initiative all inquiries that may be necessary to that end.

(ii) To bring to the notice of Heads of Departments concerned any matter of importance for them to know, with its recommendations.

(iii) To secure that in each department there shall exist efficient machinery for recognising and rewarding exceptional cases of ability and merit; and to ensure that such cases shall be brought to the notice of other Departments when the interests of the public service require this to be done.

(iv) To secure that in cases where it would be to the advantage of the Service that transfers should be made from one Department to another, such transfers shall take place.

(v) To carry out inquiries and investigations into any matters connected with Departmental administration or methods of working."[1]

This proposed special section is the obvious forerunner of the Treasury's Management Services Division and also of some of the present arguments for the establishment of a Civil Service Department.

84. The Commission also surveyed the organisation of various Departments. One of their most interesting comments was that while opportunities should be provided for promotion from the Second Division it was unreasonable to expect that large numbers of them would merit such advancement. The Commission quoted the experience of the Customs and Excise Department.[2] In 1898 this Department gave up taking recruits from the Class I Examination and decided to fill its higher posts from the best officers in its Second Division and Departmental Staffs. Much of the Departments' work was specialised and it seemed reasonable to suppose that the few men of high quality who were needed could be found among the existing staff. Yet experience showed this was not so, and the Customs and Excise reverted after a dozen years to taking recruits from the Class I Examination.

85. Another subject dealt with by the Commission was the rapid expansion that had to be undertaken to secure staff to implement the Old Age Pension Act, the Labour Exchange Act and the National Insurance Act. When the Labour Exchanges were set up, a new system of recruitment was devised under which applications were invited from persons with relevant experience, and interviews were held to select men for appointments. The qualifications looked for were general administrative capacity; people who could "take charge and responsibility, who could control a staff, and who had initiative".[3] Interviewing at the

---

[1] Cd. 7338, Chapter IX, para. 101.
[2] Cd. 7338, Chapter III, para. 43.
[3] Ibid. Chapter IX, para. 57.

final stages was done by the Permanent Secretary of the Board of Trade and final selections were made by the President himself.

86. The Commission recognised that there was a good case for the staff engaged on these duties to have a knowledge of work people and their conditions, and of the industrial conditions in their localities. But they thought that some suitable managers might be taken from existing departmental staffs and that "tried service and knowledge of official procedure should have been a recommendation for appointment to this new staff".[1] In short, they were anxious that the qualifications of existing Civil Servants should not be overlooked when setting up new departments and undertaking new types of work, though they fully accepted that some new staff with specialised or professional knowledge might be required as well.

87. Pressure for greater opportunities for women was strong at the time the Commission was sitting and they inevitably paid a good deal of attention to the subject of the employment of women. They argued in favour of maintaining the rule that established service should terminate on marriage. They also said that where women's work approximated to that of men, then they should have the same pay. But where the efficiency of men was higher then their salaries should be higher also. They recommended that the Treasury should hold an inquiry to determine which positions could be filled by women and what salaries they should receive.

88. The Commission noted that increasing numbers of women typists were being employed. They thought this practice should be extended; it was, of course, the final solution to the problem of finding the right kind of staff for copying documents which had so exercised previous inquiries. The Commission proposed that the female typists should be recruited by tests both of education and of manipulative skill. They should have the opportunity of promotion to shorthand writer typist and, for the very best of them, promotion should be allowed to the clerical class.

89. In addition to the majority report there was a minority report and a number of other reservations. The minority report differed from the majority in the number of classes proposed for the lower members of the Civil Service. The majority report had proposed the replacement of the four existing classes of Boy Clerks, Assistant Clerks, Second Division Clerks and Intermediate Clerks by a Junior Clerical Class recruited from boys of 16 and a Senior Clerical Class recruited at 18. The Junior Class would take the place of the Boy Clerks and the Assistant Clerks and would be recruited from boys with an abridged secondary education. The Senior Class would take the place of the Second Division and Intermediate Clerks and would be recruited from those who had completed a full secondary education. The minority report proposed instead that the second grade clerks should take the place of the Boy, Assistant and Second Division Clerks and that the first grade clerks should be much the same as the Intermediate Clerks. The main reason for the difference was that the minority report argued that the work of the existing three lower classes was much the same and that could all be brought within the same class.

---

[1] Ibid. para. 58.

90. Some of the other points brought out in notes of reservation are worth mentioning. First, there was a reservation, signed among others by Philip Snowden and Graham Wallas, about the administrative class. Its signatories said that they agreed with the majority report that this class should continue to be relatively small. Nevertheless, they believed that there were a fair number of officers recruited in other ways than the Class I Examination whose work was closely associated with the work of the administrative class. They gave as instances the District Auditors in the Local Government Board and the Director of the Census of the Production of the Board of Trade. The signatories said that " We believe that if the term ' Administrative Class ' were used as a description of the work done by the members of the class, instead of as a ' nomenclature . . . based on the normal method of recruiting ' that class, a considerable proportion of these important and highly paid officials would be classed as ' administrative ' and that the rest could be classed as ' professional ' in the sense in which that term is used in Clause 7 of the Order of the Council, and we are of the opinion that such a classification should be made ".[1] In short, all who carried out work of an administrative nature should be deemed members of the administrative class. They did not, however, propose that all the professional and technical staff should be grouped in this administrative class, but only that proportion of them whose work was closely allied to that of the administrative class.

91. Another reservation related to the employment of women. A group of Commission members said that it was unfair to draw inferences about the relative efficiency of the two sexes by comparing the work of existing women clerks and of existing male clerks.[2] Under the existing conditions of work, the male clerks deserved the high salary in terms of the Commission's principle. But if the women's conditions of work were improved, then their productivity would increase and they would be justified in receiving a greater salary.

VII. Developments from 1915–1929

92. The outbreak of the First World War prevented any action being taken on the MacDonnell Report. The War led to immense changes in the Civil Service; its numbers doubled and the number of Departments substantially increased. Another change was in the type of work it had to undertake. It has already been noted that the administration of the Acts of Parliament, the staple work of the Civil Service of the nineteenth Century, had been supplemented by work arising from the measures relating to social welfare and national insurance. But during the First World War the Service had to involve itself even more deeply in the activities of the country, as it had to assume responsibility for the disposition of the nation's economic resources and for ensuring that the Government's plans for the use of manpower and the production of war material were carried out as effectively as possible. This entailed close dealings with the private sector of the economy, and large numbers of people with commercial and industrial experience were brought into the Civil Service, usually on a temporary basis, to help with these tasks.

---

[1] Cd. 7338, 1st Reservation.
[2] Cd. 7338, 6th Reservation.

93. At the end of the war the Civil Service was faced with the task of retrenchment, not to the pre war position but to a smaller size and lesser power than it had exercised in the war. It was also necessary to deal urgently with a number of problems arising from the war.

94. One of the first enquiries to deal with these problems was that of the Committee on Staffs, whose Chairman was Sir John Bradbury.[1] The Committee issued a number of reports, the most important of which were a first interim report in 1918[2] and a final report the following year.[3] The interim report recommended that, save in exceptional cases, the recruitment of clerks and typists for all London departments should be centralised in the Civil Service Commission. The final report proposed that Departmental Establishment Officers should be appointed at a senior rank and with direct responsibility to the Permanent Head of the Department. A special Establishment Division should be set up at the Treasury to maintain close relations with the Establishment Officers of the various department, to acquire full knowledge of their office methods, and to act as a clearing house for information on all staff questions. A standing Committee of Establishment Officers should be established to assist and advise the Treasury. These recommendations were accepted. Establishment Officers were introduced, a special Establishment Division was set up at the Treasury, and a standing Committee of Establishment Officers came into existence in 1919. The Committee also recommended that full Treasury control over the staffing of the public service should be resumed following the break in application of this principle during the First World War. This too was accepted. Again, a recommendation was accepted that a special inquiry should be set in hand to standardize registry and accounting processes, and a more systematic effort should be made to extend the Service's knowledge of labour saving machinery. The Treasury investigation section was set up in 1919 to do this.

95. These reports show a desire to re-establish Treasury control over the Civil Service and to put recruiting on more orthodox lines than had been possible during the war. Similar support for the strengthening of Treasury control came from the Haldane Committee on the Machinery of Government which reported in 1918[4]. And further important measures were taken under the direction of Sir Warren Fisher, who was appointed Permanent Secretary to the Treasury in 1919. In September 1919, at the time of Fisher's appointment, it was laid down in a Treasury minute and circular that the Permanent Secretary to the Treasury should be the Permanent Head of the Civil Service and advise the Prime Minister on Civil Service appointments and decorations. And in 1920 another Treasury circular said that the Prime Minister's consent was necessary for the appointment or removal of Permanent Secretaries, Deputy Secretaries, Principal Establishment Officers and Principal Finance Officers. By this combination of measures the Treasury succeeded in establishing a formal control over senior appointments throughout the Civil Service. However, it has been argued that Fisher's object in making these changes was to promote the unity of the Civil Service rather than the domination of the Treasury.[5]

---

[1] Later Lord Bradbury; 1872–1950. Joint Permanent Secretary to the Treasury 1913–1919.
[2] Cd. 9074 of 1918.
[3] Cmd. 62 of 1919.
[4] Cmd. 9230 of 1918.
[5] Lord Bridges " The Treasury " 1964, pp. 169–179.

96. Another Committee to be set up was on Recruitment to the Civil Service after the War, under the Chairmanship of Lord Gladstone.[1] This was set up by a Treasury minute on January 2nd, 1918, and issued a series of reports.[2] The interim reports were mainly concerned with the problems of recruiting ex-Servicemen into the Civil Service on special terms but the final report dealt with the organisation of the clerical classes, and with the employment of women. It is not necessary to go into these recommendations in detail because they were very largely overtaken by events. Immediately after the issue of the final report, for example, the War Cabinet Committee on Women in Industry, under the Chairmanship of Lord Justice Atkin, presented its report and this made several recommendations about the employment of women in the Civil Service. And in October 1919 the National Whitley Council Committee, the so called Re-organisation Committee, was appointed. Its terms of reference included the organisation and duties of the clerical classes and its report also contained a section on the recruitment and status of women in the Civil Service. The action that was taken on this report led to the acceptance of many of the recommendations of the Gladstone Committee.

97. It is interesting to note that the Re-organisation Committee was a Committee of the new Civil Service National Whitley Council and consisted of representatives of both Official and Staff interests. It thus represented a new form of reviewing Committee, and was certainly the first time that members specifically representing the staff were appointed to such a body. The Committee did not undertake a great deal of research of their own, but drew on their own working knowledge and on the fairly recent work of the MacDonnell Committee and that of the Committees under Sir John Bradbury and Lord Gladstone.

98. In their interim (and main) report, dated 17th February 1920, the Committee set out the main principle which they believed to apply to Civil Service work. " The administrative and clerical work of the Civil Service may be said, broadly, to fall into two main categories. In one category may be placed all such work as either of a simple mechanical kind or consists in the application of well defined regulations, decisions and practice to particular cases; in the other category, the work which is concerned with the formation of policy, with the revision of existing practice or current regulations and decisions, and with the organisation and direction of the business of Government ".[3]

99. The Committee concluded that in order to undertake these two kinds of work the Civil Service would have to be divided into four classes:

a. A writing assistant class for simple mechanical work;
b. A clerical class for the better sort of work included in the first category;

---

[1] Herbert Gladstone, 1st Viscount, 1854–1930. Son of Rt. Hon. W. E. Gladstone, Secretary for Home Affairs, 1905–1910.

[2] Cmd. 34 of 1918.
Cmd. 35 of 1918.
Cmd. 36 of 1918.
Cmd. 164 of 1919.

[3] Civil Service National Whitley Council. Report of the Joint Committee on the Organisation of the Civil Service (H.M.S.O.) 1920 para. 16. The Committee's final report was published by HMSO in 1921. The Chairman of the Committee was Sir Malcom Ramsay, Controller of Establishments in the Treasury at the time, and later Comptroller and Auditor-General. The Vice-Chairman, and chief representative of the staff side, was G. H. Stuart-Bunning.

c. An executive class and
d. An adminstrative class, both of which should be for the work in the second main category.

100. In addition to these four classes the Committee also recommended that two other classes should be formed; Shorthand Typists and Typists.

101. So far as the work and recruitment of these classes were concerned, the Committee recommended that the writing assistants should be employed on duties of a very simple kind, such as handwriting and transcribing work, and it was recommended that they should be recruited by open competitive examination, with age limits of 16–17. The class should not be recruited on a national basis and the regulations should be framed so as to secure for this work people resident within the locality where they would be employed. Members of the class should be established, and there should be machinery for promoting writing assistants to the clerical class. The clerical class should be recruited by open competitive examination with age limits of 16–17 for boys, and 16½ and 17½ for girls. The syllabus should be framed with reference to the standard at the end of the intermediate stage of the secondary school course. The clerical class should be employed on simple duties, such as dealing with particular cases in accordance with well defined regulations, preparation of material for returns, accounts and statistics, simple drafting and precis work and supervising the Writing Assistants.

102. The work assigned to the executive classes has been described by the Treasury in the following terms:

> " To the executive class the Reorganisation Committee assigned the higher work of supply and accounting Departments, and of other executive or specialised branches of the Civil Service. The Committee considered that this work covered a wide field and required in different degrees qualties of judgment, initiative and resource. In the junior ranks it comprised the critical examination of particular cases of lesser importance not clearly within the scope of approved regulations or general decisions, initial investigations into matters of higher importance, and the immediate direction of small blocks of business. In its upper ranges it was concerned with matters of internal organisation and control, with the settlement of broad questions arising out of business in hand or in contemplation and with the responsible conduct of important operations. For these jobs the Committee considered that, in so far as it might be desirable to appoint men from outside the Service, recruitment should be by open, competitive, written examination between the ages of 18 and 19. The Committee considered that the duties appropriate to the administrative class were those concerned with the formation of policy, with the co-ordination and improvement of Government machinery and with the general administration and control of the Departments of the Public Service. Members of the class should be recruited by means of an open, competitive examination in the subjects embraced by the various honours courses of university institutions at the university leaving age and from persons already employed in the Service."[1]

103. The Committee thought that duties appropriate to the administrative class were those concerned with the formation of policy, with the co-ordination and improvement of Government machinery and with the general administration and control of the Departments of the public service. For the effective performance of these duties, officers of the highest standard of qualification were needed; and the Committee proposed that such officers be obtained partly by selection from within the Service and partly by recruitment from outside the Service.

---

[1] H.M. Treasury, Introductory Factual Memorandum on the Civil Service prepared for the Committee on the Civil Service, Vol. 4, Memorandum No. 1, p. 16,

104. The report of the Committee was accepted by the National Whitley Council and, in April 1920, Departments were invited to prepare schemes on the lines laid down in the report. The organisation proposed by the Committee still forms the basis of Civil Service organisation today. Indeed, it is remarkable that a scheme of organisation which has been in operation for approaching half a century should have been worked out largely by the Civil Service itself. Though whether the community's interests were best served by so interested a reviewing body is a point of legitimate argument.

VIII. The Royal Commission on the Civil Service 1929–1931

105. The next full examination of the Civil Service was conducted by the Royal Commission under Lord Tomlin[1] from 1929–1931. This Royal Commission saw their main task as to take stock of the structure introduced as a result of the re-commendations of the Re-organisation Committee. Their terms of reference required them to enquire and report on:

a. The structure and organisation of the Civil Service including methods of recruitment:

b. Conditions of service in the Civil Service with particular reference to:
   (i) the general standard of remuneration of Civil Servants and the existing differentiation between the scales of remuneraion payable respectively to men and women;
   (ii) the machinery for the discussion and settlement of questions relating to conditions of service; and
   (iii) the position of ex-Service Civil Servants in unestablished employment.

c. Conditions of retirement from the Civil Service, including the retirement of women Civil Servants on marriage.[2]

106. It will be convenient to discuss the recommendations of the Tomlin Commission under a number of headings. First, recruitment. The Commission re-affirmed the principle of open competition and stated that it would " be impracticable and undesirable to introduce any other method ".[3] The Commissioners did not take a particular view on the question which had interested the MacDonnell Commission, as to whether the examinations for the administrative class provided fair opportunities for graduates from all universities to compete. The Commissioners felt this was a matter for the Civil Service Commissioners to look into, and they thought they should keep in close touch with educational bodies throughout the country. On the problem of opening more avenues for graduates to the Service and on the recruitment of graduates generally, the Commission pointed out that there were opportunities for graduates to join the Departmental classes as well as the Administrative.

107. The Commission suggested a number of changes in the age limits for the various competitions. They believed that, generally speaking, written examinations were unsuitable for recruitment to the professional and technical staffs.

---

[1] Thomas James Cheshyre Tomlin, Baron Tomlin of Ash (1867–1935), Lord of Appeal in Ordinary from 1929 to 1935.
[2] Cmd. 3909 of 1931.
[3] Ibid. para. 240.

They also considered the use of the interview which had been introduced as a supplement to written papers for the administrative class examination. It was suggested in evidence that the interview might diminish the objectivity of the selection process by allowing the personal preferences of class bias of the examiners to affect the outcome. The Royal Commission did not agree with this view.[1] They recommended that the interview should be retained, but suggested that particular care should be exercised in the selection of interviewers.

108. Generally speaking, therefore, the Commission were satisfied with existing methods of recruitment. They proposed a number of marginal adjustments, but showed no particular concern with such questions as whether the general classes should recruit people with a knowledge of the subject matter of the problems with which they would have to deal or whether entrants to the Service were coming from too narrow a section of the community.

109. On the question of promotion, the Commissioners approved the recently instituted practise of making annual reports on the work of all officers receiving a salary of £700 or more. They reaffirmed the principle that merit should be the basis of all promotion in the Service. They also received evidence from official witnesses in support of the procedure introduced in 1920 under which the Prime Minister was required to give his consent to the appointment of Permanent Heads of Departments, their deputies, Principal Finance Officers, and Principal Establishment Officers. These appointments were made on the recommendation of the Permanent Secretary to the Treasury, following consultation with the Minister of the Department concerned.

110. The Commission also considered the arrangements which had been introduced in the Treasury for the control and co-ordination of other departments. They noted the creation of the Establishments Department of the Treasury in 1919, and received evidence about work of the departmental Establishment Officers and the Standing Committee of Establishment Officers in controlling and improving office organisation and dealing with questions of personnel management. They also heard evidence as to whether the Treasury control was too tightly exercised. As might be expected, the evidence was divided and the Permanent Secretary of the Treasury, Sir Warren Fisher, said that there was some truth in the accusation that the Treasury tried to control other departments in too much detail. He was anxious that this should not happen, and he explained some of the steps that he had taken to try to prevent it, including the practice of recruiting men to the Treasury following experience in other departments, rather than directly from the open competition for the administrative class.[2] The Commissioners concluded that the arrangements were generally satisfactory, but they emphasised that Heads of Departments should have reasonable latitude in staff matters. One interesting suggestion they put forward was that " provision should be made for the continuous overhaul of the machinery of Government, by a small specially trained staff recruited from the Service generally . . . this staff should be borne on the Treasury Vote . . . (and) . . . the necessary surveys should be carried out jointly by members of this specially trained staff and of the Department for the time being under review ".[3] The Commission said that this was

---

[1] Ibid. paras. 253–256.
[2] Royal Commission on the Civil Service 1929–1931 Minutes of Evidence p. 1270 et. seq.
[3] Cmd. 3909, para. 595.

only an extension of the Treasury's existing work as a clearing house for questions concerning improved organisation, labour-saving devices and so forth.

111. On the organisation of the Service, the Commission endorsed in broad principle the scheme recommended by the Re-organisation Committee and subsequently adopted. Under this scheme the Civil Service was divided into six main general classes: writing assistants, the clerical class, the executive class, the administrative class, and the typists and shorthand typist classes. On the executive class, they said that there was no advantage in allotting University graduates a proportion of the relatively small entry to the executive class from the open competition. The Commissioners considered the present field of recruitment was satisfactory.

112. While the Commission believed that all Departments should be organised on the same basic lines and that the broad similarity between the work of many departments justified this uniformity of organisation, they did appreciate that ... " it is necessary to leave room for a good deal of elasticity in the organisation of individual Departments. In our view, speaking generally, uniformity in organisation and grading cannot be carried any further in the Service than at present ".[1] They therefore endorsed the setting up of Departmental classes where there was a good case for them. " In regard to the departmental clerical class organisations, we therefore reach the conclusion that they are necessary for the proper performance of the work of certain Departments and we recommend:

(i) That they should continue;
(ii) That there should be no standard type of departmental clerical class organisation, but that variations should be made to meet the type of work ".[2]

113. This endorsement of the principle of Departmental classes may well have been influenced by the fact that there were in total only 17,000 people in them[3] rather than the 124,000 today. They therefore presented a much easier management problem.

114. The Tomlin Report also contained a fairly detailed survey of the problems of the professional, scientific and technical classes in the Service. The Commission noted that " In recent years there has been a marked increase in the number of specialist officers more particularly in scientific and technical appointments, owing to the assumption by the State of new or extended spheres of activity, more particularly in connection with various forms of research work ".[4] The Commission concluded that the specialist classes of the Service could not be appropriately organised on the basis of a single graded technical service, and that in general they must remain organised on a Departmental basis. But they endorsed the conclusion of the Committe under the Chairmanship of Professor Sir H. C. H. Carpenter, which had reported in 1931 that a considerable measure of uniformity in grading and salaries could be introduced among the scientific

---

[1] Cmd. 3909, para. 153.
[2] Ibid. para. 156.
[3] Ibid. para. 141.
[4] Ibid. para. 172.

and technical research staff.[1] Indeed, these recommendations were accepted in due course, when two service wide classes, scientific officers and scientific assistants were established with common pay scales and conditions of service. Some years later, in 1945, following the report of a Committee under Sir Alan Barlow[2] the scientific classes were re-organised into the scientific officer class, the experimental officer class, and scientific assistant class. Centralised recruitment was then introduced in line with the recommendations of the Tomlin Report, which had supported the pooling of vacancies.

115. Another important recommendation related to the ratio between the number of senior and junior posts in the scientific classes. The Commission noted the relatively small number of higher posts and they said that as their total ought not to be increased simply for career reasons, a great effort should be made to reduce the number of junior posts and to carry out as much work as possible by those without qualifications of a professional or technical nature.

116. However, it is interesting that the Tomlin Commission did not discuss the kind of issues about the relationship between technical and administrative work which were discussed by the Bridgeman Committee on the Post Office in 1932.[3] This Committee said that the administrative class had insufficient experience of the actual executive work of the Post Office, and that engineering experience was not brought sufficiently closely into the formulation of policy. They proposed that careful training should be given to newly recruited administrative staff and that no officer should fill a responsible post at Headquarters until he had worked in the regions. The Committee also said that, " we consider that there should be no bar to a Technical Officer holding such posts, i.e. administrative posts, provided he has shown himself to possess administrative ability ".[4] They further recommended that a functional board should be set up as the governing authority of the Post Office. It should consist of the senior officers in charge of the various activities of the Department, and so bring technical expertise directly into the senior policy-making body at the Department.

117. However, the Tomlin Commission did not go as far as this. They did not endorse the view put to them by the Institution of Professional Civil Servants that the Board System should be extended and that specialists should have the right of access to the Minister on all important questions involving technical considerations. The Tomlin Commission believed " that, in the normal type of administrative Department, there should be one officer responsible to the Minister for the advice tendered to him and for the conduct of the Department. That officer must be the Permanent Secretary. We do not, therefore, recommend any extension of what is known as the board system. Such a step would not be to the advantage of Ministers and would tend to delay public business ".[5] But the Commissioners did say that " we regard as conducive to good administration the system of periodic informal conferences, presided over by the Minister or the Permanent Head of the Department and attended by heads of branches. We note

---

[1] Ibid. para. 192.
[2] This report is included in " The Scientific Civil Service: Reorganisation and Recruitment during the Reconstruction Period." Cmd. 6679 of 1945.
[3] Report of the Committee of Inquiry on the Post Office—Cmd. 4149 of 1932.
[4] Cmd. 4149, para. 122.
[5] Cmd. 3909, para. 177.

that this procedure is already in force in several Departments ".[1] They went on to say that they did not believe that the advice of specialists was ignored in policy making and that, in their view, there was no real danger that their advice would not be placed before the Minister or official to whom fell the responsibility for the final decision. They realised that this was not appreciated by specialists, and this is why they recommended informal conferences should be held. They also said that administrators should take special precautions to consult specialists, so that they are given " no ground for feeling that their value is not appreciated. It is important that specialists, as well as other officers whose duty is to give advice, should be made aware of the decision taken by the responsible authority."[2]

118. It is noteworthy that in this respect the Commission should have taken such a different line from the Bridgeman Report, which formed the basis of a Post Office reorganisation, and also from the line taken by Sir Robert Morrant who, when taking office as the first Permanent Secretary of the newly created Ministry of Health in 1919, took steps to ensure that the Chief Medical Officer should be of the same salary and status as the Permanent Secretary and should have the right of direct access to the responsible Minister.[3]

119. Another subject considered by the Tomlin Commission was the Whitley machinery. In 1917 the Whitley Committee of the Ministry of Reconstruction had proposed the creation of joint councils of employers and employees, representing different sections of each industry, to settle wage claims and discuss working conditions. The Committee recommended that this system should not only be applied in industry but also in central and local government. The Government had some initial hesitation about applying this principle to its relation with its own employees and the proposal was finally referred to an Inter-Departmental Committee, who supported it. It was then accepted by the Government and a National Whitley Council was created to deal with questions affecting the Service as a whole. The most important piece of work carried out by this Council in its early years was the production of the Re-organisation report, which led to the introduction of Civil Service classes on the basis that it recommended. In spite of the acceptance of this scheme, the Whitley Council was never subsequently entrusted with any similar task. And when the Tomlin Commission took evidence about the Council's work there were mixed views on the success of the Whitley system. Some even suggested that it was a failure, and should be dismantled. But others supported it, and the Commissioners themselves concluded that the present arrangements were satisfactory, subject to amendment on certain points of detail.

120. One of the matters the Commission were particularly asked to survey was the position of women in the Civil Service. Theoretically, of course, the Sex Disqualification (Removal) Act of 1919, eliminated all discrimination. It stated that " a person shall not be disqualified by sex or marriage from the exercise of any public function or from being appointed to or holding any civil or judicial post ".

121. But the passage of this Act did not remove all the disadvantages from which women suffered. In 1921 the Treasury issued new regulations concerning the

---

[1] Cmd. 3909, Para. 177.
[2] Ibid. para. 178.
[3] Sir George Newman, " The Building of a Nation's Health ", 1939, pp. 112 and 119.

admission of women and their place in the Service. Under these, they were excluded from the Foreign Office, the Diplomatic Service and from certain other posts and grades in the Service. The regulations also laid down that all women candidates for posts should be single or widowed and that they should resign on marriage; exceptions to the latter rule could only be made on the recommendation of the Head of a Department.

122. The more highly placed women Civil Servants were themselves in favour of abolishing the bar, but the lower staff were in favour of retaining it. The Civil Service Clerical Association carried out a ballot among their women members, which showed a ratio of three to one in favour of maintaining the Marriage Bar, although they were also in favour of exceptions for women who had to maintain husbands who were sick or who were otherwise unable to support them.[1] The Commission's recommendation was to retain the present regulations but to modify them to make it easier for specially qualified women to remain in the Service. This recommendation was accepted.

123. Another matter on which the Commission was asked to report was remuneration. As a general principle they stated that " broad general comparisons between classes in the Service and outside occupations are possible and should be made ".[2] They admitted the difficulty of making these comparisons so far as work special to the Government was concerned, and they noted that in the business world payments for senior staff were related to particular circumstances in a way which they regarded as inappropriate for the Civil Service, where they believed that fixed scales of pay for grades were the best method of determining the remuneration of individuals. They also said that for various reasons, including the greater security of tenure and the relationship between Permanent Secretaries and Ministers, the highest posts in the Service should not carry a rate of remuneration as high as that of posts of corresponding responsibility in outside employment.

124. The Commission also considered the question of temporary employment. They recommended that it was a useful expedient when work had temporarily increased by they hoped it could be reduced to a minimum. They condemned the practice of appointing officers by any other means than open competition and they emphasised that, where the temporary employment was unavoidable, recruitment should be on a basis which afforded no grounds for a claim to retention or to special consideration. The broad principle of this recommendation was accepted, although its implementation took a number of years in view of the large number of temporary staff employed by the Government and the need to deal with them on a fair and equitable basis.

125. On the question of inter-Departmental transfers the Commission said that " any scheme of inter-Departmental transfer on a large scale would necessarily involve extremely cumbersome machinery ".[3] They also thought that most departments offered a sufficient variety of work to make it unnecessary to move officers in order to provide for the acquisition of wide experience. They recognized that different considerations applied to promotions from one class to

---

[1] Question 6124 of Minutes of Evidence taken before the Royal Commission.
[2] Cmd. 3909, para. 308.
[3] Cmd. 3909, para. 281.

another and that special arrangements might be needed for Executive officers of Administrative quality working in Departments without any Administrative posts.

126. The Tomlin Commission also considered superannuation. Under the Superannuation Act of 1859 and subsequent legislation, Civil Servants who fulfilled certain conditions received a non-contributory pension. This pension scheme was one of the most important ways in which the unity of the Service was preserved, since all Departments had to follow the same procedure.

127. However, the scheme was not fully acceptable to the staff since it did not provide for the pensioning of the dependents of those who died before their service was completed. The staff argued that a pension is deferred pay and that a man's dependents should be entitled to draw upon it. In 1898 a memorial was sent to the Treasury pressing this point of view, but it was rejected on the ground that Civil Servants should cover the risk of premature death by insurance and that to meet this demand would cost more money than it was fair to expect the taxpayer to provide. In 1902 a Royal Commission was appointed on Civil Service pensions.[1] The majority of the Commission recommended that the existing scheme should remain but that the calculations should be amended so that funds would be available for the payment of a cash benefit to the representatives of those who died in Service or shortly after retiring, and also to those retiring for reasons of ill-health. In this way the desire of the Civil Servants to provide for dependants would be met without increasing the burden on the taxpayer. This report was not unanimous, and action was deferred until 1909 when a Superannuation Act was passed which was based on the Commissioners proposals, although it was more generous than they had suggested.

128. The Tomlin Commission considered the working of the existing scheme and proposed ways of amending it so that a Civil Servant might surrender a portion of his pension in return for a pension for his wife or dependants. They also proposed the extension of the provisions of the 1909 Act to women; a uniform method of reckoning unestablished Service for pension purposes; and the creation of reciprocal arrangements for pensions with local authorities. These proposals were implemented in the Superannuation Act of 1935.

129. Although the Tomlin Commission made these recommendations for improving the existing pension arrangements, they believed that the best solution would be to make Civil Service pensions contributory. They said that, in refurbishing the existing scheme, they had faced many difficulties in determining the extent to which unestablished service should count for pensions, and they concluded that " the most satisfactory solution of these difficulties lies in the introduction of a contributory system. Under such a system the emoluments on which contributions have been paid are the emoluments reckonable for pension, and the period in respect of which contributions have been paid is the reckonable period ".[2] In making this recommendation the Commission considered the argument that the non-contributory pension induced Civil Servants to make a life-time's career in the Service. They were opposed to any change which might tend to deprive the state of the service of persons of mature experience, but they believed that " the benefits payable on voluntary retirement are

---

[1] Its report appeared as Cd. 1744 of 1903.
[2] Cmd. 3909, para. 715.

unlikely to prove so attractive as to result in the loss to the Service of a large proportion of experienced servants ".[1] They also believed that it was wrong to weigh the scales too heavily against voluntary retirement, and that they were some officials who would find other employment better suited to their abilities " To the extent that this obtains and that such persons remain in the Service, the effect appears likely to be harmful ".[2] No action was taken on this proposal to introduce a contributory pension scheme.

130. The general conclusion of this survey of the work of the Tomlin Commission is that it marked and recorded the culmination of the changes that were recommended by Northcote and Trevelyan and took the best part of eighty years to bring to full fruition. All the main principles in this report received the endorsement of the Tomlin Commission and, on the whole, the Commissioners felt that the arrangements for the classification and grading of work, for recruitment and promotion, and for securing the unity of the Service were satisfactory. The Report contained a number of interesting ideas for change, but these were on matters of marginal rather than central importance.

IX. Conclusion

131. Since the Royal Commission of 1929/31 there has been no fundamental review of the structure of the Civil Service until the appointment of the Committee under the Chairmanship of Lord Fulton in 1966. There have, of course, been many reports on particular aspects of the Service, among the most important of which have been the reports of the Committee on Higher Civil Service Remuneration (Chorley) in 1949;[3] the Committee on the Organisation, Structure and Remuneration of the Works Group of Professional Civil Servants (Gardiner) in 1951;[4] the Committee on Pay and Organisation of the Civil Service Medical Staffs (Howitt) in 1951,[5] and the Committee on the Organisation, Structure and Remuneration of the Professional Accountant Class in the Civil Service (Gardiner) in 1952.[6] The principal theme of these reports is their support for the creation and consolidation of service wide grades of specialists.

132. There have also been reports on other aspects of the Service; for example, the Committee on the Training of Civil Servants (Assheton) of 1944,[7] underlined the need for more training for Civil Servants, and the Royal Commission on the Civil Service of 1953/55 (Priestley)[8] was largely concerned with matters of pay. It endorsed the principle of fair comparison and made proposals for keeping the pay of Civil Servants under constant review. Following this report, the Pay Research Unit was established and a Standing Committee on the Pay of the Higher Civil Service was also set up. The Royal Commission also made a number of suggestions on structure. They recommended, for example, that the Civil Service should not lag behind outside employers in improving the attractions and rewards of a scientific and professional career, and that the scope for transferring specialist staff to administrative posts should be carefully considered.

---

[1] Ibid. para. 718.
[2] Ibid. para. 717.
[3] Cmd. 7635 of 1949.
[4] Published by H.M.S.O., reference 63–124.
[5] Published by H.M.S.O., reference 63–126.
[6] Published by H.M.S.O., reference 63–127.
[7] Cmd. 6525 of 1944.
[8] Cmd. 9613 of 1955.

133. But all these reports, though concerned with important questions, dealt essentially with matters of detail. The general re-organisation of the British Civil Service on the principles of Northcote and Trevelyan was complete by 1930. A survey of all the reports considered in this note suggests a number of general reflections.

134. It took nearly 20 years from the publication of Northcote and Trevelyan report in 1854 to secure the acceptance of the principle that open competition should be the basis of recruitment to the Civil Service instead of patronage. This was secured by the Order in Council of 1870 but, by that date, very little had been done to implement the other ideas in the Report, i.e. to secure promotion by merit; to divide the work between the intellectual and the routine; and to secure the unification of the Service. All the reports from 1870 to 1914 are concerned with these three principles. They affirm their importance and they detail the ways in which the Service of their time had not fulfilled them. There is a constant stress on these ideas, particularly on the importance of dividing the work between the intellectual and the routine, and recruiting and appointing officers of different abilities for these different tasks.

135. The reports devoted a good deal of attention to matters which are now mainly of historical interest. The foremost example, of course, is the problem of how best to arrange for the copying of documents, which was finally solved by the invention of the typewriter. Other examples are problems connected with the employment of boys for limited periods of service after which most of them had inevitably to be discharged, and the many questions connected with the employment and pay rates of women.

136. This concentration on these issues of the day was inevitable in the circumstances, but the reader of these reports today finds it hard to resist the conclusion that many important matters received surprisingly little attention.

137. The first matter that received comparatively little treatment was the place of the specialist officers in the Service. It was perhaps natural that the early reports would make little reference to these officers, since few of them were then employed. But even in the reports of the late nineteenth and early twentieth centuries it is clear that specialist officers were regarded as advisers rather than in the main line of policy-making and execution.

138. In a paper read to the Institute of Public Administration in 1923, Sir Francis Floud[1] said:

> " At the same time, if specialists are to be mainly employed as advisers I consider that there are certain conditions which they are entitled to demand. In the first place they have a right to demand that their advice should be sought. I have known cases in which administrative officers have come to decisions on technical questions without ever consulting the technical advisers of the Department ".

Sir Francis continued by outlining other cases where the technical staff's advice was not properly sought and, when sought, not properly acted upon. The Tomlin

[1] Sir Francis Floud was, successively, Permanent Secretary of the Ministry of Agriculture, Chairman of the Board of Customs and Excise, and Permanent Secretary of the Ministry of Labour. He was, throughout his career, a member of the administrative class.

Report quoted this paper,[1] but their recommendations showed that, while they appreciated the points that were made, they were unwilling to recommend changes in structure to give effect to them.

139. Another area which could have been given more attention (although an exception must be made here in the case of the MacDonnell Report) was recruitment to the highest posts in the Service. The main emphasis in most reports was on ensuring that men of intelligence were recruited by open competitive examination. Little attention was paid to the question whether the examinations offered a fair chance to all candidates or to the wider question of whether University degrees were the best preparation for work in the Government Service.

140. The general assumption was that competitive examinations would produce the best men and that any problems connected with the fairness of the examinations could be met by widening the syllabus of subjects and extending educational opportunities to a larger section of the community. It was assumed that action on these lines would result in Civil Servants coming from a wide variety of social backgrounds and being schooled in a large number of subjects.

141. Training was another subject that received little attention. It was assumed that a Civil Servant would be able to learn all that he needed by concentrated application to the work of his Department. The Reports continually emphasised the value of Departmental experience and, though the evidence to the MacDonnel Report contains references to the number of young men who obtained degrees and other qualifications, it was not until the Assheton Report of 1944 that a clear recommendation was made on the need for Civil Servants to acquire further knowledge and undergo extra training once they had obtained their positions. This line of thought did not, of course, apply so much to the specialist officers. They were naturally expected to have professional qualifications, though here too the assumption seemed to be that they would be obtained before entering the Service and that there was little need to keep them up-to-date by further training.

142. The relative neglect of training and certain other matters by previous Commissions and Committees does not of course mean that there have been no further developments in these fields. In fact, there has been a great expansion of training, and many other matters have undergone developments which have not been directly inspired by formal, external review. For instance, the Method II entry to the administrative class was a new approach to selective competition.

143. Finally however perhaps the most striking omission of the past reports is an examination of the tasks carried out by the Civil Service. Northcote and Trevelyan themselves were an exception: their final report was based on a thorough inspection of the current work of the departments at the time. In general, however, it was only to a surprisingly small extent that the Commissions and Committees saw it as their business to examine and set out what the Service had to do before considering how it should be structured and organised.

144. This seems to have led to two main consequences. First, the reviewing bodies did not, for the most part, distinguish at all finely between the different

---

[1] Cmd. 3909, Para. 175.

kinds of jobs and the different kinds of qualifications and experience which they called for. They mentioned of course that some Civil Servants work in industrial establishments, but tended to treat all " office " work as being of the same kind. The common assumption seems to have been that the general distinction between intellectual and routine work was sufficient. This reliance on an excessively general principle of classification may be one of the main reasons why it proved difficult in the past to match talents and jobs.

145. Secondly, the reviewing bodies did not in general attempt to consider the work of the Civil Service in the context of the changing social, industrial and political environment in which it had to operate. There are occasional references to the expansion of Government work in the spheres of public health and social insurance and during the First World War. But the social developments which accounted for the new demands that were made on the Service were very much a secondary theme in the reports of those who had to make proposals for its future. They tended to see the Civil Service as a machine to be adjusted in accordance with the principles of Northcote and Trevelyan, rather than as an institution that must inevitably change with the development of society and the articulation of the community's needs.

Appendices

(1) A list of some of the most important events and Acts that affected the development of the Civil Service, the dates of the most important inquiries into it, and statistics of the growth of the Service.

(2) Membership of some of the most important Committees and Royal Commissions on the Civil Service.

(3) Bibliography.

Appendix 1

List of Events affecting the Civil Service

Date	*Event*	*Enquiries into the Civil Service*	*Number of Non-industrial Civil Servants*
1832	Reform Act.		
1833	Factory Act (part time education for children in factories).		
1834	Poor Law Amendment Act.		
1835	Municipal Reform Act.		
1848	Public Health Act.		
1851	Great Exhibition.		
1853/4		Northcote–Trevelyan.	16,000.
1854/56	Crimean War.		
1860		Select Committee in Civil Service Appointments.	

Date	*Event*	*Enquiries into the Civil Service*	*Number of Non-industrial Civil Servants*
1866	Sanitary Act.		
1867	Reform Act.		
1870	Education Act (Local School Boards established)		
1870/71	Franco/Prussian War		
1872	Ballot Act.		
1874/5		Playfair Commission.	
1875	Public Health Act—(consolidated legislation in this sphere).		
1884	Representation of the People Act.		
1886/90		Ridley Commission.	
1888	Local Government Act—(setting up of County Councils and County Boroughs).		
1891	Fair Wages Resolution passed by Commons, recognising duty of Government Departments to see that those doing business with them should pay fair wages.		
1897	Workmen's Compensation Act.		
1899/ 1902	Boer War.		
1902	Education Act (Local Education Authorities Established).		
1908	Old Age Pensions Act.		
1909	Local Employment Exchanges Established. Housing and Town Planning Act.		
1911	National Insurance Act.		
1912/15		MacDonnell Commission.	280,000 Non-industrials (209,000 in the GPO: 71,000 in other Departments).
1914/18	First World War.		

Date	*Event*	*Enquiries into the Civil Service*	*Number of Non-industrial Civil Servants*
1918	Education Act (School leaving age raised to 14).		
1918	Representation of the People Act (universal male suffrage; votes for women of 30).		
1919	Formation of Ministry of Health.		
1920		Re-organisation Report.	381,000 Non-industrials (210,000 in the GPO).
1928	Representation of the People (Equal Franchise) Act (votes for women of 21).		
1930			306,000 Non-industrials (195,000 in the GPO).
1929/31		Tomlin Commission	
1931	Statute of Westminster.		
1939/45	Second World War.		
1942	Ministry of Town and Country Planning formed.		
1944	Education Act.		
1946	National Health Service Act.		
1946	Coal Industry Nationalised.		
1947	Railways and other Transport Nationalised.		
1947	Electricity Nationalised.		
1948	Gas Nationalised.		
1950			575,000 Non-industrials (250,000 in the GPO).
1951	General Certificate of Education introduced.		
1953/6		Priestley Commission.	
1960			637,000 Non-industrials (255,000 in the GPO).

Note: Size of the Non-Industrial Civil Service

There are no reliable figures for the size of the Civil Service in the nineteenth century. Classifications changed frequently over the years and the line between what are now called " industrial" and " non-industrial " Civil Servants was by no means clear. The figure of 16,000 for 1854 used in the table was put forward by Northcote and Trevelyan in their report. The figures for the twentieth century are taken from the statement " Staff Employed in Government Departments " which has been published annually, or more frequently, by the Treasury as a Command paper since 1919. The first issue included retrospective figures. The figures are of estimates of staff rather than numbers actually employed. Nevertheless, they serve as a broad guide.

Appendix 2

Membership of some of the Most Important Committees and Royal Commissions on the Civil Service

1. One interesting aspect of a study of the reports on the Civil Service since Northcote and Trevelyan concerns the membership of the various commissions and committees which examined the Civil Service.

2. In terms of membership, the committee fell into two classes: the first consisted of those whose membership was predominantly official and expert. Within this category, is the Northcote and Trevelyan's investigation itself; the Playfair Commission, the majority of whose members were official Heads of Departments; and the Reorganisation Committee, the official and staff side members of which were naturally well acquainted with the Civil Service of their day.

3. The other category of committees is where the membership consisted predominantly of people from outside the Civil Service. In this category come the Ridley Commission, the MacDonnell Commission and the Tomlin Commission. One of the features of the Ridley Commission was the importance of politicians among its members. Sir Matthew White Ridley was himself a Conservative Member of Parliament, and Home Secretary from 1895–1900. Among his colleagues was Lord Rothschild, the Lord Lieutenant for Buckinghamshire from 1889 and Lieutenant for the City of London; the Rt. Hon. Robert Hanbury, a Conservative Member of Parliament from 1872, Financial Secretary to the Treasury from 1895–1900 and President of the Board of Agriculture from 1903; and Earl Brownlow, a Conservative Member of Parliament and the holder of junior ministerial offices after he had succeeded to the title. In addition to being politically active, all these men had substantial means. Hanbury was a landowner with private wealth, derived from collieries, and Earl Brownlow was the owner of some 60,000 acres. It would, of course, be wrong to suggest that the Ridley Committee had no other experience available among its membership. It included Lord Lingen, who had been Permanent Secretary to the Treasury from 1869–85, and Sir John Maclure, the joint founder of the Manchester and Salford Sanitary Association, the Hon. Secretary of the Fund for Relief of Distress during the Cotton Famine 1862–1866, and a Conservative Member of Parliament from 1886.

4. The MacDonnell Commission had a wide range of experience among its membership. The Chairman had extensive official experience as a civil servant in India and Ireland, and his colleagues included the Duke of Devonshire; the Bishop of Southwark; Lord Muir Mackenzie, who was Permanent Secretary to the Lord Chancellor from 1880–1915; Sir Henry Primrose, who had been Permanent Secretary to the Viceroy of India and to Mr. Gladstone, and was subsequently Secretary to H.M. Office of Works, Chairman of the Board of

Customs and Chairman of the Inland Revenue. Members with political experience included three who were subsequently to reach high office; Philip Snowden, the future Labour Chancellor, J. R. Clynes, subsequently Chairman of the Parliamentary Labour Party and Secretary of State for Home Affairs, and the future Lord Templewood, later to become the Foreign Secretary. Other members included Sir Arthur Shipley, the Master of Christ's College Cambridge, a zoologist and member of numerous committees on education and scientific matters; Sir Donald MacAllister, the Principal and Vice-Chancellor of Glasgow University for over 20 years, the author of a number of medical works and the member of many committees in the fields of medicine and education; Graham Wallase, one of the leading members of the Fabian Society and Professor of Political Science at the London School of Economics; and Elizabeth Haldane, who was the first woman J.P. for Scotland.

5. The Tomlin Commission also included a wide range of experience. Its Chairman was a judge; and its members included Sir Christopher Needham, Chairman of insurance and many other companies, and a prominent figure in Lancashire affairs during the first third of the century; the Duchess of Atholl, a Conservative Member of Parliament from 1923–38, Parliamentary Secretary of the Board of Education from 1924–29, and the member of many committees and institutions, especially concerned with Scotland. Other members included John Bromley, the General Secretary of the Associated Society of Locomotive Engineers and Firemen, 1914–1936; Mrs. Eveline Lowe, a member of the London County Council from 1922–46 and Chairman of the Education Committee; and Robert Richards, Labour M.P. for Wrexham, Under-Secretary for India in 1924 and a university Lecturer in Economics. The Commissions Secretary was Edward Bridges, later Permanent Secretary of the Treasury and subsequently Lord Bridges.

6. It is hard to correlate the kind of experience possessed by the members of these committees with the action taken on their reports. Prima facie, it would seem that those committees with a high official membership were productive of more long-term results. This is certainly the case so far as Northcote–Trevelyan and the Reorganisation Committee are concerned; the exception is the Playfair Committee. On the other hand, although not a great deal of action seems to have resulted from the work of the committees in the other caregory, it is only fair to say that action was suspended on the MacDonnell Commission by the outbreak of the First World War and that, by and large, the Tomlin Commission did not seek many significant changes in the existing arrangements.

Bibliography

I. Books

The most helpful books in preparing this study have been Professor H. R. G. Greaves's " The Civil Service in the Changing State ", 1947, and Emmeline W. Cohen's " The Growth of the British Civil Service 1780–1939 ", 1941. Both these works are of great assistance to the student of the history of the British Civil Service. Earlier works which are still valuable are Professor W. A. Robson's " From Patronage to Proficiency in the Public Service ", 1922, and R. Moses's " The History of the British Civil Service ", 1914.

2. Official Papers

(Only the more important papers and works are listed; other references are in footnotes.)

Report from the Select Committee on Miscellaneous Expenditure. Parliamentary Papers P.P., 1847–48, xviii.

Reports from the Committees of Inquiry into Public Offices and Papers connected therewith. P.P., 1854, xxvii.

Papers on the Reorganization of the Civil Service. P.P., 1854–55 xx. The Northcote Trevelyan Report itself was published as C. 1713 of 1854.

Report from the Select Committee on Civil Service Appointments. P.P., 1860, ix.

Reports from the Civil Service (Playfair) Inquiry Commission P.P. 1875. (First Report issued as C. 1113 of 1875 and Second Report issued as C. 1226 of 1875).

Reports from the Royal (Ridley) Commission on Civil Establishments. 1st Report, P.P., 1887, xix, (C. 5226, 1887). 2nd Report P.P., 1888, xxvii, (C. 5545). 3rd Report P.P., 1889, xxi, (C. 5748). 4th Report, P.P., 1890, xxvii, (C. 6172 1890).

Papers showing the Manner in which the Recommendations of the Royal Commission with respect to the Civil Service have been dealt with. P.P., 1893–94, lxxi.

Report of the Royal Commission on Superannuation in the Civil Service. P.P., 1903, xxxiii. (Cd. 1744 of 1903).

Reports from the Royal (MacDonnell) Commission on the Civil Service. P.P., 1912–13, xv, and P.P., 1914, xvi. (Reports issued as Cmds. 6209, 6534, 6739, 7338, 7748, 7832. Evidence issued as Cds 6210, 6535, 6740, 7338, 7340, 7749, 8130).

Report of the Committee on the Machinery of Government. P.P., 1918, xii. (Cd. 9230 of 1918).

Reports of the Committee appointed to Inquire into the Organization and Staffing of Government Offices. (Bradbury) 1st, 2nd and 3rd Interim Reports, P.P., 1918, vii (Cmd. 9074, 9219, 9220, of 1918). 4th Interim and Final Reports, P.P., 1919, xi (Cmd. 61 and 62, 1919).

Reports of the Committee on Civil Service Recruitment after the War (Gladstone) P.P. 1919, xi (Cmd. 34, 35, 36 of 1918 and Cmd. 164, 1919.)

Report of the Sub-Committee of the Inter-departmental Committee on the Application of the Whitley Report to Government Establishments. P.P., 1919, xi.

Civil Service National Whitley Council. Interim Report of the Joint Committee on the Organization, etc., of the Civil Service (H.M.S.O. 1920). Final Report (H.M.S.O. 1921).

Report of the Royal (Tomlin) Commission on the Civil Service. P.P., 1930–31, x. (Cmd. 3909 of 1931).

Report of the Committee of Inquiry on the Post Office. P.P., 1931–32, xii. (Cmd. 4149 of 1932).

Report of the Committee on the Training of Civil Servants (Assheton) Cmd. 6525 of 1944. The Scientific Civil Service: Reorganisation and Recruitment during the Reconstruction Period. Cmd. 6679 of 1945.

Report of the Royal (Priestley) Commission on the Civil Service Cmd. 9613 of 1955.

Printed in England for Her Majesty's Stationery Office.
By McCorquodale and Company Limited, London.

HM 2040 Dd. 142272. K22. 7/68 McC. 3336/2